Politics and International Relations of Southeast Asia

GENERAL EDITOR

George McT. Kahin

Burma: Military Rule and the Politics of Stagnation
    by Josef Silverstein

Malaysia and Singapore: The Building of New States
    by Stanley S. Bedlington

Indonesian Foreign Policy and the Dilemma of Dependence:
    From Sukarno to Soeharto
        by Franklin B. Weinstein

The Army and Politics in Indonesia
    by Harold Crouch

THE ARMY
AND POLITICS
IN INDONESIA

HAROLD CROUCH

Cornell University Press | ITHACA AND LONDON

First published 1978 by Cornell University Press.
Published in the United Kingdom by Cornell University Press Ltd., 2-4 Brook Street, London W1Y 1AA.

International Standard Book Number 0-8014-1155-6
Library of Congress Catalog Card Number 77-90915
Printed in the United States of America
Librarians: Library of Congress cataloging information appears on the last page of the book.

Contents

Foreword, *by George McT. Kahin*   7
Preface   11
Note on Spelling   14
Abbreviations   15
Introduction   21
1. The Army as a Social-Political Force,
   1945–1965   24
2. Guided Democracy: The Uneasy Balance
   of Power   43
3. The Army Stands Firm   69
4. The Coup Attempt   97
5. The Aftermath of the Coup Attempt   135
6. President Sukarno's "Comeback"   158
7. The Disguised Coup of 11 March   179
8. The Fall of Sukarno   197
9. The Consolidation of Power   221
10. The Emasculation of the Political
    Parties   245
11. The Army's Economic Interests   273
12. Policies and the Struggle for Power   304
13. Conclusion: The Army and Politics   344
    Appendix. Institutions and Organizations   353
    Bibliography   357
    Index   369

Foreword

That broad area lying between China and India which since World War II has generally been known as Southeast Asia is one of the most heterogeneous in the world. Though it is generally referred to as a region, the principal basis for this designation is simply the geographic propinquity of its component states, and the fact that collectively they occupy the territory between China and the Indian subcontinent. The fundamental strata of the traditional cultures of nearly all the numerous peoples of Southeast Asia do set them apart from those of India and China. Beyond that, however, there are few common denominators among the states that currently make up the area except for roughly similar climatic conditions and, until recently at least, broadly similar economies and economic problems.

The political systems presently governing the lives of Southeast Asia's 300 million inhabitants have been built on considerably different cultures; the religious component alone embraces Buddhism, Confucianism, Christianity, Hinduism, and Islam. Except in the case of Thailand, the politics of all these countries have been conditioned by periods of colonial rule—ranging from little more than half a century to approximately four—each of which has had a distinctive character and political legacy. Even the nature of the Japanese wartime occupation, which covered the entire area, varied considerably among the several countries and had different political consequences. And after Japan's defeat, the courses to independence followed by these states diverged widely. Only through revolutionary anticolonial wars were two of the most populous, Indonesia and Vietnam, able to assert their independence. Although the others followed routes that were peaceful, they were not all necessarily smooth, and the time involved varied by as much as a decade.

Moreover, subsequent to independence the political character of these states has continued to be significantly affected by a wide range of relationships with outside powers. In a few cases these have been largely harmonious, attended by only relatively minor external efforts to influence the course of local political developments. However, most of these countries have been the object of interventions, covert and overt, by outside powers—particularly the United States—which have been calculated to shape their political life in accordance with external interests. Thus the range of contemporary political systems in Southeast Asia is strikingly varied, encompassing a spectrum quite as broad as the differing cultures and divergent historical conditionings that have so profoundly influenced their character.

This series, "Politics and International Relations of Southeast Asia," stems from an earlier effort to treat the nature of government and politics in the states of Southeast Asia in a single volume. Since the second, revised edition of that book, *Governments and Politics of Southeast Asia,* was published in 1964, interest in these countries has grown, for understandable reasons especially in the United States. This wider public concern, together with a greater disposition of academics to draw on the political experience of these countries in their teaching, has suggested the need for a more substantial treatment of their politics and governments than could be subsumed within the covers of a single book. The series therefore aims to devote separate volumes to each of the larger Southeast Asian states.

Presumably one no longer needs to observe, as was the case in 1964, that the countries treated "are likely to be strange to many of our readers." But even though the increased American interaction with most of the countries has clearly obviated that proposition, many readers are still likely to be unacquainted with their earlier histories and the extent to which their pasts have affected the development of their recent and contemporary political character. Thus all these volumes will include substantial historical sections as well as descriptions of the salient features of the present social and economic setting. In order to provide as much similarity of treatment as is compatible with the range of cultures and political systems presented by these states, the authors will follow a broadly similar pattern of organization and analysis of their political history, dynamics, and processes. This effort to achieve some basis of comparability may appear rather modest, but to have attempted any greater degree of uniformity would have militated against the latitude and flexibility required to do justice to the differing characteristics of the political systems described. All the books are to be written by political scientists who have lived and carried out research in one or more of the countries for a considerable period and who have previously published scholarly studies on their internal politics.

Although each of these volumes will include a section on the foreign policy of the country concerned, the increased importance of Southeast Asia in international relations that transcend this area has suggested the need for the series to include a few books focused on the foreign relations of its major states. As is true elsewhere, the foreign policies of these countries are heavily influenced by their own domestic politics; hence all contributors to the volumes that are concerned primarily with international relations are also specialists on the internal politics of the country, or countries, about whose foreign policy they write.

In addition, the series will include some in-depth treatments of particular aspects of the politics of the major states of the area. In these cases the focus is on an element of central importance in the political life of the country concerned, the understanding of which helps illuminate its government and politics as a whole.

The present volume by Harold Crouch is one of these in-depth treatments. For more than a decade before Sukarno's fall from power the army had begun to play an increasingly significant part in the political life of Indonesia. But since 1966, when the Suharto regime took over, it has come to dominate the country's government almost completely. Indeed, the army has emerged as the major political institution, decisively overshadowing and controlling—if not in a functional sense subsuming—all others.

It is, therefore, appropriate that this series should include a separate monograph focused on the army's political role, this being additional to a more comprehensive study of Indonesian government and politics that is expected to appear later.

Harold Crouch is especially well qualified to undertake the present study. Over most of the past ten years he has been engaged in research on the political role of the army in Indonesia, his most recent visit there having been in late 1976.

GEORGE McT. KAHIN

Ithaca, New York

Preface

The origin of this book can be traced back to February 1968, when I took up an appointment as lecturer in political science on the University of Indonesia's Faculty of Social Sciences. After teaching for three years in Jakarta, I enrolled in March 1971 as a graduate student in the Department of Politics and the Centre of Southeast Asian Studies at Monash University in Melbourne and in March 1975 submitted a thesis entitled "The Indonesian Army in Politics: 1960–1971." This book is both a contraction and an expansion of that thesis—some of the detail of the thesis having been removed, and the time period extended. The study has been long in preparation. The first material was collected in 1968, the first draft chapters were written in 1971, and the final additions to the manuscript were made in January 1977.

Between 1968 and 1977, I was helped in many ways by many people. I had the double advantage of association with both the University of Indonesia and the Centre of Southeast Asian Studies at Monash University. Apart from their hospitality and friendship, I am deeply grateful to my colleagues and students at the University of Indonesia for teaching me much about Indonesian politics. At Monash, I was able to study with others sharing my interests in a truly *gotong-royong* atmosphere of mutual aid and cooperation, and to my friends there I am also most indebted.

My largest debt, however, is to Herbert Feith, who arranged my job in Jakarta in 1968, discussed my work during several visits to Indonesia, supervised my research at Monash, and has continued to provide stimulating comments and criticism of my work. While he in no way bears responsibility for what is written in this book, his influence on its writing has been very great.

Apart from the three years spent in Indonesia from 1968 to 1971, I was able to visit Indonesia for four months from June to

October 1973 and made shorter visits in January 1975 and October–November 1976. During these visits I conducted many interviews and participated in many conversations with political activists and observers of various persuasions. It would be impossible to list them individually, but I am very grateful to all of them.

Several people have read and commented on one or more draft chapters. Apart from Herbert Feith, the others include J. A. C. Mackie, Ulf Sundhaussen, Ken Ward, Nazaruddin Sjamsuddin, Roeslan Abdulgani, Cosmas Batubara, George McT. Kahin, and Daniel S. Lev. Whether in agreement or disagreement, their comments have been very valuable, and to them I express my thanks. In addition, others have given, lent, or otherwise made available material of one sort or another. Among them are Charles Coppel, Andrew Gunawan, Stuart Graham, George Miller, Frank Palmos, Buddy Prasadja, Dorodjatun Kuntjoro Jakti, Victor Matondang, Molly Bondan, Cornelis Zebua, and General A. H. Nasution. I am also grateful to the editors of several newspaper who permitted me to read through their files, including those of *Angkatan Bersenjata, Kompas, Nusantara, Harian Kami, Surabaya Post,* and *El Bahar.* Other newspapers were read in various libraries in Indonesia and Australia.

I also express thanks to the Faculty of Social Sciences of the University of Indonesia, which employed me during my first stay in Indonesia, and the Indonesian Institute of Sciences (LIPI), which sponsored my second visit. My second visit was financed by the Myer Foundation (Melbourne) and the Centre of Southeast Asian Studies, Monash University. My fourth visit was financed by the National University of Malaysia, where I am now lecturing in the Department of Political Science. To all these institutions I express my gratitude.

I also wish to thank the editors of *Pacific Affairs, Indonesia, Dyason House Papers,* and the *Current Affairs Bulletin* (University of Sydney) for granting me permission to use material already published in their journals. The articles from which material has been drawn are "Another Look at the Indonesian 'Coup,'" *Indonesia,* no. 15 (April 1973); "The '15th January Affair' in Indonesia," *Dyason House Papers,* 1 (August 1974); "Generals and Business in Indonesia," *Pacific Affairs,* 48 (Winter 1975–1976), and a shortened version of the *Pacific Affairs* article in *Current Affairs Bulletin*, 54 (June 1977).

Finally I must express my great appreciation of the assistance given by Ong Beng Thye of the History Department, University of Malaya, in preparing the manuscript.

HAROLD CROUCH

Kuala Lumpur

Note on Spelling

In 1972 the Indonesian and Malaysian governments implemented a common system of spelling. The main changes are that the old *dj* becomes *j*, *j* becomes *y*, and *tj* becomes *c* (pronounced *ch*). I have adopted the new spelling except for the names of individuals and the PKI newspaper, *Harian Rakjat,* which was banned in 1965. Use of the new spelling for personal names was made optional, and many individuals continue to use the old spelling. In the interests of consistency, I have retained the old spelling for all personal names. I have also used the Indonesian *u* although many individuals continue to spell their names with the Dutch-derived *oe.*

Abbreviations

Akabri	Akademi Angkatan Bersenjata Republik Indonesia (Indonesian Armed Forces Academy)
Apodeti	Associcao Popular Democratica Timorense (Popular Democratic Association of Timor)
ASEAN	Association of South East Asian Nations
Aspri	Asisten Pribadi (Personal Assistant)
Bakin	Badan Kordinasi Intelijens Negara (State Intelligence Coordinating Body)
Bapilu	Badan Pengendalian Pemilihan Umum (Body to Manage the General Elections)
Bappenas	Badan Perencanaan Pembangunan Nasional (National Development Planning Board)
BE	Bonus Ekspot (Export Bonus)
Berdikari	Berdiri diatas kaki sendiri (Stand on your own feet)
BPI	Badan Pusat Intelijens (Central Intelligence Board)
BPK	Badan Pemeriksa Keuangan (Financial Inspection Board)
BPS	Badan Pendukung Sukarnoisma (Body to Support Sukarnoism)
BTI	Barisan Tani Indonesia (Indonesian Peasant Front)
Bulog	Badan Urusan Logistik Nasional (National Logistics Board)
BUUD	Badan Usaha Unit Desa (Village Unit Enterprise)
CGMI	Consentrasi Gerakan Mahasiswa Indonesia (Indonesian Student Movement Center)
CIA	Central Intelligence Agency (US)
Conefo	Conference of New Emerging Forces
CV	Commanditaire Vennootschap (limited company)
DPR-GR	Dewan Perwakilan Rakyat Gotong Royong (Mutual Assistance People's Representative Council)
Dwikora	Dwi Komando Rakyat (People's Double Command)
Fretilin	Frente Revolucionaria de Timor Leste Independente (Revolutionary Front for Independent Timor)
G.30.S., G.30.S./PKI	Gerakan 30 September (Thirtieth of September Movement)

Gerwani	Gerakan Wanita Indonesia (Indonesian Women's Movement)
Gestapu	Gerakan September Tigapuluh (Thirtieth of September Movement)
Gestok	Gerakan Satu Oktober (First of October Movement)
GMNI	Gerakan Mahasiswa Nasional Indonesia (Indonesian National Student Movement)
Golkar	Golongan Karya (Functional Groups)
GSNI	Gerakan Siswa Nasional Indonesia (Indonesian National High School Student Movement)
GUPPI	Gabungan Usaha-usaha Perbaikan Pendidikan Islam (Association to Improve Islamic Education)
Hankam	Departemen Pertahanan-Keamanan (Department of Defense and Security)
HMI	Himpunan Mahasiswa Islam (Islamic Student Association)
IGGI	Inter-Governmental Group on Indonesia
IMF	International Monetary Fund
Inkopad	Induk Koperasi Angkatan Darat (Army Central Cooperative Board)
IPKI	Ikatan Pendukung Kemerdekaan Indonesia (League of Upholders of Indonesian Freedom)
Ir.	Ingenieur (Engineer, a Dutch academic title)
KAMI	Kesatuan Aksi Mahasiswa Indonesia (Indonesian Student Action Front)
KAP-Gestapu	Kesatuan Aksi Pengganyangan Gestapu (Action Front to Crush the Thirtieth of September Movement)
KAPPI	Kesatuan Aksi Pelajar Pemuda Indonesia (Indonesian Student and Youth Action Front)
KASI	Kesatuan Aksi Sarjana Indonesia (Indonesian Graduates' Action Front)
Kko	Korps Komando (Commando Corps, marines)
Kodam	Komando Daerah Militer (Regional Military Command)
Kodim	Komando Distrik Militer (District Military Command)
Koga	Komando Siaga (Vigilance Command)
Kogam	Komando Ganyang Malaysia (Crush Malaysia Command)
Kokarmenda-gri	Korps Karyawan Departemen Dalam Negeri (Department of Internal Affairs Employees Corps)
Kolaga	Komando Mandala Siaga (Mandala Vigilance Command)
Komstradaga	Komando Strategis Darat Siaga (Vigilance Land Strategic Command)
Kopkamtib	Komando Operasi Pemulihan Keamanan dan Ketertiban (Operations Command to Restore Order and Security)

Koramil	Komando Rayon Militer (Rayon Military Command)
Korem	Komando Resort Militer (Resort Military Command)
Kosgoro	Koperasi Serba Usaha Gotong Royong (Mutual Aid All Purpose Cooperative)
Kostrad	Komando Cadangan Strategis Angkatan Darat (Army Strategic Reserve Command)
Koti	Komando Operasi Tertinggi (Supreme Operations Command)
Kotrar	Komando Tertinggi Retooling Alat Revolusi (Supreme Command for Retooling the Tools of the Revolution)
Kowilhan	Komando Wilayah Pertahanan (Regional Defense Command)
Mahmillub	Mahkamah Militer Luar Biasa (Special Military Court)
Malari	Malapetaka Januari (January Disaster)
Manipol	Manifesto Politik (Political Manifesto)
MKGR	Musyawarah Kekeluargaan Gotong Royong (Mutual Aid Family Conference)
MPRS	Majelis Permusyawaratan Rakyat Sementara (Provisional People's Consultative Assembly)
Nasakom	nasionalis, agama, komunis (nationalist, religious, Communist)
Nefos	New Emerging Forces
Nekolim	neokolonialisma, kolonialisma, imperialisma (neocolonialism, colonialism, imperialism)
NU	Nahdatul Ulama (Muslim teachers' party)
Oldefos	Old Established Forces
Opsus	Operasi Khusus (Special Operations)
Paran	Panitiya Retooling Aparat Negara (Committee to Retool the State Apparatus)
Parmusi	Partai Muslimin Indonesia (Indonesian Muslim party)
Partindo	Partai Indonesia (Indonesia party)
Pekuneg	Team Penertiban Keuangan Negara (Team to Regularize State Finances)
Pepelrada	Penguasa Pelaksanaan Dwikora Daerah (Regional Authority to Implement Dwikora)
Peperda	Penguasa Perang Daerah (Regional War Authority)
Peperpu	Penguasa Perang Pusat (Central War Authority)
Peperti	Penguasa Perang Tertinggi (Supreme War Authority)
Peta	Pembela Tanah Air (Defenders of the Fatherland)
Petir	Pembina Tenaga Inti Revolusi (Protectors of the Essence of the Revolution)
PKI	Partai Komunis Indonesia (Indonesian Communist party)
PN	Perusahaan Negara (state corporation)
PNI	Partai Nasional Indonesia (Indonesian National party)
PRRI	Pemerintah Revolusioner Republik Indonesia (Revolutionary Government of the Republic of Indonesia)

PSI	Partai Sosialis Indonesia (Indonesian Socialist party)
PT	Perusahaan Terbatas (limited company)
RPKAD	Resimen Para Komando Angkatan Darat (Army Para-commando Regiment)
Sekber-Golkar	Sekretariat Bersama Golongan Karya (Joint Secretariat of Functional Groups)
Seskoad	Sekolah Staf Komando Angkatan Darat (Army Staff and Command College)
SOBSI	Sentral Organisasi Buruh Seluruh Indonesia (Central Organization of Indonesian Workers)
SOKSI	Sentral Organisasi Karyawan Sosialis Indonesia (Central Organization of Indonesian Socialist Workers)
Spri	Staf Pribadi (Personal Staff)
TPK	Team Pemberantasan Korupsi (Team to Eliminate Corruption)
UDT	Uniao Democratica Timorense (Timor Democratic Union)
USDEK	Undang-undang Dasar 45, Sosialisma a la Indonesia, Demokrasi Terpimpin, Ekonomi Terpimpin, Kepribadian Indonesia (1945 Constitution, Indonesian Socialism, Guided Democracy, Guided Economy, Indonesian Personality)

THE ARMY AND POLITICS
IN INDONESIA

Introduction

The year preceding 30 September 1965 was marked by a widespread feeling in Indonesia that the political system could not last as it was for very much longer. The economy appeared to be approaching collapse as inflation raged out of control, production in many fields declined, the neglected economic infrastructure deteriorated, foreign exchange reserves were depleted, and foreign aid became increasingly difficult to obtain. The machinery of government had ceased to carry out many of its functions as pervasive corruption permitted officials at the top to enrich themselves while impoverished lower-level employees barely survived. President Sukarno's endeavors to unite the nation behind his ideological slogans had restricted political and intellectual life but failed to prevent growing tension in the rural areas, where violent clashes between peasants and landholders were frequent. At the same time the president's campaign to "Crush Malaysia" showed no signs of bringing tangible results, and Indonesia became more and more isolated from most of the rest of the world. Overshadowing all else was the ominous polarization of political forces around the two outstanding rivals for the succession. The antagonism between the army leaders and the Communist party seemed unlikely to admit of any resolution short of the victory of one and the elimination of the other.

The disintegration of the Guided Democracy system in the cataclysm that followed the 1965 coup attempt left the army as the dominant political force. The experience of Guided Democracy left a widespread hope that the army-dominated government would establish a "New Order" that would at last open the way to prosperity and progress. Members of anti-Communist civilian groups who had felt disadvantaged under the old regime naturally looked to the army with high expectations. These were shared by many Western observers who, perhaps influenced by the recent writings of political scientists about developing countries generally,[1] regarded the army as a likely agent of progress and modernization. Now that the army had acquired the power to overhaul the political system and the economy, there seemed to be few obstacles in the way of a complete break with the politics and policies of the past.

The "New Order," however, was not as new as had been anticipated. As this book will attempt to show, the army's rise to power was the culmination of a long process during which the army had acquired characteristics that conditioned its performance after 1965. The Indonesian army had acquired a political orientation and political interests at the time of the revolution against the Dutch. Later, after the introduction of martial law in 1957, the army and the other branches of the armed forces became deeply involved in politics, civil administration, and economic management with the result that the army became a key element in the government coalition under Guided Democracy. The military's experience in nonmilitary activities had two major consequences that affected its political behavior. First, its prolonged involvement in politics, administration, and business led to a politicization of the officer corps and the interpenetration of military and civilian factions that impaired the capacity of the military to act as a cohesive political force and hindered its drive to take complete power. Second, army officers had acquired extramilitary interests which they sought to further. As a political organization the army naturally sought to strengthen its own position at the expense of its rivals, while the expansion of the military's role into the economy gave army officers a personal stake in many business enterprises. As a consequence, military men became part of the political and economic elite with an interest in defending the existing social order which they felt was threatened by both the Communists and Sukarno's chaos-inducing policies.

The sudden elimination of the Indonesian Communist party (PKI) in the last months of 1965 and the drawn-out process that led to the dismissal of President Sukarno in 1967 left the army as the dominant political force. But the army had not gained control of the government by means of a Nasserite coup in which an

1. See, for example, Pauker 1959, Pye 1962, Janowitz 1964.

"outside" reforming elite overthrew a reactionary and incompetent establishment.[2] The army had already become part of the ruling elite under Guided Democracy. Its rise to a position of dominance did not follow the elimination of the old elite, but rather strengthened one section of it at the expense of other parts. The process was gradual because factionalism produced by politicization prevented the army leaders from taking decisive action.

Under the New Order army officers consolidated their political power and expanded their economic interests. Although many of the policies the new government implemented contrasted sharply with those of the old regime, they did not arise from the adoption of a new philosophy of social reform but because they were better suited in the new circumstances for the furtherance of interests that had been established for many years. Adopting economic development as its principal goal, the military-dominated regime pursued policies designed to expand the modern sector of the economy with the aid of foreign capital. As the economy grew rapidly the regime expected to attract support from urban white-collar and professional strata while avoiding political crises caused by food shortages and other reasons for extreme mass discontent. The chief beneficiaries of the New Order, however, were members of the higher echelons in the army and their bureaucratic and business associates, because foreign-financed economic expansion opened up vast new opportunities for business enterprises in which military officers had interests.

This book deals with the Indonesian army's role in politics during three periods. The first four chapters deal with the expansion of the army's involvement in politics and its position under Guided Democracy, including the activities of army officers in the events surrounding the abortive coup attempt of 1 October 1965. The next four chapters are devoted to the period of transition between October 1965 and March 1967, when the army under the leadership of General Suharto gradually eased President Sukarno out of power and finally dismissed him from office. The third phase is covered in chapters nine to twelve, in which the army-dominated New Order is examined. The conclusions of the study are summarized in the last chapter.

2. See Vatikiotis 1961.

1 | The Army as a Social-Political Force, 1945–1965

The Indonesian army has never restricted itself to an exclusively military role. During the "revolutionary" period from 1945 to 1949 the army was engaged in the struggle for independence in which politics and military action were inseparably intertwined. In the period immediately after the transfer of sovereignty at the end of 1949 the army formally accepted the principle of civilian supremacy, and its officers assumed a role on the edge of political life with sporadic but mainly unsuccessful forays into the center of the political arena. As the weaknesses of the parliamentary system became increasingly obvious, however, the conviction was strengthened among army officers that they bore the responsibility to intervene in order to "save" the nation. Although the army leaders were not directly responsible for the collapse of the parliamentary system in 1957, they were able to turn the situation to their advantage with the introduction of martial law, which enabled army officers to take on broad political, administrative, and economic functions.

In order to justify the army's continued role in these functions after the initial crisis had passed, the army chief of staff, Major General Abdul Haris Nasution, formulated the concept of the "Middle Way," according to which the army would neither seek to take over the government nor remain politically inactive. Instead the military claimed the right to continuous representation in the government, legislature, and administration.[1] At its first seminar, held in April 1965, the army produced a doctrine that declared that the armed forces had a dual role as both a "military force" and a "social-political force." As a "social-political force" the

1. Sundhaussen 1971:398.

army's activities covered "the ideological, political, social, economic, cultural and religious fields."[2]

The Origin of the Army's Political Role

The army's perception of itself as a political force arose from the blurred distinction between its military and political functions during the revolutionary war against the Dutch. By its very nature the struggle for independence was political as well as military. The youths who took up arms against the Dutch were motivated less by the desire for a military career than by a patriotism that expressed itself in support for the republic proclaimed by the nationalist politicians. The character of the fighting further strengthened the military's concern for political matters. Lacking professional training and low in modern armaments, the Indonesian resistance took the form of guerrilla warfare in which there was no clear boundary between military and civilian life, and the active fighters were heavily dependent on the support of the local population. Because the guerrilla fighters, organized into politically aligned irregular units as well as regular army forces, were always concerned to rally popular enthusiasm around their cause, military leaders performed political functions as well. In many cases the roles of political and military leader became almost indistinguishable.

The absence of an apolitical military tradition made it easier for army officers to accept their role during the revolution. The republic's pressing need for the quick mobilization of a large fighting force had meant that there was no opportunity for the gradual growth of a "professional" army around the nucleus of young officers from the Dutch colonial army who had chosen the nationalist side. The small group of academy-trained officers in the new national army was heavily outnumbered by youths who had received military training in auxiliary military organizations (especially Defenders of the Fatherland [Peta]) set up by the Japanese during the occupation or who had taken up arms in local laskar or irregular units formed spontaneously throughout the country in the months after the proclamation of independence.[3] In contrast with the Western ideal indoctrinated in the Dutch

2. Angkatan Darat 1965: Main book (Buku Induk), chap. 3.
3. See Pauker 1962:187–192, Anderson 1972a:chaps. 2, 11.

academies that the army should be politically neutral, the "non-professional" officers trained by the Japanese saw no particular merit in abjuring politics, while the youths who had joined *laskar* units often did so as members of one political organization or another. Thus, the officer corps included few officers whose backgrounds inclined them to be receptive to the concept of the army as an apolitical tool of the state and many who were ready to involve themselves in political affairs.

The circumstances under which military officers acquired their political orientation during the revolution gave them a sense of having their own political purposes that could differ from those of the civilian politicians in the government. The military nature of the struggle for independence had inevitably involved the army leadership in national politics, where their views often conflicted with those of the government. The government leaders, who had joined the nationalist movement during the 1920s and 1930s, were derived mainly from the urban, Dutch-educated elite, whereas the senior officers of the army were rarely more than thirty years old and usually came from the small towns of Java, where they had been steeped in traditional culture, obtained only secondary schooling, and learned little Dutch. The lack of rapport that derived in part from this generational and cultural gap was exacerbated by the not unnatural feeling of army officers in the field that they had at least as much right as civilian politicians in the government to decide how the struggle was to be pursued. After asserting themselves by electing their own commander in chief in 1945, the army leaders joined other political groups in expressing strong dissatisfaction with the government's readiness to offer concessions to the Dutch in the interests of a negotiated settlement. The leaders of the government had perceived the struggle in its broader international setting and therefore tended to take a more detached view of diplomatic retreats; these were regarded as betrayals by guerrilla fighters, who were willing to risk their lives for nothing less than total victory. The alienation of army officers from the government reached its peak when the army fought on after the leaders of the government had allowed themselves to be captured by the Dutch in December 1948. The new round of negotiations that commenced in 1949 was regarded with great suspicion by many army officers, who nearly rejected the cease-fire ordered by the government and felt cheated by the terms of the transfer of sovereignty in December 1949. Thus, by the end of the revolution, many army officers had become deeply distrustful of the civilian politicians who had led the government.

The Expansion of the Army's Political Role

Since its foundation the Indonesian army had thus regarded itself as a political as well as a military force, and for most of its history it did indeed play a major political role. During the first few years of full independence, the army saw itself in an essentially "guardian" role, but it later asserted its right to participate continuously in political life. The political orientation of the officer corps had made its members receptive to the idea of actively participating in the affairs of the state, but it also led to a weak hierarchical structure and to sharp rivalries between groups of officers which limited the army's effectiveness as a political force. Aware of the army's lack of internal cohesion, its leaders felt deterred from taking the initiative in order to expand their political role. The activities of politically oriented dissident groups within the army, however, contributed to a series of national crises that created the conditions that enabled the army leaders to take wider powers. Thus, the expansion of the army's political role took place gradually and almost inadvertently as the weaknesses of successive political systems provided opportunities that military leaders exploited.

Although the experiences of army officers during the revolution tended to produce common attitudes to some questions, the army was far from a politically cohesive force. Apart from the Japanese-trained recruits, who often had their own political sympathies, many of the guerrilla fighters had not joined the army as individuals but had been incorporated en bloc at one time or another as members of party-affiliated youth organizations that had set up their own *laskar* units. Therefore many units had extramilitary political loyalties and soldiers often had a stronger sense of commitment to their unit commander than to the army as a whole. It was not uncommon for conflicts between civilian political groups to be reflected within the army, leading to the involvement of military units on both sides during such crises as the "July Third Affair" in 1946 and the Communist-supported

"Madiun Affair" in 1948.[4] Although the Madiun Affair and the conflict with Muslim *laskar* units supporting the Darul Islam movement enabled the army to rid itself of its ideological extremes, it continued to be divided into factions based on personal, regional, divisional, and political loyalties. Of some importance was the fact that all the young officers who had been thrust into the senior posts of the army were of about the same age and had more or less equal claims to the mantle of General Sudirman, the army's commander throughout the revolution, who died in January 1950, the month after the transfer of sovereignty.

Despite its political orientation and the distrust of politicians that many officers had acquired during the revolution, the army accepted the subordinate role to which it was assigned under the new parliamentary Constitution of 1950. The army leadership had been taken over by a small group of "military technocrats," most of whom had attended prewar Dutch academies and whose technical proficiency had given them preference over less well-trained officers. Some of these technocrats preferred to withdraw from a directly political role and to concentrate on molding the army into a cohesive and effective military force. Still very young (in 1950 the new army chief of staff, Colonel Nasution, was thirty-one and the armed forces chief of staff, Colonel T. B. Simatupang, thirty) and probably lacking confidence in their ability to tackle the complex problems of government, the military leaders were willing to leave the government in the hands of the older, better-educated, and more experienced politicians. Most important, circumstances left them very little choice. They were well aware that they were not representative of the officer corps as a whole and had no mandate to take political action on its behalf. The army was still more an alliance of local fighting units than an integrated force. Unit commanders often had little in common with the army leadership in Jakarta and could not be relied upon to support political initiatives taken in their name. In the absence of a common political program, the army had no alternative but to accept a subordinate, formally apolitical role. The acceptance of the principle of civilian supremacy by the army leaders, however, did not mean that the "nonprofessional" officers in com-

4. For the political crises during the revolution, see Kahin 1952.

mand of troops in the regions had ceased to feel that the army's
contribution during the revolution entitled them to a continuing
political role now that independence had been won.
The army's apolitical stance did not last long. The army soon
found itself drawn back into the political arena not primarily as a
result of the political ambitions of officers or the shortsighted
machinations of politicians, but because the complex of circumstances contributing to the fluidity of the power structure did not
allow the army to isolate itself from politics. Successive governments took the form of uneasy coalitions that were under constant
parliamentary attack, while the group controlling the army headquarters was unable to assert its authority over rival factions in the
regions. In such a situation it was only to be expected that the
rivalry between factions in the army would become enmeshed
with the struggle between government and opposition in parliament as each group sought allies.

The first major political crisis involving the army was the "Seventeenth of October Affair" of 1952.[5] With the support of successive
governments between 1950 and 1952, the technocratic military
leadership had been aiming to create a smaller, more disciplined,
and "professional" force. Their plans for rationalization and demobilization were resisted by many of the less well-trained former Peta
officers, who felt that their status would be downgraded in com-
parison with the "Westernized" officers of Jakarta and Bandung.
When opposition politicians took up the cause of dissident former
Peta officers as part of a general attack on the government, the
army dissidents naturally welcomed parliamentary support in their
struggle against the army leadership. But what the parliamentary
opposition regarded as the legitimate exercise of civilian authority
over the armed forces, the army leadership regarded as unwar-
ranted and intolerable "interference" in the army's internal affairs.
Already unimpressed by the performance of the parliamentary
system, a group of army officers in Jakarta organized a large civilian demonstration in front of the Presidential Palace on 17 October
1952 while a delegation of senior officers was meeting President

5. For an account of the Seventeenth of October Affair emphasizing civilian
"interference" in army matters, see Sundhaussen 1971:205–236. For an account
stressing army factionalism, see McVey 1971b:143–152. See also Feith 1962:246–
273.

Sukarno to request that he dissolve the parliament. The Seventeenth of October Affair was not so much an attempt by the army leaders to overthrow the government as an expression of their resentment, as military technocrats, at civilian attempts to obstruct them from carrying out what they regarded as necessary policies. They cannot have been unaware, however, that the dissolution of the parliament at their behest would have placed them in a very strong position from which to make further political moves. In any case, Sukarno not only refused to dissolve the parliament but encouraged the former Peta dissidents, who organized a series of coups against several regional commanders aligned with the central army leadership. At the end of the year the army chief of staff, Colonel Nasution, who had been powerless to intervene on his supporters' behalf, was himself dismissed along with his closest colleagues from the technocratic faction. The Seventeenth of October Affair had shown that as long as the army was divided into more or less evenly balanced factions, officers would make the most of political opportunities provided by the unrestrained competition between civilian political groups to further their own factions' interests even if they were not yet envisaging a much wider political role as a long-term goal.

During the following years the conception of the army as an apolitical tool of the state quickly gave way to the older idea that the army was the guardian of the national interest with the responsibility to intervene in political affairs whenever the weaknesses of civilian government made it necessary. Dissatisfaction with the parliamentary system was becoming widespread within as well as outside the military. Since independence a series of coalition governments had failed to hold power long enough to implement their programs and establish moral authority. Reflecting the cultural, regional, and ideological diversity of the nation, the many political parties represented in the parliament were unable to work out long-term alignments among themselves; as a result governments rose and fell as rival groups maneuvered for short-term advantage. Increasingly the parties came to be seen as patronage machines chiefly concerned with furthering the interests of their own supporters without regard for the "good of the nation." As the legitimacy of the parliamentary system was thrown into doubt, the search for an alternative accelerated.

Disillusionment with the government and the parliamentary system was strong among army officers of both major factions involved in the dispute of 1952. Although the conflicts surrounding the Seventeenth of October Affair had embittered the relations between rival groups of officers, the growing sense of disaffection gradually helped to bridge the gap. The Ali Sastroamidjojo government, which had come to power in July 1953, had managed to stay in office longer than any of its predecessors, partly through its flexibility in distributing benefits to its supporters, but many army officers felt that it neglected the military in the allocation of funds. Further, the defense minister had caused much resentment with his attempts to play off army factions against each other. Army officers accused the government of weakness, incompetence, corruption, and, not least, disregard of military interests. Disaffection spread, and army officers became more conscious of their common interests as members of a currently ineffective but potentially powerful political force. Early in 1955 a formal reconciliation of factions took place, and senior officers of all groups pledged to uphold unity in a ceremony at the grave of the late commander in chief, General Sudirman.

This new awareness of common purposes reached its peak when the coalition government led by the Indonesian National party (PNI) appointed Colonel Bambang Utojo, a PNI-sympathizing but relatively junior officer, as the army's new chief of staff in June 1955. Despite a number of unresolved differences, officers of both major factions joined to reject the appointment, with the result that a humiliated government soon fell from office. The fall of the Ali government produced an atmosphere of self-confidence in the army, and officers became convinced that they could have far more political influence in the future. Reports circulated that several senior officers had gone so far as to discuss the possibility of a coup against the government.[6] In fact, the brittle quality of the army's new-found unity virtually precluded the possibility of a successful coup, but many officers had clearly become very receptive to the view that the parliamentary system should be abandoned and replaced by a system permitting the army to play a more active political role. The army was less sharply divided than

6. See Pauker 1962:211. On the basis of interviews, however, Sundhaussen suggests that no such discussions took place (1971:268).

before, but the balance between its factions made consensus on the nomination of a new chief of staff difficult. Eventually it was agreed to recall Nasution, despite his central role in the controversies of 1952, and in the years after 1955 Nasution led the army into its vastly expanded political role.

Despite the disfavor into which the parliamentary system had fallen in army circles, the collapse of the last parliamentary government and the introduction of martial law in early 1957 were not the results of a deliberate move by the army leadership to overthrow the system. The system collapsed because of its inability to cope with regional military commanders who challenged the authority of both the government and the army leadership. Paradoxically, the continued factionalism within the army both prevented the army leadership from moving against the civilian government and created the conditions leading to the substantial enhancement of the army's political role. As in 1952, intra-army rivalry once again became entangled in broader national politics, but this time the conflict brought the nation to the point of civil war.

After the interlude in 1955, factional conflict in the army had revived in response to Nasution's moves to strengthen the authority of the army headquarters over the relatively autonomous regional commanders—some of whom had supported Nasution in 1952—by transferring well-entrenched regional commanders to new positions. Like the rationalization plans of 1952, Nasution's policies were opposed by senior officers who, feeling their positions threatened, sought political support from outside the army. The dissident officers' antagonism toward Nasution was aggravated by his willingness to cooperate with the second Ali Sastroamidjojo government, which had taken office in early 1956 after the general elections of the previous year. Although the second Ali government was more broadly based than the first, many officers, especially among the non-Javanese, considered it no better than the earlier government they had successfully undermined in the middle of 1955. At the same time, regional commanders outside Java shared the growing resentment in the Outer Islands against the central government, which was regarded as dominated by Javanese intent on "exploiting" the natural wealth of the export-producing areas.

When Nasution began to transfer regional commanders and other senior officers, his rivals, including some disappointed former allies, were ready to move into action. After a coup attempt planned by the dismissed deputy chief of staff, Colonel Zulkifli Lubis, had failed to get off the ground in the latter part of 1956,[7] several regional and local commanders in Sumatra and Sulawesi took control of local governments and succeeded in rallying considerable popular support behind their defiance of the central government. The crisis continued until 1958, when a meeting of military dissidents together with several leading politicians from the Muslim Masyumi and one from the Socialist party set up the Revolutionary Government of the Republic of Indonesian (PRRI) based in West Sumatra. When defiance turned to unambiguous rebellion the government felt compelled to act decisively. Let by Nasution's first deputy, Colonel Achmad Yani, central government forces quickly occupied rebel-held towns in Sumatra, and shortly afterward rebel strongholds fell in Sulawesi. Most of the rebel forces were soundly defeated within a few months, but guerrilla activities continued until 1961.

The events of 1956–1958 had far-reaching consequences both for the Indonesian political system and the role of the army in it. The emergency conditions had opened the way to a sudden expansion of the army's role not only in politics but also in the broader fields of general administration and economic management after the introduction of martial law in 1957. By proving its indispensability in the crisis caused by the rebellion, the army leadership had underpinned its claim to a more permanent role in the government. Further, the involvement in the rebellion of Nasution's most prominent opponents had left him in unchallenged control of the army and made it more united and more capable of promoting its political interests than ever before. Convinced that its participation in the government was necessary, and less inhibited by the old internal fissures, the army took advantage of the disrepute of the parliamentary system to press for a new government structure in which the army's place would be central. Together with President Sukarno the army led the way to the

7. See the contrasting emphases on interest and ideology in the explanations of events leading to the "Lubis affair" by McVey 1971b:157–170, Feith 1962:500–507, and Sundhaussen 1971:290–310.

reintroduction of the presidential 1945 Constitution, which provided the institutional framework for Guided Democracy.[8]

Under Guided Democracy politics revolved around the army and the president as the two pillars of the system, with the PKI rapidly emerging as the army's only rival for the ultimate succession. The army's political role came initially from its martial law powers, but soon officers were given substantial representation in the formal institutions of government, such as in cabinet and parliament, and were appointed as provincial governors and other regional officials. The army continued to exercise its emergency powers under martial law until 1963, and again after the reintroduction of a modified form of martial law in 1964. Army officers also played a major role in the newly created National Front,[9] especially in the regions, and their activities in the economy expanded as a result of their powers under martial law and their position in former Dutch enterprises placed under state control after 1957. Thus by 1965 the army was well entrenched. Indeed it had become so much a part of the power structure of Guided Democracy that many officers were reluctant to support political initiatives by army leaders for fear of upsetting their own highly satisfactory arrangements. Although the army always stood firm when its own interests were directly challenged and was steady in its resolve to check the advance of its outstanding rival, the PKI, it was reluctant to act against the PKI's protector, President Sukarno. The army leaders feared that precipitate action on their part might be exploited to their disadvantage by Sukarno, whose prestige remained high in many sections of the armed forces, including the army itself. Not only was the army's power checked by the growth of the navy, air force, and police, but it was dissipated by essentially personal rivalries between army officers. In any case most senior officers felt confident that the army's superior military might would guarantee victory for them in the end, so that drastic action against the PKI in the short run was unnecessary.

8. See Lev 1966:chap. 5.

9. The National Front was set up in 1960 to mobilize all political parties and other organizations, including the armed forces, behind the government's policies. It replaced the army-sponsored National Front for the Liberation of West Irian, which had been based on the army-led military-civilian "cooperation bodies" set up after the introduction of martial law. See Lev 1966:65–67.

During the two decades since 1945 the army had acquired political ambitions and a strong distrust of civilian politicians, but its internal disunity had prevented it from taking decisive action to consolidate its power. The expansion of the army's political role had not been a planned process in which its leaders took deliberate steps to fulfill their political ambitions. Rather it took the form of a series of responses to particular crises arising, in the main, from the actions of dissident officers. Although the circumstances that were favorable for the expansion of their power were not essentially of their own making, the army leaders had always been ready to exploit unexpected opportunities to the full.[10]

By the end of the Guided Democracy period many officers had become experienced and adroit politicians. Unlike army officers in countries where the military has taken power suddenly in a coup against a civilian government, Indonesian officers had undergone a lengthy period of preparation, during which they learned the skills of negotiating, bargaining, and compromising. Their experience of nonmilitary activities before 1965 had shaped a political style more suited to the advancement of officers' interests within the existing structure than to the creation of an entirely new political order. Scattered through the regional administration, central bureaucracy, nationalized business corporations, parliament, and cabinet, army officers had become adept at intrabureaucratic maneuvering and political intrigue to achieve short-run objectives. Alongside obligations to their military superiors, officers formed extramilitary loyalties as they identified with the civilian institutions in which they were placed and allied themselves with civilians sharing their immediate interests. Integrated into the Guided Democracy regime, army officers had been beneficiaries under it. Thus, when they strengthened their grip on the government after 1965, they did not suddenly become the

10. For a contrasting interpretation, see Sundhaussen 1971. Sundhaussen concludes that "the army involved itself in politics, and finally usurped power, because civilian elites had failed to set up workable political systems" (p. 706). "In the last analysis it must be said that civilians bear a considerable amount of responsibility for the army's assuming power in Indonesia. . . . In most clashes between civilians and the army, officers reacted rather than acted, responded to challenges rather than themselves initiated challenges" (pp. 714–715). This view, however, overstates the passive quality of the army's political activities and tends to overlook the involvement of sections of the military in most of the crises which nonmilitary governments were unable to handle.

bearers of new values and ideals but were more inclined to concern themselves with the consolidation of their power and the advancement of their existing interests.

The Army's Extramilitary Interests

The Indonesian army was, in a sense, a "people's army." Its officer corps had not been a carefully selected elite intended to protect the status quo but had arisen spontaneously during the revolution. Although the revolutionary period inclined the army toward political activity, it failed to provide officers with a clear ideological conception of their own interests and objectives. Unlike the revolutionary army in China, for example, which had grown over a period of two decades under the leadership of a single political party committed to a clearly defined ideology, the Indonesian army emerged from its revolutionary experience with little more than a strongly felt but vaguely articulated creed of nationalism. The urgency of the circumstances in which the army had been mobilized had not permitted attention to ideological indoctrination, and, in any case, the diversity of the units incorporated into the new army made adoption of a uniform political outlook impossible. Although officers later believed themselves obliged to ensure that the rather amorphous "ideals of the 1945 revolution" continued to be upheld, they lacked a convincing vision of the future and a program to attain it. Despite its origins as a people's army during a revolution the army never created a revolutionary ideology to guide its postrevolutionary political activities.

The army's political outlook reflected the cultural roots of its officers, among whom orthodox *santri* Muslims were underrepresented while, especially at the higher levels, Javanese of *priyayi* outlook were heavily overrepresented.[11] The preponderance of Javanese officers, which occurred originally because most of the fighting during the revolution took place in Java, became even more pronounced when many non-Javanese lost their positions

11. In Java the term *santri* is applied to those who fully identify themselves with Islam and conscientiously carry out their religious obligations. Non-*santris*, who are nominally Muslim but more influenced by pre-Islamic beliefs and practices, are known as *abangan*, while the upper stratum of this group is known as *priyayi*. These social groupings are usually referred to as *aliran* (streams). See Geertz 1960.

because of their involvement in the 1958 rebellion. By the 1960s it was estimated that some 60 to 80 percent of army officers were Javanese.[12] The overrepresentation of the Javanese meant that not only the non-Javanese but also strong Muslims were under-represented. Whereas Outer Islanders are generally identified with Islam, a majority of the ethnic Javanese, while still nominally Muslim, are not so much secular in outlook as they are attracted to the mystical practices and beliefs found in the variants of what is known as "Javanese religion." Further, even among the ethnic Javanese, strictly Muslim youths tended to leave the army after the revolution, possibly because many army activities during the 1950s were directed toward the suppression of Muslim-backed rebellions.[13] Although the *priyayi* Javanese character of much of the officer corps did not prevent non-Javanese Muslims, such as General Nasution, from rising to important positions, the army has always, and especially since 1958, aligned itself with the secular forces in society in obstructing Muslim political ambitions. There was never any possibility that the army would adopt an Islamic political ideology.

The political and social perspectives of the officer corps were also conditioned by their social backgrounds. Although some officers, especially in West Java, were from the lower aristocracy and a few had attended university-type institutions established by the Dutch in Jakarta and Bandung, the social origins of the majority were less elevated. In East and Central Java, most of the officers were local youths who had joined Peta during the Japanese period. Usually they were the sons of local officials, school-teachers, and traders, and most had spent at least a few years at secondary school, which gave them claims to elite status in the small towns where they lived. During the revolution some *laskar* units had been commanded by less-educated officers from the lower classes, but very few held responsible positions after the fighting ceased. Thus the officer corps was recruited largely from the upper strata of the small towns of Java. Most had little sense of identity with the mass of the people in the villages and were uninterested in turning the revolution against the Dutch into a

12. Sundhaussen 1971:63. About 45 percent of the population is ethnically Javanese.
13. McVey 1971b:138–139.

true social revolution. While they recognized that they occupied a less-privileged position than the civilian elite in power in Jakarta, they were usually more interested in the possibilities that a military career offered for social mobility than in its potential for carrying out social transformation.

As members of an organization dependent on the government for its funds, army officers naturally had an interest in gaining substantial allocations for defense in the government's budget, and the failure of the government to provide what officers considered to be adequate funds lay behind much of the rising disaffection in the army during the mid-1950s. Not only did the army feel deprived of new equipment, weapons, and other facilities, but both ordinary soldiers and officers found themselves unable to live in a style to which they felt entitled. Some military commanders, especially in the Outer Islands, felt compelled to resort to unorthodox sources of supply in order to maintain the functioning of their units and the loyalty of their troops. In the export-producing regions, such as North Sumatra and North Sulawesi, the military could raise funds quite easily by sponsoring semiofficial smuggling, while in other areas regional commanders made irregular arrangements with local businesses, usually ones owned by Chinese. These economic activities of military men, although arising originally out of necessity, opened up opportunities for individuals to benefit personally, with the result that some army officers wanted to continue the emergency arrangements.[14]

The limited involvement of the military in economic affairs suddenly expanded after the introduction of martial law in 1957. Martial law put military men in positions of considerable power, especially in the Outer Islands, where countervailing civilian forces were relatively weak. Although regional commanders did not always exercise their emergency powers to the full, they often took a direct interest in the administration of such economic matters as tax collection, the issuing of licenses, and the granting of other facilities.[15] Not until the end of 1957, however, when nationalist demonstrators took over Dutch enterprises following an adverse vote on West Irian in the United Nations, did vast new economic opportunities present themselves. Acting against the

14. Ibid., pp. 152–153.
15. Lev 1966:60.

PKI and other left-nationalist groups, the army immediately used its martial law powers to place all Dutch enterprises under military supervision. Later, after the nationalization of these enterprises, army officers continued to participate in the management of the new state corporations that had inherited the dominant position of the Dutch in such fields as plantations, mining, banking, and trade. During the 1960s the army's role in the economy further expanded when British enterprises were placed under military supervision in 1964 and American enterprises in 1965. In addition, an army-sponsored oil corporation, which had been set up in 1957, continued to expand its activities, and at the regional level individual military units set up their own business concerns, usually in association with Chinese partners.

The army's participation in the economy was, in part, another aspect of the implementation of Nasution's "Middle Way" concept, whereby army officers played a role in all civilian areas but did not seek a position of exclusive domination. The openings in economic management that became available to army officers had a further function in that the army leadership was able to shift less competent middle-ranking officers out of active military service to make way for more efficient officers. The most important purpose seems to have been to utilize many of the new state corporations, as well as military-owned business concerns, as sources of funds for the army. Officers involved in economic management were entrusted with the task of siphoning off funds and transferring them directly to the army rather than to the government, so that the army's dependence on allocations from the central government budget was reduced. As the Dutch had previously owned some of the nation's most profitable concerns, the resources coming under the control of army officers were substantial, although some enterprises soon fell into financial difficulties as a result of mismanagement and the excessive diversion of funds.[16]

The army's new role in the economy not only gave it, as an institution, a large stake in the economy, but also put many individual officers into an environment where they could advance their own material interests. The army's role in civil administra-

16. McVey 1972:159–161.

tion under martial law enabled officers to continue already established corrupt practices of their civilian predecessors. There was
little to prevent an officer entrusted with the duty of transferring
funds from a state corporation and other businesses to the army
from taking a cut for himself and his colleagues. Many senior
officers took a tolerant view of these activities, which gave lower-
ranking officers a stake in the status quo and helped to ensure
their loyalty to the army leadership, and some senior officers were
among the beneficiaries. The corrupting consequences of the sudden increase in the army's economic role were of great concern to
the army chief of staff, Nasution, who took several measures
against high-ranking offenders, including the suspension of a
member of the general staff, Colonel Ibnu Sutowo, in 1958 and
the transfer of several regional commanders in 1959, among them
the Central Java commander, Colonel Suharto.[17] After relinquish-
ing command of the army to Major General Yani, Nasution, as
minister for defense and security, headed the Committee for Retooling the State Apparatus (Paran) that conducted inquiries into
the activities of corrupt army officers and other officials in state
corporations, but the body was dissolved in 1964 partly because of
the opposition of highly placed officers who did not approve of its
purpose. Although Nasution received some support from officers
who were disturbed by the loss of integrity and reputation caused
by the army's economic activities, too many officers had become
beneficiaries for Nasution's efforts to win widespread sympathy.

The involvement of so many officers in economic affairs
brought about a striking change in the army's ethos. Before 1957
most officers had been concerned primarily with the army's function as a security force, despite the growing determination of
senior officers to assert themselves politically and the limited involvement of some officers in fund-raising activities. The rapid
expansion in the number of officers concerned with financial matters, whether in state corporations, civil administration, or busi-

17. In an interview with the former U.S. ambassador to Indonesia, Howard
Jones, Suharto suggested that he had been shifted prematurely from his command
because he was strongly anti-Communist (Jones 1971:438, 444). It is difficult to
believe that the army chief of staff, Nasution, would have dismissed a regional
commander for this reason. Several sources stated in interviews that Suharto had
been involved in a smuggling scheme ostensibly to raise funds for the "welfare" of
his troops.

nesses owned by local military units, led to a new perception of the army officers' functions. Alongside the earlier view of the officer as a "freedom fighter" and the "guardian" of the state appeared the images of the manager and the bureaucrat. As officers gained a deeper understanding of the workings of the commercial world it was not a big step for many to adopt the role of the businessman as well. Officers increasingly became involved in a private capacity as partners or bogus partners in business concerns that were usually run by Chinese. While the Chinese provided the business acumen, officers were able to ensure that bureaucratic obstacles to profit making were overcome.

The rapid expansion of the army's role in the economy after 1957 had accompanied its rising political power. As army officers joined the political and economic elite, they became accustomed to the privileges and wealth that elite status provides. As a political force the army had growing interests to defend and, like any other political organization, it naturally sought to place its members in such influential offices as the cabinet, the upper echelons of the civil service, and the regional administration, where they were able to safeguard and promote the army's position. Having become part of the social elite and beneficiaries of the existing social order, army officers had little interest in seeking a change from the status quo. Their interests were served by the system as it stood.[18]

Concerned to preserve the existing social order and political arrangements that supported it, army officers were well satisfied by the system of Guided Democracy during its first few years. Together with President Sukarno, the army leaders had played a major role in the introduction of the new system, and they had reached a satisfactory understanding with him on the general rules under which the system would operate. The president was aware of his dependence on the army for the maintenance of internal security and the achievement of his foreign policy objectives, while the army leaders acknowledged Sukarno's role in providing legitimacy and popular support for the system. As long as the president and his civilian allies did not seek to restrict the

18. For similar conclusions see Lev 1966:73–74, McVey 1972:160–161, G. Pauker 1962:223–224. Pauker, however, took a different view when the army came to full power after 1965. See, for example, Pauker 1967.

range of the officer corps' activities and privileges, its members preferred to cooperate with him in preserving mutually advantageous arrangements. In the latter period of Guided Democracy, however, tensions arose that made the indefinite continuation of the system unlikely. Based on its ability to draw support from the rural and urban poor who stood well outside the elite, the PKI posed a threat to the system that could not be met by making a bit more room in the elite for its leaders. As President Sukarno aligned himself more closely with the PKI, which had become the main counterbalance to the army, the struggle for power eventually became too much for the system to bear.

2 | Guided Democracy: The Uneasy Balance of Power

Guided Democracy was initially a means of overcoming the disunity that had become apparent in Indonesian politics in the mid-1950s. To replace the parliamentary struggle between parties, a new, more authoritarian system was created in which the central role was played by President Sukarno. Sukarno had reintroduced the presidential 1945 Constitution in 1959 on the strong urging of the army leaders, and the army provided the major organizational backing for the regime. But Sukarno was well aware of the potential danger to his own position of excessive reliance on the army, so, in addition to exploiting rivalries within the armed forces, he encouraged the activities of civilian groups as a counterweight to the military. Of these groups by far the most important was the PKI. Although both the army and PKI leaders professed loyalty to Sukarno as the "Great Leader of the Revolution" they were themselves locked in irreconcilable conflict.

Sukarno sought to hold together the competing political forces of Guided Democracy by fostering an overriding sense of national purpose. Describing himself as the "Mouthpiece of the Indonesian People," he created a national ideology to which all loyal citizens were expected to give allegiance. The Panca Sila (Five Principles), which he had "dug up" in 1945, were followed by a series of doctrines, each one complementing but also to a certain extent superseding the others, such as Manipol-USDEK, Nasakom, and other formulations that were joined together in the "Five Magic Charms of the Revolution."[1] Rallying widespread

1. Manipol stood for Political Manifesto, a program based on Sukarno's Independence Day speech in 1959. Its main provisions are represented in USDEK: U (Undang-undang Dasar 1945, 1945 Constitution), S (Sosialisma a la Indonesia,

public support for his campaigns against the Dutch in West Irian and the British in Malaysia, he claimed for Indonesia a role as a leader of the "New Emerging Forces" of the world with the destiny of destroying the remaining influence of the Nekolim (neocolonialists, colonialists, and imperialists). As the symbol of the nation Sukarno aimed to create a sense of national purpose that would transcend the political rivalries threatening the survival of the system.[2]

Guided Democracy can also be seen in more traditional terms. Despite his radical slogans and political alliance with the PKI, Sukarno often behaved more as a traditional Javanese sultan than as a modern nationalist leader.[3] Apparently unconcerned with the mundane problems of economic development and rational administration, Sukarno emphasized the holding of grand ceremonies and the construction of magnificent monuments and buildings in his capital, where his court gathered around a ruler regarded as possessing exceptional—even magical—qualities. Like the traditional sultans, he appointed ministers to take care of the affairs of state while he laid down the general line of policy. Following the examples of his Majapahit and Mataram predecessors, he secured his position by carefully balancing the roles played by rival groups of courtiers. Just as the traditional court advisers sought to influence rather than depose the sultan, the day-to-day conflict between the army and PKI leaders became a struggle for the president's ear.

Guided Democracy, whether couched in modern or traditional terms, ultimately failed. Although all groups mouthed approval of the president's ideological precepts, his doctrines often became weapons in the hands of the army, the PKI, and other groups in their efforts to demonstrate each others' disloyalty. While political leaders in the capital often behaved like traditional court advisers, the rival groups of courtiers were backed by nationwide organiza-

---

Indonesian Socialism), D (Demokrasi Terpimpin, Guided Democracy), E (Ekonomi Terpimpin, Guided Economy), K (Kepribadian Indonesia, Indonesian Personality). Nasakom (Nasionalis, nationalist; Agama, religion; Komunis, Communist) denoted the unity between the three major sociopolitical tendencies in Indonesian society. See Weatherbee 1966 for explanation of these and other ideological formulations.

2. For an elaboration of Sukarno's use of symbols to mobilize voluntary support, see Feith 1963b.

3. See Geertz 1968, Willner 1970, and Anderson 1972b.

tions confronting each other throughout Indonesia. Despite Sukarno's untiring efforts to reconcile the army and the PKI, neither ideologizing and national campaigns on one hand nor neotraditional ritual and court politics on the other were able to settle the conflicts between the organizations and interests represented by the rivalry between the army and the PKI.

During the early years of Guided Democracy an uneasy but fairly stable balance of power developed among the president, the army leadership, and the PKI. With the intensification of the struggle for West Irian in 1960 the climate facilitated mutual accommodation between the main political forces. But the successful conclusion of the campaign in 1962 introduced a period of uncertainty that was resolved only when Indonesia launched a crusade against the formation of Malaysia in September 1963. The commencement of the anti-Malaysia campaign created conditions that permitted the rapid advance of the PKI and the undermining of the old, relatively stable balance. Tensions rose, and a polarization of political forces took place as the army leadership prepared to meet the PKI challenge.

The Stable Balance (1960–1962)

The stability of the balance of power under Guided Democracy depended on continued cooperation between President Sukarno and the army leadership. As the two most powerful political forces, they had worked together to replace the old system and were concerned to preserve the new arrangements, but their interests did not always coincide. Although they were partners in upholding the system, they were also rivals for power under it. They had a mutual need for each other, but each was wary about the other's ambition to gain the upper hand. Under these circumstances the balance of power initially was uneasy as the two sides explored the extent of the leeway permitted to each by the other. By the latter part of 1960 it seemed that mutual understanding had been reached on the broad outline of the way power would be distributed. There developed between the president and the army leadership what Herbert Feith called "a 'stable conflict' relationship characterized by both common endeavor and continuing competition and tension between more or less equally matched partners."[4]

4. Feith 1963a:325. This article surveys the early years of Guided Democracy before the tilting of the balance in 1963.

The relationship between President Sukarno and the army leadership was founded on a mutual awareness that one could not easily do away with the other. The political power of the army leaders, based on their control of a nationwide organization capable of using force, was a fact of life that the president had to accept. On the other hand, the army leaders recognized that Sukarno's authority as president gave the regime an aura of legitimacy it would not have without him. They knew that he had the support of most of the political parties and that these regarded him as the main obstacle to further military encroachments at their expense. Moreover, the army leaders were conscious of the president's popularity among sections of the officer corps, with the result that the loyalties of many officers were divided. Thus both Sukarno and the army leaders preferred to reach an accommodation of shared power rather than attempt to establish their own unchallenged hegemony.

The readiness of Sukarno and the army leaders to cooperate with each other had been facilitated by the atmosphere of crisis prevailing since 1957. After their success in abolishing the parliamentary system and defeating the regional rebels, Sukarno and the army were drawn together in the campaign to recover West Irian. The continued occupation of West Irian by the Dutch had been a source of national humiliation to almost all political groups. The campaign came to be seen as a continuation of the 1945 revolution that would once again inspire the people to subordinate their immediate interests in order to fulfill the nation's destiny. Open rivalry between the main political forces was subdued and the expression of opposition to the government acquired an air of disloyalty.

The continuing atmosphere of crisis after 1957 had permitted the rapid expansion of the army's political power. Under the provisions of the state of war and siege, local military commanders had almost unlimited powers to take action for the preservation of "security." The administration of martial law after 1957 was supervised by Nasution, who, as army chief of staff, headed the army's Central War Authority (Peperpu), to which the Regional War Authorities (Peperda) were responsible. In an effort to assert his control over the implementation of martial law, President Sukarno dissolved the Peperpu at the end of 1959 and established the Supreme War Authority (Peperti) headed by himself, with the first minister, Djuanda Kartawidjaja, and Nasution as his deputies. Day-to-day control of the new authority remained largely with the army, especially in the regions where the regional commanders continued to head the Peperda.[5]

The army's political position was strengthened further as the emphasis in the conduct of the West Irian campaign moved from diplomatic to military means. In December 1961, Sukarno established the Supreme Command for the Liberation of West Irian (Koti) under his own leadership, with Nasution as his deputy and Major General Yani as chief of staff; operations were placed under Major General Suharto as commander of the Mandala Command for the Liberation of West Irian.[6] Backed by Indonesian military pressure in the form of the landing of infiltrators in the jungles of West Irian and American diplomatic pressure on the Dutch, agreement was finally reached between Indonesia and the Netherlands on 15 August 1962 for the immediate transfer of the administration of West Irian to the United Nations, which would transfer authority to Indonesia on 1 May 1963. Thus the campaign ended in a victory for Indonesia and a further increase in the army's prestige.

The army's growing political strength was reflected in the formal institutions set up under Guided Democracy. In the cabinet appointed in July 1959, immediately after the restoration of the 1945 Constitution,[7] nearly one-third of the ministers were drawn from the armed forces in contrast with only three in the previous cabinet and none before 1958. The armed forces were also well represented in the new appointed Gotong-Royong People's Repre-

5. Sundhaussen 1971:466.
6. Following his removal from command of the Diponegoro Division in Central Java in 1959, Suharto took a course at the Army Staff and Command College (Seskoad) and in March 1960 was appointed to command the new General Reserve Corps, which was the forerunner of the Army Strategic Reserve Command (Kostrad) formed in 1963. See Roeder 1969:195.
7. The 1945 Constitution provided the institutional framework for Guided Democracy. The republic's original constitution, it had been withdrawn later in 1945. Under the Constitution, the government was headed by the president who was elected by the People's Consultative Assembly (MPR), which was obliged to convene at least once every five years. Legislation had to be passed by the People's Representative Council (DPR) or parliament. After the reintroduction of the 1945 Constitution in 1959, provisional bodies, the MPRS and the DPR-GR, were created to carry out the functions of the MPR and DPR until elections could be held.

sentative Council or Parliament (DPR-GR) and in the Provisional People's Consultative Assembly (MPRS), while five army officers were appointed as provincial governors in 1960. The political weight of the army was most deeply felt, however, in such bodies as the Koti and Peperti. The Koti increasingly came to rival the cabinet as the most important decision-making body, while the Peperti continued to supervise the administration of martial law until the transfer of authority in West Irian in May 1963.

As the army consolidated its power, Sukarno sought to strengthen his side. Most of his closest associates at the beginning of the Guided Democracy period were politicians who, like himself, lacked organized mass support. Such men as Djuanda, Johannes Leimena, Chaerul Saleh, Mohammad Yamin, Subandrio, and Ruslan Abdulgani formed a diverse group of intelligent and able politicians who were highly skilled in elite-level political maneuvering but could not provide Sukarno with the organized grassroots support he needed to maintain the balance with the army.[8] For this he turned back to the political parties, especially to the PKI. Although the president had worked with the army to push the parties off the center of the political stage, he did not want them entirely eliminated. He envisaged that the PNI, Nahdatul Ulama (NU), and PKI would become the organizational channels for cooperation between the nationalist, religious, and Communist elements in society to which his Nasakom slogan referred,[9] and he expected that the parties would usually align themselves with him against the army. In particular, Sukarno expected the firm support of the PKI, which was more able to mobilize mass support and more in fear of the army than the other parties.

The army leaders already regarded the PKI as their main long-term rival and wanted to limit its potential for growth. Because Sukarno recognized the PKI as one of the three components of Nasakom, plans began to be formulated in some army circles to check its advance. When the PKI issued an extremely critical eval-

8. Of these leaders, only Ruslan Abdulgani was an important figure in a major party, the nationalist PNI, while Leimena, an Ambonese Christian, led the small Protestant party, Parkindo. The others were not party leaders.
9. The nationalist Partai Nasional Indonesia (PNI), the Muslim Nahdatul Ulama (NU), and the PKI were the strongest of the ten legal parties under Guided Democracy. Another strong party, the Muslim Masyumi had been banned following the participation of some of its leaders in the PRRI revolt.

uation in July 1960 of the achievements of the cabinet, several leaders, including D. N. Aidit and Njoto, were summoned for interrogation by army intelligence officers headed by Colonel Achmad Sukendro while another, Sakirman, was arrested. Responding to the challenge, Sukarno quickly intervened and persuaded the wavering Nasution to have them released. Meanwhile, several regional commanders continued to favor direct action against the PKI, and in August the party was banned in South Sumatra, South Kalimantan, and South Sulawesi and its activities restricted in East Java. Again Sukarno intervened, and despite the feeling within the army against the president's policy toward the PKI, Nasution decided to bow to his wishes. Later in the year the bans were lifted in two of the regions—although the third commander held out until the following August—and Colonel Sukendro, who was regarded as the main initiator of the anti-PKI moves, was dismissed from his position and sent abroad.[10]

The test of strength between the president and the army leadership in 1960 gave both a clear understanding of their own and the other's power. Sukarno, conscious of his need for strong civilian support, had saved the PKI from army repression, but he was made aware of the depth of anti-Communist sentiment felt by many army officers who might well be provoked into taking more drastic action if he insisted on further strengthening the PKI. On the other hand, events had shown that the army leadership was not at that moment willing to risk an open confrontation with the president in order to ban the PKI. In the circumstances the army leaders could not rely on a united front of support in standing up to the president although further moves favoring the PKI, such as the appointment of PKI leaders to the cabinet, could be expected to lead to a hardening of feeling against him.

The mutual understanding reached between the president and the army leadership during the latter half of 1960 formed the basis of the relatively stable, if somewhat uneasy, balance of power that continued until the end of the West Irian campaign in 1962. Protected by the president and contained by the army, the PKI became a key factor in the balance. It was permitted to continue its activities as a legal party, and its members held a substantial

10. See Hindley 1966:294–295, Feith 1963a:338–339.

share of seats in the main representative bodies. Although the
PKI leaders, Aidit and M. H. Lukman, were accorded ministerial
status as deputy chairmen of the MPRS and DPR-GR respectively,
the PKI continued to be excluded from cabinet posts entailing
executive authority. Despite the recognition and security that the
party had obtained, its prospects of breaking out of the Guided
Democracy system and taking power for itself seemed very poor.
In the 1950s it had opted for the "parliamentary road" to power
and had adjusted its organization accordingly, with an emphasis
on expanding the quantity rather than the quality of its mass base.
While its following continued to increase in the 1960s, it was no
longer competing for votes with political parties but was engaged
in a power struggle with the army. In these circumstances it was
compelled to moderate its tactics. As Donald Hindley concluded,
the PKI became "domesticated."[11] It had a large mass following,
representation in the main councils of the state, and a warm relationship with the president, but no credible strategy for attaining
power. The best it could hope for seemed to be to gain more
influence with the president in exchange for political support,
while at the worst it had "become something of a bird in a gilded
cage with only a process of slow atrophy lying ahead."[12]

   The balance of power in which the PKI's role was relatively
subordinate did not last long. The campaign to recover West Irian
had attracted enthusiastic support from almost all quarters and
had been of major importance in creating the sense of national
purpose that President Sukarno hoped would prove strong
enough to hold the major political forces together despite their
differences. As long as the campaign continued, Sukarno was
confident of his ability to retain the loyalty of the army leadership
and still protect the PKI, but the successful conclusion of the
campaign introduced a strong sense of uncertainty felt by all
groups. The president was concerned that the delicate balance
might be upset in the army's favor as the armed forces turned
their attention back to domestic matters. The army was worried
that the end of the crisis might be used by the president to
weaken the army's scope for political action by lifting martial law.

   11. Hindley 1962.
   12. Van der Kroef 1965b:263. In the same work, however, van der Kroef
argued that the PKI began to dominate the political scene after 1964.

A technocratic group around the first minister, Djuanda, hoped that the new circumstances would enable emphasis to be placed on Western-financed economic development. The PKI realized that concentration on economic matters could lead to dependence on the West, and it feared that renewed moves against the party might be made by army officers. Thus the victory on West Irian ushered in a highly fluid period in which a number of very different courses seemed open. The apparently stable balance of power was shown to be resting on foundations that were far from firm.

The Balance Turns (1962–1964)

Although the conclusion of the West Irian campaign had serious implications for the domestic balance of power, the relative strengths of the contending forces were not suddenly transformed. For more than a year after the ending of the campaign the key relationship continued to be that between Sukarno and the army leadership, while the PKI refrained from taking major initiatives of its own. Although President Sukarno succeeded in weakening the position of the army leadership during this period, his moves were aimed less at turning the balance of power in his own and the PKI's favor than at preventing it from tilting back in the army's direction. Only after the sudden escalation in the campaign to Crush Malaysia in September 1963 were conditions created that permitted a much more drastic turning of the balance of power and enabled the PKI to emerge from under Sukarno's protective wing as a dynamic force in its own right.

Sukarno and the Army

As the West Irian campaign drew to a close, the army seemed to be in a position to play a much more assertive role than earlier. The military build-up had led to a rapid increase in the number of troops to over three hundred thousand, and new armaments and equipment had been obtained from the Soviet Union. The army's prestige had been further enhanced by the victory in the struggle for West Irian as well as the successful suppression of local rebellions in West Java and Sulawesi in 1961 and 1962. While the campaign was in progress the army felt inhibited from taking action against its domestic enemies, but in the new atmosphere both the president and the PKI were apprehensive about the army's intentions. It did not seem unlikely that the group of officers who had favored early action against the PKI in 1960 might find themselves in a better position to persuade their colleagues to stand up to Sukarno. Thus the president felt compelled to attempt to whittle away at the army leadership's power.

Sukarno's first move was directed against the minister for defense and security and army chief of staff, General Nasution, whom he regarded as the officer most capable of turning the army against him. Sukarno calculated that Nasution's power as minister for defense and security could be reduced by divesting him of the position he concurrently held as army chief of staff with direct control over troops.[13] Sukarno wanted to replace him with an officer more amenable to his own influence, preferably a Javanese from the group in the army which was most reluctant to consider action against the president. Sukarno knew that Nasution was not universally popular among the officer corps, partly because of his disapproval of the corrupt commercial activities in which many officers engaged. However, he was still the army's outstanding general and the architect of the army's rise to power. Thus Sukarno could not simply dismiss him without alienating the entire officer corps, and there seemed little prospect that the forty-three-year-old Nasution would resign voluntarily.

Toward the middle of 1962 an opportunity for the president arose from Nasution's own plan to consolidate his power as minister for defense and security. The initial agreement was that Nasution be appointed to the new post of commander of the armed forces with full authority over all four services. After Nasution had agreed to relinquish his position as chief of staff of the army in June 1962, however, the recently appointed air force chief of staff, Omar Dhani, protested—possibly at the instigation of Sukarno himself—that the air force could not serve under a commander from another service. After consulting the chiefs of staff of the navy and police as well as Nasution's proposed successor, Yani, Sukarno altered the plan to preserve the autonomy of the four services. The four chiefs of staff were transformed into commanders of their respective services responsible only to the presi-

13. In 1959, Sukarno had appointed Nasution as minister for defense and security in the expectation that he would resign as chief of staff of the army, but Nasution insisted on holding both positions; see Lev 1966:279.

dent as supreme commander of the armed forces. While Nasution retained his position as minister for defense and security, the proposed post of commander of the armed forces with operational authority over the four services was changed to chief of staff of the armed forces with functions limited to administrative coordination and civil defense.[14] Thus Nasution was outmaneuvered by the president and "kicked upstairs" to a relatively powerless although still influential role.

Of crucial importance in the success of the president's maneuver was the willingness of the new army leader, Yani, to go along with the plan. Nasution had originally proposed the appointment of his first deputy, Major General Gatot Subroto, as his successor, but Sukarno had been unwilling to accept Gatot, whom he regarded as completely loyal to Nasution. Fate intervened when Gatot suddenly died at the beginning of June. Nasution then proposed several more names from among whom Sukarno selected Nasution's second deputy, Major General Yani. Yani had gained a good reputation when he commanded the forces that easily put down the PRRI rebellion in 1958, and, as a strong anti-Communist, he had the confidence of Nasution and the officer corps in general. He also enjoyed the confidence of the president, with whom he had worked closely as chief of staff of the Koti. Yani had identified himself with the "moderate" group in the army who "realized that the President was essential"[15] and, as a Javanese, who lacked Nasution's Islamic puritanism, he was more at ease in Sukarno's palace circle.

The elevation of Yani to the army command had reduced the likelihood that the army would take direct action in conflict with the president's wishes. Although Yani was as strongly opposed as Nasution to Sukarno's policy toward the PKI, his personal style differed from that of his predecessor. As a Javanese he tended to treat Sukarno with the respect due to a *"Bapak"* (father) who might be wrong but should not be openly contradicted. Moreover, his easygoing and flexible personality enabled him to develop a rapport with the president which soon made him subject to the

14. For Nasution's own account, see Nasution 1967:I, 35–37.
15. Lev 1966:71, quoting an interview with Yani in 1961. Yani was referring to the 1956–1957 period, but his outlook in regard to Sukarno appears to have remained unchanged.

kind of personal pressures that Sukarno often brought to bear on his colleagues. Further, it was natural that Yani, as the new commander, would hesitate to take drastic initiatives until his authority had been fully established, especially as the circumstances of Nasution's "promotion" and Yani's apparent complicity in it had led to a strong sense of resentment among Nasution's followers. Nevertheless, the army under Yani remained an essentially autonomous center of power which continued to defend its interests.[16] If Yani was more "Javanese" in his style than Nasution, he was no less firm. While the Sumatran Nasution bluntly rejected policies proposed by Sukarno with which he did not agree, Yani was more inclined to accept them subject to his own interpretations. The president, of course, knew that Yani made his own interpretations, but both preferred to maintain the façade of unanimity in the spirit of *musyawarah* (consultation) and *mufakat* (consensus), as neither took action that went further than the other was prepared to accept.

Having succeeded in neutralizing the threat he perceived in Nasution's leadership of the army, Sukarno further sought to limit the army's capacity for taking political action against his interests by lifting martial law and abolishing the Peperti/Peperda institution. The president's case for revoking martial law had been strengthened by the army's success in suppressing a series of rebellions in Sumatra, Sulawesi, and, most important, the Darul Islam revolt in West Java. When the West Irian campaign ended in August 1962, there appeared to be no further justification for the continuation of martial law. Although the army leaders wanted to retain their emergency powers, they were able to achieve only a postponement of the return to civilian authority until 1 May 1963, the day that Indonesia took control of West Irian from the transitional United Nations administration.

The dissolution of Peperti/Peperda was followed by the reorganization of the Koti in July 1963. The transformation of the Koti was in part a countermove to Nasution's scheme to have the remaining functions of the old Supreme Command for the Liberation of West Irian transferred to his own Department of Defense and Security.[17] By preserving the Koti as the Supreme Op-

16. See Sundhaussen 1971:525–527.
17. Nasution 1967:I, 37–38.

erations Command, with Yani retaining his post as chief of staff and Nasution losing his as deputy commander, Sukarno strengthened the Yani faction and exacerbated the growing disunity within the army. At the same time he ensured that the new Koti was not dominated by the army. Although organized along military lines, only two of its five divisions were headed by army officers. The foreign minister, Subandrio, was placed in charge of intelligence, the minister of information, Achmadi, became responsible for "mobilization," and Air Commodore Sri Muljono Herlambang headed the division for operations. With broad and general functions, the Koti's role came to surpass that of the cabinet. The main cabinet ministers, including Nasution, became members of its Advisory Council, and many of the most important government decisions were taken at its sessions.[18]

After the completion of the West Irian campaign, Sukarno successfully reduced the army's capacity to seize the initiative. By fostering conflict between groups within the army, Sukarno contributed to circumstances that drew the army commander into his own circle. Under Yani the army was prepared to cooperate with the president, but its cooperation was dependent on Sukarno's refraining from moves that fundamentally affected the balance of power in a way unfavorable for the army. As long as the army's basic interests were undisturbed and its main rival, the PKI, was not permitted to make rapid advances, the Yani leadership was willing to support the status quo in which the army was still the most powerful organized force.

Confrontation

Sukarno's moves to limit the army's capacity to take the initiative against him had taken place as the government stood poised between two sharply contrasting courses for the future containing very different implications for the domestic balance of power as well as for foreign relations. The ending of the West Irian campaign opened the possibility that the government would concentrate on economic development supported by substantial American assistance. The economy had suffered during the West Irian mobilization as the rate of inflation approached 100 percent per

18. For the presidential decisions establishing the Koti and appointing its members see Nasution 1967:I, 136–140.

annum. But as long as the campaign was in full swing, there was no prospect of introducing an austerity program designed to achieve economic stabilization. Following the end of the campaign for West Irian, the first minister, Djuanda, and his colleagues felt that the atmosphere was more hopeful because the United States and the International Monetary Fund (IMF) expressed interest in providing aid. In May 1963 relatively liberal economic regulations were introduced, and in June an agreement was reached with three foreign oil companies permitting them to continue their operations in Indonesia. As Indonesia turned to what the Western governments regarded as "responsible" economic policies, the IMF indicated its approval by granting a "standby loan" of $50 million and the United States prepared to substantially increase its aid program.[19]

The success of the new economic approach, however, had been threatened by growing suport for a policy of "confrontation" against Malaysia. The Indonesian government had not shown interest in opposing the proposed formation of Malaysia until after a revolt in Brunei had been put down by British troops in December 1962, but even then official Indonesian policy had remained fairly ambivalent until September 1963. Indonesian-sponsored incursions soon commenced into the British territories of Borneo. The first clash, which occurred at Tebedu in Sarawak on 12 April when a band of Indonesian-led intruders captured weapons from a local military outpost, was followed by thirty-four small-scale incidents before the formation of Malaysia on 16 September 1963.[20] The incidents fell far short of full-scale war and were accompanied by signs that Indonesia was seeking a face-saving formula to call off the campaign, especially as Sukarno seemed to be backing Djuanda's efforts to rehabilitate the economy.

At the end of May, Sukarno had held an apparently amiable discussion with the Malayan prime minister, Tunku Abdul Rahman, in Tokyo, which was following by a meeting of the foreign ministers of Indonesia, Malaya, and the Philippines in June and a conference of the three heads of government at Manila in August which endorsed President Macapagal's proposals for regular con-

19. See Mackie 1967:30–37.
20. See the British "Incident Log for Eastern Malaysia, April–September 1963," in Boyce, ed. 1968:84–87.

sultations and cooperation between the "Maphilindo" countries. It was further agreed that the UN secretary-general be asked to send a mission to Sarawak and Sabah to ascertain the wishes of the people on the question of joining Malaysia. The mission was expected to find in favor of the formation of Malaysia, thereby enabling Indonesia to recognize the new state without severe loss of face. After brief hearings with local politicians the UN mission concluded that the "majority" wanted to join Malaysia, but these conclusions were immediately denounced by Indonesia, which had been antagonized by the Tunku's announcement before the mission had completed its work that Malaysia would be formed in any case on 16 September. Taking the view that Malaysia was a "British project" designed to create a "puppet state" to perpetuate "neocolonialism," Indonesia launched a campaign to Crush Malaysia, and mobs in both capitals immediately attacked each other's embassies. In the aftermath the IMF suspended its credit and the Americans abandoned their intention of providing new aid. The plans of the technocrats to stabilize and rehabilitate the economy were lost in the rush to Crush Malaysia.[21]

Despite the dramatic events of September, military confrontation during the following months meant little more than the continuation of the policy of sending into Sabah and Sarawak small groups of "volunteers" who had undergone training in Indonesia and whose forays were often led by Indonesian officers. The incursions seemed intended to keep the issue alive by giving encouragement to local dissidents and increasing the cost to Britain and Malaysia of protecting the two territories. There was no sign that Sukarno wanted to expand the conflict into a full-scale war, and during the first half of 1964 Indonesia seemed responsive to diplomatic moves toward a settlement. A cease-fire was announced in January 1964 following mediation by the American attorney general, Robert Kennedy, but meetings between the Indonesian, Malaysian, and Filipino foreign ministers in February and March and a meeting of the three heads of government in Tokyo in June failed to find a solution.

Instead of easing the tension, the Tokyo summit was followed by an exacerbation of the conflict. On Indonesia's Independence

21. See Mackie 1974:chap. 7.

Day, 17 August 1964, a small group of Indonesian infiltrators
landed by boat at Pontian in Johore, and a fortnight later, on 2
September, thirty members of the air force paratroop force, together with ten Malaysian Chinese, were parachuted into southern Malaya. Both groups of infiltrators were quickly rounded up
and either killed or captured by Malaysian security forces. Indonesia apparently expected the infiltrators to make contact with
local dissidents in the Johore jungles, where they could support
expanded guerrilla activities against the government. After the
dismal failure of the landings on the Malay Peninsula, confrontation proceeded as before with Sukarno and his ministers calling
on the people to Crush Malaysia while small-scale incursions continued in Sarawak and Sabah and some Indonesian saboteurs
slipped into Singapore.

President Sukarno's motives in opting for confrontation rather
than economic rehabilitation were complex. His ideological outlook certainly inclined him toward leading a struggle against the
"old established forces" of imperialism, colonialism, and neocolonialism, which he saw as standing behind the formation of Malaysia, but at the same time he seemed very hesitant to embark on a
course that would prejudice Indonesia's prospects of obtaining
funds from the leading "imperialist" power. While the need for
foreign funds to finance the economic stabilization program
curbed the trend toward confrontation, other domestic factors
hastened it. The president had appreciated the stabilizing impact
of the earlier West Irian campaign on the domestic balance of
power, and he may well have envisaged that a similar issue might
serve to preoccupy the army while the PKI became an accepted
part of the political establishment. It may also have been calculated that far from holding the nation together, a concentration
on economic reform as prescribed by the World Bank and the
IMF would have exacerbated domestic conflict by imposing sacrifices in the interests of stabilization and by seeming to imply that
the country had been ensnared in the imperialist embrace. Thus a
continuing low-level crisis might have seemed more effective in
gaining support for Sukarno than a program involving economic
deprivation.[22] The success of this strategy, however, depended on

22. For discussions of Sukarno's motives, see Hindley 1964, Kahin 1964, Bunnell 1966, Legge 1972:370–373, Mackie 1974:179–183.

the continued support of the main domestic political forces for the policy of confrontation.

The attitude of the army toward both the proposed economic program and confrontation was ambivalent. At the end of the West Irian campaign many officers had looked with sympathy on the plans to concentrate on economic development, but as the details of Djuanda's proposals were revealed, it became clear that the austerity program would lead to a cut in funds for the armed forces, making a measure of demobilization unavoidable. Thus, as the campaign against Malaysia gathered momentum during the early part of 1963, the attitude of army officers became more positive despite its consequences for the economic program.

The army leaders certainly did not want to go to war, but, short of its becoming a large-scale military conflict, many officers were not unsympathetic to the campaign against Malaysia. Army officers, like other nationalists, regarded Indonesia as the natural leader of Southeast Asia. They tended to see the formation of Malaysia as a means of prolonging British influence, and they particularly resented the presence of British bases both as an obstacle to Indonesia's long-term aspirations and as a short-term threat. Officers also remembered that foreign aid had been channeled to the PRRI rebels through Malaya and Singapore in 1958. Further, many officers feared that the new state's large Chinese minority would draw Malaysia into the sphere of the People's Republic of China and believed, or professed to believe, that this could somehow be prevented by a policy of confrontation.[23]

Some senior officers, including, it seems, the army commander, Yani, saw the campaign mainly in the context of its impact on the domestic balance of power.[24] The new crisis would justify the continued central role of the army in politics and administration and might even permit a return to martial law. The planned cut in the military budget and demobilization would be abandoned, and more armaments might be offered by the Soviet Union. Possi-

23. One Indonesian officer told the American ambassador, "I don't understand why you Americans, who profess to be so anti-Communist, don't see that in supporting Malaysia you are running the risk of the establishment of a Chinese Communist state right in the heart of Southeast Asia" (Jones 1971:270). A similar view was held by the former vice-president, Hatta. See Hatta 1965.
24. According to Nasution, Yani was less concerned with the principle of confrontation than with the advantages it offered to the army both politically and in terms of armaments (interview with General Nasution, 20 August 1973).

bly some officers anticipated that British investments might suffer the fate of Dutch enterprises taken over during the West Irian campaign and transferred to army control. Thus there were many, in part conflicting, reasons why army officers and their leaders were able to accommodate themselves to the intensification of confrontation.

The principal leaders of the army gave verbal support to confrontation from the outset, but they differed over what action was to be taken. In January 1963, Yani had announced his "fullest moral support" for the opponents of Malaysia in the Borneo states and declared that his troops were "awaiting the order" to move,[25] but he appears to have been reluctant at first to permit the direct involvement of the army. At this stage Nasution seemed to favor a more forthright policy. Nasution, who appears to have been more apprehensive than Yani of what he saw as the strategic dangers of the formation of Malaysia, had known the Brunei rebel leader, A. M. Azahari, for many years and sympathized with his aspirations for an independent state of North Kalimantan. Together with his former intelligence chief, Colonel A. E. J. Magenda, Nasution attempted to gain influence with Azahari and, through the army interregional commander for Kalimantan, Colonel Hassan Basri, he established active contact with dissidents in Sarawak from February 1963. Nasution evidently hoped to prevent Subandrio's Central Intelligence Board (BPI) from monopolizing contact with the rebels, but increasingly the BPI gained control in this field.[26] The BPI took charge of military training given in Indonesia to rebel youths, mainly of Chinese descent, from Sarawak and Sabah, and the BPI apparently organized the raids into these territories which commenced in April 1963. Yani, who reportedly was angered by Nasution's early initiative in contacting the dissidents,[27] later acquiesced in Sukarno's policies and decided to make the most of the situation to strengthen the army's domestic position.

After the escalation of confrontation in September 1963, the

25. See Gordon 1966:94.
26. Interview with Nasution, 20 August 1973. Cf. Legge 1972, who states rather baldly that Nasution "sent the first Indonesian infiltrators across the Sarawak border" (p. 365), and Polomka 1969, who says that "Iban infiltrators" were sent into Sarawak by Nasution probably for intelligence purposes (p. 93). See also Sundhaussen 1971:546.
27. Sundhaussen 1971:546.

army continued to go along with President Sukarno's policies. Together with the BPI the army continued to train Chinese "volunteers," and army officers participated in the raids into Sabah and Sarawak. Like Sukarno, the army leaders were careful to avoid action that might provoke British retaliation against Indonesia, and when Sukarno appeared to move toward negotiations during the first half of 1964 there was no indication that the army leaders did not fully agree with this policy. Only when the president appointed Omar Dhani, the air force commander, to head the new Vigilance Command (Koga) in May 1964 and the conflict was expanded to the Malay Peninsula in August and September 1964 did the army leaders' attitude begin to diverge sharply from that of the president.

The origin of the decision to land infiltrators on the Malay Peninsula remains somewhat obscure, but it was certainly not supported by the army leadership. According to Peter Polomka, the original proposal came from the intelligence division of the Koti, which was headed by Subandrio, and the actual planning was done by his deputy, Brigadier General Magenda.[28] Apparently they convinced Sukarno that dissident groups in West Malaysia were ready to take to the jungles, where they would welcome Indonesian support, while he calculated that the small number of infiltrators would not be considered serious enough by the British to merit counteraction against Indonesia itself. The plan was supported by the new Koga commander, Omar Dhani, who apparently welcomed the opportunity for the air force to play a more important role. It has also been suggested that General Nasution, who had worked closely with Magenda earlier, may have participated in the planning of the new raids,[29] but this has been denied by Nasution.[30] Indeed, Nasution seemed anxious at the time to dissociate the armed forces from the new policy. After the first landing on 17 August he had denied a Malaysian report that members of the Indonesian armed forces had landed in West Malaysia, although he added that "if it [that is, the landing] happened, possibly they were volunteers," implying that they were not under his or the army's control.[31] Nevertheless, in contrast

28. Polomka 1969:169–170.
29. See Polomka 1969:169–170, Sundhaussen 1971:577–578.
30. Interview with Nasution, 20 August 1973.
31. *Antara Ichtisar Tahunan*, 19 August 1964.

with Yani, Nasution was more a "hawk" than a "dove" on Malaysian policy and had even suggested to the Koti that forty-kilometer missiles be purchased from the Soviet Union in order to close the port of Singapore.[32]

The expansion of the conflict to the Malay Peninsula was a considerable setback for Yani and the "doves," who were predominant in the army leadership. Yani had gone along with confrontation in the expectation of gaining political benefits for the army, but as the campaign progressed the army's position seemed to grow weaker. The policy of dropping infiltrators into West Malaysia did not have the approval of the army leadership, and the American ambassador at the time, Howard Jones, has suggested that Yani was not even consulted before the second raid on 2 September.[33] The new policy raised the possibility that the army would be drawn into a much wider conflict than it was prepared for. The army leaders suddenly realized that they were being bypassed in the decision-making process and had become much less able than before to exercise a moderating influence on the course of the campaign.

The PKI's Advance (1964–1965)

While the army had accepted the policy of confrontation reluctantly, the PKI supported it from the start with enthusiasm. Once again the nation had embarked on a campaign in which all the major political forces felt compelled to rally to the defense of the nation's honor. Like the struggle for West Irian, the new campaign created an atmosphere that made it very difficult for the army leaders to envisage moving against the PKI. They could not afford to appear lacking in dedication to the national cause by hitting at the cause's most ardent supporter. The PKI, however, departing from the tactics it adopted during the earlier campaign when its primary concern was to maintain its position, opted to take advantage of the sense of invulnerability provided by the anti-Malaysian crusade to press its demands for greater influence in the government. In so doing it had the encouragement of the president, whose own position was enhanced by the growing

32. Interview with Nasution, 20 August 1973. According to Ruslan Abdulgani, who attended the meeting, President Sukarno had seemed startled by Nasution's proposal (interview with Ruslan Abdulgani, 13 July 1972).
33. Jones 1971:354.

strength of the PKI. While the PKI's new tactics brought it into sharp conflict with other political forces represented in the government, the aim was not to overthrow the regime but to join it. The PKI envisaged that its new militancy would enable it to expand its mass base and thereby strengthen its claim to be recognized as an indispensable component of the government under Sukarno's leadership.[34]

The PKI's new militancy was expressed initially in January 1964, when PKI-led unions took over a number of British plantations and other enterprises as part of the campaign against Malaysia. This was followed by an anti-American campaign that was also presented as support for the government's line. As United States sympathy for Malaysia became obvious, anti-American sentiment in Indonesia became widespread. PKI-led demonstrations were held against American films, and a series of attacks were made on United States Information Service branches in Jakarta and regional centers. In February 1965 the anti-American campaign reached new heights. In response to the American bombing of North Vietnam, a fresh wave of takeovers led by Communist and nationalist unions took place in which the targets were American plantations and other property, which were eventually placed under government supervision. The rapid spread of anti-American sentiment, which was encouraged by both the PKI and the president, presented the party with almost unlimited opportunities to mobilize its supporters in a way that did not invite army repression.

In extending its new militancy to the rural areas the PKI took up another issue that enabled it to present itself as the upholder of the government's policies. In 1959 and 1960 crop-sharing and land reform legislation had been passed, but the laws had been only marginally implemented.[35] The inability of the government to ensure the implementation of this legislation provided the PKI with a major issue on which to rally support in the rural areas. Like the takeovers of British and American property, which were presented as actions in support of the government's foreign policy, the campaign for land reform was presented as support for the government's rural policies that were being obstructed by local "counterrevolutionaries." Unlike the takeovers of foreign prop-

34. For an explanation of the PKI's position in ideological terms, see Mortimer 1974:132–140.
35. See Utrecht 1969.

erties, however, the land reform campaign directly hurt powerful domestic interests and led to an extraordinary increase in tension and sharpening of conflict.

During 1964 the PKI's *aksi sepihak* (unilateral action) campaign commenced on a large scale. The main campaigns took place in the PKI stronghold areas of Central and East Java, but important actions were held in West Java, Bali, and North Sumatra. The targets were landlords holding surplus land who were usually associated with either the PNI or the NU. Encouragement was also given to "squatting" on government-owned estates that were often managed by military personnel. The form of the *aksi sepihak* varied from place to place and "ranged from holding a deputation, presenting a petition, or staging a demonstration, to the unilateral seizure of land by force and the refusal to pay the landowner more than a certain percentage of the crop."[36] Naturally, the sharpest conflicts took place where land was forcibly seized by PKI-led peasants, often leading to fighting and occasional fatalities. In the latter part of the year violence became more common when landlords associated with the PNI and the NU mobilized their supporters against the PKI-led campaign. In strongly *santri* areas, particularly in East Java, resistance to the PKI was strongest and conflict most widespread, and by early 1965 the PKI, not the NU, was on the defensive.[37]

The PKI's new militancy and self-confidence met with resistance not only in the rural areas but also in the capital, where opposition was spearheaded by the small Murba party. The Murba, as a "national-Communist" party, had always been despised by the PKI.[38] Although small, it had a number of capable leaders who enjoyed good relations with Sukarno, such as the party chairman, Sukarni, and the trade minister, Adam Malik. In addition, the third deputy prime minister, Chaerul Saleh, was generally identified with the party and helped it in its maneuver-

36. Mortimer 1969:18.
37. See Walkin 1969, Mortimer 1974:chap. 7.
38. The Murba party was formed in 1948 by supporters of the "national-Communist" Tan Malaka. For Tan Malaka's background, see Anderson 1972a:chap. 12. For the Murba party's early outlook, see Feith 1962:131–132. After the clear alignment of the PKI with the Chinese Communist party in 1963, contacts were made between some elements in the Murba party and the Communist party of the Soviet Union with a view to the Murba replacing the PKI in international Communist bodies such as the World Federation of Trade Unions (interview with Adam Malik, 22 October 1973). See also McVey 1968:376.

ing against the PKI. Like the army commander, Yani, the Murba leaders felt at home in the subtle maneuvers of court politics in the later Guided Democracy period. Treating the president like a traditional sultan, they understood that it was futile to oppose him directly. Sukarno had to be praised and flattered, and any new initiative had to be presented as flowing from the "Mouthpiece of the Indonesian People." They knew that they could not hope to persuade the president to denounce the PKI, so they tried to maneuver him into reaffirming his own statements from the past in a way that would—apparently inadvertently—contradict stands taken by the PKI.

In April 1964, the Murba party proposed the creation of a one-party system involving the dissolution of the existing ten parties. The proposal echoed Sukarno's call in 1956 to "bury" the parties,[39] but its main purpose was to eliminate the PKI as an autonomous organization. The proposal was opposed by such parties as the PNI and NU with large mass bases and was soon rejected by the president.

The controversy over the proposal to set up a one-party system had led to a polemical debate in June between the PKI newspaper, *Harian Rakjat,* and *Merdeka,* a newspaper owned by B. M. Diah, the anti-Communist Indonesian ambassador in London. *Merdeka* was supported by a number of other newspaper editors, who in September established an organization known as the Body to Support Sukarnoism (BPS). Led by the trade minister and former journalist, Adam Malik, B. M. Diah of *Merdeka,* and Sumantoro, a member of the Murba party and editor of *Berita Indonesia,* the BPS attempted to put forward "Sukarnoism" as an alternative to Marxism. The BPS quickly received support from much of Jakarta's press and had the unofficial backing of Chaerul Saleh. Yani was kept informed by Colonel Suhardiman, the SOKSI leader who attended the BPS meetings as the representative of a SOKSI-owned newspaper.[40]

39. See Sukarno's speech in Feith and Castles, eds. 1970:81–83.
40. Interview with Brigadier General Suhardiman, 23 August 1973. According to Howard Jones, "General Yani told me the movement had the army's sympathy and support, although it would not join the front line" (1971:355). The SOKSI (Central Organization of Indonesian Socialist Employees) had been formed by army officers in 1961 to combat the PKI's labor organization, SOBSI (Central Organization of Indonesian Workers). Most of the SOKSI's members worked in army-controlled enterprises and plantations. Its leader, Colonel Suhardiman, was also the director of one of the nationalized trading corporations.

Although Sukarno had raised no objection to the BPS when informed of its formation by Adam Malik,[41] he soon appreciated that its main aim was to weaken the PKI and that it was probably receiving encouragement from the army. The BPS was accused of wanting "to kill Sukarno with Sukarnoism," and on 17 December 1964 the president issued an order banning it. This was followed by an order "freezing" the Murba party on 6 January 1965, and a number of Murba leaders were arrested. The final blow to the BPS group came in February, when eleven newspapers in Jakarta, including *Merdeka* and *Berita Indonesia,* and ten in Medan had their publishing licenses revoked.

These developments meant a further advance for the PKI in that its most vocal critics were silenced. The anti-Communist motives of the PKI's critics had been denounced by the president, who regarded their activities as inimical to the achievement of his concept of national unity involving the cooperation of the PKI along with the other political forces. The banning of the BPS and the newspapers associated with it together with the "freezing" of the Murba party marked the beginning of a period in which ideological conformity reached new heights. Nasakom at last joined the Panca Sila and Manipol-USDEK as unquestioned doctrines of the state, while the president regularly denounced "Communistophobia" as disloyalty to the doctrines of the revolution. In the new atmosphere the ideological polemics that had been possible in 1964 were no longer permitted in 1965.

The PKI stepped up its campaign against its opponents in 1965. During January and February 1965, numerous PKI-affiliated organizations called for the "retooling" of the minister of trade, Adam Malik, and the third deputy prime minister, Chaerul Saleh, who was also minister for basic industry and mining. At the end of March both lost much power in a cabinet reshuffle although they retained positions in the cabinet.[42] During the year, similar campaigns were conducted for the "retooling" of anti-PKI officials and those—often military men—accused of being corrupt "capitalist-

41. Interview with Adam Malik, 22 October 1973.
42. Adam Malik was moved from the Trade Department and became minister for the implementation of the guided economy. Chaerul Saleh remained as third deputy prime minister, but his Department of Heavy Industry and Mining was divided into three. He retained the new Department of Oil and Natural Gas but lost the Departments of Heavy Industry and Mining.

bureaucrats" and part of the "economic dynasty." Numerous demonstrations were held to demand the dissolution of the Islamic Student Association (HMI). The PKI also called for "Nasakomization in all fields," with the appointment of nationalist, religious, and Communist representatives to all kinds of bodies ranging from the leadership of regional parliaments to the directorship of state enterprises. The PKI's strength was displayed in Jakarta on the occasion of its forty-fifth anniversary in May, when elaborate celebrations were held with many foreign guests and a mass rally addressed by Aidit, the North Vietnamese leader, Le Duc Tho, and Sukarno. The party claimed to have three million members and some twenty million in affiliated organizations.[43]

The rapid changes in the political atmosphere at the end of 1964 and in early 1965 coincided with the culmination of trends that had been apparent for some time in Indonesian foreign policy. The changing ideological climate in Jakarta as the president praised the PKI and silenced its critics was accompanied by the development of what amounted to an informal alliance with the People's Republic of China, while relations with the United States deteriorated rapidly.[44] In January 1965, Indonesia moved close to China by withdrawing from the United Nations, and with China's support Sukarno pursued his plans to hold a Conference of the New Emerging Forces in Jakarta as an alternative to the United Nations, which was considered to be dominated by the "old established forces." By August 1965 the new "special" relationship between China and Indonesia had developed to such an extent that Sukarno was able to announce in his Independence Day address that "we are now fostering an anti-imperialist axis, an anti-imperialist axis—the Jakarta-Pnompenh-Hanoi-Peking-Pyongyang axis."[45] Although in fact no formal "axis" had been established, China had become Indonesia's closest foreign friend.[46]

Indonesia's moves toward alignment with China had followed naturally from Sukarno's foreign policy outlook and the circumstances in which Indonesia found itself. The policy of confrontation had antagonized Britain and increasingly alienated the

43. *Harian Rakjat,* 14 May 1965.
44. See Bunnell 1966.
45. President Sukarno's speech, 17 August 1965, p. 16.
46. See Mozingo 1965 for a survey of Sino-Indonesian relations between 1955 and 1965.

United States, while the Soviet Union gave only lukewarm support. Of the great powers only China showed full sympathy for the campaign, which it saw as aiming to reduce Western influence in Southeast Asia. Thus it was to be expected that Indonesia would draw closer to China. Although the PKI naturally welcomed the trend, its role in having the new policy adopted was small. Like the launching of confrontation, the alignment with China was not the work of the PKI, although the party benefited enormously from the climate created by the new friendship. The apparent identity between the national interests of Indonesia and those of China gave the party special prestige, while the accompanying anti-American atmosphere meant that there was no shortage of themes for rallies.

The domestic impact of foreign policy developments in 1964 and 1965 had reinforced the trends already set in motion by the PKI's new militancy. The PKI had exploited the atmosphere created by the confrontation campaign to rally support by spearheading the takeover of British and American property and leading the anti-Western campaign in general. Although it had met with serious resistance in the rural areas, its *aksi sepihak* movement had served to mobilize support among the rural poor, which could be expected to expand in the future. Further, the party had won the president's support against its critics in Jakarta. As China became Indonesia's main foreign friend, the PKI became established as Sukarno's chief domestic ally. By 1965 the trend of events seemed to be very much in the PKI's direction as the president denounced "Communistophobia" at home and the Nekolim abroad. Informed observers had already begun to conclude that not only was the PKI succeeding in establishing itself as part of the regime but that the political initiative had passed into its hands and soon the party would be in a position to take power for itself.[47]

47. Ewa Pauker concluded that the PKI's "patient, careful and extremely dexterous" leaders "may well succeed in making Indonesia the fifteenth Communist state" (1964:1070). At the beginning of 1965, Guy Pauker speculated that "Indonesia may not celebrate, in its present form, the twentieth anniversary of its 17 August 1945 Proclamation of Independence" (1965:96). Van der Kroef interpreted "recent events as a continuation of the PKI's steady climb to power" (1965a:232). According to Sullivan, many American policy makers in Washington also accepted this view and felt that nothing much could be done to prevent it (1969:159).

3 | The Army Stands Firm

The rapid advance of the PKI in 1964 and 1965 had taken place under the cover of the confrontation campaign against Malaysia. It had been made possible by the encouragement the party received from the president and the apparent acquiescence of the army leadership. During 1964 and 1965, President Sukarno had allied himself more and more closely with the PKI, while the army leaders seemed inhibited from taking action to prevent the growth of the PKI's power. This alliance between the president and the PKI together with the army leaders' apparent inability to take counteraction led some observers to conclude that the trend would continue and that the PKI's ultimate victory could not be avoided. In retrospect, it is clear that despite their reluctance to challenge Sukarno openly, the army leaders had no intention of abdicating their claim to the succession in favor of the PKI. While they gave verbal support to Sukarno's slogans, they were making their own plans to meet the challenge they faced.

The Army and Confrontation

The army's initial response to the moves to "confront" Malaysia were unenthusiastic, but the army leaders had gone along with the gradual increase in military pressure on Sabah and Sarawak during 1963. After the sudden switch to a more militant posture in September 1963, the army leaders took the view that as long as the conflict did not escalate into a "real" war, the atmosphere could be exploited to strengthen the army's political position as well as gain new armaments and equipment. Thus the army leaders accepted the policy of low-level confrontation while keeping their eyes open for the possibility of a negotiated settlement. But the decision of the president and his closest advisers to land armed infiltrators on the Malay Peninsula was an escalation of the military conflict that lacked the approval of the army leadership and showed they no longer controlled the conduct of hostilities. Their readiness to go along with the president's policies was suddenly brought into question when the prospect arose of their becoming involved in a conflict larger than they were confident of being able to handle successfully.

The first strong indications that Sukarno was considering the adoption of more aggressive tactics in confronting Malaysia appeared in May 1964. On 3 May the president announced the "People's Double Command" (Dwikora), calling on Indonesian volunteers to help "dissolve the puppet state of 'Malaysia' " and on 16 May he established the Vigilance Command (Koga), headed by the air force commander, Air Marshal Omar Dhani, with broad powers over operations against Malaysia and authority over forces in Sumatra, Kalimantan, and Java.[1] Although an army officer, Brigadier General Achmad Wiranatakusumah, had been appointed as second deputy commander of the Koga, the establishment of the new command was seen by the army leadership as a move to reduce their capacity to restrain the military side of the campaign. Appreciating the possible implications of the Koga's formation, Yani objected immediately and persuaded Sukarno to issue a new order on 2 June in which the Koga's function was limited to "retaliation" in the event of a British attack.[2] The Koga remained a paper organization until the crisis caused by the first landing on the Malay Peninsula on 17 August.

The decision to land infiltrators in West Malaysia on 17 August and again on 2 September had greatly disturbed the army leaders, who immediately began to consider ways of preventing further provocative attacks in the future. Moves were quickly made to win Sukarno's approval for a reorganization of the Koga that would enable the army to exercise a controlling influence over its operations. The army leaders had to disguise their real intentions by putting their proposals in the form of recommendations designed to improve the efficiency of the command. Following the dismal failure of the landings in West Malaysia, Omar Dhani was in a

1. See Omar Dhani's "Pleidooi" in Omar Dhani trial (I, 250), and Polomka 1972:374.
2. Polomka 1972:374.

weak position to resist army pressure for a change, and the president was more receptive to new proposals.

After discussions within the Koga, Sukarno gave his approval in October to a plan to replace the Koga with the Mandala Vigilance Command (Kolaga) modeled on the Mandala Command headed by Suharto during the West Irian campaign. Whereas the Koga had been a "functional" command charged with repulsing a British attack if it occurred, the "mandala" concept meant that the Kolaga had authority over all troops from all four services within the area of its command but no authority outside that area. Sumatra and Kalimantan were covered by the Kolaga, but not Java.[3] In addition, it was decided to provide the Kolaga with two Combat Commands, one of which was placed in Sumatra and the other in Kalimantan. Finally, the status of the Kolaga's leadership was raised by the appointment of Major General Suharto as first deputy commander from 1 January 1965.

At his trial in 1966, Omar Dhani said of the reorganization that "on paper there was progress and improvement but in practice 1001 difficulties remained."[4] The appointment of Suharto, who, as commander of the Army Strategic Reserve Command (Kostrad), was one of the army's most senior officers, weakened Omar Dhani's authority, particularly because all army troops involved in operations were first transferred to the Kostrad before being sent to the "mandala" areas.[5] The explicit limitation of the Kolaga's authority to Sumatra and Kalimantan meant that it had no authority to mobilize troops from Java but had to request forces from the service commanders. At his trial Omar Dhani complained that by March 1965 not all the troops requested by the Kolaga in October 1964 had been sent by the army and that the brigade from Central Java that arrived in December 1964 was not in fighting condition.[6] Omar Dhani's complaints were supported

3. Polomka 1969:170–171, Omar Dhani trial (I, 252). Although the "mandala" concept took effect in October 1964, the Kolaga was not officially established until March 1965 (*Berita Yudha,* 18 March 1965).

4. Omar Dhani trial (I, 252).

5. At his trial Omar Dhani said, "No matter what General Suharto asked for, no one dared contradict him" (Omar Dhani trial [I, 254]).

6. Omar Dhani trial (I, 252–253). Omar Dhani further suggested that combat-ready troops were available in Java. He said that one Diponegoro officer had asked, "Why is it our unprepared infantry brigade that is sent when many other troops are ready for action; is something going to happen in Java?"

during the 1967 trial of Brigadier General M. S. Supardjo, who
had been the commander of the Combat Command in Kalimantan.
According to Supardjo, the army leaders had been "sabotaging"
operations by permitting local commanders to retain control of
troops despite formal orders that they be transferred to the Combat Command.[7] During 1965 the army leaders continued to challenge Omar Dhani's authority. In July, Yani implied limitations on
the Kolaga's role when he stated that its "single task" was "at the
right moment to attack and destroy Singapore."[8] After a meeting
with the president at which Suharto described Omar Dhani as an
"inappropriate" leader, a committee headed by Nasution was established to inquire into the Kolaga's failure to work smoothly.[9]

The Kolaga's operations were carried out by the two Combat
Commands in Sumatra and Kalimantan. The command in Sumatra, which was stationed near Medan, had been given the formal
task of "preparing itself to invade Malaysia in order to destroy
what is known as the Puppet State."[10] The commander, Brigadier
General Kemal Idris, had been a long-time opponent of the president and appears to have had little sympathy for the campaign
against Malaysia.[11] According to Omar Dhani, Kemal Idris had
delayed the transfer of troops to Sumatra on the pretext that
accommodation was not available.[12] Further, the plans to prepare
for an invasion never reached an advanced stage because of the
failure of the army leaders to supply the means for crossing the

7. Supardjo trial (I, 8). Nevertheless, by the middle of 1965 troops were being
placed under Supardjo's command. In July all units assigned to Supardjo's Combat Command were transferred from the East Kalimantan command (*Berita Yudha*,
21 July 1965), and in August, Major General Suharto officiated at a ceremony in
Kalimantan in which two units of Sarawak Chinese joined the command (ibid., 23
August 1965).

8. Ibid., 9 July 1965.

9. Omar Dhani trial (I, 254).

10. Panitia Penyusun Sejarah Kostrad 1972:50. This work is an official history of
the Kostrad.

11. Kemal Idris had been close to the banned Socialist party and had earned the
president's ire by his participation in the Seventeenth of October Affair in 1952
and the Zulkifli Lubis Affair in 1956. Between 1956 and 1963 Sukarno had refused to permit him to receive any military appointment and had even vetoed an
attempt by Yani to have him appointed as a military attaché abroad. In 1963,
Kemal was permitted to return to active service as a member of the Indonesian
contingent in the UN force in the Congo.

12. Omar Dhani trial (I, 253). Omar Dhani had learned from another source
that vacant barracks were falling into disrepair in North Sumatra.

straits.[13] Thus it appears that the army leaders had deliberately selected Kemal Idris to head the "invasion" force with the purpose of ensuring that the invasion would never take place because they knew he would never fall under Sukarno's spell. In Kalimantan, however, the appointment in November 1964 of Brigadier General Supardjo was probably a concession to Omar Dhani and the president. Supardjo was widely regarded as a leftist officer completely committed to the president. But the army leaders apparently calculated that they could "starve" him of properly equipped troops so that he would be limited to using units from the air force, navy, and police as well as "volunteers." Further, Yani had ensured the appointment of reliable regional commanders in the border areas. The interregional commander for Kalimantan, Major General Maraden Panggabean, and the West Kalimantan commander, Brigadier General Ryacudu, both had Yani's confidence, while the left-leaning East Kalimantan commander, Brigadier General Suharjo, was sent to study in Moscow in February 1965 and replaced by Brigadier General Sumitro.[14] Finally, in September 1965, Supardjo's independence was further restricted when a new command was established within the Kolaga under the leadership of Kemal Idris, with authority over all ground forces in Sumatra and Kalimantan.[15]

Thus during 1964 and 1965 the army leaders carried out a series of maneuvers designed to obstruct the effective implementation of the policy of confrontation. While they probably appreciated that the president himself did not want Indonesia to slip into a full-scale war, they had little faith in his judgment after the militarily ineffective but provocative landings on the Malay Peninsula. Thus the army leaders sought to contain the authority of officers like Omar Dhani and Supardjo, who were in positions where they could take initiatives that might lead to an expansion of the conflict, which would inevitably involve the army. The success of the army leaders in limiting the active participation of army personnel during the campaign was indicated when pris-

13. Interview with Kemal Idris, 9 December 1970.
14. See Sundhaussen 1971:578. Panggabean had previously served as chief of staff successively to Yani and Suharto in the Interregional Command for East Indonesia.
15. The new command was the Vigilance Land Strategic Command (Komstradaga); see Panitia Penyusun Sejarah Kostrad 1972:44–48.

oners were returned after the settlement in 1966. Of 546 Indonesian prisoners, only 21 were from the army.[16]

While the army leaders succeeded in restricting the army's involvement in the conflict, their endeavors to subvert the conduct of the campaign were not limited to maneuvers and countermaneuvers over the structure of commands, the appointment of commanders, and the dispatch of troops. The landings on the Malay Peninsula in August and September had so disturbed the army leadership that it decided to develop secret contacts with the Malaysian leaders to inform them that the army was not supporting the expansion of the conflict. The exact circumstances of these top-secret contacts are not completely clear. In one account, "much" of the initiative came from Kuala Lumpur, where Des Alwi, the adopted son of the imprisoned Indonesian Socialist party leader, Sutan Sjahrir, was employed in the Malaysian Foreign Ministry after moving to Kuala Lumpur following the collapse of the PRRI revolt. Contact was originally made with Yani, during a visit abroad, and he then entrusted the matter to Suharto, whose "right-hand man," Lieutenant Colonel Ali Murtopo, organized the continuation of the contacts through his intelligence group known as Opsus (Special Operations).[17] In another account, Ali Murtopo is said to have been smuggled into Malaysia, where he met senior officials in September and October 1964.[18] Early in 1965, a permanent liaison group was sent to Bangkok, headed by Ali Murtopo's associate, Lieutenant Colonel Benny Murnadi, traveling in the guise of a Garuda Airways employee. A separate team in Hong Kong also kept contact with Singapore after its separation from Malaysia. Exactly what business transpired during these contacts is not clear, and it has even been suggested that one of the main activities of the Opsus was smuggling.[19]

16. The other categories of prisoners were 189 "volunteers," 117 members of the air force, 109 "fighters from various agencies," 72 from the police, 34 from the navy, and 4 customs officials (Weinstein 1969:7).

17. Weinstein 1972:597–599.

18. Polomka 1969:176–177.

19. This was suggested by two army officers in separate interviews. In a speech on 1 February 1966, President Sukarno had referred to "smugglers" taking "peace feelers" to Malaysia when Ali Murtopo was attempting to seek a basis for settlement (Sukarno's speech, 1 February 1966). According to Weinstein, Opsus's activi-

The contacts established by the Opsus with Malaysia were highly secret and unknown outside a tiny circle of top army leaders. The purpose was to keep the Malaysian leaders informed of the army's reluctance to give full support to Sukarno's campaign in the hope of avoiding misunderstandings that could have led to wider warfare. Thus the army leaders were able to reduce the risks of the confrontation campaign while they continued to go through the motions of supporting it. The army leaders were not in a position to persuade Sukarno to call off the campaign, so these early Opsus contacts were probably not intended to pave the way to negotiations. Although the army leaders made some progress in the early part of 1965 in encouraging the president to consider negotiations, these efforts failed to bear fruit as was shown when Brigadier General Sukendro was sent secretly to Malaysia—with Sukarno's approval—in April 1965, to explore the possibility of a new summit meeting.[20] Although the Malaysians showed some interest in new talks, they were not prepared to meet Sukarno's conditions.

The moves made by the army leaders to reduce the likelihood of further provocative attacks by Indonesian forces and their attempt to assure the Malaysians of their own unwillingness to expand the conflict showed that they had hardly been reduced to passive agents of Sukarno. They had a clear conception that their own interests diverged from those of Sukarno and his closest advisers, including the air force commander. Unable to reject the president's policies openly, they nevertheless succeeded in obstructing them.

ties were financed by "rubber smuggling" (Weinstein 1972:598). Much of this smuggling apparently was carried out under the cover of "intelligence operations" in Malaysia conducted by the Combat Command stationed in North Sumatra. According to the official history of the Kostrad, "95% of the manpower used to carry out this task [i.e. intelligence operations] were Chinese fishermen with whom our volunteers went disguised as traders" (Panitia Penyusun Sejarah Kostrad 1972:50–52). Some sources have hinted that their trading activities may have taken precedence over intelligence gathering. In 1967 the North Sumatra regional commander, Brigadier General Sarwo Edhie, referred to "112 cases of smuggling on official orders" which took place before the end of confrontation in August 1966 (*Harian Kami,* 8 July 1967).

20. Interview with Brigadier General Sukendro, 14 December 1970. See also Polomka 1969:245 and Weinstein 1972:597. Sukendro had returned from exile at the end of 1963 and was appointed as a minister of state in September 1964.

The Army's Domestic Position

The atmosphere created by the Crush Malaysia campaign had been very favorable for the PKI, which was able to identify itself with the national cause and strengthen its position in the domestic balance of power while the army leaders were forced to turn their attention to the expanding military conflict. Despite their preoccupation with preventing operations against Malaysia from running out of hand, the army leaders continued to obstruct the PKI's efforts to gain a foothold in the administration of the state.

Although the army leaders had been opposed to the landings of infiltrators on the Malay Peninsula, they were quick to make the most of the resulting sense of crisis to add to the army's legal powers. The army's capacity to check the activities of the PKI had been weakened with the lifting of martial law in 1963. But the expansion of the conflict with Malaysia permitted the army leaders to reverse this trend by insisting on the partial restoration of martial law. Under the new system, which came into effect in late September 1964, Pepelrada (Regional Authorities to Implement Dwikora) were formed in each region with such broad but specific emergency powers as to detain individuals for up to thirty days, impose curfews, restrict the movements of "dangerous" people, and seize property.[21] In all except four minor regions, army commanders were appointed to head the new bodies. Although the Pepelrada were responsible to Sukarno as supreme commander of the Koti, they usually took their orders from the army commander, Yani, in his role as chief of staff of the Koti. In practice the Pepelrada enjoyed considerable autonomy, which sometimes was used against the army's political opponents in conflict with the president's policies.[22]

The army's position in the executive machinery of the state continued to be strong during the latter phase of Guided Democracy both in the national cabinet and in regional administration. In the cabinet the army had about a quarter of the places, includ-

21. The Pepelrada regulations are in Muhono, ed. 1966:1244–1248.
22. For example, after the governor of North Sumatra had banned the newspaper, *Tjahaja*, on 4 June 1965 for its alleged association with the BPS, the Pepelrada gave it permission to appear again on 6 June (*Harian Rakjat*, 9 June 1965). In Solo a journalist was arrested for mocking Yani (ibid., 29 July 1965), and in East Kalimantan a SOBSI leader was arrested after a May Day speech (ibid., 28 May 1965).

ing the key departments of defense and security and internal affairs, although Sukarno had prevented it from gaining a dominant position. In November 1963 the sudden death of the first minister, Djuanda, whose relations with the army leaders were good, was followed by the appointment of a three-member Presidium to lead the cabinet, consisting of Subandrio, Leimena, and Chaerul Saleh but excluding the army. Despite this setback, the army's position was very strong in the Koti, which was becoming a more important policy-making body than the cabinet. At the provincial level, the number of army officers appointed as governors had risen to twelve out of twenty-four by 1965, including the important provinces of Jakarta, West Java, and East Java.

Despite the changes in the political climate that had permitted the PKI to rally popular support behind its drive for stronger representation in the government, the army leaders were successful in obstructing the president's attempts to form a "Nasakom cabinet" with substantial PKI representation. Although Aidit and Lukman had attained ministerial status in 1962 as deputy chairmen of the MPRS and DPR-GR respectively, the army had blocked the appointment of PKI ministers with executive responsibilities. In November 1963, Sukarno had pushed in the direction of a PKI appointment when he selected the deputy governor of West Java, Achmad Astrawinata, as minister for justice. Although Astrawinata was not a member of the PKI, he belonged to the PKI-aligned Indonesian Graduates' Association. The following year, in August 1964, Sukarno went further when he appointed the third member of the PKI's leadership, Njoto, as one of three ministers seconded to the Presidium with supervisory responsibilities in the field of land reform; later Njoto's importance grew when he became a senior aide to the president. Not until May 1965, when a leader of the PKI's youth organization, Pemuda Rakyat, Ir Setiadi Reksoprodjo, became minister for electricity and energy, was a PKI minister given control of a department. Thus the progress made by Sukarno and the PKI in moving toward their goal of a Nasakom cabinet was extremely slow.

At the level of provincial administration the PKI's progress was only slightly faster. None of the provincial governors was a member of the PKI although a leftist army officer, Brigadier General Ulung Sitepu, appointed as governor of North Sumatra in 1963, and Anak Agung Bagus Sutedja, of the small left-nationalist party, Partindo, who was appointed as governor of Bali in 1964, were regarded as allied to the PKI, while the deputy governors of Jakarta, West Java, and Central Java appointed in 1960 and the East Java deputy governor appointed in 1963 were all closely identified with the party.[23] In 1965 the minister for internal affairs ordered that the Nasakom concept be applied with the appointment of representatives of the Nasakom forces, including the PKI, to the executive councils of all provincial governors.[24] At the district level the PKI was better represented. By 1965 eight of thirty-seven mayors and *bupatis* in East Java, six of thirty-nine in Central Java and Yogyakarta, and two of twenty-three in West Java were from the PKI. Despite these marginal gains, the PKI's representation in formal positions in the government remained very small when compared with the major parties and especially the army.

Though the PKI still was far from being in power, its rapid advance had worried the army leaders. They were concerned by the PKI's successful demonstration of its ability to mobilize popular support in the takeovers of both foreign property and surplus land. Many officers had sympathized with the Murba proposal for a single party and the activities of the BPS, and most were disturbed by Indonesia's growing alignment with China and withdrawal from the United Nations. Nevertheless, while some senior officers became increasingly critical of the way the army leadership seemed to have lost the initiative to the PKI, the officers close to Yani were inclined to regard the PKI's advances in a broad perspective. Having set out on the risky course of undermining the president's campaign against Malaysia, Yani saw little benefit in confronting Sukarno directly over such relatively minor matters as the fate of the Murba or the BPS.

23. They were Henk Ngantung (Jakarta), Achmad Astrawinata (West Java), Sujono Atmo (Central Java), and Satrio Sastrodiredjo (East Java). When Astrawinata was appointed to the cabinet in 1963, he was succeeded by the former Jakarta garrison commander, Colonel Dachjar Sudiawidjaja, who had since become a left-wing member of the PNI. The deputy governor of East Java, Satrio, despite his PKI connection, was the brother of Brigadier General Ibnu Sutowo, the head of the oil corporation, Permina.

24. *Harian Rakjat,* 17 June 1965. This instruction does not appear to have been widely implemented before October 1965.

Yani, whose personal relations with Sukarno were warm, had avoided taking an alarmist view of the president's friendliness toward the PKI. Convinced of the PKI's vulnerability in the event of a showdown, Yani calculated that as long as the army could maintain its internal cohesion it would win in the end. Aware that Sukarno had encouraged the PKI's new militancy, Yani saw the president's moves as directed toward short-term tactical advantage for himself rather than reflecting interest in the ultimate victory of the PKI. Treating Sukarno like a sultan who could not be forced out of power, Yani preferred to keep close to his ear rather than permit access to him to be monopolized by the army's rivals. Despite the PKI's advance during 1964, Yani continued to believe that his policy was succeeding. Just as he was undermining the confrontation campaign behind a show of compliance with the president's commands, he was confident that the PKI could be kept in check by similar means without the necessity of standing up directly to Sukarno.[25] The apparent complacency of Yani and his group as the PKI made its gains had led to growing dissatisfaction in high army circles centered around Nasution, the minister for defense and security. Although Nasution did not question Yani's commitment to anti-Communism, he claimed that Yani had fallen under Sukarno's influence, with the result that he felt inhibited from resisting the president's policies.[26] The critical generals, who sympathized in varying degrees with Nasution's attitude, did not fear an immediate bid for power by the PKI, but they were concerned that if current trends were permitted to continue the PKI's position might grow very much stronger during the next few years.

The rivalry between Yani and Nasution, which originated in Nasution's loss of control over the army to Yani in 1962, had resulted in the army's losing much of its political cohesiveness. Nasution felt that he had been "stabbed in the back" in 1962 when Yani agreed to the president's plan to limit Nasution's role as chief of staff of the armed forces to administrative matters with

25. This summary of Yani's approach is based on interviews with a number of generals and political figures.
26. Interview with Nasution, 20 August 1973. There appear to be no grounds for the view that Nasution was "probably also more anti-communist than Yani" (Dake 1973:357).

no authority over operations. After his appointment as army commander, Yani had strengthened his position by replacing several of Nasution's supporters among the regional commanders, and he had cooperated with Sukarno and Subandrio in relegating Nasution to an advisory position in the Koti in 1963. Relations between Nasution and Yani had deteriorated further in May 1964 when the anticorruption Committee for Retooling the State Apparatus (Paran), headed by Nasution, was dissolved and replaced by the Supreme Command for Retooling the Tools of the Revolution (Kotrar), headed by Subandrio with Yani as its chief of staff. The Paran had been the target of a PKI campaign, but Yani's approval of its dissolution had arisen from his concern that Nasution's investigations into the corrupt activities of army officers in state enterprises might hurt his own supporters.[27] Nasution and Yani had also differed in their attitudes to the confrontation policy, with Nasution supporting it in principle despite reservations on the conduct of the campaign, while Yani's approach was more flexible and pragmatic. The key difference between them, however, was over their attitudes to Sukarno and the tactics to be adopted in meeting the challenge from the PKI.

The political advances made by the PKI during the latter part of 1964 and the leftward push in foreign policy led to a feeling within the army that steps had to be taken to overcome the friction between Nasution and Yani. A number of senior officers, including Suharto and the East Java commander, Basuki Rachmat, visited Nasution to urge him to take a more accommodating line toward the president,[28] and a meeting of about a dozen generals was held on 13 January 1965 to explore further steps that could be taken.[29] Although neither Yani nor Nasution was present, Yani's inner circle of advisers attended, and Nasution's point of view was represented by five officers, who, while in no sense

27. Among those whose activities were investigated were Brigadier General Ibnu Sutowo of Permina, Colonel Suhardiman of PT Djaya Bhakti (a state trading corporation), and Colonel Surjo, the head of finances in the Koti, all of whom became prominent under the New Order. See Chapter 11.

28. Interview with Nasution, 20 August 1973.

29. See Sundhaussen 1971:584–585, Dake 1973:357–358. Sundhaussen and Dake both report that Yani and Nasution also attended the meeting but their source, Ujeng Suwargana, stated in a later interview that this was not so (interview, 15 August 1973). Nasution also denied having attended such a meeting (interview, 20 August 1973).

part of Nasution's "group," all had grievances of one sort or another against Yani.[30] The meeting did not resolve the difference in approach, as the Yani group insisted on preserving its close relationship with Sukarno.

Despite the failure of the supporters of Yani and Nasution to overcome their differences in regard to the army's relationship with the president, there was a broad consensus on other major issues. At the army's first seminar held in April 1965 some two hundred officers participated in formulating the army's official doctrine, which was given the Sanskrit title Tri Ubaya Cakti (Three Sacred Promises). Although in his opening address to the seminar Sukarno had sharply criticized those officers who continued to think that "the possible enemy will come from the north,"[31] few officers in fact looked with favor on Indonesia's growing friendship with China. While the army adopted a new "offensive-revolutionary" strategy in line with the president's views in order to meet situations like the West Irian and anti-Malaysia campaigns, it restated its old "defense doctrine" based on its experience of guerrilla warfare during the revolution, which required the army to prepare itself by maintaining close ties with the people through political, social, and other activities. Thus, in the esoteric fashion typical of late Guided Democracy, the seminar

30. Among the members of Yani's group who attended were Suprapto (second deputy), Harjono M. T. (third deputy), S. Parman (first assistant, intelligence), Sutojo Siswomihardjo (prosecutor general for the army), J. Muskita (deputy to second assistant, operations), and Achmad Sukendro (minister of state for the Supreme Command for Economic Operations). The critics' point of view was put by Sudirman (commander of Seskoad), Sarbini Martodihardjo (minister for veterans' affairs), Basuki Rachmat (commander of the Brawijaya Division, East Java), Suharto (commander of Kostrad), and Sumantri. See Dake 1973:370, where Suharto is strangely omitted from the list. Dake is wrong in describing the critics as members of the "Nasution group." It seems that Nasution had hoped that their lack of personal identification with him would give their views more weight with Yani. All five were religious men who disapproved of Yani's libertine style of life, Sudirman and Sarbini being strong Muslims, Sumantri the head of a Javanese mystical group (Pangestu), and Suharto a follower of traditional mystical practices (interview with Ujeng Suwargana, a civilian working in the Armed Forces Intelligence Service at the time, 15 August 1973). Apart from general grievances, it seems that Suharto had quarreled with Yani in 1963 over the proper role of the Kostrad (see Panitia Penyusun Sejarah Kostrad 1972:22–24), while Sarbini, who had been Yani's commanding officer during the revolution, had been offended by his former subordinate's "interference" in veterans' affairs.

31. Sukarno's speech on 2 April 1965 in Angkatan Darat 1965:21.

reaffirmed the army's claim to an independent political role.[32]
Divided as the army leaders evidently were over tactics to meet
the immediate challenge, the new doctrine indicated a deep sense
of determination to preserve the army's political power.

The inability of the army leaders to reach agreement on tactics
for dealing with immediate issues put the army at a considerable
disadvantage in day-to-day maneuvering with Sukarno and the
PKI. In advancing the interests of the PKI, Sukarno had been
careful to avoid pushing Yani into a position where he felt compelled to take action. Aware of Yani's reluctance to force a showdown, Sukarno refrained from pressing him to the breaking
point. The drift to the left was not permitted to become a leap.
Despite the PKI's demand for the formation of a Nasakom cabinet, Sukarno's appointments of a Communist here and a sympa-
thizer there had not forced the generals to draw together as they
would have in the event of a more drastic swing in the PKI's favor
or a direct assault on their own position.[33] The army leaders were
unwilling to risk a showdown on the banning of the BPS and the
Murba, and their lack of a common approach had prevented
them from matching the PKI in taking political initiatives to advance their own position. Thus the army found itself in a position
where it was reacting defensively to the initiatives of the president
and the PKI. Nevertheless, the army's problem was not whether it
should resist the PKI but when and where to draw the line.

The PKI and the Armed Forces

The PKI leaders were well aware that their party would be very
vulnerable in the event of a showdown in which the army leaders
found an issue enabling them to use force. As long as President
Sukarno was able to exercise a restraining influence on the dominant group in the army, the PKI leaders felt secure, but they
feared that Sukarno's death or incapacitation or an open break
between him and the army leaders would put the party into a
position where it was virtually defenseless. The PKI therefore
naturally redoubled its effects to seek friends in the armed forces,

32. The doctrine is in Angkatan Darat 1965:3–18.
33. Legge suggests that Sukarno did not really want to appoint a Nasakom
cabinet (1972:327). Interviews indicated that many leading political figures at the
time do not accept this interpretation.

despite the formidable barriers to be overcome in winning officers
to its side. Inhibited by military discipline and usually unattracted
by the party's egalitarian ethic, the officer corps was not a promising recruiting ground for the PKI, although the party's nationalism, dynamism, and loyalty to Sukarno contrasted favorably, in the
view of some officers, with the qualities of the army leadership.

The PKI had been exploring the possibility of gaining influence
among officers in the armed forces since at least 1957, when several party workers were secretly assigned to this field. The story is
clearly a difficult one to trace, but it seems that the key figure was
Aidit's aide, Sjam (Kamarusaman bin Ahmad Mubaidah), who
had managed to get himself appointed in 1957 as an informant to
the head of intelligence in the army's Jakarta garrison. He was
joined in his efforts by another of Aidit's assistants, Walujo, who
was concerned mainly with the air force, and Pono, who concentrated on the navy and police. In November 1964, the PKI's Politburo decided to coordinate its clandestine activities within the
armed forces through a Special Bureau headed by Sjam with
Pono and Walujo as his deputies. According to Sjam at his trial in
1968, the Special Bureau's secret operations were "running
smoothly" in seven provinces by the middle of 1965. Through its
agents in the regions it had succeeded in establishing regular contact with about 250 officers in Central Java, 200 in East Java, 80–
100 in West Java, 40–50 in Jakarta, 30–40 in North Sumatra, 30
in West Sumatra, and 30 in Bali. Many of the Special Bureau's
contacts, however, were not fully committed to the PKI but were
regarded by Sjam only as "sympathizers" who "were not anti-
Communist and agreed with the program of the PKI."[34] It is
difficult, therefore, to determine how many of them were in fact
supporters of the PKI rather than dissidents who were willing to
accept the PKI as a useful ally in efforts to weaken the army
leadership. In any case, the PKI's influence among members of
the armed forces remained very limited.

Although the officers in the armed forces who were prepared
to commit themselves fully to the PKI made up a tiny proportion
of the officer corps, the party could feel encouraged by the presence in all four services of leftist and Sukarno-oriented factions.

34. See the summary of Sjam's testimony at his trial in "Mahkamah Militer Luar
Biasa: *Putusan,* Perkara Sjam."

These were fairly small in the army, navy, and police but dominant in the air force. The air force's leftist-Sukarnoist orientation had been derived in part from the personal outlook of its first chief of staff, Air Marshal Surjadi Surjadarma, who had been close to Sukarno politically and whose sympathies lay with the left.[35] As he was the leader of the air force from the time of its formation until 1962, his personality naturally influenced the outlook of the service, which had grown in size since the revolution with the recruitment of officers who were younger and more highly trained than those in the army. Surjadarma had been in conflict with the army leadership under Nasution and had resisted the tendency of the army to treat the air force as a junior service. Following the sinking of an Indonesian ship during the West Irian campaign, the army leaders blamed the air force for failing to provide air cover and successfully pressed for Surjadarma's dismissal, but his successor, Omar Dhani, shared his predecessor's dislike of the army leadership and became very dependent on Sukarno, especially after his appointment as commander of the Kolaga in 1964. While there is no evidence to show that Omar Dhani and other senior air force officers were ideologically committed to the PKI, their antagonism toward the army had placed them beside the PKI as supporters of the president against the army leadership, and by June 1965 air force leaders were discussing the possibility of a confrontation between the air force and the PKI on one side and the other branches of the armed forces on the other.[36] Although not all air force officers were as enthusiastic as their commander in cooperating with the PKI, the air force leadership was clearly on the PKI's side in the conflict with the army leadership.

In contrast with Omar Dhani, the navy commander, Vice Admiral Eddy Martadinata, sided with the army leaders and was particularly close to Nasution.[37] Martadinata's grip on the navy was

35. Sukarno had saved Surjadarma from dismissal in 1955 (see Feith 1962:447–448). Surjadarma had very poor relations with Nasution who, after the Madiun affair in 1948, had ordered the arrest of leaders of the Indonesia-Soviet Friendship Society, including Surjadarma's wife. Mrs. Surjadarma continued to be active in left-wing causes and was a leader of the campaign against American films in 1964. Her brother, Utomo Ramelan, was a member of the PKI and mayor of Solo.
36. Omar Dhani's testimony at Omar Dhani trial (II, 33).
37. Nasution said that Martadinata was the only service commander with whom he had regular informal contact (interview 20 August 1973).

not unchallenged, as was shown when discontented junior officers at the main naval base in Surabaya sent a delegation, which included a son of the second deputy prime minister, Leimena, to Jakarta to complain about Martadinata's leadership. In a meeting with Sukarno on 8 February 1965, they had been disappointed by his advice to hold consultations with Martadinata,[38] so they returned to Surabaya where a "strike" involving some seven hundred junior officers took place on 2 March. The "Progressive-Revolutionary Officers' Movement" was believed to have planned a similar mutiny in Jakarta to be followed by the "arrest" of Martadinata and other officers, but this part of their plan was not carried out. Backed by the army leaders, Martadinata survived the challenge. On 5 March, Sukarno announced that he had "fully entrusted" the navy commander with the responsibility for settling the problem,[39] and eventually some 145 officers were dismissed and transferred to the Department of Maritime Affairs headed by Major General Ali Sadikin, a senior officer in the navy's Commando Corps (Kko).[40] Although it seems that a few of the movement's leaders had PKI sympathies, the majority were motivated by such internal naval dissatisfactions as concern at the state of the fleet, which they claimed had been neglected by Martadinata.[41] The movement was encouraging from the point of view of the PKI in that it demonstrated the existence of discontent among junior naval officers, but the incident also suggested that Sukarno was not in a position to dismiss a commander who was regarded as an ally by the army leaders.

Similarly, Sukarno did not feel able to appoint a commander of the police who was unacceptable to the army leadership. The police force was probably the most faction-ridden of the four services during the Guided Democracy period, and its commanders were continuously subject to attempts by rivals to undermine their authority. In May 1965, following the resignation of Sutjipto Danukusumo, who had held office for only a year and a half, the president selected the apolitical Sutjipto Judodihardjo as the new commander. Although one of the strong candidates had

38. See testimony of Leo Darsa, one of the members of the group, at Sutarto trial, reported in *Kompas*, 25 August 1973.
39. *Berita Yudha*, 8 March 1965.
40. Ibid., 3 September 1965.
41. See Polomka 1969:205–206.

been Subandrio's chief of staff in the BPI, Brigadier General Sutarto, who supported Sukarno's position toward the PKI, Sukarno knew that Sutarto's candidature was opposed by the army leadership,[42] while Sutjipto's image as a "servant of the state" made him acceptable. Although the endemic factionalism in the police force was largely devoid of ideological content, such officers as Sutarto and Brigadier General Sawarno Tjokrodiningrat, who was appointed in June as police commander in Jakarta, were regarded as willing to cooperate with the PKI, and sometimes local rivalries led police officers to side with the PKI against commanders of local army units, especially in East and Central Java.

The PKI had many high-ranking friends in the air force and some potential allies in the navy and police, but these forces were in no position, in the event of a showdown, to stand up to the army in which the party had few supporters. The main factions in the army were unambiguously anti-Communist despite their differences over how the PKI should be opposed. Among senior officers only a few, such as Brigadier General U. Rukman, the interregional commander for East Indonesia, and Brigadier General Supardjo, the combat commander in Kalimantan, were regarded as "leftist" by their colleagues, although in retrospect it is clear that dissident colonels and lieutenant colonels enjoyed much more support, especially in Central Java, than the army leaders in Jakarta had supposed.

The PKI leaders realized that their influence in the armed forces was still too limited to guarantee the party's protection if Sukarno should die. Apparently worried by indications that his health was failing, they seem to have decided to take advantage of the atmosphere that had won them the president's support against their civilian opponents in 1964 to launch an offensive in 1965 designed to check the power of their adversaries within the military. Not only did they intensify their propaganda campaign against the "bureaucratic-capitalists" who dominated the state corporations,[43] but they put forward two proposals that seemed to have the support of the president and could conceivably take

42. See testimony at Sutarto trial reported in *Kompas,* 20, 21 August 1973.
43. The PKI referred to the "bureaucratic-capitalists" as "*kapbir*" with its suggestion of "*kafir*" (infidel) for Muslims. The *kapbir* were army officers and their associates in the state corporations.

them over the hump of the army's near monopoly of arms. In January 1965, Aidit proposed to the president that "organized workers and peasants" be armed and given military training.[44] Later the PKI gave full support to the president's suggestion that the armed workers and peasants form a "fifth force" in addition to the army, navy, air force, and police. Further, the PKI suggested, as part of its campaign for "Nasakomization in all fields," that the principle be expanded to the armed forces by establishing advisory teams representing the elements in Nasakom to work with the commanders of the four services.[45] The PKI leaders apparently envisaged that the creation of the advisory teams might give the party some influence and would at least enable it to keep informed of developments within the armed forces and particularly the army, while the proposed fifth force would form a powerful counterweight to the army and might come under leadership favorably disposed to the PKI.

In contrast with the PKI's earlier advances, which had been tolerated by the army leadership, the new proposals were aimed not at foreigners or the army's civilian allies but directly at the army. As 1965 progressed the disunity among senior generals gave way to a new sense of determination to prevent the implementation of the PKI's proposals even if it brought the army into open conflict with the president. The new, aggressive mood in the army quickly came to the surface in May 1965 in the reaction of army officers to the killing of a pensioned noncommissioned officer in a clash with Communist-led peasants who had occupied land on the Bandar Betsy plantation at Simalungun in North Sumatra.[46] At a meeting of regional commanders held at Jakarta at the end of May immediately after the PKI's anniversary celebrations, officers

44. *Harian Rakjat,* 15 January 1965. Aidit said that there were ten million peasants and five million workers ready to be armed.
45. Ibid., 19 May 1965.
46. Land used by peasants since the Japanese occupation had been plowed up for the plantation's use in 1963 but was then replanted by the peasants. On 13 May 1965 the land was plowed up again, but the next day peasants returned to sow new seeds. Pensioned Warrant Officer Sudjono and some colleagues then attempted to obstruct the peasants. The army claimed that Sudjono was unarmed and had been attacked by the peasants (*Berita Yudha,* 27 May 1965), whereas the Communist peasant organization, Indonesian Peasant Front (BTI), and witnesses at the trial said that he had a pistol and had beaten several peasants before they attacked him (*Harian Rakjat,* 31 May, 25 June 1965).

pressed Yani to take a more forthright line. In reply he declared that the army would no longer tolerate the PKI's challenge. The trial of peasants responsible for the murder of the former soldier in North Sumatra was held immediately as a symbolic indication of the army's resolution,[47] and at the same time the army leaders made it clear that they rejected the Nasakomization and fifth force proposals. Expressing the army's mood, Yani's second deputy, Major General Suprapto, said that "if the army is put under pressure and that pressure is wrong, we will put pressure on them in return."[48]

The PKI's proposal for Nasakomization in the armed forces—part of a campaign to achieve Nasakom representation in all kinds of bodies—was soon blocked by the army leaders. If in 1964 the anti-Communist groups had taken up Sukarnoism as a stick with which to beat the PKI, in 1965 the PKI exploited the concept of Nasakom to force its opponents into a corner. The PKI's proposal, which would have given formal representation to the political parties within the army's structure, was completely unacceptable to the army leadership. Nasution declared that "it is not possible for a force to work if its commander must be from the PNI with deputies from the religious and Communist groups."[49] Yani then devised the clever verbal formula that enabled the army

47. At the trial of the thirty-six peasants accused of killing Sudjono, thirty-eight witnesses were heard over a period of only two days. The defense counsel was given only an hour to prepare his reply to the charges, and the judgment was announced on the same evening. The peasants received sentences from between five and fifteen years (*Harian Rakjat*, 24, 25 May 1965). That pressure was exerted on the judge was admitted by the interregional commander for Sumatra, Lieutenant General Mokoginta, who related that the judge had been reluctant to give his judgment because he feared a PKI demonstration, but had eventually agreed to make the announcement when Mokoginta threatened to arrest him if he did not (interview with Mokoginta, 9 August 1973). In July, the minister of law, Wirjono Prodjodikoro, instructed the High Court in Medan to reopen the case (*Berita Yudha*, 5 July 1965) and in August the judges were brought to Jakarta (*Harian Rakjat*, 3 August 1965), where a new trial opened in September (*Antara Ichtisar Tahunan*, 28 September 1965). Van der Kroef has argued that the transfer of the court to Jakarta was an indication of the "direction of prevailing political winds," that is, toward the PKI (1966:463). I would be more inclined to regard the conduct of the original trial in North Sumatra as a better indication of the "prevailing political winds" and the transfer of the case to Jakarta as an admission by the government of its inability to protect its court in North Sumatra.

48. *Berita Yudha*, 16 July 1965.

49. Ibid., 25 May 1965.

leaders to pay lip service to the Nasakom concept while sidetrack-
ing the proposal. After meeting Sukarno on 24 May, he told re-
porters that "Nasakom refers to its spirit and not division into
compartments."[50] Yani apparently had succeeded in convincing
Sukarno of the depth of feeling within the army against the PKI's
proposal. When the president addressed the regional commanders on 27 May he explained that he never intended that "if
the commander is from the nationalist group, his deputy must be
from the religious or Communist group," but rather, echoing
Yani, "What I meant was that all branches of the armed forces
must be committed to the spirit and unity of Nasakom."[51] In his
speech to the commanders, Yani declared that "the army must
always be ready to fight to death in defense of Nasakom as a
distillation of the Panca Sila,"[52] and a few days later the army
spokesman, Brigadier General Ibnu Subroto, announced that the
army was "already truly Nasakomist as a distillation of Panca Sila"
and was "Nasakom in spirit."[53] As the "spirit" of Nasakom that
was "distilled" from the Panca Sila had already been instilled in all
of its members, there was no need to introduce the Nasakom
principle into its organizational structure.[54]

Having successfully blocked the Nasakomization idea, the army
leaders were immediately faced with the proposal to form a fifth
force, which the president had taken up as his own. Although
Aidit had proposed to Sukarno in January 1965 that the peasants
and workers be armed, the president claimed that Chou En-lai
had first suggested the idea of a fifth force consisting of the
twenty-one million volunteers who had registered themselves during 1964.[55] Possibly the matter had been raised when Sukarno
met Chou at Shanghai in November 1964: at his trial in 1966,
Subandrio acknowledged that during his visit to China in January
1965, Chou En-lai had offered one hundred thousand light arms

50. Ibid.
51. Ibid., 29 May 1965. Legge, however, suggests that this was Sukarno's view in
any case and that he needed no convincing by Yani (1972:379).
52. *Berita Yudha*, 28 May 1965.
53. Ibid., 2 June 1965.
54. The army's sophistry did not fool the PKI. The Politburo member, Rewang,
said, "In their effort to reject Nasakomisation in all fields the hypocrites are now
conducting a campaign for the idea that the important thing is that each individual
should be 'Nasakom in spirit' " (*Harian Rakjat*, 8 July 1965).
55. *Berita Yudha*, 2 June 1965.

for the purpose of "arming the people."[56] When Aidit made his proposal in January, Sukarno had remained noncommital,[57] and in February he had said that the peasants and workers would be armed "if necessary," while pointing out that Indonesia already "possessed the strongest armed forces in Southeast Asia."[58] Only after the army leaders had firmly rejected the Nasakomization proposal did the president, in an address on 31 May to the new National Defense Institute, refer favorably in public to Chou En-lai's suggestion and call for proposals from the four commanders on the implementation of the scheme.[59]

The army leaders' initial public response to the proposal had been cautious, but they soon devised arguments that permitted them to endorse it in principle while obstructing its implementation in practice. After the PKI had suggested arming the workers and peasants in January, the interregional commander for Sumatra, Lieutenant General Mokoginta, had ordered that one company of peasants and workers should be formed in every military district command (Kodim) in Sumatra,[60] but by July only four companies had been trained in North Sumatra and another six were undergoing training.[61] By implementing the PKI's proposal in his own way, Mokoginta had ensured that the number of trained peasants and workers would be very small and under the army's control. When Sukarno raised the issue of forming a separate fifth force consisting of twenty-one million volunteers, the army leaders were faced with a much more serious challenge because the force envisaged by Sukarno might not be under their control. In response Yani argued "with no doubt" in favor of arming "not only one or two sections of society but all the people

56. Mahmillub trial of Subandrio (I, 198–199). See also Dake 1973:331–332. Dake's account is based in part on the unpublished transcript of the Chou-Subandrio talks in January 1965, which was made available to him by Indonesian officials in 1968.

57. According to Aidit, Sukarno had "laughed and nodded his head" (*Harian Rakjat,* 15 January 1965).

58. Ibid., 12 February 1965.

59. *Antara Ichtisar Tahunan,* 31 May 1965.

60. *Berita Yudha,* 1 March 1965. The area of a Kodim usually corresponded to that of a *kabupaten* (district). There were seventeen *kabupaten* in North Sumatra. Mokoginta's announcement was welcomed by the PKI trade union, SOBSI (*Harian Rakjat,* 2 March 1965).

61. *Berita Yudha,* 21 July 1965.

of Indonesia."[62] On another occasion he supported the arming of
the peasants and workers "provided they fight the nekolim."[63] In
similar vein Nasution said that "all the people" should be armed
"in an extremely pressing situation."[64] Citing the constitution,
which entitled and obliged "every citizen" to participate in national defense,[65] and an MPRS decree in 1960, which provided
for defense based on "the entire people,"[66] Yani and Nasution
suggested that there was no need to form a new force that would
arm only part of the population. Thus the army leaders accepted
the concept of "arming the peasants and workers" as well as all
the rest of the "people," while remaining implacably opposed to
the creation of a fifth force outside the control of the army. As in
their response to the Nasakomization proposal, the army leaders
endorsed the scheme in principle with the purpose of killing it in
practice.

Unlike the navy commander, Vice Admiral Martadinata, whose
pro forma and qualified support for the Nasakomization and fifth
force proposals followed the example set by the army leaders, the
air force commander, Omar Dhani, placed himself unambiguously on the president's side. Although the army leaders
and the navy commander were carefully distinguishing between
"Nasakom in spirit" and the appointment of Nasakom advisers,
Omar Dhani told journalists that he was willing to accept Nasakom advisers and added that "Nasakom in a physical sense" would
be beneficial for the armed forces.[67] He had welcomed the idea of
a fifth force in a speech on 4 June in which he said, "How tremendous our strength would be if the People, as the fifth force, were
armed like the other four forces."[68] At his trial in 1966, however,
Omar Dhani claimed that he had never advocated the formation
of the fifth force as a separate service.[69] In his comments to re-
porters after his speech on 4 June 1965, his concrete proposal for

62. Ibid., 16 July 1965.
63. Ibid., 30 July 1965.
64. Ibid., 19 July 1965.
65. 1945 Constitution, chap. XII, Clause 30 (i).
66. MPRS Decree II/1960, chap. II, Clause 4(5). See *Antara Ichtisar Tahunan*, 30
July 1965.
67. Omar Dhani at Omar Dhani trial (II, 13), *Harian Rakjat*, 23 June 1965.
68. *Harian Rakjat*, 7 June 1965.
69. Omar Dhani at Omar Dhani trial (II, 9).

arming the peasants and workers was limited to training civilians living in the vicinity of air force bases for guard duty.[70]

In practice the air force training program for "volunteers" was more ambitious than stated publicly by Omar Dhani. In March 1965, the deputy for operations, Commodore Sri Muljono Herlambang, had instructed that civilian units be formed at air force bases for guard duty because of the lack of air force personnel available for the task.[71] Although this instruction envisaged the formation of only a company of 120 men at the Halim air base in Jakarta, the scheme implemented by Major Sujono, the commander of Air Base Defense at Halim, trained recruits far in excess of the number required to protect the base. Commencing on 5 July at Lubang Buaya (Crocodile Hole)[72] on the outskirts of the base, Sujono ran two courses a month with two to three hundred participants in each batch until September when the numbers increased sharply to twelve hundred in the last group.[73] According to Commodore Ignatius Dewanto, who had replaced Sri Muljono Herlambang in May, he had discovered that Sujono's volunteers were drawn mainly from the "kom" element in Nasakom, so on 21 September he ordered that the training be stopped and that future trainees should be taken from nationalist and religious organizations.[74] Meanwhile, Omar Dhani and Sri Muljono Herlambang had been secretly sent by the president to China from 16 to 19 September, where, in addition to discussing Chinese and Indonesian aid to Pakistan, they discussed the earlier Chinese offer of one hundred thousand light arms.[75] It has been

70. *Harian Rakjat,* 7 June 1965.

71. Sri Muljono Herlambang at Omar Dhani trial (III, 489).

72. Strangely, on the same day Yani officiated at a ceremony at Lubang Buaya in which Siliwangi and Brawijaya troops were transferred to the command of Major General Suharto as commander of Kostrad (*Kompas,* 6 July 1965).

73. Sujono at Njono trial (pp. 207, 214, 223).

74. Dewanto at Omar Dhani trial (III, 47). A scheme to train members of Pemuda Marhaen (PNI youth organization) and Ansor (NU youth organization) was due to commence on 1 October (Sujono at Njono trial [p. 213]).

75. At his trial, Omar Dhani said that he did not officially discuss "the arms question" in China (II, 74), although it was raised during a two-hour courtesy call on Chou En-lai (II, 76–79). Sri Muljono Herlambang said that they "explored developments" in regard to the arms (III, 468), while the third member of the party, Commodore Andoko, the deputy for logistics, said that he had been asked by Omar Dhani to make inquiries about the arms (III, 81). Although the three officers went to China without reporting to the defense minister, Nasution, Omar Dhani casually informed Nasution on his return when both were guests at a wedding. See Nasution's written statement to the Omar Dhani trial (III, 608).

alleged and is not improbable that Omar Dhani envisaged that volunteers trained at Halim would form the core of the fifth force and that the Chinese arms were intended for their use.

Despite his apparent enthusiasm for the fifth force idea, Sukarno hesitated to announce its formation. In taking up the idea publicly at the end of May he had apparently envisaged the force as a means of undermining the power of the army leaders and thereby facilitating the development of a more enduring balance in which the PKI would be assured a secure place.[76] While Sukarno could not have expected the army leaders to accept the proposals immediately without modifications, he had apparently hoped that they would be unable to resist popular pressure for the establishment of some kind of permanent body in which to organize the "volunteers" who had registered to fight against Malaysia. Although the army leaders had not rejected the idea outright, they had refused to countenance the creation of a new armed organization over which they did not exercise direct control. By 17 August, when the president gave his Independence Day speech, the question was still undecided. Sukarno referred to "the concept which I launched about the fifth force" and stated that "we cannot defend our Nation's sovereignty without the People, who should be armed if necessary." After expressing his gratitude "for the support that has been given to my idea," he promised only that "after considering the matter more deeply, as the Supreme Commander of the Armed Forces, I shall make a decision on this matter." While he did not say that the army leaders were obstructing his policy in regard to the fifth force, he made little secret of his resentment at their attitudes in general when he said, "Even if you were a scarred general in 1945 but now you break up national-revolutionary unity, now you upset the Nasakom front, now you show your enmity for the pillars of the revolution, then you have become a reactionary."[77]

By the middle of 1965 the army leaders, Yani as emphatically as Nasution, had decided to stand firm against the challenge that

76. In contrast, Legge takes the view that Sukarno did not really want to form the fifth force. Because "such a force would inevitably have been open to communist techniques of infiltration," Legge suggests that Sukarno did not want "to give in to this demand" from the PKI. He says that Sukarno "seemed thus to want to retain the possibility as a means of disciplining the army, but not to want it as an actuality" (1972:379–381).

77. President Sukarno's speech, 17 August 1965, pp. 43–44, 24.

they faced not only from the PKI but also from the president. Although the air force leadership was openly antagonistic toward the army, Sukarno had apparently felt unable to replace the navy commander against the army leadership's wishes and had avoided appointing a new police commander unacceptable to the army leaders. When the PKI called for the creation of Nasakom advisory boards in the armed forces, Sukarno not only failed to indicate sympathy for the proposal but publicly endorsed the army leadership's concept of "Nasakom in spirit," and after months of declaring his support for the fifth force idea he was still unwilling to announce its implementation. The army leaders had been put under heavy pressure, but they were far from disposed to giving way.

The Prospect

During 1965 politics had become more polarized than ever before as President Sukarno aligned himself more openly with the PKI against the army leadership, while the PKI's moves were increasingly directed against the army itself and not just against the army's allies. Although the army leadership continued to be confident that the army's overwhelming military might would guarantee that the PKI could never gain the ascendancy, they were beginning, especially since May 1965, to consider taking more active measures to protect their position. As the PKI's influence grew beneath the cover provided by the president, the army leaders felt compelled to reassess their relationship with Sukarno. If the army were not prepared to move against the president and he continued to encourage the PKI, it seemed to some officers that the PKI's advance might go on indefinitely. Thus opinion was building up within the army that something had to be done, even if it meant an open break with Sukarno. In addition, the president's support for the fifth force proposal posed a long-term threat to the army's supremacy in the military field which was the basis of its political power. As the "obstinacy" of the army leadership became increasingly blatant, the president naturally began to think of replacing Yani with a more pliable army commander, and rumors about the possibility of a military coup were heard more frequently.

Although the PKI had made considerable and even spectacular progress since 1963, especially in its influence on Sukarno's ideological formulations, its position was still far from secure. The ideological climate in which political debate took place had changed vastly as Sukarno adopted attitudes and policies in line with those advocated by the PKI. Especially in the field of foreign policy, Indonesia's alignment with China and the movement to "confront" the imperialists had created an atmosphere very favorable for the PKI, while the similarity between the president's outlook and that of the party had made domestic anti-Communism seem disloyal. Nevertheless, the PKI's advance was still limited. It was excluded from the Koti, had four members in a cabinet of eighty, and was unrepresented among the provincial governors. Despite its campaign for Nasakomization in all fields, the PKI had no base of support within the government machinery, and with the army ranged against it, its strength was derived from a mass base geared to demonstrations rather than armed resistance. Heavily dependent on the president's goodwill, the PKI was engaged in a race against time. While Sukarno lived, the party wanted to become as firmly entrenched in the machinery of government as the army was. If it could become a major force within the cabinet and obtain a substantial share of the positions in regional government, it could hope to gain the legitimacy and power that would compel the army to accept it as a partner in the future. By September 1965, however, its achievements in these fields were still very slight and, more crucially, its offensive since 1963 had alerted its opponents not only in the army but also in the NU and the PNI, especially in the rural areas.

The political polarization had taken place against a background of rapidly accelerating economic decline. The stepping up of confrontation in September 1963 had wrecked the May 1963 attempt to rehabilitate the economy, and the government had lost control over the rate of inflation. In both 1963 and 1964 the budget deficit alone exceeded revenues, and although the 1965 budget provided for revenues to cover nearly 70 percent of planned expenditures, a "Special Budget" of undisclosed proportions "over which the President exercises full control" was also passed, making it unlikely for the "real" deficit to decline. Inflation of 119 percent in 1963 and 134 percent in 1964 was followed by a 50 percent rise between January and August 1965.[78] While prices continued to rise, exports fell and foreign governments became less willing to make new credits available. As the capacity to pay for imports declined, the president made a virtue of necessity by

78. Penny 1965:5–7, 9.

announcing the principle of Berdikari (Standing on Our Own Feet) as one of the Five Magic Charms of the Revolution and declared that imports of rice would be stopped in 1965 followed by imports of textiles in 1966.[79] Although in fact new credit agreements for nearly $300 million were signed during the first nine months of 1965,[80] repayments of some $230 million had to be rescheduled during the year because foreign exchange resources were exhausted. Meanwhile, the government's capacity to raise revenues declined, and roads, railways, ports, and other infrastructure facilities fell into disrepair.

With the president and the army leadership confronting each other over the proposed formation of the fifth force and the urban sector of the economy moving to the point of breakdown, the prospect of some kind of showdown loomed large. In this atmosphere, on the morning of 4 August, Sukarno vomited and collapsed while receiving a delegation led by Brigadier General Djuhartono of the Joint Secretariat of Functional Groups (Sekber-Golkar).[81] An announcement came immediately that the president had "begun to concentrate all his attention on his 17 August speech" and had therefore stopped all other activities.[82] Although Sukarno recovered quickly enough to give his Independence Day oration thirteen days later, his collapse had reminded everybody that he was not immortal. During the following month the political atmosphere became extremely tense. With the president's health in doubt and various rumors of coups in the air, the armed forces were preparing for a massive celebration of Armed Forces Day on 5 October to match the PKI's huge anniversary celebrations of the previous May. As some twenty thousand troops concentrated in Jakarta there was a feeling that "something might happen."[83] According to an American political scientist who was in Jakarta at the time, "My interview notes and general observations of October 1 reveal not a single instance of individuals who expressed surprise at the course of events publicly disclosed early that day."[84]

79. Gibson 1965:1.
80. See table in *Bulletin of Indonesian Economic Studies,* no. 2 (September 1965), 6. More than half of the new credits came from Japan and West European countries.
81. Testimony of Brigadier General Djuhartono at Subandrio trial (II, 163).
82. *Berita Yudha,* 5 August 1965.
83. Omar Dhani at Omar Dhani trial (II, 88).
84. Paget 1967:297.

4 | The Coup Attempt

Following the radio news broadcast at 7 A.M. on 1 October, a special statement was read, announcing that "a military movement has taken place within the army assisted by troops from the other branches of the Armed Forces." It stated that the "Thirtieth of September Movement" headed by Lieutenant Colonel Untung, a battalion commander in the Cakrabirawa palace guard, had arrested members of the "Council of Generals," which was said to have been sponsored by the CIA and to have become very active following the illness of the president in early August. The statement claimed that the Council of Generals had brought troops from West, Central, and East Java to Jakarta to carry out a coup on about 5 October, the Armed Forces Day. The generals were accused of being "power-crazy, neglecting the welfare of their troops, living in luxury over the sufferings of their troops, degrading women and wasting the nation's money." The Thirtieth of September Movement had taken action to prevent such a coup. Thus, "this movement is purely a movement within the army directed against the Council of Generals." President Sukarno was "safe under the protection of the Thirtieth of September Movement," and a Revolutionary Council would be established in Jakarta followed by provincial and lower-level Revolutionary Councils in the regions. The Revolutionary Council would carry out President Sukarno's policies, such as the "Five Magic Charms of the Revolution" and an "independent and active foreign policy opposed to the Nekolim."[1]

This announcement was followed by the broadcast of a decree at 11 A.M. according to which "all power in the Republic of Indonesia" had passed to a Revolutionary Council which would

1. Announcement of the Thirtieth of September Movement in Puspenad 1965:19–22.

hold authority until elections could be held. Meanwhile, the cabinet was placed in "demissionary" status, meaning that the ministers were permitted to carry out only routine activities. The decree was issued in the names of Lieutenant Colonel Untung, as commander of the Thirtieth of September Movement, Brigadier General Supardjo, Lieutenant Colonel (air) Heru Atmodjo, Colonel (navy) Ranu Sunardi, and Adjutant Senior Commissioner (police) Anwas Tanuamidjaja.[2] At 2 P.M. two decisions of the movement were broadcast. In the first the names of the forty-five members of the central Revolutionary Council were announced. The Presidium of the council consisted of Untung as chairman with Supardjo, Heru Atmodjo, Sunardi, and Anwas as deputy chairmen. Among the council's members were twenty-two officers of the armed forces, including the commanders of the air force, navy, and police, together with five regional army commanders. Two of the three deputy prime ministers (Subandrio and Leimena but not Chaerul Saleh) were included and the main parties were represented, including three from the PKI. The most notable name missing from the list was that of President Sukarno.[3] A second decision announced that all military ranks above that of lieutenant colonel had been abolished and that all noncommissioned officers and privates who participated in the movement would be promoted.[4]

Later in the afternoon an order of the day issued that morning by the air force commander, Omar Dhani, was broadcast. In the order he referred to the Thirtieth of September Movement, which had "protected and safeguarded the Revolution and the Great Leader of the Revolution against CIA subversion" by carrying out "a purge within the army." He declared that the air force "has always and will continue to support all progressive-revolutionary movements."[5]

2. Decree of Thirtieth of September Movement in ibid., pp. 22–24. Heru was an air force intelligence officer and Sunardi a naval intelligence officer. Anwas was a senior police officer in Jakarta. It appears that neither Sunardi nor Anwas played an active role in the movement, while Heru's was marginal.
3. First Decision of the Thirtieth of September Movement in ibid., pp. 24–25. It appears that hardly any of the members of the Revolutionary Council had been consulted about their proposed membership, and during the next few days most of them explicitly denied having any knowledge of how their names were included in the list of members.
4. Second Decision of the Thirtieth of September Movement in ibid., pp. 25–26.
5. Order of the Day of the commander of the air force in ibid., pp. 26–27.

Finally, at about 9 P.M. Major General Suharto, the commander of the Army Strategic Reserve Command (Kostrad), made a brief speech on the radio. He said that "a counterrevolutionary movement" had kidnapped six generals including the army commander, Lieutenant General Yani. He described the formation of the Revolutionary Council as a coup against President Sukarno and then announced that he had taken over command of the army and that an understanding had been reached between the army, navy, and police to crush the Thirtieth of September Movement. He claimed that "we are now able to control the situation both at the center and in the regions" and that the army was united.[6]

The six generals mentioned by Suharto had been taken from their homes by small groups of soldiers in predawn raids. They were Lieutenant General Yani (minister/commander of the army), Major General Suprapto (second deputy), Major General Harjono M. T. (third deputy), Major General S. Parman (first assistant), Brigadier General D. I. Pandjaitan (fourth assistant), and Brigadier General Sutojo Siswomihardjo (prosecutor general of the army). The raiding soldiers told the generals that they had been summoned to the palace by the president. Almost every general doubted the story, but each was overpowered and taken out to a waiting truck or jeep. In this process, three (Yani, Harjono, and Pandjaitan) were killed either by bullets or bayonets, while the other three were taken alive. The house of General Nasution was also raided. Nasution, however, managed to escape over the wall of his house into the residence of the Iraqi ambassador next door. During the raid on Nasution's house his five-year-old daughter was mortally wounded, and a policeman was killed at the nearby house of the second deputy prime minister, Leimena. The raiders captured one of Nasution's aides, First Lieutenant P. Tendean, who was living at Nasution's house, and took him away instead of Nasution. The six generals and the lieutenant were brought to the area known as Lubang Buaya at the edge of the Halim air force base on the outskirts of Jakarta where those still alive were killed and all were dumped into an unused well.

Meanwhile, two battalions of about a thousand men each had been placed in the Merdeka Square. These were Battalion 454

6. Radio speech by Suharto on 1 October, ibid., pp. 32–33.

from Central Java and Battalion 530 from East Java. They were in
Jakarta to take part in the Armed Forces Day celebrations on 5
October, but their commanders had agreed to support the Thirtieth of September Movement. Occupying the Merdeka Square,
they were in a position to control the Presidential Palace on the
north of the square, the radio station on the west, and the telecommunications building on the south. The Kostrad headquarters
overlooked the square from the east.

The Thirtieth of September Movement had its headquarters at
the Halim air force base first in the Aerial Survey building and
then in the house of a noncommissioned air force officer. Elsewhere at the base the chairman of the PKI, Aidit, had spent the
night. A little after 9 A.M. President Sukarno arrived at the base,
where he was welcomed by the air force commander, Omar
Dhani, who had also spent the night there. Sukarno then spent
the day at the house of a senior air force officer at the base.

Opposition to the Thirtieth of September Movement was centered at the Kostrad headquarters where Major General Suharto
was in command. During the afternoon he managed to persuade
one of the battalions in the Merdeka Square to join him, but the
other fled to Halim. In the evening Suharto issued an ultimatum
to Halim with the result that Sukarno, Omar Dhani, Aidit, and
the leaders of the Thirtieth of September Movement evacuated
the base, which fell under Suharto's control shortly after dawn the
next day.

The action in Jakarta was supported by a similar movement in
Central Java. At 1 P.M. while the regional army commander, Brigadier General Surjosumpeno, was out of Semarang, a radio announcement declared that Colonel Suherman, the division's head
of intelligence, had been appointed as the leader of the Thirtieth of
September Movement in Central Java and that Lieutenant Colonel
Usman Sastrodibroto, another member of Surjosumpeno's staff,
had been placed in command of the Diponegoro division. Elsewhere in Central Java a number of garrison commanders, including two of the three military resort commanders, were deposed by
their subordinates. The commander of the resort at Salatiga was
arrested in the middle of the day, and the commander and chief of
staff of the Yogyakarta resort were abducted in the late afternoon
and killed during the night. Only the resort commander at Purwokerto in the western part of the province succeeded in foiling an

attempt to depose him. In Solo, the commander of the 6th Infantry Brigade was arrested. Of the seven infantry battalions in Central Java on 1 October, five were under rebel command by the evening and one of the two "loyal" battalions was stationed at Purwokerto away from the Central Java "heartland." In Semarang, Solo, Yogyakarta, and other towns it was announced that local Revolutionary Councils had been established.

Outside Jakarta and Central Java, very little activity took place in support of the movement. In Surabaya, the capital of East Java, a junior army officer forced his way into the local radio station and made a broadcast in support of Untung, but his action was accompanied by no other overt activity. At Cimahi, near Bandung in West Java, it was reported that about thirty soldiers paraded around the town shouting "Long Live Bung Karno" and "Long Live the Revolutionary Council," but they were quickly brought under control.

Theories about the Coup[7]

The attempted coup has been subject to a wide range of conflicting interpretations. The Indonesian army's version, which gained universal public acceptance in Indonesia, identified the PKI as the *dalang* (puppetmaster or mastermind). On the other hand, two scholars at Cornell University, Benedict Anderson and Ruth McVey, produced papers in January 1966 (but not published until 1971) in which they put forward a provisional interpretation suggesting that the PKI played no role in the planning of the coup attempt. Unlike the unanimity that characterized public discussion of the affair in Indonesia, sharp controversy arose among Western scholars between those who accepted the interpretation in the so-called "Cornell Paper" and those who took the view that the PKI was deeply involved. Later the testimony of PKI leaders at the Mahmillub (Special Military Court) trials as well as the opinions expressed by PKI émigré groups in Europe and elsewhere made the "Cornell" thesis very difficult to defend in its original form. While it appears clear that the PKI was indeed involved, the circumstances and extent of its involvement are still unclear.

7. The assassination of the generals on the morning of 1 October was not really a coup attempt against the government, but the event has been almost universally described as an "abortive coup attempt," so I have continued to use the term.

Initially the PKI was linked to the coup attempt through a number of circumstances. It became publicly known that Aidit had been present at the Halim base on 1 October and that members of such Communist mass organizations as Gerwani (women) and Pemuda Rakyat (youth) had been present at the murder and burial of the generals. PKI elements had also given public support to the Thirtieth of September Movement. In Central Java, the PKI mayor of Solo had broadcast in support of Untung, and on the 2 October a PKI-led demonstration occurred in Yogyakarta, while in Jakarta the PKI newspaper, *Harian Rakjat,* published an editorial praising Untung. These early indications of PKI involvement and support were followed by the "confession" of a PKI leader, Njono, which was published in early December,[8] and the "confession" of Aidit, allegedly extracted before he was shot, which appeared in the Japanese press in February 1966.[9] In these "confessions" both admitted that the PKI had played a major role in organizing the coup attempt. It was on evidence of this sort that the army's case was originally built.[10]

The authors of the Cornell Paper put forward an alternative hypothesis which they felt conformed with all the facts that had been made known about the coup attempt by the beginning of 1966.[11] They argued that the coup attempt was an "internal army affair" in which discontented and frustrated Javanese colonels revolted against the generals in the army leadership, who had been corrupted by the fleshpots of Jakarta and failed to give more than lukewarm support to the confrontation campaign. The paper argued that the PKI had no motive for holding a coup. It had been making great gains under the existing system so its best strategy was to maintain the status quo rather than upset it by supporting a coup. Thus the involvement of the PKI was incidental. The authors hypothesized that Aidit had been taken to Halim, first, to prevent the PKI from exploiting the situation and, sec-

8. The "confession" is in *Angkatan Bersenjata,* 3 December 1965. At his trial Njono withdrew the confession and claimed that it had been made in an atmosphere of "Communistophobia" in which Communist prisoners were being beaten during interrogation (Njono trial [pp. 59–60]).
9. Aidit's "confession" is in Hughes 1968:168–172.
10. For an early statement of the army's case see Nugroho Notosusanto 1966.
11. The Cornell Paper was eventually published in 1971. See Anderson and McVey 1971.

ond, to put pressure on the president to support the movement. The Pemuda Rakyat and Gerwani members were used to supplement the very small forces that the movement leaders had under their command in Jakarta. The PKI supporters were being trained at Halim at the time as part of the air force's preparations for the creation of a fifth force, so it was not the PKI that arranged for their participation but certain air force officers. PKI support for the Thirtieth of September Movement in Central Java and in *Harian Rakjat* was dismissed as not proving or even indicating PKI involvement in the assassination of the generals. The authority of the Njono "confession" (which Njono withdrew during his trial in February 1966) was doubted because of a number of blatant inaccuracies, such as references to Politburo meetings attended by Aidit and Njoto in July when in fact both were abroad and Njono's apparent confusion as to the identity of members of the Politburo. The Aidit "confession," which appeared after the Cornell Paper was prepared, certainly would not have been accepted by the authors as authentic.

The view that the PKI took no part in the planning of the coup attempt was seriously challenged when important PKI leaders appeared before the Mahmillub court set up to try those alleged to have been involved in the coup attempt. As sources, the trial evidence must be treated with caution because many of the witnesses may well have had reason to mislead the court. The army, which conducted the trials, had already blamed the PKI as the *dalang,* and the prosecution and judges spared no effort in driving this point home. Further, some witnesses claimed to have suffered beatings during pretrial interrogation. However, it is too easy simply to dismiss the trial evidence out of hand. Important admissions were made by those alleged to have been directly involved, both military and Communist, although they often rejected the interpretations made by the prosecution. In particular, the testimony of such PKI Politburo members as Sudisman and Njono and the candidate member, Peris Pardede, in which they admitted involvement in one way or another, greatly strengthened the army's case.[12] That these prisoners were not merely reciting previously rehearsed "confessions" was indicated by the

12. The "involvement" of the PKI was also admitted in statements by PKI emigre groups in Europe and elsewhere (see Mortimer 1968:347).

frequency with which they made statements that were unwelcome
to the court, such as Njono's withdrawal of his original confession,
and the way they continued to justify their actions on the grounds
that there really had been a Council of Generals.

While the testimony of these PKI leaders at least implicated the
PKI, the army's case went much further.[13] According to the army,
the PKI was the sole *dalang* that had initiated the planning and
organization of the coup attempt. The key figure linking the PKI
to the Thirtieth of September Movement was the head of the
PKI's secret Special Bureau, who was known by a number of
pseudonyms but generally referred to as Sjam. Sjam was responsible only to Aidit, and the details of the Special Bureau's contacts
with members of the armed forces were unknown to most PKI
leaders. When Sukarno suddenly fell ill in August 1965, Aidit
feared that he might die or become incapacitated, in which case
the army leadership could be expected to move to consolidate its
position at the expense of the PKI. To forestall such a possibility,
Aidit ordered Sjam to mobilize the PKI's supporters in the armed
forces to take action against the army leadership. Thus the PKI
was responsible for the coup attempt. The military participants
were mere puppets in its hands. Much of the evidence for this
version came from Sjam himself.

Doubts have been cast on the army's version on the grounds of
its improbability. While the involvement of the PKI in one way or
another has been widely accepted, the view that it was the sole or
even principal *dalang* has been doubted, and the theory that all
the military participants were acting on the instructions of the
PKI through Sjam has been considered unconvincing.[14] The trial
evidence hardly proved that Untung, Supardjo, and others were
conscious agents of the PKI while such other important participants as the members of the Central Java group led by Colonel
Suherman were killed before their motives could be examined,
and a key Jakarta plotter, Colonel A. Latief, has never been
brought to trial. It seems quite possible that these officers may
have participated in the coup attempt for their own reasons, re-

13. The most complete statement of the army's case is in Nugroho Notosusanto
and Ismael Saleh 1968.
14. See, for example, Hindley 1970:35, Mortimer 1971:99, Legge 1972:392–
395.

gardless of the PKI. This theory leads to the further possibility that the movement was under way before the PKI became involved. Possibly Aidit learned of the plans of the "progressive officers" from Sjam and decided to support them as the PKI might be blamed in the event of their failure even if it had not participated. Thus it is quite possible that the main initiative came from the "progressive officers" rather than the PKI or that they were more or less equal partners.

Another theory puts the view that neither the dissident officers nor the PKI would have been likely to take drastic action against the army leadership without some assurance of the president's approval and argues that Sukarno's alignment with the PKI during 1965 and the firmness with which the army leadership was resisting the president's policies had made a confrontation inevitable. Fearing that the abrupt dismissal of Yani and Nasution may have provoked them to take countermeasures, Sukarno encouraged others to do the job for him. On one hand, Arnold Brackman suggests that Sukarno gave his approval to the PKI's plan to move against the generals, and on the other, A. C. A. Dake argues, on the basis of the interrogation of Colonel Bambang Widjanarko in 1970, that the president's wishes were conveyed to Lieutenant Colonel Untung and that the PKI played a relatively minor role. Although Suharto at the 1967 MPRS session absolved Sukarno of direct responsibility for the coup, these writers argue that Suharto's purpose was less to explain the president's role than to meet the political needs of 1967, when Sukarno's supporters were threatening to move in his defense.[15]

Finally, a highly speculative hypothesis has been put forward by W. F. Wertheim, who accepts the idea that Sjam did play a crucial role in organizing the coup attempt, but suggests that he may have been an army agent who infiltrated the PKI rather than a PKI agent working in the army. Through Sjam army officers fed Aidit with rumors about an impending coup and convinced him that there were enough dissident officers to carry out a successful countercoup. The aim was to provoke the PKI into making a move that would permit the army to retaliate by crushing the PKI. They calculated that in such circumstances the president would be

15. See Hughes 1968, Brackman 1969, Dake 1973.

in a weak position to protect the PKI. The initial objection to this theory is, of course, that, if it is true, the generals were too clever by half, as six of them lost their lives in the maneuver. Wertheim overcomes this by following the method of a detective story and asking who benefited from the crime. The answer is obviously Suharto, who had personal links with the main plotters.[16] Wertheim's theory, however, is unsupported by positive evidence.

The "Council of Generals"

According to the original announcement of the Thirtieth of September Movement, the Council of Generals was planning to carry out a coup against Sukarno on about 5 October. For this purpose, elite troops from West, Central, and East Java had been brought to Jakarta under the guise of participating in the Armed Forces Day parade. At the Mahmillub trials most of the participants in the Thirtieth of September Movement justified themselves on the grounds that there really was a Council of Generals that was planning a coup, but very little evidence was presented in support of this claim.[17] Most of the participants seemed to have based their belief in the existence of the Council of Generals on political intuition rather than hard evidence.

Rumors about the existence of a Council of Generals had been circulating since early in 1965, and at a meeting of the commanders of the four services on 26 May, Sukarno had raised the question with Yani. Asked whether some generals met to evaluate the president's policies, Yani replied that there was indeed a Council of Generals that considered promotions and appointments in the army but did not discuss political questions.[18] Despite Yani's denial, rumors about the Council of Generals continued to circulate as the conflict between the army leaders and the president became more serious in the middle of 1965.

16. Wertheim 1970.
17. At his trial Njono said that he had heard that the Council of Generals had met at the Military Law Academy on 21 September (Njono trial [pp. 116, 276]) and at the Untung trial, a defense witness, Major Rudhito Kusnadi Herukusumo, claimed he had heard a tape recording of the meeting at the academy at which General Parman read out the names of ministers to be appointed after the coup (Untung trial [pp. 170–171]). It is hard to believe that the plotting generals tape recorded their meetings.
18. See statement of Admiral Martadinata read at the Subandrio trial, (I, 99–101), and the testimony of Air Vice Marshal Sri Muljono Herlambang (II, 113).

Although Yani had denied its existence, it was logical to believe that the army did indeed have its own "politburo" which was concerned with planning its political moves. While there is no evidence to show that a formal body had been established, it is very likely that the politically inclined generals often met informally to discuss the latest developments. Given the differences between Yani and Nasution, it is unlikely that Nasution was among these generals, but the six generals killed on 1 October and Brigadier General Sukendro, who would have been a target if he had not been in Peking for China's National Day celebrations, made up the core of Yani's political advisers and met together frequently. However, no evidence has appeared showing that the Council of Generals was in fact planning a coup at the beginning of October. At the trials the participants in the coup attempt were unable to produce evidence in support of their assertion that the Council of Generals had been about to carry out a coup, and the claim of the original announcement that the battalions from West, Central, and East Java had been brought to Jakarta for the purpose of supporting a coup was particularly dubious in view of the use made by the Thirtieth of September Movement of the battalions from Central and East Java. Fearing a real coup later, it seems that they fabricated the story of the coup to take place on Armed Forces Day in order to justify their own movement.

The PKI

The case that the PKI was consciously involved in the planning and organization of the coup attempt had to overcome a number of substantial objections. First, all the overt participants were members of the armed forces, mainly from the army but also from the air force. No PKI members appeared to be associated with the leadership of the coup attempt. If the PKI really did play a major role, why was it so heavily disguised and what did it actually do? Second, apart from one PKI-led demonstration in Yogyakarta on 2 October, the PKI refrained from mobilizing its mass support behind Untung's movement. If the PKI were involved, why did it not utilize its most effective weapon in support of the movement? Third, as the Cornell Paper said, the PKI "had been doing very well by the peaceful road." Political developments in 1964 and 1965 had seemed very favorable to the PKI, so why did it take the risk of initiating or supporting a movement aiming to upset favorable circumstances?

The argument that the PKI took part in the planning and implementing of the coup attempt rests on evidence presented at the Mahmillub trials held in 1966 and later. Such PKI leaders as Njono, Sudisman, Peris Pardede, and Sjam stressed that the party really believed that there was a Council of Generals planning either to take over when Sukarno died or to depose him before he died, although it seems doubtful that they really expected a coup on 5 October. They were convinced that such a takeover would be disastrous for the PKI. When the president's health gave cause for concern in early August, the PKI's fears became acute. Thus, despite the favorable atmosphere of the preceding year, the PKI had a pressing reason for supporting a move against the army leadership. The PKI, however, did not have the physical resources to challenge the army leaders in a direct confrontation. The picture that emerges from the testimony at the trials is that the PKI leaders wanted the coup to take the form of an "internal army affair" in which dissident middle-level officers would take action against the top army leadership. The PKI's role in the movement would remain hidden and the PKI's mass organizations would not be mobilized immediately so as to create the impression that the PKI was not involved. By disguising its role, the PKI hoped that the movement would win acceptance more easily within the armed forces and from non-Communist political groups. The movement was essentially defensive in that the aim was to protect the PKI from the Council of Generals.[19] No suggestion was made that the PKI aimed at taking over the government, although the PKI's position would have been much stronger if the move had succeeded.

19. Pauker and van der Kroef have put forward an "offensive" interpretation of the PKI's involvement. Because both had argued earlier that the PKI was becoming the dominant influence in Sukarno's government, it was difficult for them to argue that the PKI's involvement was "defensive." Pauker was "inclined to believe that Aidit was preparing his own offensive against the Army leadership before rumors about the Council of Generals spread in late May 1965" (1969:298). Van der Kroef saw the coup attempt as part of "the final acceleration of the PKI's drive to power, which began almost exactly two years to the day before the September 30 coup" (1966:459). There are no indications in the trial evidence that the coup attempt was the culmination of a PKI "offensive" that commenced before August 1965. Instead the evidence suggests it was an almost desperate defensive move.

The evidence presented by Communist leaders at the Mahmil-lub trials clearly implicated the PKI. Their testimony demonstrated that the PKI had a motive and that its tactic of disguising its role was logical. The testimony of key witnesses at the various trials, however, did not lead to identical conclusions about the nature and extent of PKI involvement. Thus Njono confessed that he personally had assisted the rebel officers and had arranged for members of PKI mass organizations to be trained as a reserve force, but he denied that the PKI itself was involved in any way. In contrast, Sudisman and Peris Pardede said that the PKI leadership had decided to support the coup attempt, but they claimed that the initiative came from the "progressive officers." Finally, the Special Bureau chief, Sjam, gave evidence that led to the conclusion that the officers involved had been manipulated by the PKI. Thus the trials seemed to establish that at least some PKI leaders were "involved" in the coup attempt but the precise nature of that "involvement" was still subject to varying interpretations.

While the PKI leaders' statements at the trials differed over the character of the party's relationship with the dissident officers who carried out the coup attempt, none of them suggested that the party's involvement in the plot commenced earlier than August 1965 when Sukarno fell ill. Indeed, if Aidit and Njoto had really believed that the Council of Generals was planning a coup against Sukarno or if they were planning a major move of their own before August, it seems inconceivable that they would have spent the entire month of July abroad. Both Aidit and Njoto had been instructed to return by Subandrio in the name of the president on 31 July,[20] but it was only after 4 August, the day of Sukarno's collapse, that they rushed back to Indonesia, Aidit arriving from Peking on the seventh and Njoto from Moscow on the ninth.[21] Possibly fearing that the seriousness of the president's condition might be withheld from him by Sukarno's Indonesian doctors, Aidit arranged for a team of Chinese physicians, who had treated Sukarno earlier, to accompany him back to Jakarta. After discussing Sukarno's condition with the Chinese doctors as well as meeting with the president on the eighth and again together with

20. Subandrio at Subandrio trial (I, 139–140).
21. *Harian Rakjat*, 9, 10 August 1965.

Njoto on the tenth,[22] it seems that Aidit gained the impression that Sukarno's health was precarious. At a Politburo meeting later in the month he is reported to have said that the doctors informed him that it was likely that the president would either die or be paralyzed unless he changed his style of life.[23]

According to Sjam, he was called to Aidit's house on 12 August, a few days after Aidit's return from abroad. Aidit spoke about the president's serious illness and the likelihood that the Council of Generals would take immediate action if he died. He told Sjam that he had obtained information about the Council of Generals from Sakirman, a member of the PKI's Politburo and the older brother of Major General Parman, the head of army intelligence and supposedly a member of the Council of Generals. Aidit then ordered Sjam to "review our forces" and to "prepare a movement." On 13 August, Sjam and his Special Bureau colleagues, Pono and Walujo, discussed possible participants in "a movement" and decided to approach Colonel Latief, the commander of the 1st Infantry Brigade attached to the Jakarta Military Command, Lieutenant Colonel Untung, commander of one of the three battalions of the Cakrabirawa palace guard in Jakarta, and Major (air) Sujono, commander of Air Base Defense at Halim. All three were regarded as sympathetic to the party, and they quickly agreed to join the movement. Aidit, however, felt that more officers should be approached, so contact was made with Major Sigit, the commander of one of the battalions in Latief's infantry brigade, and Captain Wahjudi, who commanded an air defense battalion in the Jakarta Military Command. The five military conspirators met for the first time with Sjam and Pono on 6 September at Wahjudi's house, and during the next few weeks they assessed the forces that could be won over to their side. Although both Sigit and Wahjudi withdrew, apparently because they were not confident that they could commit their troops to the movement, the plotters were able to recruit Brigadier General Supardjo, com-

22. See ibid., 11 August 1965.
23. Testimony of Peris Pardede (a candidate member of the Politburo) at Njono trial (p. 131) and Subandrio trial (II, 205). It appears that the doctors had asked the president to curb his sexual activities. At the Njono trial Peris Pardede delicately referred to "the problem of his family," but at the Subandrio trial he quoted Aidit as saying that "what most disturbed his health was a private matter, that is meeting the desires of his wives."

mander of the Combat Command under the Kolaga in Kalimantan, whom Sjam said he had known since the mid-1950s.[24]

Aidit called several meetings of the PKI Politburo during August at which he reported his assessment of the president's illness.
In this context, Aidit discussed the probability that the Council of
Generals was preparing for a coup if the president died, and he
informed the Politburo that a group of "progressive officers" was
planning to take preventive action against the Council of Generals
and had requested the PKI's support. Although Njono claimed at
his trial that on 28 August the Politburo had accepted Aidit's
advice to report these matters to Sukarno and await his decision,[25]
Peris Pardede said that Aidit had indicated his preference for
supporting the "progressive officers" rather than risking that the
Council of Generals would move first. When no one objected,
Aidit asked that the matter be left with the four-member executive consisting of Aidit, Lukman, Njoto, and Sudisman.[26] At his
trial, Sudisman endorsed Pardede's account and added that the
executive decided to meet the request of the "progressive officers"
to support their preventive action. In September, Njono, the
party chairman in Jakarta, was asked to mobilize two thousand
members of PKI-affiliated mass organizations to be trained as part
of a reserve force at the disposal of the "progressive officers," and
Sudisman sent couriers to the regions, where local leaders were
told to cooperate with other parties and groups in issuing statements and holding demonstrations in support of the Revolutionary Council after its formation was announced in Jakarta.[27]

In the version of Sudisman and Peris Pardede, the PKI leadership consciously supported the coup attempt. Sudisman, however,
claimed that the PKI had only assisted what was essentially a
movement carried out by "progressive officers." In contrast with
the picture of marginal involvement of the PKI presented by
Sudisman, Sjam's version suggests that the PKI's role was crucial
because the "progressive officers" commenced their plotting and
carried out their scheme under Sjam's leadership. According to

24. See summary of Sjam's testimony in the Putusan (Judgment) of the Sjam
trial (pp. 52–71).
25. Njono at Njono trial (pp. 33–37).
26. Peris Pardede at Njono trial (pp. 130–134).
27. Sudisman at Sudisman trial (I, 12–49).

Sudisman, the PKI Politburo decided to assist a movement already set in motion by the "progressive officers," but Sjam claimed that the PKI's Special Bureau set the "progressive officers" in motion. According to Sjam's version, the "progressive officers" were little more than puppets manipulated by the PKI.

The "Progressive Officers"

The Indonesian army's version of the coup attempt follows the interpretation implied in Sjam's testimony. Based on the evidence presented to the Mahmillub trials and the results of pretrial interrogation, two army officers, Colonel Nugroho Notosusanto and Lieutenant Colonel Ismael Saleh, published an account of the coup attempt in which they argued, "The coup, staged to look like an 'internal army affair,' [was] executed by the PKI men in the officer corps." These officers "were either Communists or at least Communist sympathizers, who accepted systematic 'management' by the PKI." Thus the Nugroho-Ismael version puts the view that the army and air force officers involved in the coup attempt were conscious agents of the PKI without independent motivation of their own.[28]

The evidence presented to the Mahmillub trials, especially the testimony of the officers involved, did not prove that the coup attempt was masterminded by the PKI. Although the army's aim in conducting the trials was to demonstrate that the PKI initiated the coup attempt, there were indications that the idea to purge the top army leadership had originated among the "progressive officers" as suggested by Sudisman rather than in the PKI as claimed by Sjam. Given the purpose of the trials, it is only to be expected that the evidence for this interpretation is inconclusive, but it is nevertheless not untenable. Although the trials showed that the military plotters in Jakarta were in league with Sjam and his colleagues from the PKI's Special Bureau, the links between the "progressive officers" and the PKI in Central Java were far from clear.

The authors of the Cornell Paper took the view that the coup attempt was a move by discontented officers, mainly from the Diponegoro division, against the top army leadership. According to to them, the Diponegoro division had its own values and traditions which set it apart from the other divisions. Its officers have

28. Nugroho Notosusanto and Ismael Saleh 1968, quotations from pp. 10, 93–94.

been "inward-looking" and proud of Central Javanese culture and history. They have tended to scorn the "outward-looking" cosmopolitanism of Jakarta and Bandung, where "one finds a majority of officers with Westernized outlooks, expensive big-city tastes, ready access to the funds and resources of the capital, and a relatively good technical military eduation." In contrast, "The language of Diponegoro is Javanese, not Dutch or Indonesian." The Diponegoro officers have felt closely integrated with Javanese society, and among them the "mystique of the revolutionary army" remains strong. A number of Diponegoro officers were appointed to senior positions in the army's headquarters in Jakarta, however, and in 1962 a Diponegoro officer, Yani, became commander of the army and appointed a staff that was drawn heavily from the Diponegoro division. According to the Cornell Paper, the new army leadership "underwent rapid Djakartanization" and Yani himself became "almost a caricature of the 'corrupted' Diponegoro officer," with immense wealth, two wives, palatial homes, several cars, ties with the Americans, and a flair for the cynical politics of Jakarta. The "corruption" of the army elite which had forsaken "the spirit of Djogja" (Yogyakarta, the Republican capital during the revolution) for the "spirit of Menteng" (an elite suburb in Jakarta) led to resentment on the part of those officers who remained true to "Diponegoro values."[29]

The view that the coup attempt arose essentially from discontent within the Diponegoro division was strengthened by the widespread activity in support of the Thirtieth of September Movement in Central Java compared with an almost total lack of support elsewhere.[30] In Central Java the movement took control of the

29. Anderson and McVey 1971:2–6.
30. There was a somewhat similar dissident group in the Brawijaya division of East Java. According to First Lieutenant Ngadimo, at the Untung trial, junior officers from Surabaya, Malang, Jembar, Basuki, and Madiun had met to discuss their grievances. The highest-ranking officer among them was a major, the rest being captains and lieutenants. According to Ngadimo, they received advice from two members of the PKI (Ngadimo at Untung trial [pp. 125–126]). See also report of trial of Captain Sumbodo and Lieutenant Sudono in *Surabaya Post*, 8, 9 February 1967. There is little reason to believe that the PKI was the inspiration behind the group, which bore much affinity with the "Progressive-Revolutionary Officers' Movement" in the navy that had called a "strike" in Surabaya in March 1965. The movement in East Java differed from that in Central Java in that it contained no senior divisional officers and it took no action to depose regional and local commanders on 1 October.

divisional headquarters in Semarang, two of the division's three military resorts, and the headquarters of the infantry brigade in Solo, while the attempted takeover of the third resort at Purwokerto failed. The leader of the movement in Central Java was Colonel Suherman, the head of the division's intelligence section, and his chief associates were fellow members of the headquarters staff, including Colonel Marjono, who was in charge of the personnel section and Lieutenant Colonel Usman, who headed the section dealing with extramilitary functions. After the collapse of the movement all three fled from Semarang with their supporters to the mountainous area around Mount Merapi and Mount Merbabu, where they were captured and summarily executed in December. Their execution without trial gave them no opportunity to explain their motives publicly and it obviated the need for the army to demonstrate their connections with the PKI.

Although the army has asserted that Suherman and his colleagues were "controlled" by the PKI, the available evidence is not strong. In the case of Suherman, his position as head of intelligence and the fact that he had only recently returned from a course at Fort Leavenworth in the United States suggest at least that no one suspected him of being a supporter of the PKI before the coup attempt. The only important Diponegoro officer to be tried during the first few years after the coup attempt was Major Muljono Surjowardojo, who deposed the commander of the military resort in Yogyakarta and proclaimed himself as chairman of the local Revolutionary Council. Muljono admitted to being a supporter of the PKI, and it was shown that he had regular contact with a PKI member, Wirjomartono (alias Sujono), who had the task of cultivating sympathizers in the armed forces.[31] It was not demonstrated that Muljono was acting on Wirjomartono's instructions on 1 October, but seemed more likely that he was taking

31. Major Muljono at Muljono trial (pp. 59–60). According to Nugroho, Wirjomartono was the Special Bureau leader in Yogyakarta (Nugroho and Ismael 1968: 45). This allegation, however, was not made at the Wirjomartono trial in 1966. Wirjomartono contacted Muljono and other officers after 25 September on the instruction of Sudijono, the party secretary in Yogyakarta (Wirjomartono trial [pp. 48–49]). As the Special Bureau operated independently of the party branches, it seems highly improbable that Wirjomartono was acting for the Special Bureau. Rather, he seems to have been acting on the information sent by Sudisman to the regional branches.

orders from Suherman and his colleagues in Semarang. At the trial it was shown that Wirjomartono sent a message to Muljono at about 3 P.M. advising Muljono to support the Revolutionary Council, but not until about 9 P.M. was an announcement broadcast in the name of Muljono as commander of the local Thirtieth of September Movement. This announcement followed a telephone call from the divisional headquarters in Semarang in which instructions were conveyed to support the Revolutionary Council.[32]

In view of the widespread and coordinated nature of the support for the movement within the Diponegoro division and the lack of similar activity within other divisions, it is reasonable to believe that the Diponegoro officers had their own motives, especially in the absence of evidence to show that they were acting on instructions from the PKI. Possibly their motivation was as described in the Cornell Paper, or they may have had more specific grievances not only against the army leadership in Jakarta but in Central Java as well. Most likely they felt that senior officers were neglecting the welfare of their troops, and they probably shared the widespread devotion to Sukarno found among the people of Central and East Java and considered Nasution and Yani to be disloyal. While it seems certain that the PKI leaders in Central Java, and especially the Special Bureau men, were aware of the discontent within the division and naturally had an interest in assisting the dissidents, there is a lack of convincing evidence that the PKI had a crucial influence on the decisions made by these officers.

At his trial, Sjam said that he approached Untung, Latief, and Sujono after his meeting with Aidit on 12 August. Thus his testimony leaves open the possibility that a dissident group of officers had been formed before then. At his trial, Supardjo said that he had been told by Latief in March 1965 that there was a Council of Generals[33] and, according to Omar Dhani, Supardjo had often spoken well before August of discontented officers in the army who wanted to oppose the Council of Generals.[34] At his trial, Untung claimed that the original meeting of the plotters had been

32. Muljono at Muljono trial (p. 35), Major Surono Hartono at Muljono trial (pp. 354–356). Major Surono Hartono was the officer who made the telephone call from Semarang.
33. Supardjo's testimony (as summarized in the Judgment) at Supardjo trial (p. 6).
34. Omar Dhani at Omar Dhani trial (II, 21–23).

called on his and Latief's initiative after Untung had heard of plans for a coup by the Council of Generals,[35] and Sujono said that Latief had invited him to the meeting.[36] Although it is, of course, possible that Untung and Sujono were lying in order to hide their own connections with Sjam and the PKI, it is equally possible that they and Latief had taken the initiative themselves. Sjam and Pono may have attended the original meeting at the invitation of the military plotters rather than the reverse. Having been instructed by Aidit to seek supporters in the armed forces for a "movement," Sjam naturally approached the group around Latief, which was known to be already considering action, and was asked by them to participate in their movement. Thus it is possible that it was Latief who invited Sjam and Pono to the meeting rather than Sjam who invited Latief and the others.

In the army's version of the coup attempt, Sjam's Special Bureau played a vital role in coordinating the activities of the dissident officers in Jakarta and their supporters from the Diponegoro division in Central Java. It seems improbable, however, that the Special Bureau's assistance was required because both Untung and Latief were former Diponegoro officers who were personally acquainted with the dissidents in Semarang. Untung had once been a company commander in a battalion commanded by Suherman, and twice during 1965 he had visited Central Java, where he was able to discuss developments with his former colleagues, the last time being when he accompanied the president to Yogyakarta on 29 July.[37] It is therefore quite possible that Untung had been assured of support from his colleagues, which he conveyed to Latief in Jakarta. If the Special Bureau in Central Java had an important role, it may have been to inform Sjam of the links between the Diponegoro dissidents and Untung and Latief rather than to have been the means through which the links were established.

Although there is no strong evidence to show that the officers involved in the Thirtieth of September Movement were committed supporters of the PKI, it is clear that they were willing to

35. Untung at Untung trial (pp. 35–36, 55, 58).
36. Sujono at Untung trial (p. 102).
37. Captain Kuntjoro at Untung trial (p. 146). According to Kuntjoro, Untung went to Central Java with the president in "about August." In fact, Sukarno did not visit Central Java in August but had been there on 29 July, a few days before his collapse (*Berita Yudha*, 30 July 1965).

cooperate with representatives of the party in order to achieve their ends. It seems probable that all the main participants in the movement had been sounded out by the Special Bureau much earlier and were regarded favorably by Sjam and his colleagues, but there is little to indicate that they were prepared blindly to follow instructions from the party. Although the Special Bureau's role in Central Java may have been very limited, it seems that Sjam and Pono were present at all meetings held by the plotters in Jakarta and played a major role in formulating the final plan. According to Sjam, he drew up the list of generals to be abducted in consultation with Aidit, who insisted on the removal of the names of former Vice-President Hatta and Chaerul Saleh from Sjam's original list in order to preserve the appearance of an "internal army affair."[38] While the Special Bureau representatives were important members of the plotting group, there is little evidence to show that their role was dominant.

In addition to the "progressive officers" directly associated with the Thirtieth of September Movement, the coup attempt had the support of the air force leadership. Although only one of the main conspirators, Major Sujono, was an air force officer, the coup movement set up its headquarters at the Halim air force base where PKI "volunteers" had been trained and the bodies of the generals found. Moreover, on 1 October, the air force commander, Omar Dhani, issued an order of the day in which he supported the movement. At his trial in 1966, Omar Dhani said that he had been shocked to hear of the president's illness on 4 August and had immediately called a meeting of senior officers to discuss what might happen if the president's condition deteriorated or if he died. They concluded that some kind of physical clash might occur and in order to meet this contingency prepared a plan known as "Operation Unity" (Operasi Utuh) to safeguard the president and to act as a deterrent against fighting. They envisaged that the president would be evacuated by air and combat-ready planes brought to Jakarta in a show of force. However, this contingency plan was not put into effect as the president quickly appeared to have regained his health.[39]

38. Sjam at Sudisman trial (I, 217, 233).
39. The plan of Operasi Utuh is among the documents of the Omar Dhani trial (I, 387–390). See also testimony of Omar Dhani (II, 59–60), Leo Wattimena (III, 7–8), Dewanto (III, 49, 66).

As Armed Forces Day approached, tensions increased again. According to Omar Dhani, on the morning of 29 September, he told Sukarno he was concerned that so many troops had been brought to Jakarta and informed the president that Supardjo had told him about a discontented group of junior army officers who "are already hot and can no longer contain their feelings."[40] The next day, Major Sujono told Lieutenant Colonel Heru Atmodjo, the acting director of air force intelligence, that the movement against the Council of Generals would commence that night, that its headquarters would be set up at the Halim base, and that air force arms and vehicles would be used. According to testimony at Omar Dhani's trial, a meeting of senior air force officers was called at the air force commander's home at about 8 P.M. to hear Heru's news. The officers felt that there was no point in refusing the arms and vehicles as the rebels would outnumber the air force guards. Commodore Leo Wattimena was given the task of reactivating Operation Unity by preparing a plane for the president and calling combat-ready aircraft to Jakarta and Bandung, and it was decided that Omar Dhani should spend the night at Halim. Thus it would appear that several senior air force officers, including the commander, knew in advance that a movement against the army leadership was about to take place, but they did nothing to prevent it and in fact gave minor assistance with arms and vehicles.[41] Despite this "involvement," none of the air force leadership had taken a direct part in the planning or implementation of the movement although it seems likely that Omar Dhani had assured the movement leaders of the air force's support.

President Sukarno

Toward the end of 1966, as the movement to dismiss Sukarno gained momentum, allegations were made that Sukarno himself had been "involved" in the coup attempt. In particular, testimony at the Omar Dhani trial in December 1966 showed that Sukarno had seemed undismayed at the news of the abduction of the gen-

40. Omar Dhani at Omar Dhani trial (II, 89–91).
41. See testimony at Omar Dhani trial: Omar Dhani (II, 96–106), Leo Wattimena (III, 10–14), Dewanto (III, 59–60), Andoko (III, 72–76), written testimony of Heru Atmodjo (III, 553–554). Despite their attendance at the meeting, only Omar Dhani and Heru were later tried; Leo Wattimena was promoted and eventually appointed as ambassador in Rome.

erals and had greeted Brigadier General Supardjo in a friendly way at Halim on 1 October when Supardjo reported to him on behalf of the Thirtieth of September Movement. Early in 1967 the parliament adopted a resolution and memorandum detailing the circumstantial evidence implicating Sukarno and calling for his trial, but Suharto, bearing in mind the strong support that Sukarno continued to enjoy not only among the people of Java but also in some sections of the armed forces, claimed that the evidence was not sufficient to charge Sukarno and thereby avoided the exacerbation of tensions that would have accompanied a trial.[42]

In the absence of clear-cut evidence, there has been much speculation about whether the president was aware of the plans of the Thirtieth of September Movement and to what extent he sympathized with them. According to a document purporting to be a record of the interrogation of Sukarno's former adjutant, Colonel (navy) Bambang Widjanarko, in late 1970, Sukarno had decided to dismiss Yani and appoint his first deputy, Major General Mursjid, as the new army commander. Sukarno had ordered that Yani be summoned to the palace on 1 October, presumably to be informed of his dismissal.[43] Sukarno had also discussed the "turmoil" in the army with Omar Dhani on 29 September and, according to Omar Dhani, had been told of the existence of a group of discontented officers including Supardjo. According to Bambang Widjanarko, Supardjo himself was present at this discussion.[44] It thus seems clear that the president was aware that some kind of move against the army leadership was in the offing, and it is reasonable to assume that he hoped to exploit the conflict at Yani's expense.

It has been argued, however, that Sukarno's role was much more than that of a third party hoping to exploit the discontent of younger officers with the army leadership. Based on the interrogation of Bambang Widjanarko, Dake has put the case that Su-

42. See DPR-GR Resolution and Memorandum of 9 March 1967 and Suharto's Written Report of 1 February 1967 in Supolo Prawotohadikusumo, ed. 1967.

43. Karni 1974:15–16. The Karni volume contains what purports to be the record of the interrogation of Bambang Widjanarko. For a critical assessment of the reliability of Bambang Widjanarko's testimony, see Utrecht 1975.

44. Sukarno's statement at Omar Dhani trial (III, 596), Omar Dhani at Omar Dhani trial (II, 89–91), Karni 1974:183.

karno was in fact the initiator of the Thirtieth of September Movement. According to Widjanarko, when Sukarno was celebrating his sixty-fourth birthday on 6 June at his palace at Tampaksiring, Bali, he complained about the attitude of the senior generals and told the Bali regional army commander, Brigadier General Sjafiuddin, to check on the "loyalty" of the army leaders, and later it appears that Sjafiuddin and the head of the military police, Brigadier General Sudirgo, were among those consulted by Sukarno on this question.[45] Bambang Widjanarko further claimed that early in the morning of 4 August, Sukarno spoke to Brigadier General Muhamad Sabur, the commander of the Cakrabirawa palace guard, and Lieutenant Colonel Untung, one of the Cakrabirawa battalion commanders. According to Widjanarko, who was present, Sukarno asked Untung "whether he was prepared, if ordered, to take action against the disloyal generals," and Untung replied that he was.[46] Then on 23 September, in the president's palace, Sukarno, together with the three deputy prime ministers, the air force commander, Sabur, and several others, heard a report from Yani's first deputy, Mursjid, who said that there was in fact a disloyal Council of Generals which opposed Sukarno's policies. According to Widjanarko, Sukarno then told Sabur to "go into action against the generals as soon as possible."[47] Finally, on 30 September, while Sukarno was attending a meeting

45. Karni 1974:14, 17–19, Dake 1973:368–369.
46. Karni 1974:21, Dake 1973:384. Shortly afterward Sukarno collapsed. According to Dake, "An infinitely short interruption of the bloodstream in the brains had occurred, a phenomenon that medical science closely links with the psychosomatic situation, both long and short term, Sukarno was then in." Dake's dramatic account is, however, marred by inaccuracies in his description of the political context of Sukarno's collapse. According to Dake, Sukarno finally made up his mind after Yani had addressed the regional commanders in Jakarta on 30 July. Yani is reported to have told them that "he had finally made up his mind on the two current issues"—the proposals for a fifth force and Nasakomization in the armed forces. On "that same day" Yani made similar comments in an address to students. Yani's attitude made Sukarno "hopping mad," so he then decided to order Untung into action (pp. 381–382). In fact, by 30 July the Nasakomization proposal had been a dead issue for two months, and it was already quite clear that Yani was opposing the fifth force proposal. The meeting of regional commanders at which Yani had made his defiant speech in fact took place at the end of May. The address given by Yani to students "that same day" was certainly reported in the press on 30 July, but was given to students in Makassar during Yani's visit to Sulawesi for the installation of a new regional commander on 27 July (see *Berita Yudha*, 29, 30 July 1965).
47. Karni 1974:13, 178–179, Dake 1973:405.

in Jakarta, Widjanarko states that he received an urgent letter for the president from Untung. Sukarno left the hall to read the letter and, at the end of his speech to the meeting, he said, "I have to arrange some matters that may keep me up until deep into the night."[48] The following day he destroyed the letter.

From this evidence Dake has drawn the conclusion that it was neither the PKI nor the "progressive officers" but Sukarno who was the initiator of the coup attempt. According to his interpretation, Sukarno had continued to consider how to deal with the "disloyal" generals after the meeting in Bali on 6 June, but did not decide that Yani had to be eliminated until the end of July. On the morning of 4 August he spoke to Untung and Sabur and, apparently finding the strain too much, collapsed shortly afterward. A few days earlier, on 31 July, he had telegrams sent to Aidit and Njoto recalling them to Jakarta, and when they returned they were informed of his decision to move against the generals. Thus, according to Dake, it was not Sukarno's collapse that motivated the PKI independently to participate in the coup attempt but the party leaders' willingness to follow Sukarno's wishes.

Dake's thesis can, of course, be questioned for its reliance on the largely uncorroborated testimony of one witness who had every reason to cooperate with his interrogators and whose earlier testimony in court gave no indication of the later revelations. Moreover, there is a lack of details on the link between Sukarno and the Thirtieth of September Movement. That Sukarno was increasingly angered by Yani's attitude after May 1965 is clear, and it is not unlikely that he often spoke of "taking action" to be rid of him. But it is not obvious that on 4 August Sukarno had in mind the movement led by Untung on 30 September. Nor does Dake explain exactly what "action" Sabur was asked to take after the meeting on 23 September.

A further examination of Bambang Widjanarko's testimony suggests an alternative interpretation to that of Dake. According to Bambang Widjanarko, in late September Sukarno had decided to dismiss Yani, and Sabur and the deputy attorney general, Brigadier General Sunarjo, were asked to prepare the order for Yani's dismissal. Sukarno would undoubtedly have been anxious to gain some assurance before taking action that his move against

48. Karni 1974:23, Dake 1973:408.

Yani would be acceptable to key sections of the armed forces. Therefore it is quite likely that Sabur's "preparations" concerned the securing of such support. According to Widjanarko, Sabur reported to Sukarno on 29 September about his preparations and at the same time Omar Dhani assured the president of the air force's support and Mursjid said that army troops would act as a reserve. Sukarno then ordered that Yani be called to the palace on 1 October when the dismissal order was presumably to be given.[49] Confident of the support of key sections of the armed forces, Sukarno apparently felt he was in a position to force Yani to accept dismissal.

Thus it is not inconceivable, if we accept the Widjanarko testimony, that two parallel movements were being planned against the generals—one by Sukarno through Sabur and the other by the Thirtieth of September Movement. When the movement led by Untung went into action first and Sukarno was so informed during the evening through Untung's letter, he apparently decided not to commit himself until the situation became clear.

On the basis of Bambang Widjanarko's testimony, it could be argued that Sukarno's encouragement to the Thirtieth of September Movement was largely unconscious.[50] He had often spoken of the "disloyal" generals in Untung's presence, and his desire to replace them was clear. Undoubtedly, Untung had informed his dissident colleagues in Jakarta and Central Java of the president's mood, so that they felt confident that an initiative on their part would meet with Sukarno's approval. It is not impossible that they had given Sukarno some idea of their plans, although there is no evidence showing that he was aware of the details. The Widjanarko evidence thus indicated that Sukarno was favorably disposed toward a movement aimed at the army leadership, but it is hardly sufficient to support Dake's conclusion that the president masterminded the affair.

49. Karni 1974:15–16.
50. Arguing that Sukarno was "involved," Hughes writes, "This is not to suggest that Sukarno wrote out an order for the generals' removal. It does not mean the plotters came to Sukarno, asked for his assent and got it. In Indonesia, things are not done that way. And in any event, Sukarno had proved himself too wily and experienced a politician for that. . . . With that remarkable Javanese capacity for evasion of direct issues, there would have been no need for Sukarno to signal in actual words his blessing for the arrest of the generals" (1968:114).

General Suharto

The suggestion that Suharto may have had a hand in the Thirtieth of September Movement is even more speculative than the case for Sukarno's involvement. As the commander of the Kostrad and the general who normally acted for the army commander in his absence abroad, Suharto was the most important general omitted from the list of those abducted on 1 October. Moreover, together with the Jakarta commander, Major General Umar Wirahadikusumah, Suharto had control of the troops that could be used to defeat the coup attempt. Thus it is necessary to explain why he was ignored by the Thirtieth of September Movement. According to Wertheim, Suharto may have been in league with the plotters. Suharto was apparently dissatisfied because the army leadership was failing to meet the Communist challenge and thus used the Thirtieth of September Movement as a means of implicating the PKI in a treacherous action that gave the army a pretext for moving against the party. In this theory, Sjam was probably Suharto's agent who had infiltrated the PKI rather than the PKI man who had become an army informant.

Wertheim has shown that Suharto had links with all the main army officers involved in the Thirtieth of September Movement. As a former commander of Central Java's Diponegoro division, Suharto was naturally well known to the dissidents in Central Java, and the three key army officers in Jakarta, Untung, Latief, and Supardjo, were all personally acquainted with Suharto. Untung, who had served with Suharto in Central Java and during the West Irian campaign, had been honored by Suharto's presence at his wedding in 1964. Latief, who was also a former Diponegoro officer, had fought under Suharto during the revolution and had been stationed at Suharto's headquarters during the West Irian campaign, while Supardjo, although from the Siliwangi division, had contact with Suharto as the commander of a combat command under the Kolaga.[51] Such evidence is hardly enough to support the view that Suharto was involved in the plotting of these officers. Wertheim discovered the "missing link" in an interview held by the American journalist, Brackman, with Suharto in 1968. Suharto told Brackman that while he was visiting his young son in hospital

---

51. Wertheim 1970:52; see also McVey 1968:384–385.

on 30 September, he met Latief, who inquired about his son's health. According to Suharto, "Today I realize that he did not go to the hospital that evening to check on my son, but, rather, to check on me."[52] Wertheim suggests, however, "There is at least reason to assume that, through this meeting, Suharto got some information about plans for a coup" and in fact the relationship between Suharto and the plotters may have been even closer. He ends his article by asking, "What if it could be proved that those who had masterminded the assassination of the generals and the massacre of the communists were the same people?"[53]

While there is absolutely no evidence to show that Suharto "masterminded the assassination of the generals," we have only Suharto's word that Latief discussed nothing more than the health of Suharto's son. The fact that Latief was never brought to trial has given rise to further doubts. Although Latief was captured a few days after the coup attempt, he was not even permitted to appear as a witness at the trials of the other plotters until January 1972.[54] Until then his testimony was in written form. Thus the impression was given that the authorities feared what Latief might say at a public hearing about his meeting with Suharto.

Suharto, therefore, may have been regarded as a potential friend of the movement. Suharto had not been given to speechmaking, and his taciturn manner had made it difficult for outsiders to know his political views. The plotters probably considered him to be an essentially apolitical general who would be unlikely to move to save Yani and Nasution once the action against them had been endorsed by the president.[55] Further, Suharto was known to be on bad terms with Nasution since his

52. Brackman 1969:100. According to a diplomatic source, Suharto later claimed that Latief met his wife, not Suharto himself, and inquired about Suharto's whereabouts.

53. Wertheim 1970:56–57.

54. A military spokesman announced that Latief deliberately disobeyed his doctors' orders so that he would not be well enough to appear in court (*Kompas,* 26 March 1966).

55. According to McVey, "It is not necessary to assume Untung's move aimed specifically at putting Suharto in power; it would seem more likely on the basis of present evidence that the conspirators assumed that, as an officer not identified with the Nasution-Yani grouping and a good field commander of strongly Javanese cultural orientation, he would share their general viewpoint and would not think of defying any decisions the President might make" (1968:385).

dismissal as Diponegoro commander in 1959 and he had apparently quarreled with Yani over the role of the Kostrad in 1963. If Latief held this view of Suharto, it is not impossible that he told him in vague terms that a movement was about to be launched against disloyal generals in order to forestall the possibility of countermeasures by Suharto due to "misunderstanding" when he heard the news next morning. Whatever Latief said to Suharto at the hospital, it seems clear that the plotters knew he was not a member of Yani's inner circle, which they regarded as the core of the Council of Generals. Like such other senior officers as Mursjid, Umar Wirahadikusumah, and several other senior members of Yani's staff, Suharto did not play an important role in formulating Yani's tactics in facing Sukarno and the PKI and was therefore not on the list of generals abducted by the Thirtieth of September Movement.[56]

The Plot Fails

The Thirtieth of September Movement presented itself as acting against the Council of Generals in order to safeguard the president. Sukarno's endorsement of their actions was crucial to the plan. The plan apparently was to arrest the seven generals and then report to the president. Ideally, Sukarno should then have issued a statement expressing his gratitude. Such presidential endorsement was expected to give the movement acceptance within the army itself and in the regions outside Jakarta. Caught off guard, the supporters of the army leadership would have been forced to accept the fait accompli. But the president failed to endorse the movement. Possibly he had concluded that Nasution's escape would mean the failure of the plot because the defense minister would certainly seek to mobilize resistance to the movement. Further, it seems that the news that at least some of the generals had been killed placed the affair in an entirely new perspective.

The evidence presented to the Mahmillub trials suggests that

56. Following the publication of Wertheim's article in 1970, Suharto began to tell foreign diplomats that he had been on the list but escaped because the plotters were confused as to his whereabouts. This story conflicts with what Suharto had earlier told his semiofficial biographer (see Roeder 1969:10–11). That Suharto was not on the list is confirmed by testimony at the Mahmillub trials.

the plotters did not in fact plan to kill the generals. At his trial, Sjam said that the aim had been to arrest the generals and hand them over to the Revolutionary Council, which would investigate their plan to carry out a coup.[57] As the commander of the military side of the plot, Untung had been responsible for planning the abduction of the generals. At his trial, he denied instructing that they be killed but admitted ordering Lieutenant Dul Arief, the officer in charge of the raids on the generals' houses, to make sure that none escaped.[58] A number of participants in the raids claimed that Dul Arief ordered them to take the generals "dead or alive."[59] In the event, three generals, including Yani, resisted and were killed at their houses, while the others were brought alive to Lubang Buaya where both Dul Arief and the officer in charge at Lubang Buaya, Major (air) Gatot Sukrisno, were very agitated to find that three had already "been put to sleep." Apparently because they had no instructions to meet such a contingency, they contacted the movement's headquarters and only then received the order to "finish off" the others.[60] The movement's leaders had begun to panic on hearing that Yani had been killed.[61]

Meanwhile, at about 6 A.M. a delegation led by Brigadier General Supardjo had left the Halim base to report on the movement's behalf to Sukarno and request that he accompany them to Halim, where, they hoped, he would issue a statement commending their actions. On arrival at the president's palace they found that Sukarno was not there, and no one seemed to know where he had spent the night. In fact, Sukarno had been with his third wife, Dewi, at her house in the south of Jakarta. On being informed

57. Sjam at Sjam trial (p. 69). See also Sjam's testimony at Sudisman trial (I, 217, 250). At the Sudisman trial, however, Sjam seems to have become confused when he said that the decision to kill the generals was taken by himself, Pono, Untung, Latief, and Sujono on 29 September (see Sudisman trial [I, 255, 268–269]).

58. Untung at Untung trial (p. 59).

59. See Untung trial (pp. 123, 133, 135, 139).

60. Gatot Sukrisno at Untung trial (pp. 68–69), Sjam at Sjam trial (p. 72), Sujono at Untung trial (pp. 96–97).

61. It is quite possible that the movement's leaders did not issue unambiguous instructions to those entrusted with implementing the plot. Referring to an earlier plot, Anderson noted, "It must be recognized, however, that in Javanese social communication, much is commonly left unsaid, great trust being put in intuitive understanding; this pattern, while sharpening subtle sensibilities, frequently leads to confusion and misunderstanding" (1972a:396).

that shots had been fired at the houses of Nasution and Leimena, Sukarno decided to go immediately to the palace, but on the way was informed of the presence of unidentified troops in the square facing the palace, so he went instead to the home of his fourth wife, Haryati, on the west of Jakarta, and from there to the Halim air base. Although Sukarno later claimed that he went to Halim in order to be near an airplane if it became necessary to evacuate, his opponents accused him of going there because the headquarters of the Thirtieth of September Movement was located at the base.

On hearing that Sukarno was moving to Halim, Supardjo and his delegation, which had spent about two hours waiting at the palace, returned to Halim, where Supardjo reported to Sukarno at about 10 A.M. Although the accounts of this meeting given by Supardjo and others, such as Omar Dhani, differ in details, it seems that Supardjo told Sukarno that junior officers had taken action against the Council of Generals but that Nasution had escaped. Supardjo did not say that the generals had been killed, but Brigadier General Sabur, who had spent the previous night at Bogor, arrived during Supardjo's report with the news that Pandjaitan had been killed and bloodstains had been found at Yani's house. After further discussion, Sukarno is reported to have said, "good, good, good" to Supardjo and asked him for evidence that the generals were involved in a plot, but Supardjo promised only to bring the evidence later. Sukarno then said, "Yes, this can happen in a revolution," and, after telling Supardjo that he wanted no more bloodshed, asked him whether he could stop the movement. Supardjo said that he could, so Sukarno patted him on the shoulder and said, "If you don't I will slaughter you later."[62] Although Sukarno's apparently calm and not unfriendly reception of Supardjo's report was later interpreted as indicating that he had been informed of the plot beforehand and had already given his approval, he nevertheless refrained from giving explicit support to their actions. Thus Supardjo returned to the Thirtieth of September Movement's headquarters, where he re-

62. Supardjo at Supardjo trial (pp. 14–15). Testimony at Omar Dhani trial: Omar Dhani (II, 131–132), Sabur (III, 320), Sunarjo (III, 153). Brigadier General Sunarjo was head of the Criminal Research Service in the Attorney General's Department. Personally close to Sukarno, he had come to Halim on his own initiative.

ported to his dismayed colleagues that instead of extending his blessing, Sukarno had asked that the movement be stopped.[63]

One could perhaps speculate that if the plot had been carried out as originally planned, Sukarno may have given his endorsement. If all seven generals, including Nasution, had been arrested but not killed, Sukarno might have taken the opportunity to dismiss all or some of them and replace them with officers more congenial to himself and the Thirtieth of September Movement. Nasution's escape must have caused Sukarno to fear that resistance was already being organized against the movement. Further, when he learned that some of the generals, possibly including Yani, had been killed, he was even more reluctant to endorse the movement. Sukarno had never been a bloodthirsty ruler, and he was probably shocked when he heard of the violence carried out against the generals. He must also have been aware of the impact that the murder of Yani and other generals would have on the army as a whole. Thus he refused to endorse the movement and, in his characteristic way, began to seek a means of achieving a compromise settlement.

After hearing Supardjo's report, Sukarno began to consider the problem of appointing a successor to Yani and summoned the commanders of the other services as well as some senior ministers, including Leimena, to discuss the matter. Several proposals were made, but Sukarno rejected all of them. Suharto was regarded as "too stubborn," Mursjid rejected because "he likes to fight," and Basuki Rachmat, the East Java commander, because he was "not in good physical condition."[64] Supardjo came again to meet Sukarno, who asked for his opinion about the caretaker commander. At his trial, Supardjo said he had initially suggested Basuki Rachmat or Pranoto Reksosamudro but then asked whether he could consult the other leaders of the Thirtieth of September Movement because the appointment could affect his efforts to stop the movement. Supardjo then returned to the movement's headquarters, where Sjam suggested Rukman, Pranoto, or Suharto.[65]

63. According to Supardjo, Untung was ready to accept Sukarno's order but Sjam was unwilling (Supardjo trial [p. 15]). The commander of Battalion 530, which was stationed in front of the palace, was also present. He testified that he had heard Latief, Untung, and Heru excitedly debating the question of Sukarno's blessings, while Supardjo sat in dejected silence (Supardjo trial [pp. 30–31]).
64. Omar Dhani at Omar Dhani trial (II, 136).
65. Sjam at Sjam trial (p. 73).

Supardjo apparently decided to suggest Pranoto, and, after talking to Supardjo again, Sukarno announced that he himself was taking over the leadership of the army and that Pranoto would carry out the routine duties of the commander. This decision was taken at about 4 P.M.[66]

One can only speculate on why Pranoto was selected.[67] He was an experienced and senior officer but not the obvious candidate for the succession. Sukarno, however, ruled out the two most senior surviving members of the army's general staff, Suharto and Mursjid. Although it seems that Sukarno may have planned to replace Yani with Mursjid before the Thirtieth of September Movement went into action, he possibly felt that Mursjid's promotion in the new circumstances would be seen as evidence of his own complicity in the assassinations. Apart from them, Pranoto's claim in terms of seniority was as great as any of the other candidates because he had been commander of the Diponegoro division from 1960 to 1962 and a member of the army general staff as third assistant in charge of personnel since then. He was also known to be sympathetic toward the president's ideas, including the concept of Nasakom, which made him attractive to the Thirtieth of September Movement. Further, if we assume that Sukarno had already been informed of the action taken in support of the coup in Central Java, he may have calculated that Pranoto would be able to exercise some authority over his former subordinates there. If Sukarno's aim was to appoint a caretaker who was acceptable both to the army as a whole and to the coup group, his choice of Pranoto was understandable. Sukarno also may have

66. Supardjo at Supardjo trial (p. 16).

67. Pranoto had been chief of staff when Suharto was commander of the Diponegoro division. Suharto was dismissed in 1959 because of his involvement in smuggling after complaints were made by Pranoto. In interviews several generals, including Nasution, said that they had not regarded Pranoto as pro-PKI before October 1965. Pranoto was widely respected because of his simple style of living and apparent incorruptibility. Pranoto was arrested in 1967 because of alleged involvement in the coup attempt. Appearing as a witness in the Pono trial in February 1972, Pranoto admitted discussing Sukarno's health with Aidit at Sjam's house on 20 September (Report on Pono trial in *Indonesian Current Affairs Translation Service* [February 1972], 133). According to Major Sujono, Pranoto was at Sjam's house with Aidit on 30 September and went with Aidit and Sujono to Halim that night (Sujono at Untung trial [p. 115]). Later Sujono told Heru that Pranoto flew with Aidit to Yogyakarta at night on 1 October (Heru's written testimony at Omar Dhani trial [III, 548]). Apparently, Sujono mistook one of Aidit's two companions for Pranoto because Pranoto spent the entire day at the Kostrad headquarters.

developed special ties with Pranoto, who was perhaps the only member of the general staff who did not share the prevailing antipathy toward the PKI.[68]

An announcement was immediately prepared stating that Sukarno was in good health "and still holds the leadership of the state and revolution." It said that "temporarily the Leadership of the Army is directly in the hands of the President" and that Major General Pranoto Reksosamudro had been temporarily appointed "to carry out daily tasks in the Army." Further, Sukarno ordered all troops "to increase their alertness, return and remain at their posts and only move when ordered." The announcement was given to the navy commander, Admiral Martadinata, to take to the radio station. When Martadinata reached the radio station at about 6 P.M., Suharto's troops had taken it over and refused to permit him to enter.

Suharto had quickly taken charge of the army early in the morning on hearing that Yani was missing.[69] He had been woken at about 5:30 A.M. by one of his neighbors, who told him that there had been some shooting nearby and that several generals had been abducted. Suharto then drove to the Kostrad headquarters from where he could see the two battalions placed in the Merdeka Square by the Thirtieth of September Movement. Meanwhile, the first announcement of the Thirtieth of September Movement was broadcast. As Yani was missing, Suharto decided that he should take over the leadership of the army. The senior generals in Jakarta who could be contacted agreed, and in addition navy and police forces in Jakarta were placed under Suharto's authority. Suharto then ordered that all troops be confined to barracks and that none should move without his explicit orders. The air force, however, did not accept his authority, and he began to suspect that the air force was somehow involved in the kidnappings.

Suharto was anxious to avoid physical conflict. Apart from the natural reluctance of a general to order army troops into action against other army troops and the fact that the battleground

68. Yani told Nasution that he had appointed Pranoto as his third assistant on the direct order of Sukarno (Nasution 1967:II, 28).
69. See Suharto's speech to National Front on 15 October 1965 in *Indonesia*, 1 (April 1966).

would have been the Merdeka Square in the center of the city, he was conscious of the possibility that precipitate action might provoke air force retaliation. He also wanted to avoid taking military action while Sukarno was still in the hands of the rebels because such action might be represented in such a way as to suggest that Suharto was the rebel. Thus he set about winning over the two battalions in the Merdeka Square by persuasion.

Messengers were sent to attempt to convince the troops in the square to move to the Kostrad compound. Perhaps the crucial factor in winning them over was the mismanagement of the coup group in failing to ensure supplies of food and drink for the troops in the square.[70] Tired, hungry, and thirsty after hours in the hot Jakarta sun, the troops from the Brawijaya battalion were won over with promises of food and, on leaving the square shortly after 4 P.M., placed themselves under Suharto. The commander of the Diponegoro battalion, Major Sukirno, however, was more deeply committed to the movement led by his former commander and friend, Untung. Eventually, most of his troops, who were also very hungry and had seen the Brawijaya battalion leave its position in the square, withdrew to Halim at about 6 P.M. Thus, without firing a shot, Suharto was able to regain control of the Merdeka Square together with the palace, radio station, and telecommunications center that adjoined it.

Meanwhile Sukarno had sent his adjutant, Colonel Bambang Widjanarko, to call Pranoto, who was at the Kostrad headquarters, to Halim. Suharto, together with Nasution, who had come to the Kostrad in the late afternoon after spending the day in hiding, decided to send Bambang Widjanarko back to Halim with the reply that the president's order could not be implemented while operations were still in progress and the fate of the missing generals still unknown. Widjanarko was given the additional instruction that Sukarno had to be taken away from Halim because Kostrad troops were planning to move in.[71] Suharto's

---

70. Untung at Untung trial (p. 48). Suharto was fortunate to have the assistance of the commander of the Brawijaya division, Major General Basuki Rachmat, who happened to be in Jakarta at the time. Basuki Rachmat, another former Brawijaya commander, Major General Sarbini, and Brigadier General Sobiran Mochtar, helped to persuade the Brawijaya troops to leave the square, but Lieutenant Colonel Ali Murtopo was less able to exert authority over the Diponegoro soldiers.
71. Bambang Widjanarko at Supardjo trial (pp. 40–41), Nasution 1967:II, 54–56.

refusal to permit Pranoto to go to Halim was clearly an act of insubordination. Not only had Suharto prevented Pranoto from going to Halim, but he also refused to recognize the appointment. Further, instead of broadcasting Sukarno's announcement—brought by Admiral Martadinata—appointing Pranoto and the order for all troops to stay at their posts, he made his own radio speech announcing that he had taken over the army leadership and was mobilizing forces to crush the Thirtieth of September Movement. In the speech broadcast at about 9 P.M., he described the Thirtieth of September Movement as a counterrevolutionary coup against Sukarno and claimed that "now we are able to control the situation both in the center and in the regions."[72]

Meanwhile, Bambang Widjanarko returned to Halim. He reported that the Kostrad was preparing to occupy Halim and the president should leave quickly. Supardjo then proposed that Sukarno be flown to Bali, though Omar Dhani suggested East Java, presumably with the aim of putting Sukarno in a position where he could rally the people against the generals in Jakarta.[73] Sukarno, conscious that the nation might be on the point of civil war, decided instead to follow the cautious advice of Leimena and go by car to his palace at Bogor.

The collapse of the coup attempt made the plotters and their associates at Halim desperate. In the late afternoon Supardjo proposed to Omar Dhani that it would be better to attack the Kostrad rather than wait for the Kostrad to attack Halim,[74] and when it was clear that Suharto intended to move in on Halim, Commodore Leo Wattimena ordered that fighter planes be sent from the Abdurachman Saleh base in Malang to Halim and Bandung.[75] After the president left Halim, Omar Dhani and Leo Wattimena took off in the Hercules aircraft that had been made available for the president, but instead of flying directly to another air force

72. Suharto's radio speech in Puspenad 1965:32–33.
73. Supardjo at Supardjo trial (p. 17), Omar Dhani at Omar Dhani trial (II, 144).
74. Supardjo at Supardjo trial (p. 16), Omar Dhani at Omar Dhani trial (II, 141–142).
75. Testimony at Omar Dhani trial: Omar Dhani (II, 157), Leo Wattimena (III, 20). That night four planes (two B-52s and two Mustangs) were sent to Jakarta (testimony of Commodore Sudarman, commander of the Abdurachman Saleh base at Malang, Omar Dhani trial [III, 393–394]).

base, they held the plane in the air for seven or eight hours until the morning, when they landed at Madiun. While in the air they kept in contact with the situation on the ground, and when they heard further reports of Suharto's preparations to attack Halim, Omar Dhani instructed Wattimena to send a radiogram to Halim ordering the base commander to "tell Major General Suharto to abandon his plan for Halim because Halim is air force territory. If General Suharto does not heed this, he will be confronted by the air force."[76]

Before dawn next morning elite Army Paracommando Regiment (RPKAD) troops led by Colonel Sarwo Edhie were advancing on Halim. They had been ordered to take Halim with as little bloodshed as possible, but as they approached Lubang Buaya, where some of the remnants of battalion 454 and the "volunteers" had spent the night, they met with some resistance, leading to an exchange of fire in which one member of the RPKAD and two members of the air force were killed. Contact was quickly established between Colonel Sarwo Edhie and Commodore Dewanto of the air force, and a cease-fire was reached at 6:10 A.M. The air force base had fallen under effective army control. Meanwhile, Aidit had flown to Yogyakarta, and the leaders of the Thirtieth of September Movement had disappeared from the base.

The coup attempt took place against the background of the strengthening alliance between Sukarno and the PKI which had enabled the PKI to make rapid advances in the maneuvering of capital-city politics. Although there is no evidence that a Council of Generals was in fact planning immediate action to counter the PKI's advances, the atmosphere permitted such rumors to be believed both by the PKI and officers in the army and the air force, who preferred Sukarno to the army leadership. There is evidence that dissident officers had begun to worry about an anticipated coup attempt by the army leadership from early in 1965, and some had probably begun at least to consider taking preventive measures, while it is quite possible that they had already formulated a plan of action by the middle of 1965. When the president fell ill early in August, the PKI decided to contact these officers.

76. The text is in Omar Dhani trial (I, 417). See also testimony of Omar Dhani (II, 155) and Leo Wattimena (III, 21).

Together they laid their final plans for the movement. Whether they received explicit encouragement from Sukarno must remain an open question, but it is clear that they expected his support.

While the full consequences of the coup attempt took many months to work themselves out, Suharto's open defiance of Sukarno marked a crucial shift in the balance of Indonesian politics. Before 1 October the army leaders had consciously worked to undermine some of Sukarno's policies but always within a framework that recognized the supremacy of the president. His commands were "interpreted" and twisted to suit the army's purposes and, in the case of contacts with Malaysia, his policies were secretly sabotaged. Although there were signs that Yani was moving toward a much firmer line, the army had never stood up to the president by openly rejecting his commands. On 1 October, Suharto blatantly disobeyed Sukarno's instructions. Pranoto's appointment was ignored, and Suharto issued a veiled command to the president that he should leave Halim. The relationship between the president and the commander of the army that had prevailed through most of the Guided Democracy period ended on 1 October 1965.

5 | The Aftermath of The Coup Attempt

The murder of the six generals on 1 October 1965 set in train a series of developments that culminated in the dismissal of President Sukarno one and a half years later. The disintegration of the Guided Democracy system had been foreshadowed on 1 October 1965, when Suharto, with the backing of other senior generals, openly defied the president, but it was not until later in the month, when the decimation of PKI supporters commenced, that the old balance of power was irretrievably upset. The elimination of the PKI as an effective political force during the last three months of 1965 left the president and the army leadership as the two surviving centers of power competing for the support of lesser political forces. It soon became clear that without the backing of the PKI, Sukarno was much less able than before to control the army leadership.

The crucial condition for the army's increasing dominance was the elimination of the PKI. While it was not clear that the army leaders intended that the postcoup massacres should reach the level of ferocity experienced in areas like East Java, Bali, and Aceh, they no doubt consciously exploited the opportunity provided by the coup attempt to liquidate the PKI leadership, both in Jakarta and at the provincial and district levels. In the rural areas of Java and elsewhere, army officers cooperated with members of anti-Communist civilian organizations to murder several hundred thousand PKI activists, resulting in the party's loss of its organized mass base of support. The PKI, which had been organized for agitation rather than warfare, was in no position to defend itself against the army-backed offensive. Its leaders wavered on whether to encourage resistance, and its friends in the armed forces were too few in numbers to provide protection. While President Sukarno repeatedly raised his voice in Jakarta against the continuing massacre in Java, his closest supporters in the armed forces and the political parties remained silent. Resenting the rise of the PKI to a position where it had become Sukarno's main ally, the leaders of other political forces closer to the president than to the army leadership behaved as if unable to appreciate that Sukarno's authority depended on the maintenance of the balance in which the PKI played an integral role. Perhaps regarding the demise of the PKI as an opportunity to strengthen their own positions as forces on which the president could rely in balancing the power of the army and preferring not to compromise themselves in the eyes of the army leaders by appearing to defend the PKI, the leaders of the navy, the police, and parties like the PNI stood aside as the balance of power that provided the basis of Sukarno's authority was overturned.

The elimination of Yani and his "inner circle" on 1 October led to an important change in the outlook of the army leadership. Although Yani and his group had been moving toward a less flexible position, they had remained unwilling to challenge the president directly to a showdown on the question of his encouragement to the PKI. As a consequence of the coup attempt, however, the leadership of the army passed to Suharto, who was backed by Nasution. Neither Suharto nor Nasution was a member of the president's court circle, and both were among the senior officers who had expressed concern with Yani's reluctance to confront Sukarno directly on the question of the PKI's advances. When the "Yani group" was eliminated in one blow on 1 October, the leadership of the army shifted to those who were more inclined to take immediate action against the PKI and much less subject to Sukarno's personal influence.

President Sukarno fully appreciated that the delicate balance upon which his own power and authority rested was in grave danger of being upset as a result of what had happened on 1 October. Suharto and Nasution had refused to recognize the president's appointment of Pranoto and had continued operations against the Halim base in direct contradiction of his orders. Sukarno realized that if he did not reestablish his authority over the army immediately, they would endeavor to purge the army, take action against the air force, and might find ways of implicating the PKI. In the weeks that followed, Sukarno's primary goal was to maintain the status quo. He called repeatedly for calm and restraint and promised to provide a "political settlement" in contrast with the more drastic solution threatened by the army leaders.

Aware that he had no time to lose in reestablishing his authority over the army leadership, Sukarno summoned the commanders of the air force, navy, and police together with Pranoto, Suharto, and Mursjid to his palace at Bogor on 2 October with the purpose of confirming Pranoto's appointment. The meeting, which lasted five hours, was held in an atmosphere of high tension as Suharto asserted that the army would not accept Pranoto's appointment and demanded that action be taken against the air force leadership. In the end, Suharto agreed to accept the president's order of the previous day, according to which Sukarno himself took formal command of the army and appointed Pranoto to carry out the "daily tasks" of the commander, but only on the condition that Suharto was given responsibility for the "restoration of security and order."[1] Suharto, with the backing of Nasution and other senior generals, was determined to conduct a purge of all whom they regarded as involved in the assassinations, and they considered it essential that they, rather than the president, should be in control.

Sukarno hoped to limit the repercussions of the coup attempt as much as possible, for he knew that the officers involved in the movement were supporters of his leadership. Although he gave refuge to Supardjo for a few days in his Bogor palace, he could do little to prevent the purge of Supardjo and the other army and air force officers directly associated with the Thirtieth of September Movement. He nevertheless needed to protect the air force leadership, which had been his strongest ally in the armed forces during the previous months. Omar Dhani was also given refuge in the president's palace at Bogor. On the third, after the discovery of the bodies of the missing generals at the Halim air force base, Sukarno made a late-night radio broadcast in which he declared that accusations about air force involvement in the 30 September incident were untrue and warned, "We must remain on guard so

1. See Sukarno's radio speech at 1:30 A.M., 3 October 1965, in Puspenad 1965:36–37.

that the air force and army are not pitted against each other with beneficial results for the Nekolim and others."[2]

As the president had feared, the opportunity provided by the discovery of the bodies at Halim was fully exploited by the army leaders.[3] The exhumation of the corpses on 4 October was delayed until a full battery of journalists, photographers, and television cameramen had been assembled. The exhumation was also witnessed by several senior generals, including Suharto, who made a short speech for radio and television in which he pointed toward both air force and Communist involvement in the murders. After stressing that Lubang Buaya, where the bodies were found, was within the limits of the air force base, he pointed out that it was also the site of an air force training center where members of PKI-affiliated youth and women's organizations had been given military training. He went on: "Possibly the training was intended for defense of the base; however, according to a member of Gerwani who was trained here and who has now been captured in Cirebon, she is from Central Java. Far from here. So, according to the facts, it is possible that what was said by our beloved president and Great Leader of the Revolution that the air force was not involved in the question possibly contains some truth but it is not possible that there is no connection between the incident and certain members of the air force."[4] When Suharto referred to the involvement of "certain members of the air force," he was thinking not only of Major Sujono and other relatively junior officers but also of Air Marshal Omar Dhani. Suharto's speech, in which he had openly suggested that "our beloved president" had not been telling the whole truth in his radio statement that had appeared in the press that morning, made it quite clear that he stood in no great awe of the president. The president would not be able to exploit feelings of personal devotion and affection in his dealings with Suharto, who publicly indicated that he was determined to purge the air force leadership even if this involved acting without Sukarno's blessings.

2. Sukarno's radio speech at 11:00 P.M. on 3 October 1965 in ibid., p. 39.
3. According to Bambang Widjanarko, Sukarno had sent aides to Lubang Buaya in an unsuccessful attempt to remove the corpses before they were discovered by the army (Karni 1974:28–29).
4. Suharto's speech on 4 October 1965 in Koti 1965.

In his speech, Suharto also suggested that the PKI had been involved in the coup attempt. Although the evidence available in the first few days seemed to indicate that dissident army officers assisted by air force officers were mainly responsible, the army was quick to suspect the involvement of the PKI and to appreciate the opportunity such involvement would provide to deal with it.

The army leaders quickly declared Jakarta to be in a "state of war," and army units began to sweep through Communist stronghold areas in the capital arresting PKI cadres. Local officials and anti-Communist citizens were encouraged to point out the homes of PKI figures, who were then arrested. On the third, the Politburo member, Njono, was captured in one such raid. PKI resistance was slight except for an exchange of shots between some troops and armed members of the PKI youth organization, Pemuda Rakyat, near the Hotel Indonesia on the second. The leftist press and all other newspapers except the military-sponsored *Angkatan Bersenjata* and *Berita Yudha* were banned.

While the president appealed for calm and restraint, the army leaders deliberately fostered a highly emotional atmosphere in which the dominant theme was the call for revenge. The widespread publicity given to the exhumation of the general's bodies on the fourth was calculated to rouse public passions behind the army's demand for retribution, and instead of the spectacular display of military might that had been planned for 5 October, Armed Forces Day, a massive funeral was held for the six generals and the junior officer. Almost the entire non-Communist elite was present at the funeral, but the president was absent. Knowing that the generals might use the occasion to try to associate him with their demand for revenge, he stayed away but sent an aide to announce that the assassinated generals had been posthumously promoted.

On the sixth, the president continued his efforts to create an atmosphere favorable for a compromise settlement by calling a full cabinet meeting at Bogor. In his address to the cabinet, Sukarno condemned the murder of the generals, whom he honored as "Heroes of the Revolution." He declared that he did not approve of the formation of the Revolutionary Council and said that a calm and orderly atmosphere must be restored so action could be taken against "individuals from all sections" who had participated in the 30 September incident. The president emphasized that "we should not be overcome by emotion, accusations, and placing blame on each other, dividing our nation, dividing our armed forces, and dividing our political life."[5] The president's speech was followed by statements by representatives of the main groups in the cabinet, including the PKI. Although Aidit did not attend the meeting, the PKI was represented by Njoto and Lukman, who read a Politburo statement in which the PKI dissociated itself from what was described as "an internal army affair."[6] It was also announced at the session that Omar Dhani had ordered the arrest of air force members who had been engaged in the training of "volunteers" at Halim.

While Sukarno sought to restore harmony at the cabinet level, the army leaders continued to stir up emotions that were increasingly directed at the PKI. On the night of the sixth, Nasution's young daughter, who had been wounded during the raid on her father's home, died, adding further to the demand for retribution. Posters began to appear in Jakarta with the message "Crush the PKI, Hang Aidit," and on the sixth the army permitted the reappearance of eight newspapers, all of which could be relied on to support the army's line against the PKI, while the ban on the leftist press continued. On the same day the army newspaper, *Berita Yudha,* suggested that there had been a *dalang* (puppeteer) behind Untung[7] and on the eighth, *Angkatan Bersenjata* editorially stated that "Gestapu" (the coup attempt) had been "masterminded by PKI-Aidit."[8] During the next few days rumors were circulated about how the generals had been tortured and their sexual organs mutilated by members of the PKI women's organization, Gerwani, and it was reported that Untung and Supardjo had planned to kill the president.[9]

The army leadership had contacted the anti-Communist parties

5. Puspenad 1965:75–76.

6. The PKI statement is in *Indonesia,* 1 (April 1966), 188–189.

7. *Berita Yudha,* 6 October 1965.

8. *Angkatan Bersenjata,* 8 October 1965. The Thirtieth of September Movement was commonly abbreviated as "G.30.S" (Gerakan 30 September) or "Gestapu" (Gerakan September Tigapuluh). The term "Gestapu" was coined by Brigadier General Sugandhi, the director of *Angkatan Bersenjata,* with the German "Gestapo" in mind.

9. Ibid., 9, 13 October 1965. No evidence supports these stories.

and mass organizations immediately after the coup attempt and encouraged them to form a front to demand action against the PKI. On 2 October the head of the Koti's political section, Brigadier General Sutjipto, had called a meeting of younger-generation leaders of anti-Communist parties and organizations, who immediately formed the Action Front to Crush the Thirtieth of September Movement (KAP-Gestapu). Led by Subchan Z. E. of the NU and Harry Tjan of the Catholic party, the KAP-Gestapu, with the encouragement of army officers in the Kostrad, held its first rally on the fourth, which was attended by about a thousand demonstrators. As the propaganda offensive against the PKI gathered momentum, another KAP-Gestapu rally was held on the eighth. In contrast with the first rally held in the uncertain atmosphere immediately after the coup, the second rally attracted tens of thousands of demonstrators. After listening to speeches attacking the PKI, the demonstrators marched through the city to the National Front headquarters for a further demonstration. Some of them, mainly members of Muslim youth organizations, went to the PKI headquarters, which they attacked and set on fire. Although they had not sought the formal permission of the leaders of the KAP-Gestapu or the military authorities, it is likely that they had been assured by junior army officers that the senior generals would not be displeased if the PKI building were "spontaneously" attacked by the "people." In any case, the army took no steps to protect the PKI building, and it did not act to stop further attacks on other buildings associated with the PKI during the next few days.

Suharto had moved cautiously in taking measures against the PKI. He was determined to utilize the new circumstances to eliminate the army's archrival, but felt unable to issue an overt order instructing the regional commanders to arrest PKI leaders and dissolve the party and was even less in a position to openly order the decimation that in fact occurred. While he, personally, had scant respect for the president, he was aware of Sukarno's popularity within the armed forces, including the army, and wanted to avoid a showdown in which the regional army commanders would be asked to choose between the president on one side and Suharto and Nasution on the other. Confident that most of the regional commanders were nevertheless keen to exploit the opportunity to hit at the PKI, Suharto did not send formal, written orders instructing them on how to deal with the PKI. Instead the message that the PKI had to be crushed was conveyed informally, leaving local commanders to decide on the means to be used. In the absence of explicit instructions from Jakarta, each regional commander reacted to the situation in his own way, with the result that the measures taken against the PKI varied markedly from place to place.

In Jakarta the army moved swiftly to arrest PKI cadres and activists in mass organizations, and by the middle of November it was announced that some 2,200 had been detained.[10] Similarly, in West Java the military authorities aimed to paralyze the party by depriving it of leaders and activists, and by December over 10,000 had been arrested.[11] Cut off from their leaders, the ordinary members of the PKI and PKI-controlled organizations were then assembled in town and village squares, where they "voluntarily" agreed to dissolve the party and its supporting organizations. By November it was announced that some two-thirds of the PKI's branches in West Java had been dissolved in this way.[12] Although some mass killings of Communists took place in West Java, especially in the northern coastal areas around Cirebon, Indramayu, and Subang, where the PKI was relatively strong, anti-Communist violence in West Java was mild compared with what happened in Central and East Java.[13] Because the army moved quickly against the party's activists, the PKI's civilian opponents did not have a chance to take matters into their own hands. The relatively weak position of the PKI in West Java had made the army's task easier.

The first full-scale massacre of PKI supporters broke out in Aceh in the first part of October. Although the PKI in Aceh was very small, the Muslim leaders in Indonesia's most strongly Islamic province regarded it as a threat to Islam, and its largely non-Acehnese following became the target of what amounted to a holy war of extermination. Although the army commander,

10. *Antara Ichtisar Tahunan,* 17 November 1965.
11. Ibid., 18 December 1965.
12. *Angkatan Bersenjata,* 21 October, 2 November 1965. See also Sundhaussen 1971:635.
13. According to Sundhaussen (1971:694), Siliwangi officers estimated unofficially that fewer than ten thousand were killed in West Java. The journalist Frank Palmos reported an army-sponsored survey's estimate of three thousand in West Java (information from Frank Palmos).

Brigadier General Ishak Djuarsa, reportedly "tried to limit the killing to only the cadres,"[14] many of his troops apparently shared the outlook of the religious leaders. Ishak Djuarsa later claimed that "due to the quick and appropriate actions of the people, Aceh was the first region to be cleansed of counterrevolutionary G.30.S elements," and by December he was able to state that "the PKI is no longer a major problem for Aceh because the region has been entirely purged in a physical sense of PKI elements."[15] According to some reports, not only PKI cadres but their entire families and even household servants were included in a massacre that liquidated several thousand people.

In Central and East Java the atmosphere was very different during the first two or three weeks after 1 October. In Central Java the PKI had grown stronger than its main rival, the PNI, and in East Java the PKI and the NU had more or less equal support, with the PNI in third position. With a strong mass following, the PKI was well represented in regional government in the two provinces. Both the deputy governor of Central Java, Sujono Atmo, and the deputy governor of East Java, Satrio Sastrodiredjo, were closely allied to the party, while six out of thirty-five district heads (*bupatis* and mayors) in Central Java and eight out of thirty-seven in East Java were from the PKI, including the mayors of Solo, Magelang, Salatiga, Madiun, and Surabaya. Further, in Central Java the support given by Diponegoro officers to the Thirtieth of September Movement indicated that sympathy for the PKI was not insignificant in the officer corps and probably even stronger at lower levels. In East Java, Brawijaya officers had been only marginally involved in the Thirtieth of September Movement and most were strongly anti-Communist, but they felt a deep sense of devotion to the president and a reluctance to take action against his wishes.

On 1 October the Thirtieth of September Movement had virtually taken power in Central Java.[16] The army's strength in Central Java had been unusually low because one full infantry brigade and all but one battalion of another brigade were stationed in

14. Sundhaussen 1971:630.
15. *Antara Ichtisar Tahunan,* 6, 19 December 1965.
16. See Nugroho Notosusanto 1966:85–93 and Nugroho Notosusanto and Ismael Saleh 1968:41–65.

Sumatra and Kalimantan, leaving only seven infantry battalions in Central Java, of which three were attached to the three military resorts at Salatiga, Yogyakarta, and Purwokerto. By the evening of 1 October the Diponegoro headquarters in Semarang had been taken over by the rebels and the resort commanders in Salatiga and Yogyakarta had been arrested, as had the commander of the 6th Infantry Brigade in Solo. Of the infantry forces, only the resort at Purwokerto and one battalion outside Semarang remained loyal to the divisional commander, Brigadier General Surjosumpeno, who had avoided arrest by evacuating to Magelang, where a loyal cavalry battalion was stationed. In Semarang the head of the division's intelligence section, Colonel Suherman, had been appointed as chairman of the newly established Revolutionary Council, and the formation of similar councils had been announced in several major towns, including Solo and Yogyakarta.

Although Surjosumpeno's position seemed desperate, he had one great asset. Suharto had broadcast from Jakarta that the coup had failed, while President Sukarno had made no statement in support of the Thirtieth of September Movement. The collapse of the movement in Jakarta had a devastating impact on the morale of the coup leaders in Semarang, who decided during the night to flee with two companies to the mountainous area around Mount Merbabu and Mount Merapi. When Surjosumpeno returned to Semarang early in the morning on 2 October, he found his headquarters empty and immediately ordered that a statement be broadcast opposing the Thirtieth of September Movement and declaring that he stood "without reserve" behind Bung Karno (President Sukarno).

During the following weeks an uneasy truce prevailed in Central Java as the divisional commander sought gradually to restore his authority. With demoralization spreading rapidly among those who had supported Colonel Suherman, Surjosumpeno individually called several rebel officers, who in some cases tearfully confessed their involvement and requested his forgiveness. By the fourth the commander of the resort at Salatiga had resumed his post without obstruction, and on the fifth Surjosumpeno held a briefing in Yogyakarta which was attended by the leader of the Yogyakarta Revolutionary Council, Major Muljono, and several of his associates. After appointing a loyal member of his staff, Colonel Widodo, to take command of the Yogyakarta resort in place of the missing commander and his deputy, who had been secretly killed by the rebels, Surjosumpeno held another briefing on the eighth at Solo, attended by officers of the two rebel battalions of the 6th Infantry Brigade stationed in the era. Although Surjosumpeno had succeeded in establishing his presence in Yogyakarta and Solo, his actual authority was still very weak because effective power remained in the hands of troops that a week earlier had sided with the coup attempt but now pledged their loyalty to him.

Tension continued to grow between the PKI on one side and supporters of the nationalist and religious groups on the other. During the night of 1 October, Aidit had flown from Halim to Yogyakarta and, apparently under the impression that the president had evacuated to Bali, ordered PKI supporters to hold demonstrations in support of the president against the generals who had seized power in Jakarta.[17] In the meantime, Lukman, who had been following developments by radio in Semarang, had instructed local branches to avoid implicating the party in the abortive movement.[18] Although Aidit quickly accepted Lukman's view, a PKI-led demonstration nevertheless took place at the military resort headquarters in Yogyakarta on the second, addressed by an army officer.[19] This "involvement" of the PKI in supporting the Thirtieth of September Movement became the pretext for attacks on PKI offices and supporters by members of Muslim and nationalist youth organizations. In an atmosphere of high tension, the province faced the prospect of wider conflict between supporters and opponents of the PKI, with the possible involvement of armed forces personnel on both sides.

In East Java, where the NU's resistance to the PKI had been turning into an offensive during the first nine months of 1965, the postcoup atmosphere provided Muslims with an opportunity to step up their pressure on the PKI.[20] Tension had been rising in Surabaya during the last weeks of September as the PKI con-

17. Sumbul Djokosawarno (PKI official) at Utomo Ramelan trial (II, 158).
18. Djoko Sudjono (member of PKI Secretariat) at Sudisman trial (I, 358–364).
19. Major Muljono at Muljono trial (pp. 47–49). See also testimony of the officer who addressed the demonstrators, Major Kartawi (pp. 149–152).
20. For discussion of Muslim resistance to the PKI before October, see Mortimer 1972:chap. 5 and Walkin 1969.

ducted a campaign against high prices, corruption, and other economic ills that culminated on 27 September when demonstrators burst into the residence of the governor, Brigadier General Wijono, and held him captive for about an hour. As part of this campaign the PKI labor organization, SOBSI, had planned a series of demonstrations in which state enterprises were to be taken over by the workers and placed under the control of boards appointed on the Nasakom principle. The first takeovers commenced on 2 October and were followed by more until on the eighth the army commander, using his powers as the regional Pepelrada, banned "takeover actions" and on the tenth the SOBSI headquarters in Surabaya was occupied by troops. Meanwhile, beginning on about the seventh, anti-PKI and anti-Chinese demonstrations began to break out in the smaller towns of East Java. Many of the demonstrations ended with attacks on PKI offices and the homes of local PKI leaders as well as Chinese shops. The main force behind the demonstrations was the NU's youth organization, Ansor.

As Muslim violence against the Communists increased, the military authorities in Surabaya appeared to be more concerned with preserving order than in moving against the PKI. Although most of the officer corps was strongly anti-Communist, many important officers had little sympathy for the Muslims, whom they regarded as fanatics and troublemakers. In Surabaya some two hundred people from the "religious group" who were carrying "sharp weapons" were detained on 16 October after an anti-Communist rally had been followed by attacks on PKI offices, and two days later the Pepelrada issued a warning against "unwanted excesses which lead to both human and property losses" and ordered the cessation of attacks on "certain groups" and the destruction of property.[21] In some of the smaller towns also there were signs that the authorities were taking steps to prevent the attacks on the PKI and the Chinese from running out of hand. Curfews were imposed after rioting in a number of towns and on the thirteenth a member of Ansor was shot dead by a policeman during a demonstration at Porong, near Bangil,[22] while two days later five young men were killed when troops fired on a demonstration at Leces,

21. *Pewarta Surabaya*, 20 October 1965, Puspenad 1965:215.
22. *Obor Revolusi*, 15 October 1965.

near Probolinggo.[23] No roundup of Communist activists had commenced by the middle of the month, and PKI members of district
assemblies were reported to be still attending sessions in several
towns.[24]

As the army leadership in Surabaya hesitated to move against
the PKI without clear orders from Jakarta, leaders of Ansor decided to take the initiative. Meeting on about the tenth, they decided to hold synchronized rallies at midday on the thirteenth at
Kediri, Blitar, Trenggalek, and other towns, after which attacks
would be made on PKI offices and PKI supporters would be
deliberately killed.[25] After local army officers considered sympathetic to their plans were informed, the demonstrations were held
and, following a "Vigilance Rally of Godly People" at Kediri,
eleven supporters of the PKI were hacked to death as they tried
to defend the besieged party office.[26] On the eighteenth a large
clash between PKI supporters and youths from Ansor, supported
by the PNI's Pemuda Marhaen, occurred in South Banyuwangi on
the eastern tip of Java. Some thirty-five corpses were discovered
on the eighteenth and another sixty-two in mass graves a few days
later.[27] During the next few days a massacre broke out in which
several thousand PKI supporters lost their lives in the South Banyuwangi area[28] and, as the news of the killings spread, Muslim
leaders in other parts of East Java, usually with the tacit or express support of local military officers, prepared for an onslaught
against the PKI that was to last for several months.

While civilians took the lead in attacking the PKI in East Java,
the balance of power in Central Java remained extremely precarious because of the dubious loyalty to the regional commander of
the five battalions that had supported the Thirtieth of September
Movement on 1 October. In particular, Surjosumpeno needed to
neutralize the three battalions of the 6th Infantry Brigade stationed near Solo and Yogyakarta. Preferring not to attempt a

23. *Pewarta Surabaya,* 23 October 1965.
24. For example, at Pasuruan and Blitar; see *Obor Revolusi,* 20 October 1965,
Manifesto, 21 October 1965.
25. Interview with an Ansor leader, October 1973.
26. *Pewarta Surabaya,* 16 October 1965; interview with an eyewitness, May 1970.
27. Ibid., 28 October 1965.
28. Unpublished report of Fact-Finding Commission appointed by President
Sukarno on 27 December 1965, p. 9.

purge of the three battalions for fear that soldiers might desert
and return to their home villages with their arms, Surjosumpeno
used the pretext of the confrontation campaign to order the three
battalions to prepare for transfer to Sumatra, Kalimantan, and
Sulawesi.[29] In the meantime, Surjosumpeno had urgently requested the recall of two Diponegoro battalions posted in Sumatra, but no means were available to transport so many troops
immediately. Troops in Jakarta were still required to maintain
security in the capital, and Suharto apparently feared that the
dispatch of Siliwangi troops from West Java to Central Java might
lead to a flareup of interethnic and interdivisional rivalry. In the
middle of the month, when Suharto's control of Jakarta was
firmly established, it was decided to send slightly more than a
battalion of elite RPKAD troops from Jakarta to join "skeleton"
RPKAD forces already stationed in Central Java, thereby forming
two full RPKAD battalions, together with a Kostrad cavalry battalion. Although the reinforcements were not enough to ensure a
decisive numerical superiority for the pro-Suharto forces in Central Java, their quality and equipment were far superior to that of
the Diponegoro troops, who would have been well aware of their
own inferiority. Thus it was hoped that the presence of the
RPKAD forces would overawe the rebels, who would then comply
with Surjosumpeno's order to leave the province.

The reinforcements reached Semarang on the eighteenth, and
on the nineteenth the newly arrived troops paraded through the
city in a show of force. Searches were carried out in various parts
of the city, and over a thousand people were detained while documents, knives, and various other weapons were seized. At the
same time nationalist and Muslim youths attacked Communist
buildings and set them ablaze. The main body of RPKAD troops
then moved on to Magelang where, on the twenty-first, the pattern of events in Semarang was repeated.

On the evening of the twentieth, the graves of the missing Yogyakarta resort commander, Colonel Katamso, and his deputy,
Lieutenant Colonel Sugijono, were discovered at the barracks of
Battalion L of the 6th Infantry Brigade outside Yogyakarta. Early
the next morning, the bodies were exhumed in the presence of

29. Interview with Major General Surjosumpeno, 26 November 1970.

Surjosumpeno, who decided to hold the funeral on the twenty-second, an event that could be expected to inflame passions against the PKI. On the evening of the twenty-first, Surjosumpeno was disturbed by reports from Solo and Boyolali, where the PKI appeared to be organizing its supporters. In Boyolali PKI supporters were attempting to release the recently captured leader of the Yogyakarta Revolutionary Council, Major Muljono, while in Solo railway workers went on strike, preventing the departure of trains to Jakarta. Reports came in that fallen trees were being laid across roads, telephone wires were cut, and traffic on the road south from Solo toward Sukohardjo was being stopped by Pemuda Rakyat youths. Further, a barricade had been erected in front of the headquarters of Battalion K in Solo.[30] These preparations were largely a response to the approach of the RPKAD and the expected repercussions of the funeral, while the railway strike was probably intended to make it impossible for Battalions K and M of the 6th Infantry Brigade to leave Solo in accordance with Surjosumpeno's order.

Fearing that the PKI and the dissident battalions would turn Solo into a bastion for a last-ditch battle, Surjosumpeno ordered the RPKAD to leave Magelang immediately and take control of Solo. Moving rapidly during the night, they met with no serious obstruction, although shortly after they had passed, the road between Yogyakarta and Solo was blocked with fallen trees, especially in the Prambanan area.[31] In Solo, the RPKAD went into action immediately. They conducted raids in areas regarded as centers of PKI strength and quickly broke the railway workers' strike. They held a show of force by parading through the city as they had in Semarang and Magelang and, as in those cities, the RPKAD parade triggered off attacks on Communist and Chinese property by members of religious and nationalist youth organizations. In Solo the anti-Chinese rioting was particularly severe, but the anti-Communist demonstration met with some resistance when a parade was fired on and six people were killed and twenty-nine wounded.[32]

30. See Boerhan and Soebekti 1966:117–118.
31. Interviews with Major General Surjosumpeno, 26 November 1970 and Brigadier General Sarwo Edhie, 5 September 1970.
32. Puspenad 1965:304–305.

With the occupation of Solo by the RPKAD, Surjosumpeno's forces had gained control in all the important towns. Unwilling to go into battle with the RPKAD, the leaders of Battalion L in Yogyakarta agreed to obey Surjosumpeno's order to leave Central Java, and in Solo telephone discussions between RPKAD officers and the commanders of Battalions K and M eventually resulted in their agreement to leave also. Thus the threatened outbreak of fighting was averted. Battalion K left Solo on the twenty-third and Battalion M two days later.[33] The agreement of the commanders of the three 6th Infantry Brigade battalions to obey Surjosumpeno's order to leave Central Java greatly eased the situation for the RPKAD commander, Colonel Sarwo Edhie, but he still felt beleaguered. He was able to control the city of Solo and had arrested its Communist mayor, Utomo Ramelan, but the surrounding village areas were centers of PKI strength. Further reports poured in of telephone wires being cut and roads being blocked by fallen trees in areas including Klaten, Prambanan, Boyolali, Karanganyar, Sragen, and Wonogiri. In addition, reports began to be received that PNI and religious leaders were being killed.[34] Although confident that he could hold the city of Solo, Sarwo Edhie felt unable to establish his authority throughout the area by sweeping through the villages to arrest PKI activists.

Colonel Sarwo Edhie was convinced that he could not successfully carry out his task of "restoring security and order" without more troops. He contacted Suharto in Jakarta and requested that reinforcements be sent, but was told that additional troops would

33. Ibid., pp. 208, 211.
34. In early November, Sarwo Edhie estimated that PKI supporters had killed about 200 of their opponents in the Surakarta area, mostly at Boyolali and Klaten (*Duta Masyarakat*, 5 November 1965). Later the governor's liaison officer for the former residency of Surakarta, Hadisukmo, reported that 369 non-Communists had been killed—21 in the city of Solo, 238 in Klaten, 98 in Boyolali, 1 in Sragen, 1 in Karanganyar, and 2 in Sukohardjo (testimony at Utomo Ramelan trial [I, 463]). This contrasts with the later claim of *Angkatan Bersenjata* that "tens of thousands died on both sides" (9 February 1970, translated in *United States Embassy Translation Unit Press Review;* hereafter cited as *USE*). See also Brackman's comment that "what happened in Indonesia, in some respects, was more akin to civil war than mass murder" (1969:117). Most misleading of all is Jones, who wrote that "Communist forces mounted sporadic attacks on their opponents in the civilian population, mostly anti-communists, mutilating and killing several hundred people, before General Sarwo Edhy and his para-commandos put an end to the carnage" (1971:391).

not be available until the end of the month. He then requested permission to arm and train youths from the religious and nationalist organizations. After a delay, permission was granted, and the youths were given two to three days of training before being sent out into the villages in units led by RPKAD men with the task of breaking the back of the PKI.[35] In each village members of Communist organizations were rounded up and taken away. After quick interrogation, those considered to be activists were killed and passive supporters were placed under detention in camps and jails.[36] During the following weeks similar operations spread out through all of Central Java. In general, the operations remained under army control and were directed mainly at PKI activists, but in some areas, such as Banyumas, it was reported that the army authorities stood aside and permitted the Muslim and nationalist youths to select their own victims, with the result that many thousands, who would have been merely arrested in areas where the army exercised close control, were killed.[37]

The army-supervised killings in Central Java, which took place with the obvious approval of the army leadership in Jakarta, removed the inhibitions of troop commanders in East Java. Arrests of Communist activists had not commenced until about the middle of October,[38] but by the end of the month large-scale swoops were being conducted by army units in many areas.[39] The regional commander, Major General Basuki Rachmat, and the chief of staff of the Pepelrada, Colonel Widjaja Sukardanu, had appeared reluctant to authorize action that might have provoked a large-scale clash, but with the commencement of operations in Central Java, Basuki Rachmat permitted his resort commanders to take similar measures, while the Sukarnoist Colonel Sukardanu was "sent to Seskoad" (the Army Staff and Command College) later in the month and then arrested.[40] While Basuki Rachmat was hesitating, two of the three resort commanders, Colonel Willy

35. Interview with Brigadier General Sarwo Edhie, 5 September 1970.
36. See Hughes 1968:chap. 13. For a horrifying account by an individual personally involved, see Usamah 1970. See also the short story, "Bawuk" by Umar Kayam in *Horizon*, 5 (January 1970), 6–15.
37. Report made available by Frank Palmos.
38. Puspenad 1965:216–222.
39. See *Manifesto*, 3, 5 November 1965.
40. *Pewarta Surabaya*, 30 October 1965.

Sudjono in Madiun-Kediri and Colonel Sumardi in Malang, had been urging strong measures, and later in the month extensive operations were carried out in their areas.[41]

Although the army usually had control of operations in the towns, religious leaders in the villages were encouraged to take their own measures. Most commonly the lead was taken by the *kiyais* (religious teachers) and *ulamas* (religious scholars) affiliated with the NU, who mobilized students from their *pesantrens* (religious schools) to drag Communists, members of pro-PKI organizations, and suspects from their homes and take them to riverbanks where their throats were cut and their bodies thrown into the river. Members of the Ansor youth organization moved from area to area inciting Muslims to exterminate "atheists," and by the middle of November killings had taken place in almost all parts of the province. In some villages the massacre even extended to children, while in others only party activists were killed. Often the army stood by, sometimes supplying trucks to cart off the victims, although it was not uncommon for soldiers to participate more actively.

The pattern of killing in East Java was followed, after a delay, in Bali, where the PKI had been challenging the PNI's ascendancy. Tension between PNI and PKI supporters had risen as rumors spread of developments in Central and East Java, and on 11 November fighting between youths at Bulelang led to seven deaths. Although surface calm was maintained until the end of the month, the explosion of mass resentments that followed a clash between an army unit and Communist youths at Jembrana in which one soldier was killed led to a massacre that spread through most of Bali during the first week of December.[42] As in East Java, army officers gave at least tacit approval to the plans of the PKI's civilian opponents, but the massacre quickly ran out of hand with an intensity that was second only to what had happened in Aceh.

In other parts of Indonesia, where the PKI was not a major political force, the army usually moved quickly in arresting PKI activists before the party's civilian rivals took more drastic action.

41. Interview with Colonel Willy Sudjono 12 October 1973.
42. See Report of Fact-Finding Commission, p. 8, and Appendix A, p. 1. See also Hughes 1968:chap. 15.

Nevertheless, killings took place in all areas, usually with the co-operation of the military authorities. In the worst-affected of the remaining provinces, North Sumatra, the PKI had become a significant political force, with strong support among Javanese plantation workers, who were the main victims of the killings. In the plantations the army-organized "trade union," SOKSI, played a leading role, while in Medan the army gave a fairly free hand to members of anti-Communist youth organizations, especially Muslim and Catholic groups and the secular Pemuda Panca Sila. The Pemuda Panca Sila appears to have included in its ranks a substantial "cross-boy" element who participated in the killings less for ideological reasons than for the opportunity that a breakdown of law and order gave for looting.

The army leadership's goal in encouraging the massacre of PKI supporters was to eliminate the PKI as a political force. The army leaders viewed operations against the PKI as tactically necessary to achieve a strategic objective. Moreover, field officers in Java were drawn largely from the *priyayi* section of society, which tended to look on the PKI's activities in mobilizing the lower classes as "non-Javanese" and a threat to the established hierarchy that placed them near the top. While the army leadership welcomed the opportunity to consolidate its political position and local commanders were pleased to get rid of troublemakers, they did not sympathize with the "holy war" fervor of the Muslims, nor did they, or at least the army leadership in Jakarta, condone the urge to extirpate all traces of the force that had been disrupting traditional Balinese society. Having crushed the PKI's leadership at all levels and destroyed the party's potential for revival in the short term at least, the army had no interest in an ongoing slaughter that strengthened the political position of organized Islam. During November there were signs that the army was seeking to reestablish its control by calling a halt to unsupervised killing, which was providing a cover for the settlement of all sorts of personal feuds.

By about the middle of November, the army leaders in Central Java had become concerned that the massacres were getting out of hand. Having whetted their appetites for blood, the youths from Muslim and nationalist organizations seemed unable to restrain themselves as they ran out of PKI "activists" and extended their net to include victims with marginal associations with the

PKI. In the middle of the month Suharto visited Central Java,[43] and on 24 November, Major General Surjosumpeno issued an order that unauthorized groups should stop making arrests. At the same time the RPKAD commander, Sarwo Edhie, warned publicly against "excesses."[44]

In East Java there were similar indications. In Madiun, Colonel Willy Sudjono said that on 15 November he had changed the name of the local "Action Command to Crush G.30.S" to the "Action Command to Restore Security," and in Malang, Colonel Sumardi acknowledged responsibility for killings that took place before 3 December but said that murders taking place after that date would be treated as criminal offences.[45] In December the new acting commander of the Brawijaya division, Brigadier General Sunarijadi, addressing a conference of the NU at Jombang, praised the NU's policy "in regard to the annihilation of G.30.S. elements which is parallel to the policy of the Brawijaya division," but added that "operations must be coordinated and guided because, if not, the wrong targets might be hit, causing unnecessary conflict between fellow instruments of the revolution."[46] At the end of December, Sunarijadi issued an instruction which "prohibits and stops individual activities by members or groups from political and mass organizations in assisting the Armed Forces to annihilate G.30.S.,"[47] and at the end of January a new instruction ordered that firm action be taken against "any individual who performs 'wild' deeds outside the law" by bringing them to court, or "if necessary individuals who do not obey orders from the authorities should be shot dead."[48] Meanwhile, the RPKAD, which had instigated the massacre in Central Java, was rushed to Bali in December to curb, or at least redirect, the killing so that only PKI activists were taken, rather than permitting it to run wild as in the first part of the month.[49]

43. *Berita Yudha,* 18 November 1965.
44. *Kompas,* 27 November 1965.
45. *Surabaya Post,* 4 January 1966.
46. *Duta Masyarakat,* 18 December 1965.
47. *Nusa Putera,* 30 December 1965.
48. Ibid., 28 January 1966.
49. In a press interview, Colonel Sarwo Edhie said, "In Central Java the people had to be aroused to oppose Gestapu whereas in Bali the spirit of the people was overflowing so that we had to control them." The interview is in Dharmawan Tjondronegoro 1966:167.

Although the worst of the killing was over by December, executions continued on a diminished scale well into 1966. Estimates of the total number killed varied from 78,500, suggested by a Fact-Finding Commission appointed by the president at the end of December, to one million, based on an army-sponsored survey conducted by students from Bandung and Jakarta. The Fact-Finding Commission, which made brief visits to only East and Central Java, Bali, and North Sumatra, noted a tendency on the part of officials "to hide or minimize the number of victims reported," and estimated that 54,000 had been killed in East Java, 10,000 in Central Java, 12,500 in Bali, and 2,000 in North Sumatra.[50] While the Fact-Finding Commission's estimate is universally regarded as too low, the estimate of a million appears to be too high. According to the survey, 800,000 were killed in Central and East Java and 100,000 in Bali, with the remaining 100,000 spread through the other provinces.[51] Although there is no way of knowing, the most commonly accepted estimate was between 250,000 and 500,000.[52] In addition, the Fact-Finding Commission reported that 106,000 supporters of the PKI had been interned in prison camps, of whom 70,000 were in Central Java, 25,000 in East Java, and 11,000 in North Sumatra, while the number taken prisoner in Bali was apparently too small to note. Later the attorney general estimated that some 200,000 people had been arrested throughout Indonesia.[53]

The PKI's supporters had been completely unprepared for the onslaught and offered almost no resistance. The party's mass base among the peasantry had been attracted by the PKI's vigor in defending the interests of the *abangan* (nominally Islamic) poor, which conflicted with those of the better-off peasantry and the Muslim community, but the party's program had been in no way "revolutionary." During the parliamentary period the PKI's rural

50. Report of the Fact Finding Commission.
51. Information from Frank Palmos. An example of overestimation is the report's estimate that "one third of the population" was killed in the Boyolali-Solo-Klaten "triangle." If it is assumed that half the population were children, this would mean that two-thirds of all adults were killed. Possibly one-third of adult men were killed, or about 8 percent of the total population, and a much smaller percentage of adult women.
52. In 1976 the head of the Kopkamtib, Admiral Sudomo, estimated that between 450,000 and 500,000 had been killed (*Tempo*, 10 July 1976).
53. *Harian Kami*, 27 July 1967.

supporters had given their votes, and later they had participated in small-scale "actions" in support of land reform and the "re-tooling" of local officials, but they had never been prepared for armed resistance.[54] The PKI's "offensive" in 1964 and 1965, however, had brought the party's supporters into bitter conflict with their rivals in other parties, and only the catalyst of the coup attempt in Jakarta was needed for anti-Communist groups to prepare to take their revenge. The driving force behind the decimation had been Muslim fanaticism, but Catholic youths were prominent in North Sumatra and the Lesser Sundas, while in Bali Hindus affiliated with the PNI played the main role. The massacre was in large part a reaction against the threat posed by the PKI's activism to traditional relationships and values in the rural areas,[55] but the huge scale of the massacre was possible only because of the encouragement given by the army. It was only after army officers indicated their approval of the killing that the isolated incidents in Java during the first half of October turned into the unbridled massacre that raged in many areas during the latter part of October and November. Moreover, the participation of the army gave the supporters of the PKI, un-armed or armed only with bamboo spears and knives, no chance of defending themselves.

As the killings continued, President Sukarno spoke out in Ja-karta against the events of the "epilogue" of the 30 September incident. The "epilogue," he exclaimed, "has disturbed my spirit, made me sad, made me worried.... Frankly, I wept to God, asked God, how, Allah, Robi, how could this happen?"[56] Again and again he quoted Abraham Lincoln as saying, "A nation di-vided against itself cannot stand," and both Gibbon and Toynbee were credited with saying, "A great civilization never goes down unless it destroys itself from within." At a meeting of provincial governors in December he said, "We are restoring law and order in a way that is too extreme ... with the result that innocent people are being put in jail. Not only put in jail, some even have their throats cut." He warned that "if a person, a group, a party is too severely persecuted and even the innocent are also captured,

54. See Hindley 1967.
55. See Sloan 1971:70–73.
56. President Sukarno's speech, 20 November 1965.

also killed, also crushed, a day will come when they might rise again and take their revenge."[57] At a women's rally he said that many people in Central and East Java who were "not directly involved" in the coup attempt were being massacred by "retrogressive-revolutionary" elements,[58] and in desperation he appealed to members of the Muslim student organization, HMI, to behave as good Muslims by at least burying the dead. He said that in East Java "many members of Pemuda Rakyat or members of the PKI or mere PKI sympathizers have been killed, slaughtered, stabbed or beaten till their heads split." Their corpses "were left under trees, beside rivers, thrown like the corpses of dead dogs." Sukarno reminded his audience that Muslims have a duty to care properly for the dead. In East Java, he said, people who wanted to carry out their obligations in regard to the corpses of Communists were themselves threatened. Sukarno called on the HMI students, "who understand the laws of Islam . . . to go on tour to East Java, to Central Java and tell the Muslims there not to neglect the corpses, not to make the orphans more miserable." He added, "If we go on as we are, brothers, we are going to hell, really we are going to hell."[59]

While there is no need to doubt that Sukarno was truly horrified at seeing his vision of a united nation shattered by the spectacle of Indonesians massacring Indonesians, he was also fully aware of the political implications of the drive against the PKI. Nasakom was more than a conception of national unity; by recognizing the PKI's integral role, it was an essential condition for the kind of political system over which Sukarno ruled. By moving to eliminate the PKI as a political force, the army was also overturning the system that gave Sukarno his power. Without the PKI to balance the power of the army, the president's own role would be limited unless he could forge a new coalition opposed to the army leadership. Toward the end of 1965 and early in 1966 Sukarno's confidence in his ability to regain his authority seemed to be growing. As he increasingly behaved as if his powers had been left unimpaired by recent developments, the conflict between the president and the army leaders sharpened.

57. Ibid., 13 December 1965.
58. Ibid., 17 December 1965.
59. Ibid., 18 December 1965.

6 | President Sukarno's "Comeback"

During the last three months of 1965, President Sukarno's position had been weakened drastically. The army had exploited the coup attempt not only to arrest those whom it suspected of direct involvement but to crush completely its main political opponent, the PKI. Despite the president's appeals to limit the retribution to those directly involved, the PKI's civilian and military opponents carried out a massacre on a scale unprecedented in Indonesia's history. As a consequence, the president was deprived of his most dynamic civilian support. Further, his scope for the kind of political maneuvering at which he excelled was restricted because the previous balance was succeeded by circumstances in which one political force threatened to become much stronger than the rest.

Although the power of the army leadership in relation to the president had increased greatly during the last quarter of 1965, the president was by no means a spent force. Sukarno had lost his most powerful source of support, but he still had friends in the armed forces and the political parties who preferred him to the army leadership. Suharto had, after all, inherited Yani's army, which had become adept at undermining the president's commands at the point of implementation but had never envisaged taking action to depose the Supreme Commander and Great Leader of the Revolution. While Suharto knew that he had the support of virtually all the senior officers in moving against the PKI and the air force leadership, he was acutely aware of the loyalty felt by many officers, especially in East and Central Java, to Sukarno, whose flamboyant nationalism appealed to an officer corps priding itself on its revolutionary origins. Many senior officers hoped that the elimination of the PKI would allow them to return to the old spirit of understanding and rapport which they had enjoyed with Sukarno before his close alignment with the PKI. Moreover, many of the generals who had risen to high positions under Yani feared that if Suharto were permitted to consolidate his power at Sukarno's expense, they too would be replaced because Suharto would want to appoint his own men to key posts. Thus, some important generals in the army were prepared to accept Suharto as commander of the army but were not willing to cooperate in moves designed to enhance his power at the expense of the president.

Support for Sukarno was much stronger within the other branches of the armed forces. During the guided Democracy period, the president had cultivated the leaders of the air force, navy, and police and fostered their independence from the army. Although officers in the navy, police, and, less unambiguously, the air force, had generally sympathized with the army's anti-Communism, they had realized that the postcoup increase in the army leadership's power might well lead to an attempt by the army to reestablish its ascendancy over the armed forces as a whole. It was therefore in their interests to support Sukarno as a bulwark against the expansion of the army's power, just as he encouraged them for the same reason. Moreover, the predominantly Javanese officers in the navy, police, and air force felt a strong sense of personal commitment to the man whom they had long regarded as their patron and *Bapak* (father) and whose position was now under threat.

For similar reasons of sentiment and interest, the leaders of the main political parties, the PNI and the NU, as well as most of the smaller party leaders, were originally inclined toward the president's side in the conflict between Sukarno and the army leadership. Although they had in varying degrees supported the army's drive against the PKI, they wanted to preserve the system of elite-level maneuvering under which they had prospered, while local party leaders in the provinces were apprehensive about the possibility of a further expansion of the military role in regional government. Like many senior officers in the armed forces, the party leaders also regarded themselves as "*Bapak*'s children" and could not easily envisage a system without him. As they contemplated the expansion of the army's power, they realized that their own room for maneuver would be wider in the context of competition between the army leadership and the president than if the army leaders succeeded in curtailing the president's role. The parties, however, were not always united internally in their attitude to the president. The lines of division ran within parties as much as between them as younger activists, especially from the religious parties, were in the forefront of the Action Fronts that sprang into existence to demand action against Sukarno and the "old order." While the established party leaders of the older generation hesitated to forsake Sukarno, the young leaders of the Action Fronts provided the army leadership with its most enthusiastic civilian support.

By the beginning of 1966 the broad features of a new balance of power were discernible. By eliminating the PKI, the army had destroyed the old power constellation and created the conditions for a new balance in which it would be the single most powerful force. The army leaders felt that in the new circumstances they would be in a position to exercise a decisive influence over the president and his policies. They expected that they would be able to force the president to condemn the PKI publicly and formally announce its dissolution. They also planned to force Sukarno to dismiss those of his ministers who had cooperated with the PKI in the past and who, with some others, were now most reluctant to accept the army's dominant influence. If the president were deprived of his old advisers and supporters, they expected that he would have no alternative but to turn to them. Thus the army leaders hoped to consolidate their power without disturbing the formal status of the president, thereby avoiding the tensions and dangers, not least within the army itself, that would inevitably accompany an attempt to depose Sukarno. The army leaders' strategy was based on the hope that the president would recognize "reality" and accommodate himself to the new circumstances.

During the latter part of 1965, Suharto had taken a series of steps to strengthen his own position within the army and the army's position in relation to the president. On 10 October he had institutionalized the authority given to him by Sukarno at Bogor eight days earlier to "restore order and security" by establishing the Operations Command to Restore Order and Security (Kopkamtib) which was recognized formally by Sukarno on 1 November. As Suharto took control of security operations it was clear that he and not Pranoto or the president was exercising the powers of the commander of the army, and on 16 October, Sukarno bowed to pressure to appoint Suharto formally as commander of the army and chief of staff of the Koti. In late November, Suharto reorganized the Koti staff after insisting on the removal of the civilians, Subandrio and Achmadi, and the transfer of Air Vice Marshal Sri Muljono Herlambang from his position as head of operations to the nominal post of deputy chief of staff. At the same time Sukarno was pressed to dismiss Omar Dhani as commander of the air force, but his successor, Sri Muljono Herlambang, was hardly more acceptable to the army.

Meanwhile, the campaign against the PKI continued. Aidit, who had flown to Central Java on 1 October, was captured and summarily executed on 22 November; Njoto, who had been taking shelter in the president's palace and the homes of leftist ministers, was captured and shot sometime after attending a cabinet meeting on 6 November. Lukman and Sudisman went into hiding in Jakarta, and Sakirman disappeared in Central Java. Of the senior PKI leaders captured by the end of 1965, only Njono and Peris Pardede were not killed immediately, and it was soon decided to bring them to trial. In late November, after a "confession" had been extracted from Njono,[1] Suharto demanded authority from the president to establish the Mahmillub (Special Military Court) to try leading prisoners, and on 4 December Sukarno conceded wide powers to Suharto to appoint the judges in such courts and determine who would be brought to trial by them.

The principal target of the crusade launched in the last three months of 1965 was the PKI, though there were signs that some civilian and military groups involved in the "anti-Gestapu" movement wanted to extend the campaign to cover other targets. The president continued to be above public criticism, but the anti-Gestapu campaign was broadened to attack some of the president's allies and policies. Clearly, the crusade against the PKI undermined one of his policies; attempts were also made to exploit the situation so as to undermine the president's policy of close friendship with the People's Republic of China. Related to

1. See *Angkatan Bersenjata,* 3 December 1965.

this goal was the propaganda launched against the foreign minister and first deputy prime minister, Subandrio, who also headed the Central Intelligence Board. In addition, moves were initiated against the PNI, which, after the PKI, was the main stronghold of civilian support for Sukarno.

As the expanding campaign spread beyond the PKI to other allies of the president, Sukarno was at pains to assert that he was still in control. At the ceremony to install Suharto as the new army commander on 16 October, he mocked rumors that he had lost power. "Ah, I want to laugh, brothers," he said, "Some people say, Sukarno? Ho, Sukarno has been overthrown . . . Sukarno is not an effective leader anymore. He is only like a father over his nation." Aiming to preserve the old status quo, he played down the significance of the coup attempt as "something ordinary and normal in a revolution." In contrast with the army leaders, who regarded the murder of Yani and his colleagues as a "national tragedy," Sukarno repeatedly spoke of the coup attempt as "a ripple in the ocean of the revolution."[2] At a cabinet meeting on 6 November, attended by Njoto, he clearly accepted that PKI members had been involved in the coup attempt when he described it as a case of "an infantile illness of Communism." "Hey, Njoto," he called, "your Communist party, yes, now the Gestapu people are stupid. Stupidity which harms Communism."[3] Nevertheless, Sukarno sought to separate the involvement of individual Communists from the question of the party's right to existence.

Sukarno's refusal to take action against the PKI was not based merely on his admiration for the party. He realized that the elimination of the PKI would undermine the entire political system that he led. Although the army leaders pressed him to announce the dissolution of the PKI, he repeatedly stressed that the forces of Nasakom existed independently of the parties that were their current organizational expression. In a number of speeches he said, "Kom does not mean the PKI, no. A does not mean only the NU, no. Nas does not mean only the PNI or Partindo, not at all, but as ideas, as principles of the Indonesian revolution."[4] The general tenor of Sukarno's speeches in late October and Novem-

2. President Sukarno's speech, 16 October 1965.
3. Ibid., 23 October 1965.
4. Ibid., 20 November 1965.

ber suggested that he was considering the possibility of a "political settlement," including action against PKI leaders who had been "directly involved" in the coup attempt, while separating these individuals from their party. He realized that it might not be possible to save the PKI, so he stressed that the Kom element of Nasakom was not identical with the PKI, and in late November he canvassed the possibility of forming a new party to represent the social force that stood behind the Kom element in Nasakom.[5]

Sukarno's continued rejection of the army's demand that the PKI be banned had antagonized not only Suharto and his colleagues but also other officers in the armed forces who had been generally sympathetic to the president. As Sukarno continued to postpone announcing the terms of his promised "political settlement," Major General Ibrahim Adjie, the commander of West Java's Siliwangi division and the president's most powerful friend among the senior army generals, announced on 17 November that he had "dissolved" the already "frozen" PKI in West Java. During the next few weeks, Adjie's example was followed by regional commanders throughout the nation. Although the ongoing massacre of PKI supporters was rapidly making the question of the party's legal existence irrelevant, the issue had become one of great symbolic significance. If Sukarno had given in to the demand that he formally dissolve the PKI, he would have openly acknowledged the army's capacity to force him to take action in direct conflict with his own publicly expressed wishes. Unable to prevent the "freezings" and "dissolutions," Sukarno refused to back down, and in a speech on 6 December he seemed to be issuing a challenge to the army leaders when he said, "Each group, every newspaper expresses its loyalty to the Great Leader of the Revolution. Loyal to the commands of Bung Karno. Faithful and loyal to every order from Bung Karno, but what I see, and I have already said this, sometimes I feel that I am being farted upon, brothers."[6]

During December the tone of Sukarno's speeches hardened as he prepared to follow up his challenge to the army leadership. If

5. Interview with Ruslan Abdulgani, 20 August 1972. Brackman says that it was envisaged that Semaun, the veteran leader of the PKI in the 1920s who had since left the party, would lead the new party (1969:165).

6. President Sukarno's speech, 6 December 1965.

he were to retain his aura of authority, Sukarno could not afford to back down on the question of the PKI's legality, but in choosing to make his defense of the PKI the central issue, he ran the risk of alienating his own potential supporters in the armed forces. In the latter part of December, Sukarno began to introduce a new theme into his speeches which even further alienated his military friends. If earlier his emphasis had been on the need to preserve the concept of Nasakom and to stop the massacres, in his speech to a student audience on 21 December he launched into the offensive. After describing the experiences of Communists at Boven Digul and other Dutch prisons during the colonial period, he reminded the students that the Communists as well as the nationalists and religious people had suffered in the struggle against the Dutch. He then claimed that "their sacrifices in Indonesia's struggle for freedom were greater than the sacrifices of other parties and other groups."[7] Many of Sukarno's stunned sympathizers in the army and the other forces felt that the president was deliberately slighting the armed forces, which they, naturally, considered had borne the greatest sacrifices during the revolution. By insulting the army as a whole, Sukarno unwittingly helped Suharto mobilize support within the officer corps for a more aggressive policy in approaching the president.

Sukarno's intransigence both forced and permitted Suharto to apply increased pressure on the president. If Suharto had failed to respond to the president's implicit challenge, he would have risked losing the momentum that had so greatly enhanced the army's power during the previous months. Sukarno's alienation of the officer corps provided the opportunity that Suharto needed. Nevertheless, Suharto continued to move cautiously, and during the first weeks of 1966 it was less the president's attitude to the PKI than sharp price increases that were made the overt issue. The issue of the price increases helped to broaden the focus of attention beyond the PKI and Gestapu to the performance of the government as a whole. When students, encouraged by the army leadership, took to the streets to protest against price increases, their demands were not limited to the removal of "pro-PKI" ministers—they called as well for the dismissal of "stupid" ministers, whom they accused of mismanaging the economy. The dem-

7. Ibid., 21 December 1965.

onstrations were not simply directed toward forcing the government to make certain changes, but tended to express a lack of confidence in the government as a whole. Although the president was not attacked directly, the competence of the government he headed was brought openly into question.

Inflation had been running out of control in the latter part of 1965, putting great pressure on the government to raise the prices of commodities and services it controlled directly. On 23 November, the coordinating minister for development, Chaerul Saleh, had announced an increase in the price of petrol from Rps 4 per litre to Rps 250; by January further increases in government-administered prices became unavoidable. On 3 January, Brigadier General Ibnu Sutowo, the minister of state for oil and natural gas, announced a fourfold increase in the price of petrol together with a rise in the price of kerosene used for cooking. At the same time postal and telecommunications charges were increased tenfold, train fares fourfold, and bus fares in Jakarta from Rps 200 to Rps 1000. Faced with inflation spiraling at an extraordinary rate, the government could hardly have avoided drastic increases in the charges for public utilities and the prices of subsidized commodities. The public, who had to pay the new prices, would inevitably lack understanding of the government's predicament. Thus the price rises created an atmosphere of discontent which could be exploited by groups wanting to put pressure on the government, and these price increases served as the catalyst for the political developments that followed.

The student demonstrations against the price increases were channeled through the Indonesian Student Action Front (KAMI), which had been established in late October by anti-Communist student organizations meeting at the home of the minister for higher education, Brigadier General Sjarif Thajeb. Although the PNI-affiliated Indonesian National Student Movement (GMNI) had been represented at the original meeting, it had refused to join the new body, which included the large Muslim organization, HMI, which had been the target of a combined Communist and nationalist campaign up to 1 October.[8] Its base consisting largely of Muslim organizations, the KAMI was actively supported by

8. The pro-PKI student movement, the Indonesian Student Movement Center (CGMI), together with the PNI's GMNI, had been campaigning for a ban on the HMI, which they claimed was a front for the banned Masyumi.

Catholic and PSI-oriented students as well as the Mahasiswa Panca Sila, affiliated with the small army-linked League of Upholders of Indonesian Freedom (IPKI).[9] Although there is no reason to doubt the spontaneity of the initial reaction of the students to the price increases, since the rise in petrol prices had led to a fivefold increase in bus fares in Jakarta directly affecting most students, it was clear that the KAMI leaders had contact with leading army officers, whom they informed of their plans to hold demonstrations and who sympathized with them. Such officers as the Kostrad chief of staff, Brigadier General Kemal Idris, the RPKAD commander, Colonel Sarwo Edhie, the chief of staff of the Jakarta regional command, Colonel A. J. Witono, and Lieutenant Colonel Urip Widodo, also of the Jakarta command, were particularly well-disposed toward the KAMI leaders and kept them informed of the views of Suharto and Nasution. Thus, when the students decided to hold massive demonstrations, they knew they had the backing of the army leadership.

On 10 January several thousand students gathered at the Medical Faculty of the University of Indonesia, where they adopted the "Tritura" (Tri Tuntutan Rakyat or Three Demands of the People) slogan. The three demands were to bring down prices, dissolve the PKI, and purge the cabinet. After an address by Sarwo Edhie, the students marched to the nearby Department of Higher Education and Science to convey their demands, and from there proceeded to the State Secretariat beside the president's palace, where Chaerul Saleh eventually addressed them. Not satisfied with Chaerul's attitude, they decided to continue their campaign, and they held more demonstrations the following days.

Meanwhile, a KAMI-sponsored seminar on the economy was held at the University of Indonesia. Most of the speakers at the seminar were economists and social scientists, but the most important was General Nasution, whose presence could hardly have failed to give the impression of tacit approval for the current demonstrations. Further, Major General Suharto sent a written message. Referring to the demonstrations, he said, "I regard these actions as manifestations of social control. I know that the demonstrations have proceeded in an orderly and highly disciplined

9. See Wibisono 1970:chap. 1. The IPKI was a small party set up by a group of army officers before the 1955 elections.

way. . . . Students in fact stand in the midst of the people, are aware of the people's difficulties and understand the wishes of the people, from whence we came, by whom we were brought up and for whom we struggle."[10]

President Sukarno was quick to appreciate the potential threat posed by the army-backed student demonstrations and complained immediately to the pliable army commander in Jakarta, Major General Amir Machmud, who criticized the "wild demonstrations" that had taken place and instructed that future demonstrations "be channeled through the proper authorities in an orderly and proper way."[11] On 15 January, however, when a cabinet meeting was held at Bogor, thousands of students from Jakarta, Bandung, and Bogor gathered in the rain outside the Bogor Palace, and when some students attempted to climb into the palace grounds, warning shots were fired by members of the Cakrabirawa palace guard. At the cabinet meeting the president delivered an extremely angry and provocative speech in which he strongly criticized the students' way of expressing their demands. At the end of his speech, he challenged his opponents to reveal themselves. He claimed that he had found pamphlets accusing him of defending the PKI. There were signs that people secretly wanted to push him out: "I will not move a millimeter . . . I am Sukarno, the Great Leader of the Revolution. As Luther, Martin Luther, said at the church in Wurtenberg—here I am, I can do nothing else. . . . Come on, whoever wants Sukarno, agrees with Sukarno as Great Leader of the Revolution, gather your forces, form your *barisan* [ranks], defend Sukarno. . . . Wait for my command. . . . Stand behind Sukarno."[12]

Taking up the president's call to "form your *barisans,*" the first deputy prime minister, Subandrio, appealed in a radio speech the following evening for the formation of a Barisan Sukarno (Sukarno's ranks) to defend the president, and on the nineteenth a rally was held at the National Front headquarters, where Sudibjo, the Front's general secretary, accompanied by Brigadier General Djuhartono, the leader of the Sekber Golkar, announced the Na-

10. The proceedings of the seminar were published in KAMI 1966. For Suharto's message, see p. 23.
11. *Angkatan Bersenjata,* 13 January 1966.
12. President Sukarno's speech, 15 January 1966.

tional Front's membership in the Barisan Sukarno. A few days later, Chaerul Saleh, who was acting as chairman of the National Front, announced the formation of an "Action Command to Defend Bung Karno" and said that the secretariat of the National Front would act as the secretariat of the new Action Command. Such anti-Communist Sukarnoists as Chaerul Saleh, Sudibjo, Achmadi, and Djuhartono appeared to be attempting to wrest control of the Barisan Sukarno from Subandrio by placing the new organization within the structure of the National Front. Meanwhile, statements were issued by dozens of organizations declaring that they stood behind Bung Karno as part of the Barisan Sukarno, and on the twentieth, ninety-two cabinet ministers assembled at the palace to present a statement to the president pledging their complete loyalty to him and declaring their readiness to form the front ranks of the Barisan Sukarno.

The president's call for a clear expression of support for his leadership caught the army leaders off balance. They had hoped to use the student demonstrations as a means of stepping up the pressure on the president, but his challenge suddenly put them on the defensive. The day after Sukarno's speech, the sixteenth, Suharto issued a statement on behalf of the army in which he declared that the entire army "stands behind the President/Great Leader of the Revolution and awaits his further commands."[13] But the minister for defense and security, Nasution, was dissatisfied with Suharto's willingness to declare unreserved support for the president, so he called Suharto and the commanders of the other three services to a meeting, where they signed a further, more guarded, statement on behalf of the armed forces, declaring their loyalty to the president "in facing all challenges to the Revolution in accordance with the *Saptamarga* and the Soldiers' Oath."[14] As numerous organizations made statements in support of the Barisan Sukarno during the next few days, the army leaders looked for a way to neutralize the president's move without a direct confrontation.

The initiative came from Major General Adjie, the West Java

13. *Berita Yudha,* 17 January 1966.
14. Ibid. For Nasution's implicit dissatisfaction with Suharto's statement, see Nasution 1971:403. The Saptmarga were general principles adopted by the army in the 1950s.

commander. Adjie had welcomed the expansion of the army's political role since October 1965, but he apparently resented Suharto's rise to power and unsympathetic treatment of the president. He had little sympathy for the KAMI students in Bandung, whom he thought were manipulated by members of the Masyumi and PSI with the purpose of undermining the president.[15] Nevertheless, although he sympathized with the president's attitude toward the demonstrating students, he did not approve of setting up the Barisan Sukarno to oppose them. He apparently regarded such an organization as a threat to the army's position, which would be used by Subandrio and others to advance their own interests at the expense of the army. On the eighteenth he issued a statement: "That all state bodies, citizens, political parties, and mass organizations which are permitted to carry out activities contributing to the defense and implementation of the Indonesian Revolution are in fact followers and supporters of Panca Sila and the Teachings of the Great Leader of the Indonesian Revolution, Bung Karno, and therefore automatically make up *barisans* standing behind Bung Karno."[16] Thus, there was no need for the Barisan Sukarno as a formal organization in West Java.

Adjie banned "the formation and every attempt to form what is called the 'Barisan Sukarno' in any form of organization whatsoever in the region covered by the West Java Pepelrada," thereby killing the proposal to set up a Barisan Sukarno, at least there. But the plan to set up the Barisan Sukarno had been supported by the president, who called Adjie to Jakarta on the twentieth. Recognizing in Adjie a vital ally who should not be alienated, Sukarno was able to reach a compromise with the Siliwangi commander on this question. They agreed that a "physical" Barisan Sukarno would be formed in West Java, but it would be directly under the leadership of the army commander.[17] This was a satisfactory compromise for Adjie because he had foiled the move to set up a mass organization independent of the army's control, while Sukarno was assured that Adjie would permit no serious moves against him in West Java.

Adjie's move to neutralize the proposed Barisan Sukarno orga-

15. See Adjie's remarks reported in *Suluh Indonesia*, 23 February 1966.
16. *Berita Yudha*, 20 January 1966.
17. Wibisono 1970:37.

nization in West Java was warmly welcomed by the army leaders in Jakarta. In its editorial on the twentieth, *Angkatan Bersenjata* said that Bung Karno belonged to all the people, not just a certain group, and warned of the danger that certain groups might try to monopolize the name of Sukarno. Brigadier General Sunarso, of the Koti's political section, said that "the Barisan Sukarno can be nothing but the Barison of Unity of all progressive revolutionary forces among the Indonesian people. . . . The Barisan Sukarno need not take the form of conventional troops and it is certainly not just 'troops' which march along in ranks carrying arms."[18] In welcoming Adjie's move, Suharto declared that "ever since the revolution, the armed forces and the political and mass organizations in West Java have been the Barisan Sukarno,"[19] and on the nineteenth, in the name of the president, Suharto requested that all loyal organizations wishing to declare their support for Bung Karno should do so by sending their declarations to the Koti. By the end of the month some two hundred organizations had registered with the Koti as part of the Barisan Sukarno. On 21 January a huge rally was held in Jakarta, where Major General Amir Machmud declared that the Barisan Sukarno covered "all the people."[20]

By the time Lebaran (the end of the Muslim fasting month) was celebrated on 23 January, the army had largely blocked the initiative taken by Sukarno when he issued his challenge at the cabinet meeting on the fifteenth. Taken off guard, Suharto had been forced to respond to Sukarno's challenge by abjectly declaring his loyalty on the sixteenth. The initiative passed to Subandrio and the National Front, which began to organize the Barisan Sukarno. Only after Adjie had first banned and then "taken over" the Barisan Sukarno in West Java were the army leaders able to counter the proposal. Instead of repressing the Barisan Sukarno, they embraced it in such a way as to eliminate its potential for independent action. They declared themselves to be the leaders of the Barisan Sukarno and the most loyal supporters of the president. The National Front's plan to embody the Barisan Sukarno in an organizational or "physical" sense was blocked by the army's con-

18. KAMI 1966:27.
19. *Angkatan Bersenjata*, 26 January 1966.
20. *Pelopor*, 22 January 1966.

cept of the Barisan Sukarno as consisting of all loyal citizens, as a "mental" concept rather than a "physical" organization.

Despite the army's success in blocking the move to set up a Barisan Sukarno in the sense originally envisaged by Chaerul Saleh, Subandrio, and the National Front leaders, Sukarno nevertheless had reason to feel encouraged. The army-backed student demonstrations had stopped, and the army leaders had felt compelled to declare their allegiance to him. Sukarno felt confident that the army leaders were in no position to move against him because they could not be sure that such a move would have united support within the army itself, let alone from the other services. Feeling assured of support within the army in East and Central Java, Sukarno was particularly concerned to retain his influence over the West Java commander, Adjie. He apparently calculated that Suharto, aware of the president's influence among East and Central Javanese officers, would be unable to move in Jakarta without a guarantee of support from the Siliwangi commander. In the weeks that followed, Sukarno kept in regular contact with Adjie, and on 28 January the president's close aide, Brigadier General Sabur, visited Adjie in Bandung "in the context of implementing more perfect preparations to face the current situation."[21]

At the same time, Sukarno seemed to be making a special effort to reinforce his influence with the older-generation leaders of the established political parties. In the middle of the month he received the PNI leaders, Ali Sastroamidjojo and Sartono, who pledged their party's support to him, and when the NU held its fortieth anniversary celebrations on 30 January, Sukarno appealed for support from the party. In a speech that avoided any references to the massacres, which had been a dominant theme of many of his earlier speeches, Sukarno said, "I love the NU, you should love me. I embrace the NU, you should embrace me."[22] In reply, the NU chairman, Idham Chalid, said that "the NU is not able to say 'live and die for Bung Karno.' But the NU will live and die together with Bung Karno for God. . . . All organs of the NU are ready all day and all night to be used by the Great Leader of the Revolution as tools for the Revolu-

21. *Antara Ichtisar Tahunan*, 28 January 1966.
22. *Duta Masyarakat*, 31 January 1966.

tion."[23] Occupying high positions under Sukarno, and publicly identified with him, the older generation of PNI and NU leaders saw little future in cooperating with the army against the president, especially when there was, as yet, no certainty that the army leaders would come out on top in the end.

During the first weeks of February, Suharto's strategy continued to be based on the hope that the president could be persuaded to recognize the new "reality" in which the army's role was much greater than before. In particular, Suharto aimed to convince Sukarno that the new balance of power required that the president publicly acknowledge the army's predominance by assenting to the formal dissolution of the PKI, followed by a cabinet reshuffle reflecting the new power realities. The army leadership's encouragement to student demonstrations had been designed to achieve these goals, and during the early part of February, Suharto's demands implied the threat of a further round of demonstrations. But the president apparently had been emboldened by Suharto's caution and his unwillingness to take direct measures to achieve his ends. Despite the massive student demonstrations, Suharto had backed down rather than Sukarno, when the army commander pledged his loyalty on 16 January. Although the army leaders had largely neutralized the Barisan Sukarno concept, Sukarno appeared confident that they would not dare take more positive steps against him.

Early in February, the president commenced a new series of moves designed to reassert his authority. Claiming that the predominance of army officers in the Koti was giving the impression that Indonesia was moving toward militarism, he proposed that its function be limited to directing the campaign against Malaysia. Thus Suharto's position as chief of staff of the Koti would presumably no longer give him the right to issue directions on domestic matters to the Pepelrada. Suharto apparently did not reject Sukarno's proposal out of hand, and on February 11 he publicly welcomed the plan on the grounds that it would dispel "slanders" about military dictatorship.

23. Ibid. Just as Sukarno had avoided references to the massacres, Idham Chalid pointedly failed to mention the NU's demand that the PKI be banned. His speech was greatly resented by younger NU supporters in Ansor, and the Ansor general secretary, Chalid Mawardi, publicly stated that the NU still wanted the PKI banned (*Suluh Indonesia,* 7 February 1966).

Possibly Suharto's apparent unwillingness to obstruct the proposed reorganization of the Koti emboldened Sukarno to assert himself further. On 13 February, the day before the opening of the first Mahmillub trial in which the PKI leader, Njono, faced the court, Sukarno made a stirring, aggressive speech to a National Front rally, in which he seemed to indicate that he was ready to challenge the army leaders to a showdown. Returning to his old theme of Nasakom and the past services of the PKI, he said, "I do not want to close my eyes to the fact that the Kom group, thank God, made a contribution and sacrifices for freedom that were very great indeed. I ask, I ask openly, where is another party, not even my own party, I was once a PNI leader, I was imprisoned, exiled, but even the PNI's contribution to Indonesia's freedom was not equal to what was proved by the PKI. . . . We must be fair, brothers, fair, fair, fair, once again, fair." Again he warned that there were people who wanted to push him aside: "If we really want to continue our revolution, if we really want to keep our revolution on the progressive revolutionary road, come on, form the Barisan Sukarno. Form the Barisan Sukarno to defend our revolution."[24]

The renewed call to set up the Barisan Sukarno was a direct challenge to the army leaders. Other regional commanders had followed Adjie's lead in emasculating the original Barisan Sukarno proposal. The interregional commander for Sumatra, Lieutenant General Achmad Junus Mokoginta, had denounced efforts to set up a "physical Barisan Sukarno" as "subversive." The regional commander for South Sumatra, Brigadier General Makmum Murod, banned the formation of any new organization on the grounds that "all progressive-revolutionary people are automatically included in the Barisan Sukarno," and in Central Kalimantan, Brigadier General Sobiran Mochtar banned the formation of a "structural or conventional Barisan Sukarno." There had been no reports of the successful formation of the Barisan Sukarno anywhere, but despite the failure of their original appeal, the president, Subandrio, and Chaerul Saleh apparently felt that circumstances were now more propitious.

Exploiting his initiative, Sukarno further decided to move toward the release of the one to two hundred thousand supporters

24. President Sukarno's speech, 13 February 1966.

of the PKI who had remained under detention and who could be
expected to support the president in any conflict with the army. A
committee of three ministers was set up to investigate the problem, and Sukarno ordered "that those who were not in fact involved in G.30.S. should be released immediately."[25] Sukarno also
ordered that the administration of civilian prisoners be transferred from Suharto as commander of the Kopkamtib to Brigadier General Augustinius Sutardhio, the attorney general.[26] Sutardhio was a Sukarnoist army officer who clearly sided with the
president against Suharto.

The president's offensive to reassert his authority culminated in
the cabinet reshuffle announced on 21 February. Ten members of
the old cabinet were dismissed, including the coordinating minister for defense and security, General Nasution, the commander of
the navy, Vice Admiral Martadinata, and such anti-Communist
civilians as Ipik Gandamana, Artati Marzuki Sudirgo, and the
chairman of the DPR-GR, Arudji Kartawinata. Others, such as the
minister for higher education, Brigadier General Sjarif Thajeb,
were transferred to less prominent posts. On the other hand,
ministers who had been the target of KAMI demonstrations were
retained, including Subandrio, Omar Dhani, Oei Tjoe Tat, and
Setiadi Reksoprodjo, who had been considered close to the PKI.
The new ministers included Sumardjo, as minister for basic education and culture, who had been associated with a pro-PKI
teachers' union and had reportedly been detained for a period
after the coup attempt, and Lieutenant Colonel Imam Sjafe'i,
known as the "Boss of Senen" because of his underworld contacts
in the seamy Senen district of Jakarta. Sjafe'i was no leftist, but it
was believed that his functions as minister for special security
affairs would be to organize underworld elements to terrorize
antigovernment demonstrators.

In reshuffling the cabinet, Sukarno had paid particular attention to the military departments. As well as dismissing Nasution
from his post as coordinating minister for defense and security,
Sukarno also abolished his position as chief of staff of the armed
forces and disbanded the staff that he had built since 1962. As the
new coordinating minister for defense and security, Sukarno ap-

25. *Pelopor* and *Duta Masyarakat*, 19 February 1966.
26. *Kompas*, 8 March 1966.

pointed Major General Sarbini Martodihardjo, the former minister for veterans' affairs and demobilization. Sarbini was widely respected within the army as a former commander of both the Brawijaya and Diponegoro divisions, but he also had great affection for the president. Another general firmly committed to the president, Major General Mursjid, the first deputy to the army commander, was appointed to the new position of deputy coordinating minister for defense and security. In the navy, Vice Admiral Martadinata, who had worked closely with Nasution in the past, was replaced by his first deputy, Rear Admiral Muljadi, who was regarded as a Sukarnoist, and the commander of the Marine Corps (Kko), Major General Hartono, who was completely devoted to the president, entered the cabinet as deputy navy minister, a position that had no equivalent in the other services.[27] The air force commander, Sri Muljono Herlambang, and the police commander, Sutjipto Judodihardjo, were both regarded as men whose ultimate loyalty rested with the president. Of the military ministers, only the army commander, Suharto, seemed to be an obstacle to the president. Further, a day later, on the twenty-second, it was announced the the Koti had been transformed into the Crush Malaysia Command (Kogam), with the implication that its functions would be restricted to the conduct of the confrontation campaign. Although Sukarno had succeeded in imposing a formal limitation on its functions, its personnel remained firmly under the control of Suharto, who was appointed as chief of staff of the new body. Most of the Koti staff retained equivalent positions in the Kogam.

The president had discussed his plans with Suharto before the announcement of the new cabinet. According to Nasution's account, the president told Suharto that he could no longer work with Nasution and offered to appoint Suharto as coordinating minister for defense and security in Nasution's place. Suharto refused, and eventually it was agreed to appoint Sarbini, with Mursjid as his deputy.[28] According to Sarbini, Suharto had in-

27. Reportedly, the president had wanted to appoint Hartono as commander of the navy but was persuaded that naval officers in general would not accept a Kko officer (Karni 1974:159–160).

28. Nasution's written answers to Howard Jones (made available by General Nasution).

formed him personally of his proposed appointment. At first, Sarbini had rejected it and asked why Nasution had to be replaced. Suharto told him that Nasution was to be appointed to a new position. Unsatisfied with this reply, Sarbini then went to Nasution, who said it was up to Sarbini whether to accept or not. According to Sarbini, this "increased my confusion." Then he met the sultan of Yogyakarta, who advised him to accept the position "if we don't want to see worse bloodshed." The sultan said that if Sarbini refused, a "Gestapu element" might be appointed. Thus convinced, Sarbini accepted the position.[29] Sarbini was never installed as the new minister because of Nasution's unwillingness to cooperate in the customary ceremony. According to Nasution, he told Suharto "that the President has the right to choose and dismiss his ministers; but in the name of justice I can not just accept this." He refused to attend both the formal announcement of the new cabinet in the palace on the twenty-first and the installation of the new navy minister on the twenty-fifth, and later, when his nominated successor, Sarbini, and Mursjid called on him to discuss the formal transfer of the Department of Defense and Security, he told them that "it would be a sin if I simply accept this unjust decision of the President."[30]

Why had Sukarno taken the enormous risk of blatantly defying the army leadership? The explanation lies partly in the president's personality and his conception of his role as president. Since the establishment of Guided Democracy, he had been the central figure in the state. His authority had continued to grow, so that his position had come to resemble that of a sultan. All political groups declared their allegiance to him, and all policies had to be justified in terms of his teachings. Suddenly, on 1 October, and especially after the ensuing massacres, Sukarno could no longer control events. Faced with the choice between resigning himself to the new circumstances or fighting back against great odds to restore his previous supremacy, his personality compelled him to choose the latter course. However, his willingness to fight back was not entirely based on blind recklessness. He calculated that he was still recognized almost universally as the legitimate head of state and that the army could not take the risk of deposing him.

29. Sarbini in newspaper interview, *Angkatan Bersenjata*, 29 August 1966.
30. Nasution's written answers to Howard Jones.

He was convinced that not only the people, especially in Java, would rise to defend him if his position were threatened, but much of the army, as well as the other three services, would refuse to support a coup against him. In this context, the consultations that he had with the Siliwangi commander, Adjie, at his Bogor palace on 19 and 23 February were probably not without significance.[31] It is also probable that Sukarno calculated that he could separate Nasution from Suharto. Once Nasution was out of the way, he may have expected that he would be able to outmaneuver the politically inexperienced Suharto. Moreover, by elevating Suharto at Nasution's expense, he hoped to create further divisions between the senior officers in the army, who did not all regard Suharto as the most talented among them.

Why did the army fail to take immediate action to prevent the dismissal of Nasution, accompanied as it was by the dismissal of other proarmy ministers, the retention of the antiarmy ministers, and the president's attempt to expand his influence over the armed forces as a whole? It has been claimed that Nasution himself was reluctant to force an immediate showdown, even though he refused to leave his office. Perhaps he still felt restrained by the memory of the abortive attempt by the army to impose its will on the president on 17 October 1952, which led to Nasution's dismissal as chief of staff of the army. Further, Nasution's dismissal may not have been altogether unwelcome to Suharto, whose grip on the army leadership tightened as a consequence. The basic reason for the army's reluctance to move, however, was that it was still unprepared for a final showdown. Since the beginning of the year, feeling had been growing that the army would have to do something to check the president. Until the cabinet reshuffle, the army leaders had still hoped that the president could be brought round to imposing a formal ban on the PKI and dismissing such ministers as Subandrio and others considered to be pro-PKI or antiarmy. While in fact there were many signs that the president would not do this, the army's tactics continued to be directed toward this goal. It was only when the new cabinet was announced that the army leaders became fully convinced that more drastic measures would be required. Suharto and his circle

31. *Pelopor,* 21 February 1966, *Duta Masyarakat,* 24 February 1966.

in Jakarta now realized that a showdown could not be avoided, but they also knew that Jakarta was not Indonesia, and particularly it was not Java. They wanted to avoid open action in the capital that might give the impression outside Jakarta that they were usurping the powers of the president or were even in conflict with him. They feared a wave of popular support for Sukarno from East and Central Java if he appeared to be under threat in Jakarta, and they were far certain that they could rely on the united support of the armed forces in such circumstances. Not only might the navy, air force, and police support the president in the event of a conflict with the army, but the army leaders doubted the reliability of many of the army's own forces, particularly those in Java, where regional commanders like Adjie and the Central Java commander, Surjo-sumpeno, were subject to the president's influence. Thus, when the membership of the reshuffled cabinet was announced, the army leaders were caught unprepared to take the decisive action necessary to back up an immediate rejection of the cabinet.

7 | The Disguised Coup of 11 March

President Sukarno's announcement of the changes in cabinet membership was the culmination of a series of moves during the previous two months to reassert his authority. His dismissal of Nasution and several proarmy ministers, while reappointing Subandrio and other implacable opponents of the army leadership, had shown that the president had no intention of accepting the army leadership's claim to a dominant role in the government. His appointments of defense and security ministers indicated that he aimed to isolate the army leadership in the expectation that Suharto would be forced to accept a subordinate position. Faced with Sukarno's intransigence, the army leaders had either to back down or to modify their strategy by taking more drastic and explicit measures against the president. They chose the latter course.

Sukarno's demeanor during the previous months had alienated many of his supporters within the armed forces and especially in the army. The president's military allies had initially been tolerant and understanding of what they regarded as his natural reluctance to lose face by openly condemning the PKI, but many of them had been dismayed by the president's effusive praise for the party's past services to the revolution, which seemed calculated as a deliberate slight to the armed forces. Further, while the pro-Sukarno officers had little sympathy for the demonstrating students, whom they tended to see as agents of the Masyumi and PSI,[1]

1. The Masyumi and PSI had been banned in 1960 after a number of party leaders were involved in the PRRI revolt of 1958, during which several thousand soldiers lost their lives. Many army officers, especially among the Javanese, regarded the revolt as unforgivable treachery. Further, they regarded the Masyumi followers as Muslim fanatics and disliked the Westernized intellectuals associated with the PSI for their alleged "superiority complex."

they did not relish the prospect of the formation of a Barisan Sukarno led by such opponents of the army as Subandrio and Chaerul Saleh and based on leftist youth organizations and the PNI. Finally, they had been shocked by the cabinet announcement, which not only reasserted the president's preeminence but blatantly ignored what most officers regarded as not unreasonable demands from the army leadership. In essence, the pro-Sukarno elements in the army were not averse to Suharto's policy of using the new circumstances to increase the army's role in the government at the expense of the Subandrios and Chaerul Salehs. But they were not willing to countenance taking direct action against the president to force him to accept army policies. They continued to hope that Sukarno could be persuaded to accept the view that his most reliable supporters were to be found within the armed forces.

Suharto was aware of the growing sense of alienation among the president's sympathizers in the army and was almost obsessed with the need to avoid premature action that might reverse the trend by making the pro-Sukarno officers feel compelled to declare themselves unequivocally for the president against the army leadership. At the same time, Suharto realized that acceptance of the new cabinet would be interpreted as an indication of weakness that might pave the way for Sukarno to reestablish his ascendency over the armed forces. Suharto needed a way to reject the cabinet without taking action that would force members of the armed forces to choose between Sukarno and Suharto. The means he chose was to give covert approval to a group of strongly anti-Sukarnoist officers who encouraged students to create an atmosphere of anarchy in the capital. As the situation began to run out of hand, the president felt that he had to turn to the apparently moderate Suharto to restore order rather than permit the army extremists to gain the upper hand.

During the three weeks after the announcement of the reshuffled cabinet, the small but influential group of anti-Sukarnoist officers in Jakarta played a crucial role. The most important of them was Brigadier General Kemal Idris, the chief of staff of the Kostrad. A former Siliwangi officer who had openly sympathized with the PSI, Kemal's participation in the Seventeenth of October Affair in 1952 and the Zulkifli Lubis Affair in 1956 had brought him into sharp conflict with President Sukarno, who refused to approve his appointment to an active military post from 1956 until 1963, when he joined the Indonesian contingent sent as part of UN forces to the Congo. Although the Kostrad was formally under the command of the moderate Major General Umar Wirahadikusumah, in practice Umar, who was appointed to succeed Suharto as commander of the Kolaga in February, was concerned with Kostrad forces engaged in the confrontation campaign, while Kemal was in direct command of Kostrad troops in Jakarta. The majority of forces assigned to the Kostrad in Jakarta were from the RPKAD under the command of Colonel Sarwo Edhie, who fully shared Kemal's view that more vigorous pressure should be put on the president. In addition, the Kostrad's forces included several Siliwangi battalions that had been sent to Jakarta earlier to help maintain security in the capital.[2] Although the Siliwangi commander, Major General Ibrahim Adjie, supported the president, Kemal Idris' outlook was shared by the former Siliwangi chief of staff who had recently been transferred to the army headquarters, Major General Hartono Rekso Dharsono, and by many junior Siliwangi officers who willingly cooperated with Kemal in Jakarta. Further, an informal agreement had been reached with the Jakarta commander, Amir Machmud, whereby operational command of all army troops in Jakarta was transferred to Kemal, while Amir Machmud remained responsible for administration and territorial matters. Although Kemal Idris sometimes appeared to be acting independently of Suharto, the army commander was kept well informed by such Kostrad intelligence officers as Brigadier General Yoga Sugama and Lieutenant Colonel Ali Murtopo, who had been close confidants of Suharto's since they had served under him in Central Java in the 1950s.

As the army leaders began to reconsider their strategy following the announcement of the cabinet changes, the army radicals let student leaders know that a new wave of demonstrations would be welcome, despite the ban imposed by Amir Machmud.[3] On 23 February, while youths from PNI-affiliated organizations demonstrated at the American embassy, KAMI students went to the State Secretariat behind the president's palace, broke into the

2. Interviews with Lieutenant General Kemal Idris, 9 December 1970, and Brigadier General Sarwo Edhie, 5 September 1970.

3. Interview with the KAMI leader, Cosmas Batubara, 26 July 1973.

building, smashed windows, and threw furniture into the street. In the confusion, some members of the Cakrabirawa palace guard fired at the students. Several were wounded but none killed, although a report appeared in the press that two students had died, and the usually reliable Radio Australia broadcast that four students had been killed by the palace guard.

The following day, the twenty-fourth, the atmosphere was electric as the president prepared to install his reshuffled cabinet at the palace. A huge student demonstration surrounded the palace from early in the morning. In the procession from the University of Indonesia the blood-stained jackets of two students, who had been wounded but not killed the previous day, were held aloft, and along the road many houses flew flags at half-mast in honor of the nonexistent martyrs. As the students approached the palace, the road was blocked by army units which tried to keep the students calm and out of reach of the palace and the Cakrabirawa guard. These circumstances made it very difficult for the ministers and other guests to reach the palace for the installation, and their problems were compounded when students deflated the tires of all cars in the vicinity of the palace. In response, the president ordered that helicopters be used to bring the ministers to the installation, and one minister, Brigadier General Sukendro, arrived on a bicycle. At the cabinet installation, the president was in an angry mood. He declared that the cabinet reshuffle had nothing to do with the demands of the KAMI. He angrily rejected the KAMI slogans accusing him of appointing a "Gestapu cabinet" or a "Communist cabinet," and then asked the new ministers one by one whether they were Communists; all answered "no." While the guests sipped tea after the installation ceremony, the sound of shooting outside the palace was heard.

The students had eventually pierced, or been permitted to pierce, the army buffer between the demonstrators and the Cakrabirawa.[4] Suddenly Cakrabirawa soldiers opened fire, killing two students, one a youth studying medicine at the University of Indonesia and the other a girl still at high school. The boy, Arief

4. See Wibisono 1970:68–69. At first soldiers blocked the students but eventually permitted them to pass. The KAMI leaders encouraged girl students to push forward on the correct assumption that the soldiers would be less inclined to take firm measures to push them back.

Rahman Hakim, was buried in a massive funeral the next day. His body was borne by a military vehicle, and flowers were sent by Nasution, Suharto, the Kostrad, the Jakarta Command, the RPKAD, the Siliwangi commander, the widows of Generals Yani and Pandjaitan, and many others. Soldiers from the Jakarta Command fired a salute at the burial. The streets were packed for the funeral procession, shops along the route were closed and flags were flown at half-mast from many government buildings. By expressing sympathy for the students, a wide range of army leaders indicated their dissatisfaction with the cabinet changes.

On the day of Arief Rahman Hakim's funeral, the newly re-organized Kogam met for the first time in a session that lasted from 11 A.M. until late at night. Although Sukarno's purpose in having the Koti replaced by the Kogam was to concentrate its attention on the question of confrontation rather than domestic matters, the first session of the new body was devoted to the domestic situation. The president insisted on the dissolution of the KAMI, and in the end Suharto agreed to go along with the president's demand. The KAMI was formally dissolved by the Kogam and once again all demonstrations were banned and students were forbidden to gather together in groups of more than five. Following this decision, Kemal Idris called the KAMI leaders and told them to move their headquarters from the University of Indonesia. They were unwilling at first, but eventually agreed to move to the headquarters of the 2nd Combat Command of the Kostrad where Ali Murtopo's Special Operations unit was based.[5] The Kostrad action was partly designed to protect the KAMI leaders and probably also to prevent premature action by the KAMI which might have upset the plans the Kostrad officers themselves were in the process of preparing.

Despite the massive student demonstrations against the cabinet and the widespread public sympathy expressed in Jakarta at Arief Rahman Hakim's funeral, Sukarno felt that he had successfully weathered the storm. Although the army leaders had been angered by the dismissal of Nasution and by the other cabinet changes, they had done nothing, and at the Kogam session Suharto had finally accepted the order dissolving the KAMI. As long

5. Interviews with KAMI leaders, including Zamroni, 4 February 1971, David Napitupulu, 11 February 1971, and Cosmas Batubara, 26 July 1973.

as the army leaders could be kept divided among themselves, the president felt secure. Although the Siliwangi commander, Adjie, had sent flowers to Arief Rahman Hakim's funeral, Sukarno still regarded him as a vital ally, and on the twenty-seventh Adjie was flattered by the president's personal attendance at a Bandung rally to express loyalty to the president.[6] On the twenty-eighth, Sukarno attended another rally in Jakarta to celebrate the anniversary of the PNI's high school student organization, GSNI. PNI supporters from Central and East Java came to Jakarta especially for the rally, which was addressed by the party general chairman, Ali Sastroamidjojo, Chaerul Saleh, Subandrio, the controversial new minister for basic education, Sumardjo, and the president. Subandrio reminded the audience that "Victory will not be given as a gift but must be fought for," and he called on the president's supporters "to destroy the counterrevolutionaries who now use terror. . . . Those who use terror must be faced with counter-terror."[7] Then Sukarno spoke. He claimed that the Indonesian revolution had been in a state of drift since 1 October, but now the turning point had been reached. "I am convinced that the majority of the Indonesian people now want to return the Indonesian revolution to its progressive-revolutionary foundations." Sukarno restated his faith in Marxism, which for many Muslims and army officers was tantamount to a declaration of support for the PKI. He said, "In fact I have repeatedly and openly declared, yes, I am a Marxist. I even said that Marhaenism is Marxism applied in Indonesia."[8] Enthused by the president's speech, PNI supporters moved on toward the University of Indonesia, where fighting broke out after they attempted to raise to full-mast a flag flying at half-mast in honor of Arief Rahman Hakim.

Encouraged by Kemal Idris, Sarwo Edhie, and Ali Murtopo, anti-Sukarno demonstrations broke out again. Following the ban on the KAMI, the demonstrations were conducted by two new bodies, the Indonesian Student and Youth Action Front (KAPPI) and the Laskar Arief Rahman Hakim. The KAPPI had been formed on 9 February to organize high school students and other

6. This rally was held in conformity with an instruction issued by Suharto as chief of staff of the Koti on 16 February, before the cabinet reshuffle.

7. *Pelopor* and *Kompas*, 1 March 1966.

8. President Sukarno's speech, 28 February 1966.

youth behind the KAMI demonstrations. It was headed by Husni Thamrin, the general secretary of the Pelajar Islam Indonesia, a Masyumi-oriented Islamic organization for high school students. Reflecting its Muslim base of support, the KAPPI's demonstrations were aimed at the newly appointed minister for basic education, Sumardjo, who was said to be both pro-PKI and an atheist, and at the coordinating minister for education and culture, Prijono, a supporter of the banned Murba party, whose secular education policies had aroused Islamic ire. Many of the participants in KAPPI rallies were university students. On 2 March a KAPPI rally at the University of Indonesia was followed by a procession through the streets in which a truck carried an effigy of Subandrio hanging from a bamboo pole. It was clear to the government that the University of Indonesia was still being used as a base by KAMI students and their colleagues from the KAPPI, so the acting minister for higher education and culture, Leimena, issued an order closing the university from 3 March, but the army guard placed at the university ignored the minister's order and the wives of many army officers, including Yani's widow, supplied food to the students, many of whom were sleeping at the university. On 4 March, one day after the closure order, the Laskar Arief Rahman Hakim was set up at the university with a militant HMI activist, Fahmi Idris, as "commandant." The laskar was formally organized along military lines, with seven "battalions" named after the six generals and the junior officer killed on 1 October, but in practice the new body was really the KAMI under another name.[9]

As the demonstrations grew in size and became increasingly anarchic, Suharto and his closest colleagues discussed what to do next. Suharto apparently still preferred to move cautiously, so he sent a letter to Sukarno listing the ministers the army wanted removed from the cabinet, but the president rejected his suggestions out of hand. The radical officers then proposed that the army should arrest a number of senior ministers, including Subandrio, and some even suggested that snipers might be used to eliminate them. By about 6 March the decision was made that troops would seize Subandrio and a number of other ministers

9. Both Kemal Idris and Sarwo Edhie were consulted before the formation of the Laskar (interview with Fahmi Idris, 31 July 1973).

and that Suharto would claim to have no knowledge of the plot.[10] The officers still assumed that, deprived of his closest advisers, Sukarno would be forced to adopt the army's policies. Outside Jakarta it would seem that the arrests had been made with the president's blessings. The implementation of the plan was left in the hands of Kemal Idris and Sarwo Edhie, while Suharto continued to play the public role of the loyal army commander. On the seventh he instructed the Pepelrada throughout Indonesia to declare that all organizations that had taken part in earlier rallies to express loyalty to the president were components of the Barisan Sukarno in each region.[11]

A few days after the decision to kidnap Subandrio had been taken, the president got wind of the discussions. He probably did not know exactly what had been decided, but he heard that the radical officers planned to capture and perhaps kill Subandrio and some others. Possibly Sukarno feared that he himself might be arrested. On the eighth President Sukarno issued an order of the day that emphasized the duty of the members of the armed forces to be loyal to the president as supreme commander. Fearing an act of insubordination, he reminded the armed forces of "the Soldier's Oath and Sapta Marga to uphold the unity between the People/Armed Forces/Great Leader of the Revolution."[12] On the same day, Sukarno addressed a women's rally, where he claimed that "the fact is my authority is being 'jacked up.' They acknowledge Bung Karno as their commander but my commands are 'jacked up.' "[13] The rally was also addressed by Subandrio, Mrs. Subandrio, Chaerul Saleh, and the new general secretary of the National Front, J. K. Tumakaka. After the rally, demonstrators attacked the American Embassy and burned several embassy cars.

While PNI supporters attacked the US embassy, the Laskar Arief

10. On 6 March, Suharto met Sukarno and warned, "I would not be responsible if some officers permit their troops to violate discipline and join the people's actions." That evening Suharto called Kemal Idris, Sarwo Edhie, Colonel Wahono (the deputy chief of staff of the Kostrad) and two junior officers and told them "to protect" KAMI students from the Cakrabirawa troops (Panitia Penyusun Sejarah Kostrad 1972:74–75). The plan to kidnap Subandrio was most likely finalized at the same meeting.

11. *Pelopor,* 8 March 1966.

12. *Angkatan Bersenjata,* 9 March 1966.

13. President Sukarno's speech, 8 March 1966, *Antara Ichtisar Tahunan,* 8 March 1966, *Pelopor,* 9 March 1966.

Rahman Hakim attacked the Foreign Affairs Department and occupied it from 7 A.M. to 1 P.M. The police were powerless to act against the students, who were protected by army forces, and, while the students rampaged through the building, military intelligence officers removed vital files.[14] The attack on the Department of Foreign Affairs set off a new wave of violence. On the ninth students from the KAPPI and the laskar occupied a building of the Department of Education and attacked the Chinese news agency, Hsin Hua. On the tenth a Chinese consulate office and the Chinese Cultural Building were attacked and damaged.

As conditions in Jakarta became increasingly chaotic, the president called a series of meetings to try to win declarations of loyalty from all major political forces. He called a meeting of party leaders on the tenth, the cabinet on the eleventh, and regional military commanders from all four services on the twelfth. At the meeting with party leaders, the president demanded that they sign a statement condemning the recent student demonstrations. After five hours, agreement was reached on the wording of the statement, in which the party representatives unanimously said, "We cannot approve of the methods used by the schoolchildren, students, and youth which directly or indirectly could endanger the Indonesian revolution and undermine the authority of the Great Leader of the Revolution, Bung Karno."[15] After signing the statement, the party representatives were permitted to leave the palace. When dismayed students and army officers heard the news, they felt the cause had been "betrayed."[16]

On 11 March a full cabinet meeting was held in Jakarta. Again students were in the streets blocking traffic and deflating the tires of cars near the palace, but despite these obstructions virtually all the ministers attended the meeting. The most notable absentee was Suharto, who was said to have a mild throat ailment. According to one source, the night before the meeting Sukarno had been

14. Interview with a KAMI leader.
15. *Angkatan Bersenjata*, 11 March 1966.
16. According to the NU leader, Subchan, who attended the meeting (interview, 16 April 1970), the statement was deliberately phrased in such a way as to permit a "correction" to be issued the next day in which representatives of all the parties except the PNI and Partindo said that the reference to student demonstrations "means that approval could be given to 'methods which do not endanger the revolution'" (*Angkatan Bersenjata*, 12 March 1966).

informed by Brigadier General Suadi, the ambassador to Ethiopia currently on leave in Jakarta, that RPKAD troops planned to attack the palace. Sukarno then contacted the Kko commander, Hartono, who assured him of the Kko's readiness to confront the RPKAD.[17]

The atmosphere at the meeting was thus extremely tense. In giving his opening speech to the cabinet meeting, Sukarno was in an aggressive mood. He called on those ministers who could not follow his leadership to resign. Once again he reaffirmed his Marxism and added that if it were "God's will" he would continue to follow Marxism until the end of his life. During this speech, one of his aides interrupted him to give him a note. Upon reading the note, Sukarno announced that something extremely important had been brought to his attention and that he would have to leave the meeting "for a moment."[18] He asked Leimena to chair the meeting in his absence and hurried out of the room. When Subandrio and Chaerul Saleh learned of the contents of the note given to the president, they, too, rushed from the meeting. The note informed the president that unidentified troops had taken up positions in front of the palace. The soldiers had removed all insignia so their identities would be unknown. The note had been shown first to the Jakarta commander, Amir Machmud, who said, "It's nothing." [19] The aide then took the note to the president, who, recalling the rumors he had heard and noting Suharto's absence, became very alarmed. After leaving the meeting, he went immediately to his helicopter and was about to take off, when he was joined by the equally alarmed Chaerul Saleh and Subandrio. Together they flew off to the Presidential Palace at Bogor.[20]

Immediately after Sukarno's flight, Amir Machmud reported the events to Suharto. Suharto ordered Amir, Major General Mohamad Jusuf (minister for basic industry), and Major General Basuki Rachmat (minister for veterans' affairs and demobiliza-

17. Karni 1974:4–8.
18. President Sukarno's speech, 11 March 1966.
19. It is not clear whether Amir Machmud was pretending not to know what was happening or whether he really did not know. According to one source, Amir Machmud had not been informed beforehand and, as the officer responsible for security in Jakarta, was as startled as the president.
20. It was rumored that Sukarno stopped at the Kko base at Cilandak on the way to Bogor to alert troops loyal to him.

tion), all of whom had witnessed the president's sudden departure, to go to Bogor to meet the president. Suharto trusted all three, though they were also known to have good personal relations with the president. Exactly what their instructions were has never been authoritatively explained. In any case, the three generals went to Bogor, where in the late afternoon they met the president, who was accompanied by three of the four deputy prime ministers—Subandrio, Chaerul Saleh, and Leimena—and one of his wives, Hartini. The outcome of their discussions was the "Letter of 11 March," in which the president "ordered" Suharto "to take all measures considered necessary to guarantee security, calm, and stability of the government and the revolution, and to guarantee the personal safety and authority of the President/Supreme Commander/Great Leader of the Revolution/ Mandatory of the MPRS in the interests of the unity of the Republic of Indonesia and to carry out all teachings of the Great Leader of the Revolution." Suharto was further ordered to report all matters concerning these duties to the president. Having accomplished their mission, the three generals brought the letter back to Suharto in Jakarta, where it became popularly known as the "Supersemar."[21]

Official and semiofficial accounts of what happened on 11 March do not go beyond the events related in the preceding two paragraphs.[22] The army has been anxious to show that it did not carry out a coup against the president and thus maintained the impression that Sukarno voluntarily handed over wide powers to Suharto, who had no connection with the "undisciplined troops" in front of the palace.

The troops in front of the palace were three companies of the RPKAD without insignia and without their famous red berets. They had been ordered there by Kemal Idris and Sarwo Edhie. According to Kemal Idris, their main purpose was to frighten the president and protect the demonstrating students from the Cakrabirawa troops, but Kemal also instructed them to arrest Subandrio and some other ministers if the opportunity arose as they left

21. The letter of 11 March is in Suripto 1969:74. The acronym "Super Semar" (*Surat Perintah Sebelas Maret*) referred to the clowngod, Semar, in the *wayang* (Javanese shadow-play) who possessed all sorts of magical powers.
22. See Roeder 1969:41–43.

the palace.[23] It is not altogether clear to what extent Kemal and Sarwo were merely carrying out Suharto's instructions and to what extent they were going beyond his orders. Suharto had approved the plan to arrest Subandrio and a number of other ministers, but he apparently left the implementation of the plan to Kemal, who said that Suharto did not order him to place the troops in front of the palace during the cabinet session. That plan was devised by Kemal and Sarwo Edhie; both claimed that they did not give details to Suharto beforehand.[24] Kemal Idris and Sarwo Edhie may have exceeded their orders by placing the troops in front of the palace, perhaps fearing that the cautious Suharto would veto their plan if he were informed beforehand. Certainly there was a great risk that fighting might break out between the RPKAD and Cakrabirawa troops, and a clash in front of the palace might have sparked off disturbances in other provinces, especially in East and Central Java.[25] A false move could have brought the nation to the brink of civil war. On the other hand, Suharto probably gave Kemal and Sarwo a free hand to do whatever they chose to heat up the situation, provided they did not implicate Suharto. Suharto's strategy was to give the impression that he was losing control of the troops led by the radical officers so that the president would turn to him as the lesser evil. Suharto may well have "not wanted to know" what Kemal and Sarwo were doing, though Yoga Sugama and Ali Murtopo were in fact keeping him informed.[26]

As soon as Suharto heard of Sukarno's flight, he set about exploiting the new development. According to Amir Machmud, Suharto instructed the three generals only to reassure the president

23. Interview with Kemal Idris, 9 December 1970.

24. Interviews with Kemal Idris, 9 December 1970, and with Sarwo Edhie, 5 September 1970.

25. Sarwo Edhie blandly stated that the risk was not great because the RPKAD could have defeated the Cakrabirawa (interview, 5 September 1970). On the other hand, a close supporter of the president asked, "What were the Cakra for anyway?" implying that the president had no need to flee to Bogor (interview).

26. Kemal Idris was the officer who pointed a cannon at the president's palace on 17 October 1952 as Sukarno stood on the palace steps. It seems that Kemal took this action without consulting his superiors, but, as McVey has noted in her discussion of that incident, "Officers frequently found it politic to feign reluctance while quietly encouraging impatience on their subordinates' part, the better to present their demands as the result of overwhelming pressure from below and to escape full responsibility if the move failed" (1971b:147).

that the army could keep the situation under control if given the full confidence of the president. According to Amir, the Letter of 11 March was formulated after the three generals had talked with the president and understood his wishes. The letter was drafted by the three generals, with the help of Brigadier General Sabur. Sukarno then showed it to Subandrio, Chaerul Saleh, and Leimena. According to Amir, Subandrio made some minor changes in the wording, and then the president signed it.[27]

Some writers have doubted Amir Machmud's version.[28] Insofar as his account suggests that the initiative to draw up the letter was Sukarno's, it is hard to believe. On the other hand, it seems unlikely that the three generals carried the draft of the letter with them from Jakarta and then presented the president with an ultimatum to sign it. Such crude behavior toward the president would have been out of character for the generals involved, and in any case such a demand probably would have antagonized a man of Sukarno's temperament so that he would have refused to sign. It seems more likely that in their discussions with Suharto before they left Jakarta the three generals were given a fairly clear idea of what Suharto wanted. The result would depend on the president's reaction, so in Bogor the generals had to "play it by ear." Suharto wanted to obtain the president's "voluntary" approval for the measures he was planning. By stressing that the situation was getting out of hand in Jakarta, the generals hoped to persuade the president to turn to them as the only way of restoring order. Amir's account of the letter's easy acceptance by Subandrio and Chaerul Saleh is most implausible. Both, especially Subandrio, must have realized the implications for them personally of the document. Other sources claimed that Subandrio strongly advised the president against signing the letter,[29] but Sukarno calculated that the least harmful solution was to hand over powers to Suharto. If the powers were not handed over, the chances were that the army radicals would have taken matters into their own hands, perhaps by assassinating their main opponents. Further, in the long run, Sukarno probably believed that he would eventually outmaneuver Suharto and revoke the powers that he was transferring.

27. See interview with Amir Machmud in *Kompas*, 15 March 1971.
28. For example, Polomka 1971:89; see also Hughes 1968:235–236.
29. See Brigadier General Sutjipto's speech reported in *Kompas*, 9 April 1966.

Suharto wasted no time in using his newly acquired powers. On 12 March he issued an order of the day addressed to the armed forces and the people of Indonesia. He claimed that the president's order to him of the previous day showed that "the voice of the heart of the people . . . is truly seen, heard, and considered by the Great Leader of the Revolution, Bung Karno, whom we love so much, and it is also evidence of the Great Leader of the Revolution's love for all of us."[30] On the same day he issued his first

order as the "Bearer of the Letter of 11 March." In the name of the president, he ordered the dissolution of the PKI and its affiliated organizations throughout the nation, while "continuing to hold steadfastly to the Panca Azimat (Five Magic Charms) of the Indonesian Revolution."[31] While he carefully avoided showing signs of disrespect for Sukarno personally, Suharto implemented what the army had been demanding and the president resisting since October 1965. The massacres, incarcerations, and regional dissolutions of late 1965 had effectively eliminated the PKI as an active political force, but the president's continued praise for the party's past services and his reaffirmation of the validity of Nasakom had transformed the issue into one of tremendous symbolic significance. When the president failed to disown the order issued in his name by Suharto, his authority suffered a shattering blow.

Suharto's move had caught the president's supporters unprepared to act in his defense. The Letter of 11 March did not have the approval of the commanders of the navy, police, air force, and the Sukarnoists in the army, but once the president had signed it, they could hardly reject it. Suharto's order dissolving the PKI placed the president's military supporters in similarly awkward circumstances. They knew that the order would undermine the president's authority, but they had no sympathy for the PKI and did not want to cast themselves in the role of its defender. Thus they were reluctant to take an immediate stand in support of the president against Suharto.

On 13 March tensions within the armed forces rose as all sides drew their conclusions about what had happened. Infuriated by Suharto's use of his new powers to dissolve the PKI in the presi-

30. Perintah Harian in Suripto 1971:87–88.
31. Decision No. 1/3/1966 in ibid., pp. 76–77. One of the Panca Azimat (Five Magic Charms) was Nasakom.

dent's name, Sukarno called the deputy prime ministers and the commanders of the navy, police, and air force to Bogor. On their return to Jakarta, further meetings were held at the house of the navy commander, Muljadi, followed by another meeting at Leimena's house. Meanwhile, rumors spread that Kostrad forces were planning to attack the Halim air force base, while Kostrad officers seemed to anticipate an attack from the air force. Army and air force troops were placed on alert, Kostrad forces occupied strategic places in the city, and Kko and police troops were prepared for action. As rival forces faced each other, General Nasution called representatives of all four forces to his house in the middle of the night. At the beginning of the meeting, Kemal Idris, representing the army, refused to shake hands with Admiral Muljadi, Major General Hartono, and the air force representative, Commodore Rusmin Nurjadin, but after a tense discussion a measure of understanding was reached and everyone shook hands.[32]

Although Nasution's initiative had defused a potential explosion in Jakarta, tension remained high as the president continued to explore means of reasserting his authority. Next morning, the fourteenth, the president called the coordinating minister for defense and security, Sarbini, and his deputy, Mursjid, to Bogor for discussions with the commanders of the navy, police, and air force; the commander of the army was notably absent. On the fifteenth a meeting was held at Bogor, attended by all four commanders, including Suharto, together with the commander of the Kko, Hartono.

On the sixteenth another meeting was held in the palace to discuss the army leadership's demand that the cabinet be reconstituted and Subandrio and other leftist ministers dismissed. Although it was probably left unstated, everyone understood that the army also wanted to arrest Subandrio, who by then had sought refuge in the palace. The meeting was attended by the four deputy prime ministers (Subandrio, Leimena, Chaerul Saleh, Idham Chalid),[33] the coordinating minister for defense and secu-

32. Interview with General Nasution, 24 July 1973. See also Nasution 1971:237–238 and Brigadier General Sutjipto's speech, *Kompas,* 11 April 1966.
33. The NU general chairman, Idham Chalid, had been appointed as the fourth deputy prime minister in the February cabinet reshuffle.

rity (Sarbini), the four service commanders, and the coordinating minister for communications with the people (Ruslan Abdulgani). Again the president refused to give way to Suharto's demands and instead ordered Chaerul Saleh to present a statement on his behalf on radio and television that night. In the announcement read by Chaerul, the president said that he was "responsible only to the MPRS and Almighty God in carrying out the mandate of the MPRS." In performing his tasks, "Bung Karno has complete freedom to appoint his own assistants." He therefore regretted that some wanted "to force their wishes on the President, even by means of an ultimatum."[34]

The president's announcement clearly gave the impression that at that moment the president was resisting pressure from certain quarters who were trying to restrict him in his choice of "assistants." Little imagination on the part of the audience would have been required to conclude that Suharto was demanding the dismissal of Subandrio and that Sukarno, supported by Chaerul Saleh, was resisting this demand.

Meanwhile, students from the KAPPI and the Laskar Arief Rahman Hakim had become restless. After consulting Kemal Idris and Sarwo Edhie, who approved their plan "provided no one gets hurt,"[35] members of the KAPPI and the laskar kidnapped several ministers on the sixteenth, including the chairman of the DPR-GR, I Gusti Gede Subamia, the justice minister, Astrawinata, a minister of state, Sudibjo, and the coordinating minister for education and culture, Prijono, while attempts to "arrest" Oei Tjoe Tat and Jusuf Muda Dalam failed. The "arrested" ministers were taken to the Kostrad headquarters.[36] The same day KAMI students demonstrated at the parliament, and further student demonstrations occurred on the seventeenth. The impatient students, supported by some elements in the army, were pressing Suharto to move more quickly.

On the evening of the seventeenth there were no news broadcasts on the radio or television. By next morning, troops and

34. The "President's Announcement" in Boerhan and Soebekti 1966:274–280.
35. Interview with Fahmi Idris, 31 July 1973.
36. *Angkatan Bersenjata*, 17 March 1966. See also *Harian Kami*, 4 March 1967. The students apparently were acting independently of the top army leadership. On the eighteenth the army arrested Astrawinata, Oei Tjoe Tat, and Jusuf Muda Dalam, but not Subamia, Sudibjo, or Prijono.

tanks were stationed in the streets. A list of fifteen ministers who
were to be arrested had been prepared. At least one had already
been "arrested" by the KAPPI students, and nine had taken refuge in the palace. Sarwo Edhie and the RPKAD were given the
job of capturing them. The RPKAD troops were ordered to sur-
round the palace and make sure that none got away, while Amir
Machmud was given the task of requesting the president to hand
over Subandrio. As Subandrio was taken away, Sukarno pleaded
with Amir not to kill him.[37] The others were arrested at the palace
or elsewhere except for Achadi and Surachman, who escaped.[38]

In a later speech Suharto placed the arrested ministers into three
categories, first, those "about whose connection with the PKI/Ges-
tapu there are sufficient indications," second, those "whose good
faith in assisting the president . . . is doubted," and third, "those
who have amorally and asocially lived in luxury over the sufferings
of the people."[39] Subandrio, Astrawinata, Oei Tjoe Tat, Setiadi
Reksoprodjo, and Sumardjo were considered to fit the first category. Chaerul Saleh and Jusuf Muda Dalam were covered by the
third category. It could be said of all that their good faith in
assisting the president rather than any lack of it led to their arrest.
All fifteen strongly supported the president in his endeavor to
bring the army back under control. Chaerul, Achmadi, A. M.
Achadi, and Tumakaka had been especilly prominent in organizing the Barisan Sukarno. Sutomo Martopradoto, Oei Tjoe Tat, and
Armunanto were members of the left-nationalist Partindo, and
Surachman, the PNI's general secretary, represented his party's

37. See Sutjipto's speech in *Kompas*, 11 April 1966.
38. Achadi (minister for transmigration and cooperatives) was arrested on 3 May
1966. Surachman (minister for public irrigation and village development) eventually joined the PKI underground and was killed at South Blitar in 1968. The other
thirteen were Subandrio (first deputy prime minister and minister for foreign
affairs), Chaerul Saleh (third deputy prime minister and chairman of the MPRS),
Setiadi Reksoprodjo (electricity), Sumardjo (basic education and culture), Oei Tjoe
Tat (minister of state), Jusuf Muda Dalam (central bank affairs), Armunanto (mining), Sutomo Martopradoto (labor), Astrawinata (justice), Achmadi (information),
Lieutenant Colonel Sjafe'i (special security affairs), Tumakaka (secretary general
of the National Front), and Major General Sumarno Sosroatmodjo (internal affairs
and governor of Jakarta). Several other ministers were arrested shortly afterward,
including Brigadier General Hartawan Wirjodiprodjo (road construction), Air
Vice Marshal Sri Muljono Herlambang (minister/commander of the air force), and
Sudibjo (minister of state).
39. Suharto's radio-TV speech in Sutjipto, ed. 1966:I, 19–20.

left wing. The two army officers arrested, Major General Sumarno Sosroatmodjo, and Lieutenant Colonel Sjafe'i, were regarded as more loyal to the president than to the army commander.

Thus, although on the sixteenth Sukarno had refused to dismiss the ministers who were unacceptable to the army leaders, on the eighteenth the army simply arrested them. Just as the president had been presented with a fait accompli in the case of the dissolution of the PKI, now he had little alternative but to accept the arrest of his ministers and the need to reshuffle his cabinet. Clearly the president had lost in the confrontation with Suharto on this issue, but Suharto continued to keep his demands as moderate as possible, as indicated by the fact that only fifteen ministers, plus a few more who were arrested later, were on the list. Thus the president was not pushed into a position where he had nothing to lose in forcing another open confrontation with the army leadership. He and his supporters could still hope that, given time, he might be able to outmaneuver the generals and restore much of his power.

8 | The Fall of Sukarno

President Sukarno knew what had happened on 11 and 18 March, but he had not been forced into a corner where he had nothing to lose by resorting to immediate counteraction. The ministers and supporters of Sukarno who had been most antagonistic to the army leadership were quickly purged, but the president remained in office and his more moderate supporters in the armed forces retained their positions. From the point of view of the moderate Sukarnoists in the army and the other branches of the armed forces, the "Eleventh of March Affair" was undoubtedly a setback, but most of them did not greatly regret the removal of Subandrio, Chaerul Saleh, and Jusuf Muda Dalam or the air force commander, Sri Muljono Herlambang, who was replaced later in the month. Indeed, the purge had provided them with new opportunities because the president brought them into his depleted inner circle of confidants. Although the army leadership's power had grown dramatically, the president's allies could still hope to benefit from future political crises which might provide openings for a comeback by the president, with the support of his friends in the armed forces.

During the months after 11 March, however, the atmosphere of Jakarta politics underwent a drastic change. The new army-dominated government reversed many of the president's principal economic and foreign policies, and youthful enthusiasts in the Action Fronts that had risen to oppose Sukarno[1] proclaimed the birth of the "New Order" in place of the discredited "Old Order."

---

1. Apart from the university students' front, KAMI, and the front for high school students and youths, KAPPI, there were several other Action Fronts, including the university graduates' front, KASI. These bodies were strongly supported by followers of the Masyumi and the Indonesian Socialist party, both of which had been banned by Sukarno in 1960.

In Jakarta and Bandung the reemergence of groups repressed under Guided Democracy coincided with the development of a movement, encouraged by several strongly anti-Sukarnoist generals, which demanded a complete break with the past, including the removal of Sukarno from office. The army leadership remained conscious of the sympathy still felt for the president through most of East and Central Java, where Javanese officers were responsive to the political sentiments of the civilian population. As anti-Sukarno feelings intensified in Jakarta and Bandung, there were signs of a backlash developing in Central and East Java, where rival youth and student organizations clashed with increasing frequency.

The reluctance of the army leadership to force a final showdown with the president was due primarily to their concern to avoid the outbreak of fighting between rival military units. The army's superiority in numbers[2] and armaments seemed to guarantee that it would win a conflict in the end, but the costs could have been enormous. Moreover, the specter always haunted Suharto of army units, especially in East Java, crossing to the other side. The air force and navy, backed by the navy's Kko, the police Mobile Brigade, and sections of East Java's Brawijaya division, had the capacity to inflict severe losses on forces supporting Suharto, although they had little prospect of achieving final victory. The army leaders, who wanted to inherit the armed forces intact rather than crippled as a consequence of civil war, realized that the legacy of bitterness resulting from such a conflict would have lasted for at least a generation and might have prevented the victors from consolidating their rule when it was over. Further, Suharto, as the leading advocate of the gradualist approach, had a personal interest in the success of that strategy. If clashes between

2. The strength of the armed forces in September 1965 was 505,300 (Angkatan Darat 1966 6:151). The police force had 125,000 members in 1966 (*Angkatan Bersenjata*, 26 July 1966), while Nasution referred to the army's strength reaching 300,000 in the early 1960s (1971:387). On the basis of rice allocations provided for the armed forces in the 1971 budget, a newspaper calculated that the relative strengths of the four forces were in the ratios of the army 30, the navy 6, the air force 5, and the police 15 (*Indonesia Raya*, 15 February 1971). Assuming that in 1966 the army numbered 300,000 and the police 125,000 and that the relative strengths of the navy and air force were much the same as in 1971, the navy's strength would have been about 44,000 (perhaps half of whom were in the marine corps, the Kko) and the air force's about 36,000.

rival units in the armed forces had in fact broken out, it was likely that the leadership of the army would have been seized by the more aggressively anti-Sukarnoist generals.

The unwillingness of the army leaders to risk a civil conflict in order to establish full control was related to their conception of their basic objectives. While some senior officers regarded the fall of Sukarno as the army's opportunity to fulfill its destiny of "modernizing" Indonesia, the aspirations of the majority were more mundane. Since entering the political elite after 1957, army officers had expanded their nonmilitary role into the administrative and financial fields, where they had acquired some of the values of the established elite which had little interest in overhauling the existing social order but sought only to consolidate and protect its position within the system. Experienced in exploiting bureaucratic positions for commercial gain during the Guided Democracy period, many officers viewed the political developments after 1965 as opening wider opportunities to pursue much the same objectives that had occupied them before 1965. The Guided Democracy period had seen the flourishing of bureaucratically based commercial empires built by Chaerul Saleh, Jusuf Muda Dalam, and other leaders, including on a lesser scale army officers like Ibnu Sutowo and Suhardiman, so the army leaders had reason to hope that the president would accept an essentially unchanged system—at least for the commercial elite—except that army officers would be much more prominent than before. Many army officers tended to view the problem as one of reconciling their material interests with those of Sukarno. If he had been able to accept the changes they considered necessary to further their interests, they would have been content to leave him in office.

The hesitancy of Suharto and the senior generals in taking decisive action to dismiss the president was reinforced by their traditional Javanese values, which gave them a sense of propriety that inhibited them from humiliating an honored elder. As much as they disliked Sukarno's behavior and his policies, they regarded themselves as his subordinates and felt compelled to seek means of reducing his power without the shame of an open confrontation. Like the *wayang* (Javanese shadow-play) hero, Raden Gatot-kaca, who was obliged to reprimand his uncle, Raja Baladewa, Suharto saw himself as a nephew approaching an erring uncle. In the *wayang* story, Gatotkaca first knelt before his uncle in order to admonish him. When Raja Baladewa took no notice, Gatotkaca rose to his feet, and after Raja Baladewa drew his sword, Gatotkaca began to fight with his uncle. Even then, as the fight progressed, Gatotkaca continued to show his respect by saluting the older man.[3] As late as February 1967 the cultural need of many Javanese officers to avoid the sense of shame they felt in taking action that would humiliate the president was illustrated again when they proposed that Sukarno should follow the example of another *wayang* figure, Habioso, the wise king who had left his palace to meditate in the mountains, but was willing to give advice to his sons whenever they consulted him. When Sukarno had finally been dismissed, Suharto called on the nation to treat him as "a president who is no longer in power."

During the months after 11 March, a purge of the government machinery was carried out, aimed primarily at the followers of Subandrio, Chaerul Saleh, and the left wing of the PNI. The dismissal and arrest of fifteen cabinet ministers on 18 March and several more shortly afterward was followed by dismissals and suspensions of officials in all government departments and the regional bureaucracy. In the armed forces a major purge took place in the air force, following the replacement of Sri Muljono Herlambang as commander by Rusmin Nurjadin at the end of March, and by mid-April it was announced that 306 officers had been arrested, including Omar Dhani and Sri Muljono Herlambang. Purges on a lesser scale were conducted in the police and navy, and the Cakrabirawa palace guard was disbanded.

The purge remained limited, however, and many "moderate" supporters of the president retained their positions. In the new six-member cabinet Presidium, Leimena, Ruslan Abdulgani, and the NU leader, Idham Chalid, were closer to Sukarno than to Suharto, although the other three deputy prime ministers, Suharto, Adam Malik as the new foreign minister, and the sultan of Yogyakarta, played the most prominent roles. Of the forty-one full ministers in the eighty-five-member cabinet "reshuffled" on 27 March, only five had not been members of the previous

3. See the article by Pranoto in *Berita Yudha*, 26 March 1970 (translated in *United States Embassy Translation Unit Press Review*). The author makes the point that young people and non-Javanese did not understand Suharto's attitude.

Sukarno-appointed cabinet and none was a reputed opponent of the president. Suharto had not insisted on the reappointment of ministers openly antagonistic to Sukarno, such as Nasution. In the bureaucracy the purge was similarly limited, although in some regions, such as West Java, supporters of the left wing of the PNI quickly lost their positions, while they were able to hold on until the latter part of the year in Central Java and even until 1967 in East Java.

The army leadership was particularly concerned with the PNI. In contrast with figures like Subandrio and Chaerul Saleh, who owed their positions largely to their ability to win the president's confidence, the PNI leaders had widespread mass support. Suharto therefore hesitated to take action against the party, whose supporters, like those of the PKI, were drawn largely from the *abangan* (nominally Muslim) community of Java. Perhaps fearing that a ban on the party would push many of its supporters into alliance with the underground PKI while removing a secular balance to the resurgence of political Islam, the army leaders wished to preserve the PNI, but under new leadership. Here their interests ran parallel with those of a dissident group in the PNI—led by Hardi and Hadisubeno Sosrowerdojo—which had been suspended from the party leadership in August 1965 because of their opposition to cooperation with the PKI. Under pressure from the army leadership after March 1966, the Sukarnoist general chairman of the party, Ali Sastroamidjojo, agreed to hold a congress in Bandung at the end of April. After blatant interference by the military authorities, Ali Sastroamidjojo and his supporters were swept out of office by the army-supported dissidents, who appointed Osa Maliki as the new party chairman. Although the new leadership was still attached to Sukarno, it was more "realistic" in its assessment of the new circumstances, in which the army and not Sukarno was the dominant force.

In order to consolidate the changes that had taken place since March, the army leaders called a session of the MPRS, which opened in late June.[4] The main purpose of the session was to obtain constitutional endorsement of Sukarno's Letter of 11

4. The MPRS was the supreme policy-making body. Its most important function was to elect the president. It also set down general policy guidelines which the parliament and government were obliged to follow.

March which, legally, the president could revoke at any time. Although the assembly was dominated by groups that had supported Sukarno in the past, its members were under great pressure to pass decisions proposed by the army leaders. The leaders of the navy, police, and air force, as well as the new leaders of the PNI and the dominant group in the NU, continued to sympathize with Sukarno, but they were not prepared to force a showdown with the army leaders by rejecting the proposal that the Letter of 11 March be incorporated in a decision of the MPRS. At the same time the MPRS passed several other decisions aimed at "returning to the 1945 Constitution," from which the president had implicitly deviated. The presidency for life bestowed on Sukarno by the MPRS in 1963 was withdrawn and the statement made that the title "Great Leader of the Revolution" entailed no legal authority. The president was explicitly forbidden to issue presidential decisions and presidential regulations, and he was reminded of an obligation to carry out MPRS decisions and report back on their implementation. Sukarno was permitted to speak to the MPRS session, but the unrepentant tone of his speech led to much dissatisfaction among the army leaders and in some Muslim circles, with the result that a further decision of the MPRS "requested the president to complete his report on his responsibilities to the MPRS, especially the causes of the G.30.S./PKI event and its epilogue as well as the decline in the economy and morals."[5]

The fourth General Session of the MPRS had thus imposed strict limitations on the president's prerogatives and given formal endorsement to the powers that Suharto had in fact been wielding since 11 March. Although the members of the MPRS had avoided language insulting to the president, they had shown that Sukarno was no longer above criticism and that they had ceased to fear him. Nevertheless, no attempt was made to remove Sukarno from office. During the three months after 11 March, Suharto had tried to prove to the president that he would have to accept the dominant role of the army leadership in the new government. Having persuaded the leaders of the armed forces to agree to a situation where the president remained in office with strictly circumscribed powers, Suharto gained the imprimatur of the MPRS for the arrangements that had evolved since 11 March. Having

5. The MPRS decisions are in Sutjipto 1966, Vols. I and II.

demonstrated his capacity to manipulate the MPRS to endorse his policies, Suharto hoped that the president would accept "reality." Such an arrangement would have been convenient for Suharto in that it would enable him to avoid the risks and tensions that would inevitably accompany an attempt to depose Sukarno. The president apparently interpreted the signs differently. Relieved that he had not been attacked more directly, he regarded Suharto's restraint as an indication of weakness. He seemed to believe that Suharto had flinched at the last moment from fear of provoking the mass of the people and the Sukarnoists in the armed forces. Thus, while Suharto hoped that the MPRS deicisions had established the basis for a permanent understanding between the president and the army leadership, Sukarno was encouraged to entertain hopes of reasserting himself in the future.

Although the army leadership had been willing to give Sukarno a place of honor within the new structure of power, the president contemptuously rejected the role of a "constitutional monarch."[6] Sukarno's personality and his conception of his responsibilities as "Great Leader of the Revolution" made it impossible for him to accept the army leadership's preferred terms. He had become accustomed to leading the government, and he was not willing to suffer the indignity of seeing his own policies reversed by his subordinates acting in his name. For him, politics were not just a matter of the distribution of the perquisites of power (although this aspect was not ignored), but also a moral crusade against colonialism and imperialism and the domestic forces that rejected his conception of the unity of the Indonesian nation. He had no interest in retaining the presidency while the army leaders destroyed his domestic allies and turned to the Western "imperialists" for economic support. In his speeches during the second half of 1966, Sukarno made it unambiguously clear that, come what may, he would not submit to the conditions required by the army leaders. He refrained from calling on his followers to rise in his defense, but he continued to express the ideological themes of the past, which were anathema to the army leaders and consequently symbols of his continued defiance.

The new government's top policy objective since March had

6. See President Sukarno's speech to the closing session of the MPRS, 6 July 1966.

been to restore some order to the economy, over which the old government had lost almost all control. In 1965 the general rate of inflation had risen to 500 percent and the price of rice rose by 900 percent. The budget deficit in 1965 had amounted to 300 percent of revenues, and the deficit for the first three months of 1966 was almost as large as for the whole of 1965. Moreover, if foreign debt repayments were to be made on schedule in 1966, almost all of the nation's export income would have been required for this purpose.[7] Clearly, the new government faced an enormous problem, and not unexpectedly it drew the conclusion that the only way out was to appeal to foreign sources of funds, first to postpone repayment of existing debts and then to supply more loans. In the circumstances not much assistance could be expected from Indonesia's main creditor, the Soviet Union, and the other Communist countries, so the countries approached for funds were the United States, Japan, and other Western states.

New foreign aid from the western countries was not likely to be forthcoming as long as Indonesia's foreign policy orientation remained unchanged and the confrontation of Malaysia continued. The army leaders had in fact lost interest in the confrontation campaign since the latter part of 1964, and secret contacts had been established with the Malaysian leaders through Suharto's aide, Ali Murtopo. Operations in Kalimantan had been curbed after October 1965, but as long as Sukarno remained in power, the prospect of a formal settlement was remote. Only after 11 March did the earlier secret contacts seem likely to bear fruit, but the question was extremely delicate, not only because of the president's opposition but also the unwillingness of many military officers to submit to what would appear as a humiliating capitulation.[8]

During April and May, Suharto and Adam Malik began to prepare Indonesian public opinion for a change in policy by suggesting that the aims of confrontation could be achieved by nonmilitary means. At the end of May, Adam Malik flew with a delegation that included important military officers to Bangkok,

---

7. See the statement of the sultan of Yogyakarta as deputy prime minister for economic, financial, and development affairs in *Statement-Statement Politik Waperdam Bidang Sospol/Menteri Luar Negeri dan Waperdam Bidang Ekubang*. The statement was made on 4 April 1966.

8. For a detailed account of the ending of confrontation, see Weinstein 1969.

where he met the Malaysian deputy prime minister, Tun Abdul Razak. In Bangkok, Malik and Razak reached agreement on three principles, known as the Bangkok Accord, which were to be submitted to their respective governments for approval. The principles, which were not announced publicly at the time, were that the people of Sabah and Sarawak be given an opportunity to "re-affirm" their status in Malaysia through general elections, that diplomatic relations be established immediately, and that hostilities cease.

On his return to Jakarta, Adam Malik faced strong criticism from several quarters. President Sukarno, sensing that the apparent capitulation at Bangkok might enable him to win back support in his struggle with Suharto, refused to endorse the settlement terms. There was a widespread feeling within the armed forces and among important party leaders that Adam Malik had gone too far, especially by agreeing to open diplomatic relations before elections were held in Sabah and Sarawak.[9] Ironically, the most outspoken critic of the agreement was the president's old foe, General Nasution, who saw the issue as one of principle. Early in May he told a Japanese journalist, "The confrontation of Malaysia is a matter of principle to implement the Manila/Maphilindo principles which have been violated by Britain and Kuala Lumpur. Peaceful means should be stressed in the settlement but don't sacrifice principles because of this."[10] During a visit to Sumatra at the end of May he once again warned, "We must not violate our principles just for the sake of peace with Malaysia."[11] Nasution's outspoken dissent had the support of many senior officers in all four services who felt that Indonesia could not simply abandon a policy to which they had all been committed, and his attitude won the approval of PNI and NU leaders.

Faced with a groundswell of opinion against the Bangkok Accord, Suharto quickly appreciated that the apparent "sellout" might well become an issue for Sukarno's supporters to rally opposition to the new government, as well as providing an opportunity for his outstanding rival within the army, Nasution, to regain ground that he had been rapidly losing. Ratification of the agree-

9. See Weinstein 1972:606–609.
10. *Angkatan Bersenjata,* 6 May 1966.
11. *Kompas,* 30 May 1966.

ment was postponed while Ali Murtopo and his colleagues held further negotiations with Malaysia. Final agreement was not reached until after the MPRS session, when Malaysia accepted a secret annex to the agreement proposed by Suharto which postponed official recognition until after the elections in Sabah and Sarawak. The agreement was eventually signed in Jakarta on 11 August by Adam Malik and Tun Razak, and shortly afterward "unofficial" diplomatic offices were established in both capitals.

Sukarno, although confirmed in his position as president by the MPRS, had lost control over policy when the government ended the confrontation campaign and turned to the West for economic assistance. Apparently emboldened by the reluctance of the army leaders to take drastic measures against him at the MPRS session, however, he quickly showed that he was not willing to give up without a fight. As Suharto's aides entered the final stages of their delicate talks with Malaysia on the terms of the confrontation settlement at the end of July, Sukarno declared once again that "Malaysia is a neocolonialist project" and proclaimed that the government had decided that "the confrontation of Malaysia will continue."[12] Although he approved the settlement a few days later, after being informed of the secret annex, he then revealed its existence to the whole nation as well as the Malaysian public in his annual 17 August speech celebrating the 1945 proclamation of independence.[13] The president's move failed to upset the agreement, but it proved beyond doubt to Suharto and his advisers that the problem of the presidency had not been settled at the MPRS session.

In his 17 August speech, Sukarno virtually challenged Suharto to test his popularity against that of the president: "Over and over again I have said that we must hold general elections as quickly as possible because general elections are the only democratic means of knowing the will of the people, to know the real wishes of the people, to clarify demands that are put forward 'in-the-name-of-the-people' and to improve the membership of our present State Bodies." As his speech drew to a close, Sukarno asked, "Why were we supreme in the past? . . . We were supreme because the entire

12. President Sukarno's speech, 28 July 1966.
13. See President Sukarno's 17 August speech entitled "Djangan Sekalikali Meninggalkan Sedjarah," pp. 27–30.

nation and all revolutionary groups were united." He asserted that they were united as bearers of the Panca Azimat Revolusi (Five Magical Charms of the Revolution), which consisted of the Panca Sila, "Nasakom, or Nasasos or Nasa-whatever," Manipol-Usdek, Trisakti, and Berdikari. These were the teachings of Indonesia's history. He warned, "There are some people who don't want to learn from history, who even want to cut themselves off from our history. That can't be done. They will fail." He then declared, "I am your Great Leader; that's what the MPRS said; I am your leader. Follow my leadership, follow all my instructions." Finally, he called on God "to bless the Indonesian Revolution under my leadership."[14]

The president's defiance continued to express itself in other speeches. Referring to the MPRS's recent ban on Marxism, he quoted Confucius as saying, "One general can destroy a thousand enemy soldiers but one thousand generals cannot uproot a man's convictions."[15] In a speech in September he again mocked the MPRS for banning Marxism and Communism. "Beforehand," he said, "I advised the members of the MPRS that if they decided to ban Marxism, Leninism, Communism, I would laugh." After restating his belief in "Nasakom, Nasasos or Nasa-whatever," he added, "I now say without beating about the bush, I am a Marxist, I have said that since the year '28, I am a nationalist, I am religious, I am a Marxist . . . Marxism is contained in my heart."[16] As the pressure increased, he became all the more unyielding. Refusing to refer to the 1965 coup attempt as "Gestapu" or "G.30.S./PKI," as preferred by the generals, he repeatedly condemned what he called "Gestok," the 1 October Movement, thereby introducing uncertainty as to whether he meant the movement launched by Untung and his colleagues in the early hours of 1 October or the movement launched later the same day by Suharto.[17]

As long as Sukarno continued to demonstrate his disapproval of the direction the generals were taking the nation, he was a potential threat to their hold on the government. For the time being,

14. Ibid., pp. 25, 40–41. Apart from Panca Sila, the other four "charms" were ideological formulations devised during the Guided Democracy period.
15. *Kompas*, 2 July 1966.
16. President Sukarno's speech on 6 September 1966. For Sukarno's 1928 formulation, see McVey 1970.
17. President Sukarno's speech, 17 August 1966, p. 19.

Sukarno was unwilling to risk mobilizing his supporters against the army leadership, but the generals could not afford to leave him in a position where he could become a rallying point for opposition to the regime in the future. While Suharto hesitated to deliver the final blow, he was under strong pressure from Nasution and a small but influential group of officers, led by the acting Kostrad commander, Kemal Idris, the new Siliwangi commander, Dharsono, and the RPKAD commander, Sarwo Edhie, who had achieved immense popularity in student and other anti-Sukarnoist circles in Jakarta and Bandung and wanted to depose the president as a prelude to a thorough reform of the political system. Further, Suharto was concerned that his failure to subjugate the president would be interpreted by the Western nations, to which Indonesia was turning for economic assistance, as an indication that the army was not really in control and that a return to the old policies was still possible. As Sukarno's intransigence continued, the need to safeguard his own position and to reassure the sources of foreign aid forced Suharto to take more decisive action.

Since March the ground for a possible final showdown had been prepared by the transfer of Sukarno's key sympathizers among the regional commanders in the army. During the month before the opening of the MPRS session in June, Suharto ordered a number of senior officers, including the West Java commander, Adjie, and the Central Java commander, Surjosumpeno, to attend a special upgrading course at the Army Staff and Command College in Bandung.[18] Their places were taken "temporarily"—but in fact permanently—by the strongly anti-Sukarnoist Major General Dharsono in West Java and the governor of the Armed Forces Academy, Major General Surono Reksodimedjo, in Central Java. At the same time, Major General Sumitro replaced Brigadier General Sunarijadi as commander in East Java, and the Sukarnoist regional commander in Bali was transferred. Adjie was soon appointed as ambassador to London, and Surjosumpeno joined the president's staff as secretary for military affairs.

The president still had sympathizers in the army. Although most army officers had supported Suharto's measures to curb Sukarno's powers, many were disturbed by the prospect that more

18. *Angkatan Bersenjata,* 17 May 1966.

severe action might be taken against him. Among them was the interregional commander for Sumatra, Lieutenant General Mokoginta, by then the only incumbent of a major command who had been appointed before Suharto became army commander in October 1965. As a general enjoying warm personal ties with the president, he must have felt that he would meet the fate of Adjie, Surjosumpeno, and others if Suharto's power continued to grow. After Sukarno's 17 August speech, Mokoginta had expressed his disappointment because of "matters which could create a negative impression," but he also noted that the speech "contained positive aspects."[19] On 13 October he and the interregional commanders of the other three services in Sumatra issued a joint statment that the armed forces "will continue to follow the leadership of Bung Karno as long as he is president and commander in chief of the armed forces in accordance with the decisions of the fourth session of the MPRS." They warned that "all actions which openly or indirectly reduce the prestige of the president/commander-in-chief of the armed forces violate the decisions of the MPRS and are therefore anti-people and anti-Ampera."[20] In November, Mokoginta issued another statement to remind the people of Sumatra that they must not "attack the reputation of the President."[21]

There were indications within the Brawijaya division that many officers were not convinced of the need for further moves against Sukarno. As were PNI members in East Java, the typical Brawijaya officer had been strongly anti-Communist but at the same time deeply attached to Sukarno, who also came from an East Javanese *priyayi* background. They were intensely suspicious of the technocratic element in the army gathered around Nasution and the PSI-influenced officers of the Siliwangi division,[22] while their *priyayi* backgrounds made them ever ready to suppress signs of a Masyumi revival, which they tended to see in the activities of

19. *Harian Kami,* 26 August 1966.

20. *Angkatan Bersenjata,* 15 October 1966. "Ampera" was the acronym for *Amanat Penderitaan Rakjat* (Mandate of the Sufferings of the People), a Sukarnoist slogan taken over by the new government.

21. Ibid., 17 November 1966.

22. This conflict had been apparent at the time of the Seventeenth of October Affair in 1952. Several of the Brawijaya officers opposing Nasution in 1952 were among those giving strong support to Sukarno in 1966. The most outspoken, both in 1952 and 1966, was Colonel Bambang Supeno. For the 1952 affair, see Feith 1962:246–273.

the KAMI and KAPPI. On 25 and 26 October a meeting was held at Tretes in East Java to discuss a plan to set up a "Great Brawijaya Family" along the lines of the Siliwangi "Guidance Body" established by former and current officers of the Siliwangi division. The meeting was attended by a number of former Brawijaya commanders, including Major General Sungkono, Major General Bambang Sugeng, Lieutenant General Sudirman, Lieutenant General Sarbini, Lieutenant General Basuki Rachmat, and the current commander, Major General Sumitro. The driving force behind the plan was the retired Colonel Bambang Supeno, an almost fanatical devotee of the president, to whom he was distantly related. Supeno, who lived in Jakarta, had gathered around him a group of middle-ranking officers known as Petir (Protectors of the Essence of the Revolution), who were determined to defend Sukarno.[23] Under his influence, the new Brawijaya body could be expected to speak out as strongly for the president as the Siliwangi body, under the Siliwangi commander, Major General Dharsono, spoke out against him.

President Sukarno had planned to go to Surabaya on Heroes' Day, the anniversary of the bloody battle fought by the youth of Surabaya against the British in November 1945. The army leadership feared that the occasion would provide an excellent opportunity for Sukarno to attempt to rally support in an area that was already well disposed toward him. Not only were there increasing signs of support for him in the Brawijaya division, but Surabaya was the main base for the navy's Kko, and another relative of the president, Brigadier General Sumarsono, was regional commander of the police. Moreover, the PNI was strong in East Java, as was the pro-Sukarno element in the NU. During the week before Heroes' Day on 11 November, it became known that Bambang Supeno and other army officers in Jakarta and East Java were cooperating with colleagues in the navy and police in a plan to abduct Sukarno during his visit to Surabaya and place him under their protection so that he could lead a resistance to Suharto. The rebellious group was apparently planning to follow the example of the militant youths in Jakarta who abducted Sukarno and Hatta on 16 August 1945, with the purpose of persuading them to issue an immediate declaration of independence. Su-

23. "Petir" also means lightning.

karno, however, told their representatives that he did not want to take action that might start a civil war.[24] Meanwhile, his planned visit to Surabaya was canceled by Suharto.

Against this background, Sukarno spoke at a meeting in Jakarta to commemorate the Isra and Miraj of Mohammed on 9 November. Extremely angry after Suharto had prevented his visit to Surabaya, he promised that "I will follow the example set by the Prophet Mohammed in all his sayings, deeds and even his silences. Am I wrong if I follow the Prophet? Am I wrong?" He then revealed the contents of a letter sent to him by the minister for religion, Saifuddin Zuhri, who had advised Sukarno "to be thankful for the times of your supremacy but be patient when you are in difficulties." "Yes," Sukarno said, "Yes, I will be patient, but patient like the Prophet Mohammed. When the Prophet was abused, mocked, slandered, and even had dung thrown at him at Thaif, he was patient; but after that the Prophet began to take action and even went to war as well as other things; I will also follow the example of the Prophet Mohammed."[25]

During the latter part of 1966, the army leaders had attempted to undermine the president by putting senior ministers of the old government on trial—though these were in fact less trials of individuals than means of discrediting the president by proxy and demonstrating his lack of power to save his most loyal colleagues. In September the former minister for central banking affairs, Jusuf Muda Dalam, was sentenced to death after being found guilty of subversion, corruption, the illegal import of arms, and having two more wives than the four permitted under Islamic law.[26] In October Subandrio was tried and found guilty of participating in the 1965 coup attempt; he, too, was sentenced to death.[27] Both trials involved the president. The Jusuf trial ex-

24. Interviews. See Karni 1974:121–122, 127–129. McVey argues that Sukarno's political style reflected "the feeling that a social breakdown and chaos could only be prevented by the negotiation of communal differences, and that for this a cohesive, representative and authoritative elite was necessary." Thus, when "confronted in the immediate post-coup period with the need to decide whether to stake all on an appeal beyond the national elite to his mass following or to try to recoup his fortunes by maneuvering the familiar entourage, he persevered in the latter course, with results fatal to his rule" (1970:6, 9).
25. *Duta Masyarakat,* 11 November 1966.
26. See Jusuf Muda Dalam trial.
27. See Subandrio trial. In fact the trial produced no evidence that Subandrio had played a role in the kidnapping and murder of the generals.

posed extraordinary irresponsibility and mismanagement in the highest circles of economic policy making and strengthened the impression that the members of the old government had been enjoying the high life at the expense of the suffering people, all of which unavoidably reflected on the president. Subandrio had been Sukarno's most trusted adviser, and his "crimes" necessarily reflected on his superior.

The final phase of the army leadership's drive against Sukarno commenced in December, when the trial of the former air force commander, Omar Dhani, was held. There was no doubt that Omar Dhani had been "involved" in the coup attempt, but the trial was directed less at proving his guilt than at revealing the activities of Sukarno on and around 1 October 1965. The suggestion was repeated throughout the trial that Sukarno had been in league with, or at least approved of, the Thirtieth of September Movement, and evidence showed that he took no action to arrest the leaders of the movement.[28] The proceedings of the Omar Dhani trial were widely publicized and were quickly accepted by Sukarno's detractors as proof of his complicity in the coup attempt. In Jakarta and Bandung, KAMI and KAPPI students, urged on by Kemal Idris, Dharsono, and Sarwo Edhie, declared their lack of faith in the president and demanded his dismissal and trial. At the same time the national associations for judges and lawyers issued a "Declaration of Justice and Truth," in the form of a detailed indictment of the president for his alleged support of the Thirtieth of September Movement.[29] The declaration was signed by the chairmen of the two bodies, one of whom was Mashuri, Suharto's former next-door neighbor and a close political adviser.

By holding the Omar Dhani trial and exploiting the resultant public indignation, Suharto put the military supporters of the president in an extremely difficult position. A new wave of massive demonstrations like those in the previous January seemed about to break out. The commanders of the navy, police, and air force thought that Sukarno would have to meet the earlier request of the MPRS to "complete" his report to it by making an unambiguous statement condemning the PKI for its role in the

28. See Omar Dhani trial (II, 33, III, 325, 371–372).
29. See *Angakatan Bersenjata,* 19 December 1966.

coup attempt. Although they realized that such a statement would deeply humiliate the president, they felt that if Sukarno continued to defy the army leaders, Suharto would take more drastic action against him, and his supporters in the armed forces would be faced with the terrible choice between acquiescence and resistance.

After a fortnight of tense meetings with the four service commanders and the members of the cabinet Presidium in late December and early January, the president finally agreed to "complete" the report which the MPRS had regarded as unsatisfactory six months earlier. The written report was finally submitted on 10 January 1967. In it Sukarno claimed that the "G.30.S. was a complete surprise for me." He said that his earlier condemnations of "Gestok" referred to the assassination of the generals, and he acknowledged that one of the factors leading to the coup attempt was the "confusion" of the PKI "leaders." He also blamed "Nekolim subversion" and unidentified "bad elements."[30] Thus Sukarno had finally bowed to the pressure that had been building up throughout the previous year. But his tone was reluctant and his condemnation still ambivalent from the point of view of the army leaders and his civilian critics. He had blamed only the "leaders" of the PKI and left open the possibility that their role had been minor compared with that of the Nekolim and "bad individuals." Thus, although Sukarno had made a humiliating concession, his opponents were not satisfied.

Anti-Sukarno demands became increasingly vociferous, and KAMI and KAPPI students began to hold demonstrations. The Siliwangi commander, Dharsono, the acting Kostrad commander, Kemal Idris, and the RPKAD commander, Sarwo Edhie, met on 25 and 26 January at Cipayung in West Java, where they discussed military preparations for facing the expected crisis. After the meeting, Dharsono said that "the agreement between the Siliwangi, Kostrad and RPKAD is expected to hasten the destruction of the Old Order."[31] Kemal Idris announced that his troops were "ready for battle,"[32] and Dharsono held a five-hour meeting with all commanders of fighting units within the Siliwangi division,[33]

30. See Sukarno's "Pel-Nawaksara" in Supolo, ed. 1967:1–7.
31. *Antara Ichtisar Tahunan,* 31 January 1967.
32. *Harian Kami,* 28 January 1967.
33. Ibid., 31 January 1967.

after which sixty-seven officers were transferred to new tasks "in order to consolidate the body of the Siliwangi in the context of winning the struggle for the new order."[34] Expressing the outlook of the militant group, Dharsono declared, "In these final moments there are only two sides confronting each other, the New Order against the Old Order. . . . It is nonsense to talk of a third party. We always doubt their claim to be in the middle and they always endanger our struggle."[35]

The rising demand in Jakarta and Bandung for the president's dismissal, however, was accompanied by signs of military support for Sukarno in East and Central Java, where clashes between PNI and Muslim youth groups became increasingly frequent. In January the Kko set up a new Eastern Regional Command, based in Surabaya under Brigadier General Suwadji, with authority over all Kko forces in Central and East Java, Sulawesi, and West Irian.[36] At the fourth anniversary celebrations of the Kko's combat-ready Armada Troop Command, its commander, Brigadier General Sumardi, emphasized that his command had been formed because "it was felt necessary to have troops ready for battle at any time."[37] Speaking to members of the PNI's high school student organization, GSNI, Suwadji reminded them that the president's Letter of 11 March had "firmly declared that it is our duty to protect the authority of the president, commander in chief of the armed forces and all his teachings."[38] In Semarang, the commander of the 8th Maritime Command, Commodore Sudjadi, warned that "rightist counterrevolutionaries" were attempting to overthrow Bung Karno.[39] The attitude of the naval leaders in East Java was shared by the regional police commander, Brigadier General Sumarsono, who declared that "Bung Karno is the only leader who is really loved by all the people of Indonesia."[40] Meanwhile, rumors spread that troops from the army's Brawijaya division were ready to rush to Jakarta if Sukarno's position were threatened.[41]

34. *Angkatan Bersenjata,* 9 February 1967.
35. *Harian Kami,* 3 February 1967.
36. *Surabaya Post,* 20 January, 3 February 1967.
37. Ibid., 20 January 1967.
38. Ibid., 13 February 1967.
39. Ibid., 9 January 1967.
40. Ibid., 27 January 1967.
41. Ibid., 18 February 1967. This rumor was publicly denied by Brigadier General Wahono, the deputy chief of staff of Kostrad and a former Brawijaya officer.

Suharto was still preoccupied with avoiding a crisis that might lead to an outbreak of fighting between sections of the armed forces, and at the beginning of February he decided to approach Sukarno with a final offer. The Legion of Veterans, meeting in Yogyakarta at the end of January, had asked the minister for veterans' affairs, Lieutenant General Sarbini, to suggest to the president that he should follow the example of the wise king Habioso in the *wayang,* who entrusted his kingdom to his sons and retired to the mountains to meditate but was available for consultations whenever his sons faced difficulties.[42] Sarbini, a former Brawijaya commander, who was known to favor a solution that did not injure the president's prestige excessively, obtained Suharto's approval before meeting Sukarno on 5 February.[43] On 3 February, a delegation of "elders" of the Brawijaya division had met the president for three and a half hours, ostensibly to report on the recent foundation of the "Great Brawijaya Family." The "elders," who were led by the current Brawijaya commander, Major General Sumitro, consisted of former commanders of the division who generally opposed the outright dismissal of the president and included Colonel Bambang Supeno, Major General Sungkono, and Major General Bambang Sugeng, whose affection for Sukarno was very strong. Shortly after the meeting, the navy-sponsored newspaper, *El Bahar,* reported that the Brawijaya "elders" had assured the president that their division stood firmly behind him.[44] Although Sumitro claimed that the report was "truly without his knowledge and permission,"[45] the attitudes expressed by the former Brawijaya commanders may have encouraged Sukarno to hold his ground when approached by Sarbini, who was not present on the third, two days later.

Although the president was reluctant to accept the "Habioso solution," Sarbini's approach was not entirely in vain. Apparently

42. Interview with Lieutenant General Sarbini, 25 August 1973.
43. Sarbini was accompanied by Suwadji, the Kko's eastern regional commander, and the retired Major General Bambang Utojo, both of whom were fervent supporters of the president (*Surabaya Post,* 6 February 1967).
44. *El Bahar* was edited by the secretary to the navy and nephew of Sukarno, Commodore Puguh. The newspaper was temporarily banned because of the report, which appeared on 14 February.
45. Sumitro said it was true that the Brawijaya division wanted to help Suharto settle the problem; however, he added, "we do not want publicity in any form whatever" (*Kompas,* 21 February 1967).

emboldened by the sympathy expressed by the Brawijaya officers and sensing that Suharto was willing to make concessions in order to avoid a showdown, Sukarno sent a confidential letter to Suharto on 8 February, offering to announce that he was entrusting Suharto with the "Daily Leadership of the Government" while he retained "the state leadership" and the right "to determine the broad outline of the government leadership in order to uphold the Panca Sila Revolution."[46] Suharto rejected the president's offer, but Sukarno's proposal gave Suharto hope that a settlement short of dismissal might still be achieved.

During the next twelve days, intense discussions took place among the army leaders, the commanders of the other three services, and the president. The parliament met (after the appointment by Suharto, using the powers acquired from Sukarno on 11 March, of a large number of new anti-Sukarno members) and passed a resolution calling for a new MPRS session to dismiss the president.[47] As the president's prospects grew darker, Suharto proposed that he retain the presidency on the condition that he declare himself incapacitated. Sukarno refused to make such a declaration, but with the support of the other three commanders, he agreed on 20 February to "transfer the authority of the government" to Suharto, who would be obliged "to report on the implementation of the transfer whenever it was felt to be necessary."[48] That Sukarno was being compelled to surrender his powers against his will was indicated when he watched a *wayang* performance at the end of the negotiations. The story was *Bambang Irawan Rabi,* in which one of the Pandawa is forced to hand over his daughter to the Kurawa. Many interpreted this as Sukarno being forced to hand over his authority to Suharto.

Sukarno and the commanders of the navy, police, and air force had been finally convinced that nothing short of an explicit "transfer of authority" could save the president from the fate that seemed to be awaiting him if the MPRS convened as called for by

46. Sukarno's letter was quoted in Suharto's speech to the DPR-GR on 4 March 1967 in *Keterangan Pemerintah pada Sidang Pleno DPR-GR Tanggal 4 Maret 1967 Mengenai Penjerahan Kekuasaan.*
47. The resolution and memorandum are in Supolo, ed., 1967:135–166. In January 1967, 108 new members were appointed, raising the total to 350.
48. *Pengumuman Presiden Republik Indonesia/Mandataris MPRS/Panglima Tertinggi ABRI, Tanggal 20 Februari 1967.*

the parliament. Their concessions came too late. While Suharto probably hoped that the transfer of authority would make the MPRS session unnecessary, Nasution, the Siliwangi "hawks," and many civilian groups demanded that the MPRS session be held as planned. As the fall of the president became inevitable, only the PNI among the political parties stood at his side. The "old guard" NU leaders who had refrained from attacking him in the past prudently revised their attitude, and their party now took the lead in demanding Sukarno's dismissal and trial.

With about eighty thousand troops from all four services concentrated in Jakarta and its environs, the Special Session of the MPRS opened in an atmosphere of pervasive tension on 8 March. As the navy's armada sailed into Jakarta Bay, rival forces prepared for the outbreak of conflict and the commanders of the navy, police, and air force warned Suharto that they might not be able to control their troops if Sukarno were dismissed.[49] Meanwhile, Nasution, the Siliwangi militants, the Muslim parties, and representatives of the Action Fronts called both for Sukarno's dismissal and for his trial.[50]

In his speech to the opening session of the MPRS, Suharto sought to head off the conflict.[51] He described two groups who made up the New Order forces as those who were "rational" and those who were "irrational." The second group was influenced by "irrational feelings which can still be understood," such as their regard for Sukarno's record in the struggle for independence, his "discovery" of the Panca Sila, and his role in proclaiming the republic and as its first president. Thus, "with deep reasons and complete understanding and knowledge of Bung Karno's present faults, they irrationally and in good faith hope that Bung Karno is not treated in an unjust way." Suharto warned that if the irrational supporters of the New Order were not taken into account, they might decide to support the Old Order, and, he added, "Frankly speaking, there are members of this irrational group within the Armed Forces also." Thus Suharto asked the MPRS to consider a decree "in the spirit of a stronger paragraph 2 of MPRS Decree No. XV of 1966 . . . without weakening the spirit of

49. See Polomka 1971:91.
50. See Nasution's speech to the MPRS in Supolo, ed., 1967:243–273.
51. Suharto's report in ibid., pp. 285–317.

paragraph 3 of MPRS Decree No. XV as intended in the Resolution of the DPR-GR." Logically, paragraph 2, which deals with the incapacitation of the president, and paragraph 3, dealing with his permanent replacement in the event of death or dismissal, could not both be implemented simultaneously. Possibly the solution that Suharto had in mind was a declaration that Sukarno was permanently incapacited.

After several days of debate, during which, according to one report, the military men argued while "beating the table,"[52] a compromise decision was produced between the two incompatible paragraphs. The decision declared "that President Sukarno has not been able to carry out his constitutional responsibilities" and "that President Sukarno has not been able to implement the sentiments and decisions" of the MPRS. It therefore "Bans President Sukarno from taking part in political activities until the general elections and, from the taking effect of this decision, withdraws the mandate of the MPRS from President Sukarno and all government authority as regulated by the 1945 constitution." It then appointed General Suharto "as Acting President." Finally, the decision provided that "the settlement of the legal problem involving Dr. Ir. Sukarno" would be left in the hands of the acting president. A "clarification" was added as an appendix stating that "the meaning of government authority" was the same as that in the constitution, so that "President Sukarno is thereby replaced by General Suharto . . . as acting president of the Republic of Indonesia."[53]

Speaking to the nation on radio and television immediately after the MPRS session, the new acting president summarized each of the paragraphs of the decision, although he omitted the "clarification" and in place of the reference to "Dr. Ir Sukarno" used the expression "Bung Karno." He then explained that "President Sukarno no longer carries out the duties of President," and he praised the wisdom of the MPRS for "not mentioning the dismissal of President Sukarno from the office of president." He also explained that a team of doctors "under oath" had reported that Sukarno's health had deteriorated. Suharto then announced that "for the time being we will treat him as a president who is no

52. *Harian Kami,* 14 March 1967.
53. Decree No. XXXIII in Supolo, ed., 1967, pp. 321–326.

longer in power, as a president who has no authority at all in the fields of politics, the state, or government."[54]

Despite the camouflage, the fact was that Sukarno had been dismissed and replaced by Suharto. While the president's critics, who dominated the membership of the MPRS, were very suspicious of Suharto's motives, his supporters felt relieved that the final result had not been worse. Aware that power had in fact passed into his hands, Suharto saw little point in taking vindictive action against Sukarno as demanded by the deposed president's opponents. If Sukarno's dismissal had been made more explicit and he had eventually been brought to trial, his supporters would have been enraged and, moreover, they would have felt that if they did not move to protect their patron, they too would be in danger after their leader had been dealt with. Instead, Suharto assured Sukarno's supporters among senior officers in the armed forces that action would not be taken against them personally. Suharto understood that the navy, police, and air force leaders were reluctantly prepared to accept the new configuration of power rather than fight, and he wanted to avoid giving offense to their feelings, which may have caused them to revise their attitude.

During the eighteen months up to March 1967, Indonesia had moved to the brink of armed conflict on several occasions, but each time the rival forces had stopped before taking the final plunge. Civil conflict had been averted, in the final analysis, because the major political forces were convinced that their losses in negotiations would be less than their losses in a war, even if it ended in victory. President Sukarno had refused to respond to the invitation of his most militant followers, who wanted him to lead the resistance from East Java; General Suharto resisted pressure from his militant allies to take action against the president and his supporters that might have provoked Sukarno's followers to rise in his defense. By resisting the advocates of far-reaching change in the ranks of his own camp, Suharto made it possible for the president's supporters to accept a compromise which was in fact a defeat.

In the weeks that followed the MPRS session, Sukarno remained in his palaces, but as time went on it became apparent that

54. Suharto's speech, 13 March 1967 in ibid., pp. 421–425.

he was in fact under house arrest. In May it was announced that he was no longer permitted to use the titles of president, commander in chief of the armed forces, and mandatory of the MPRS, nor could he use the presidential flag. Two months later the removal of Sukarno's photographs from government offices was ordered. Although Sukarno had lost all the attributes of the presidency, Suharto continued to hold the office of acting president until March 1968, when the fifth General Session of the MPRS appointed him as the republic's second president. The first president remained under effective house arrest until his death in June 1970.

9 | The Consolidation of Power

The resolution of the conflict situation achieved at the MPRS session in March 1967 was naturally resented by the supporters of Sukarno and fell far short of the demands made by his most outspoken opponents. Nevertheless, the conclusion of the session was followed by a widespread sense of relief. The extraordinary tensions that had dominated the political process during the previous eighteen months had brought the nation almost to the brink of armed conflict on several occasions. Although the desire of both Sukarno and Suharto to avoid such a conflict prevailed in the end, the period since the anti-Communist massacres of late 1965 had been marked by a series of small-scale local clashes between members of party-affiliated youth and student organizations, encouraged by rival sections of the armed forces. The appointment of Suharto as acting president finally settled the central issue, and most Sukarnoist and anti-Sukarnoist leaders realized that the power arrangements endorsed by the MPRS would have to be accepted.

Nevertheless, several potential bases of opposition to Suharto's continued grip on the government could be expected to reassert themselves if the opportunity arose. The army's pre-1965 rival, the PKI, had lost most of its leadership and at least half a million cadres and supporters during the postcoup massacres and arrests, but much of its mass base survived. Although outwardly cowed into submission after experiencing the postcoup terror, many former PKI supporters could be drawn back into an underground party if the army relaxed its repression and new Communist leadership emerged. Of more immediate concern to Suharto was the continued presence in important military positions of officers who resented his rapid rise to power. Although these officers had accepted his leadership rather than resort to civil war, they were ready to take advantage of any signs of vulnerability.

Suharto met the challenge to his position in two ways. He maintained the repressive apparatus established after the coup and directed it against the remnants of the PKI, supporters of Sukarno, and other groups challenging the army leadership, whether these were in the non-Communist parties or in the armed forces. On the other hand, Suharto preferred the Javanese principle of *alon alon asal kelakon* (slow but sure) in dealing with his military rivals who had the capacity to mobilize troops. Moving against one group at a time, he always endeavored to isolate them from their potential allies and, after convincing them of the hopelessness of their position, offered face-saving ways out in the form of prestigious and often lucrative diplomatic and administrative appointments. Many of his former rivals were given opportunities to succeed in business. A few of the more recalcitrant, however, were arrested.

The Machinery of Control

The army's political power was exercised in part through its "territorial" organization. Alongside its fighting units, the army had developed a network of territorial units concerned with internal security and watching over civilian activities generally. In accordance with its "Territorial Warfare" doctrine, which had been developed from its guerrilla experience during the revolution, the army sought to "integrate itself with the people" through its territorial organization. The territorial units were organized more or less parallel with the civilian administration. This network was most developed in Java, where regional military commands (Kodam) were established in each province, military resort commands (Korem) in the main towns, military district commands (Kodim) at the *kabupaten* (district) level, and small military rayon commands (Koramil) at the *kecamatan* (subdistrict) level. In the other islands each Kodam usually covered several provinces and the lower-level structures were less elaborate. Martial law had been administered through the territorial units between 1957 and 1963, and the reintroduction of a modified form of martial law through the Pepelrada system in 1964 during the confrontation campaign again permitted the territorial units to act as guardians of security at the local level. When the Pepelrada emergency regulations were abolished in 1967, local commanders continued to carry out internal security functions as agents of the Operations Command to Restore Security and Order (Kopkamtib).

The Kopkamtib originated in the compromise reached between Sukarno and Suharto on the morning after the coup attempt in October 1965, when Suharto accepted the president's appointment of Pranoto as "caretaker" commander of the army on the condition that he was entrusted with the "restoration of security and order." The new body was established under Suharto's command on 10 October and formally recognized by the president at the beginning of November. The Kopkamtib's security function quickly expanded beyond its original purpose of tracking down PKI supporters. The Kopkamtib became the government's main instrument of political control, dealing with a wide range of such civilian dissidents as student and Muslim demonstrators. Newspapers required Kopkamtib permission to publish, and on many occasions this permission was temporarily and sometimes permanently withdrawn. In 1971 the Kopkamtib was entrusted with maintaining "security and order" during the election campaign and made many arrests to achieve this purpose. With virtually unlimited power, the Kopkamtib was a key instrument in maintaining the government's authority.[1]

Another important army-controlled "security" body was the State Intelligence Coordinating Body (Bakin). In 1966 the new government decided to replace the dissolved Central Intelligence Board, which had been headed by Subandrio, with a new organization that commenced operations in 1967. The Bakin's role was to make intelligence assessments in fields outside those concerned directly with military affairs. It was particularly active in watching over internal developments in the political parties and the Chinese community as well as being alert for signs of a Communist revival.[2]

1. Initially headed by Suharto, the Kopkamtib was transferred to the newly appointed deputy commander of the armed forces, General Panggabean, in 1969, but day-to-day control was in the hands of his deputy, Lieutenant General Sumitro, who in 1973 replaced Panggabean as commander. Sumitro was dismissed in the wake of the Fifteenth of January Affair of 1974, after which Suharto himself resumed command of the Kopkamtib, with Admiral Sudomo as chief of staff.

2. In 1967, the Bakin was headed by the former head of army intelligence, Brigadier General Sudirgo, but he was dismissed in 1968 and arrested early in 1969—apparently for suspected Sukarnoist sympathies. His place was taken by Major General Yoga Sugama, a former member of Suharto's personal staff. At the end of 1969, Sudirgo's successor as head of army intelligence, Major General Sutopo Juwono, moved to the Bakin, but he, like Sumitro at the Kopkamtib, lost his position in the wake of the Fifteenth of January Affair. Yoga Sugama was recalled from a diplomatic appointment to take charge of the Bakin once again.

The Continued Suppression of the PKI

The chief target of the army's security drive was the PKI, which, as the army's main political opponent before 1965, had suffered most as the army rose to full power. Although the massacres of late 1965 had eliminated much of the PKI's leadership at all levels, the army's security and intelligence network continued to devote a large part of its attention to searching out and capturing those of the party's activists still at large. During 1966 there were signs that surviving leaders of the PKI had begun to take tentative steps toward reorganizing the party. After these moves failed, a more successful attempt was made to establish a base of support in the southern part of East Java, but this, too, was crushed in 1968. At the same time a Communist-supported insurgency, based on part of the Chinese minority in West Kalimantan, caused concern for local authorities, although it was not a threat to the regime as a whole. Despite the thoroughness with which the PKI had been repressed, the army leadership still continued to regard the possible revival of the party as the main long-term challenge to its grip on the government.

Many PKI activists who had survived the massacres were arrested during the last three months of 1965, and arrests continued during the following years. It was unofficially estimated that about 200,000 prisoners had been held immediately after the coup, but by July 1966 the attorney general, Major General Sugih Arto, said that the number of civilians in detention had fallen to 120,000, not including an undisclosed number from the armed forces.[3] In 1967 the prisoners were classified into three categories—Group A, those alleged to have been "directly involved" in the Thirtieth of September Movement; Group B, those who actively supported the PKI and therefore, according to official reasoning, were "indirectly involved" in the 1965 coup attempt; and Group C, those who had merely supported PKI mass organizations without playing an active leadership role. Many prisoners in the Group C category were peasants who had joined the PKI's peasant organization, the Indonesian Peasant Front (BTI), for entirely nonideological reasons. Prisoners in this group were gradually released according to local circumstances. Those in Group B, it was explained, were to be held

3. *Harian Kami,* 27 July 1967, *Angkatan Bersenjata,* 1 August 1966.

indefinitely without trial because the lack of evidence of their "direct involvement" made it impossible to charge them in court. Many in Group B were transferred to the agricultural prison camp on Buru Island, near Ambon, after 1970. Group A prisoners were gradually brought before military courts, which sentenced some to death and others to long periods of imprisonment.

The total number of prisoners gradually declined because releases apparently exceeded fresh arrests. There was a steady stream of releases after early in 1966, when inactive supporters of BTI began to be released in Central Java. In East Java, however, where the massacre had been less controlled than in Central Java, the number of prisoners was much smaller and their ranks had been further depleted during 1966 because prison-camp authorities in some areas released prisoners to members of the Muslim youth organization, Ansor, in exchange for small bribes. Reports of the killing of prisoners in other regions were not uncommon, and in 1969 the chairman of the Indonesian League of Human Rights, H. J. C. Princen, reported accounts of the killing of 860 prisoners in Purwodadi, a small town in a remote part of Central Java. In addition to the decrease due to release and unofficial execution, the number of prisoners was reduced by deaths resulting from poor conditions, inadequate diet, and lack of medical attention.[4] In 1974 the government announced that 30,000 prisoners remained—10,000 at Buru and the rest in other prisons.[5] Nevertheless, fresh arrests continued,[6] and official figures have been treated with much skepticism by such independent bodies as Amnesty International, which estimated that at least 55,000 were still being held in 1974. Following the release of Group C prisoners, the government announced in 1976 that all Group B prisoners would be "released" by 1979, but in fact many were to be sent to "transmigration" centers at Buru and elsewhere.

Although as many as half a million PKI supporters were killed in the massacres following the coup attempt and hundreds of

4. For an account of conditions in prisons, see Feith 1968b. Feith visited a number of prisons in 1967. See also Budiardjo 1974; Mrs. Carmel Budiardjo is a former political prisoner.

5. Statement by Adam Malik in *Merdeka,* 2 November 1974.

6. According to Admiral Sudomo of the Kopkamtib, about five hundred new arrests were made every year (*Kompas,* 23 December 1975).

thousands were either in prison or under surveillance as former prisoners,[7] an enormous number remained relatively unscathed. The PKI's claim of three million members and another twenty million in mass organizations was probably an exaggeration, but there is no reason to doubt that the party's potential base of support remained large after 1965. Because the party's leadership was crippled at all levels, many millions of former supporters and sympathizers were disillusioned, leaderless, and unorganized. Regardless of their innermost feelings, their recent experiences had convinced them that they had little to gain and much to lose in becoming associated with any underground network of the party. Nevertheless, surviving leadership elements did not lose all hope of reviving the party as an underground organization.

During 1966, Sudisman, the fourth-ranking PKI leader before October 1965, had attempted to revive the party organization under his own leadership. In the name of the Politburo he issued a statement on 17 August 1966 and a "self-criticism" in September 1966 in which he analyzed the party's faults in the past and pointed the way for the future. He condemned "the black line of right opportunism" adopted earlier by the party leadership in which the party identified itself with the policies of President Sukarno. He argued instead that the party had to disabuse itself of "modern revisionism" and realize that "the armed struggle of the people against the armed counterrevolutionaries is unavoidable and constitutes the chief form of struggle in the coming revolution. . . . a protracted armed struggle which is integrated with the agrarian revolution of the peasants in the countryside." Sudisman called on the party "to devote special attention to studying the Thought of Mao Tse-tung who has succeeded in brilliantly inheriting, defending, and developing Marxism-Leninism to its peak in the present era."[8]

In Jakarta, Sudisman tried to rebuild the party on a base of

7. See article in *Merdeka*, 17 September 1974, which states that a total of 540,000 prisoners had been released, implying that at least that number had been held at one time or another since 1965, although it is unlikely that the number at any one time ever exceeded 200,000–300,000.

8. See *People of Indonesia, Unite and Fight to Overthrow the Fascist Regime* for extracts from the statement (pp. 11–24) and the self-criticism (pp. 25–56). Quotations are from pp. 20, 23, 27, 49. See also Sudisman's "Uraian Tanggung-Jawab" at Sudisman trial (II, 96–141).

interlocking groups of three members, but he made little progress before he was captured in December 1966. Meanwhile, in East Java, other leaders began to apply Sudisman's ideas in the country-side. Led by the Politburo member, Rewang, the party theorist, Oloan Hutapea, and the East Java leader, Ruslan Widjajasastra, the party began to regroup in an isolated region south of Blitar in East Java. In this area the peasants were extremely poor, nearly all *abangan,* and previously identified largely with the PKI. The bad condition of roads and other forms of communication per-mitted the PKI refugees to carry out their activities unhindered, and they were joined by the former commander of the Pande-glang Military District in West Java, Lieutenant Colonel Pratomo, who helped to give military training. It seems unlikely that the PKI leaders in South Blitar ordered the opening of a guerrilla offensive, but their presence in the area and the military training they organized apparently encouraged local *abangan* peasants to take their revenge by killing Muslim leaders, whom they blamed for the earlier massacres. By March 1968, some sixty killings of NU figures had alerted the military authorities, who organized a full-scale and highly successful offensive in mid-1968. Thus the one serious attempt after 1965 to revive the PKI was crushed.

Communist-led guerrilla activities in West Kalimantan also caused concern for the government, although the Kalimantan guerrillas apparently had few links with the surviving PKI leader-ship in Java. Rather, the West Kalimantan insurgents were linked with Chinese dissidents in neighboring Sarawak, who in turn were assisted by deserters from the Diponegoro division who had been in Kalimantan during the confrontation campaign. By 1968, how-ever, the guerrilla movement had been largely defeated, although small-scale resistance continued to be reported.

The vigilance of the army's intelligence and security apparatus and its capacity to mobilize overwhelming armed strength at the first sign of Communist regrouping enabled the government to prevent an open resurgence of the PKI. Nevertheless, the potential base of support for a resurgent radical movement remained in the rural areas, towns, and cities of Java from which the PKI had drawn its support in the past.[9] Thus the army leaders' almost obses-

9. For an assessment of the PKI's predicament in 1970, see McVey 1971a.

sive concern to suppress all indications of renewed Communist activity was not entirely groundless. More importantly, the specter of a revived PKI played a vital legitimating role for the military leadership, allowing it to present itself to anti-Communist civilians as the only force capable of saving the nation from Communism.

Consolidation within the Armed Forces

In confronting the challenge posed by the PKI's potential for revival, Suharto used unrelenting and often brutal repression. But in consolidating his control over the armed forces, he followed the Javanese principle of *alon alon asal kelakon* in moving step by step against successive groups of rivals. After establishing his control over the army headquarters in late 1965, he moved against his potential rivals among the regional commanders during 1966 and simultaneously succeeded in easing Nasution into a prominent but relatively powerless civilian position. The few remaining officers who had held senior positions under Yani were soon replaced, and the process of consolidation was gradually completed during the next few years with the removal of the "New Order militants," who had called for more far-reaching reform than Suharto and his colleagues wanted. Meanwhile, Suharto sought to force the other branches of the armed forces to accept his authority. After he was appointed as minister for defense and security in 1966, he at first permitted the other branches to retain their formal independence, while he was moving to undermine their capacity to take independent action. In 1969 the long-promised integration of the armed forces took place, with the transfer of full operational command of all four branches to Suharto as commander of the armed forces.

The emergence of Suharto from relative obscurity to the command of the army in October 1965 had been partly fortuitous. It seems most unlikely that he would have succeeded to the army leadership if Yani and his colleagues had not been assassinated on 1 October, even though Suharto was one of the army's most senior and experienced officers. He had gained a good reputation as a young officer during the revolution, especially when he led an assault on Yogyakarta in March 1949. After serving as commander of the Diponegoro division in Central Java from 1956 to 1959, he had been appointed—after taking a course at the Seskoad—as first deputy to the army chief of staff in 1960 and then, in 1962, as commander of the forces preparing for the invasion of West Irian. Later, as commander of the Kostrad, he had authority over all army troops involved in the "confrontation" campaign against Malaysia, and acted in Yani's stead when the army commander's travels prevented him from carrying out his official duties in Jakarta.[10] Despite his seniority, however, he was not a member of Yani's inner circle of political advisers, and his failure to establish warm rapport with President Sukarno had made it improbable that he would ever be called upon to take command of the army.

The assassination of Yani and his closest colleagues and the disappearance of Nasution into hiding had given Suharto the opportunity to take effective command of the army on the morning of 1 October 1965. As the most senior officer in Jakarta with direct control of troops, Suharto had immediately asserted his authority. The other generals with whom he had contact accepted his authority, apparently preferring him to the only other available general with comparable status, Yani's Sukarnoist first deputy, Major General Mursjid. During that day, Suharto's stature had been enhanced by his cool-headed moves to bring Jakarta under control without bloodshed. With the support of Nasution, Suharto rejected Sukarno's appointment of Pranoto, and on 16 October he was installed as the minister/commander of the army in place of Yani.

The circumstances of his appointment as army commander gave Suharto an exceptionally free hand in appointing the members of his general staff. Of the old general staff, the commander, two of the three deputies, and two of the seven assistants had been killed on 1 October, while another assistant, Pranoto, had been compromised so that his replacement was easily justified. In reorganizing the general staff, Suharto replaced three of the remaining assistants, leaving only the Sukarnoist Mursjid as the first deputy for operations and Major General Alamsjah Ratu Perwiranegara, an old associate of Suharto's, as the seventh assistant for finance, from Yani's staff. By the beginning of November 1965, the army's general staff consisted almost entirely of officers handpicked by Suharto himself.

10. For biographical data on Suharto, see Roeder 1969.

Suharto's grip on the army headquarters was not matched by similar authority over the regional commanders, who had become accustomed to the enjoyment of considerable autonomy and many of whom had built up personal bases of support in their areas. Further, some of the commanders had warm ties with Sukarno, whose antagonism toward Suharto was becoming increasingly apparent in the weeks and months after 1 October. The regional commanders had been adept under Yani at blocking initiatives from the PKI while voicing support for the policies espoused by the president and had endorsed Suharto's policy of crushing the PKI, but they showed far less consensus on how to deal with the president. Several commanders in areas such as Central and East Java where popular support for Sukarno was strong were reluctant to back Suharto's moves against the president, and some, whose qualifications were comparable to Suharto's, hoped that Suharto would overplay his hand and give Sukarno the opportunity to appoint a new commander. Such regional commanders as Adjie in West Java, Mokoginta in Sumatra, and Rukman in East Indonesia had enough prestige and authority that they might be able to act independently of Suharto.

Suharto moved against his potential challengers and their supporters among the regional commanders gradually during 1966 and the first part of 1967. As the movement against the president gathered momentum, his friends in the army found themselves increasingly isolated, and the more important among them were usually willing to accept ambassadorships or other rewarding posts. The leftist Brigadier General Rukman had been transferred in January 1966 from the interregional command in East Indonesia to the headquarters staff,[11] but not until after 11 March when tension increased as the fourth session of the MPRS approached in June did Suharto feel both able and compelled to transfer several pro-Sukarno regional commanders, including those of the key provinces of West Java and Central Java, both of whom lost effective command of their division in May 1966. Major General Adjie, the Siliwangi commander, who had openly expressed his support for Sukarno, was appointed in July 1966 as ambassador in London. The Diponegoro commander, Major

11. Rukman was appointed as inspector general of the army in July 1966 and arrested in 1968.

General Surjosumpeno, became the president's military secretary and, in 1967, a senior official in the Department of Internal Affairs. Also in May, Major General Mursjid was relieved of his post as first deputy and later sent as ambassador to the Philippines.[12] Finally, early in 1967, the strongly Islamic but pro-Sukarno interregional commander for Sumatra, Lieutenant General Mokoginta, was appointed as ambassador to the United Arab Republic after the United States had made known its reluctance to accept him as ambassador in Washington, presumably because of his military background. With the removal of Mokoginta, all the regional commanders appointed by Yani had been either moved to new commands selected for them by Suharto or transferred to civilian posts. The seventeen regional commands and three interregional commands were thus all filled by Suharto's appointees.

The consolidation of Suharto's hold on the regional commanders was accompanied by moves to curb Nasution's influence. As the army's most senior general, it might have been expected that Nasution should have taken over command on 1 October 1965. But, injured and concerned about the condition of his mortally wounded five-year-old daughter, Nasution had not challenged Suharto's right to lead the operations against the Thirtieth of September Movement. Moreover, in view of Sukarno's undisguised distrust of Nasution and the army's strategy of avoiding an open rift with the president, the senior army generals may have calculated that it would be better to keep Nasution in the background. After Sukarno had rejected Suharto's suggestion that Nasution be reappointed as army commander in October 1965,[13] Nasution apparently sought to turn the Department of Defense and Security into a major focus of power. Suharto, however, had not pushed Nasution's candidature with much vigor in October, and following Nasution's dismissal as minister for defense and security in February 1966, Suharto had not insisted on his reappointment when the opportunity arose in the cabinet reshuffle after 11 March. Apparently realizing that Suharto was using Sukarno's objections as a pretext to prevent his return to office, Nasution accepted the prominent but not powerful position of chairman of the MPRS. Although Nasution's prestige was very

12. Mursjid was arrested on his return from the Philippines late in 1969.
13. Nasution 1971:402.

great, his disapproval of the corrupt commercial activities of army officers, which had expanded during Yani's period in office, had made many officers reluctant to see him return to real power in the army. Further, the army leaders felt that in the circumstances of 1965–1966, the army needed a Javanese commander in facing President Sukarno, whose strongest supporters were Javanese.

In gradually establishing his preeminence among his former peers, Suharto had initially used more carrot than stick. As his potential rivals were isolated one by one, each was offered an attractive alternative appropriate to his standing and inclinations. As long as Sukarno retained the presidency, Suharto had felt inhibited from taking more drastic measures, but during 1967 he turned increasingly to coercion in consolidating his position in the army. During the movement against Sukarno, the president's main support lay in Central and East Java and to a lesser extent in North Sumatra, all areas where the PKI formerly and the PNI currently had substantial influence. In these areas also sympathy for Sukarno within the armed forces, including the army, had been significant.

Although popular support for Sukarno had been very strong in Central Java, the Diponegoro division of this province was not a major source of resistance. It had been largely neutralized by the internal turmoil that followed the 1965 coup. According to the new Diponegoro commander, Major General Surono, about 20 percent of the division had been regarded as "involved" in the Thirtieth of September Movement.[14] Many officers and men were arrested and eventually some 1,500 were dishonorably discharged and another 1,100 were suspended, pensioned, or otherwise punished.[15] The appointment of Surono in June 1966 had placed the division under the command of a loyal supporter of Suharto's leadership, and he had little difficulty in asserting his authority over the division's largely demoralized officer corps.

Conditions were very different in the Brawijaya division of East

14. *Api Pantjasila,* 26 September 1966. Following this report, a spokesman for the division said that only 6 percent of its members had been "involved" (ibid., 1 October 1966). The 6 percent figure probably refers to those against whom disciplinary action was taken and who therefore, presumably, were mainly officers. The 20 percent figure apparently referred to the proportion of troops mobilized by the Thirtieth of September Movement.
15. Military source.

Java, where few officers had been more than marginally associated with the Thirtieth of September Movement, so that during
the purges that followed the movement's defeat, the division had
remained more or less intact. Unlike many middle-level and junior officers in Central Java, the Sukarnoists in East Java had
been steadfastly anti-Communist; thus many Brawijaya officers
with pro-Sukarno sympathies retained local commands during
1966 and resented Sukarno's deposition in 1967. They regarded
the East Javanese Sukarno as in some way their own patron and
saw his fall as a threat to their own position within the army.

The central army leadership had made no attempt to weed out
Sukarnoist influence in the Brawijaya division during 1966. In the
middle of that year, Sumitro, who had close family connections
with PNI leaders in the province, was placed in command of the
division, but his role was limited to preventing the outburst of open
defiance rather than purging the division of potential dissidents.
Only after Sukarno's dismissal, when the former military attaché in
Moscow, Major General Jasin, took command were preparations
commenced for what was called the "New Orderization" of East
Java.

The purge in East Java followed a meeting in July 1967 of the
four regional commanders in Java (Jakarta, West Java, Central
Java, and East Java) and the commanders of the Kostrad and
RPKAD. In a statement issued after the meeting at Yogyakarta on
7 July, they said that "it is clear that there are forces which still
undermine the decrees of the Special Session of the MPRS, 1967,"
and they announced their intention to "take firm action against
anyone or any group which tries to restore the authority of the
Old Order leader, Dr. Ir. Sukarno."[16] In August, RPKAD units
were placed at the disposal of the Brawijaya commander, Jasin.
Jasin, who had already replaced three of the four resort commanders and sent five senior officers to "study" at the army college, Seskoad, in Bandung, then began the long-expected purge,
arresting a number of officers, including the newly dismissed Surabaya resort commander, Colonel Willy Sudjono. In addition,
the governor of East Java, Major General Wijono, who had just
completed three months of study at Seskoad, was replaced, and
the regional police commander, Brigadier General Sumarsono,

16. *Nusantara*, 10 July 1967.

was dismissed and then arrested. The PNI, which had occupied a strong position in local government, was the main civilian target of the purge. Its activities were "frozen" and its leaders given an ultimatum to rid themselves of Sukarnoists by the end of the year, while many of its supporters were dismissed from public office and some were arrested.

While the New Orderization of East Java was taking place, the former RPKAD commander, Brigadier General Sarwo Edhie, commenced a similar purge in his new command of North Sumatra. Following the lead of the Java commanders in July, Sarwo Edhie announced that he was "declaring war on supporters and remnants of the Old Order whose exalted leader is Dr. Ir. Sukarno," and at the end of September fifty-one members of the army and forty-one civilians had been arrested.[17] At the same time Sarwo Edhie banned the PNI from organizing activities.

In eliminating Sukarnoist influence from the army, Suharto had made use of a number of strongly anti-Sukarnoist officers on whom he could rely to carry out a thorough program of "de-Sukarnoization." At the core of this group were two PSI-influenced Siliwangi officers, Major Generals Dharsono and Kemal Idris, who held the extremely important Siliwangi and Kostrad commands. Closely allied to them was the new North Sumatra commander, Sarwo Edhie, a Diponegoro officer whose charismatic qualities had become apparent during his term as RPKAD commander. Other regional commanders who shared the general outlook of this group were such Siliwangi officers as Brigadier General Ishak Djuarsa, the Aceh commander until May 1967 and then commander in South Sumatra, Witono, the new West Kalimantan commander, and Solihin Gautama Purwanegara, the commander in South and Southeast Sulawesi. In addition, the new commanders in Aceh and East Java were broadly sympathetic to the "militant" group, especially in their antagonism toward Sukarnoist remnants.

Although the militant officers were never a tightly knit group, they shared some attitudes. During 1966 they had been impatient with Suharto's cautious strategy in dealing with the president, and at the time of the 1967 MPRS session they had called not only for Sukarno's dismissal but also his trial. They had great contempt for the party politicians, whom they regarded as opportunists lacking

17. Ibid., 30 September 1967.

the moral strength to stand up to Sukarno. They particularly disliked the PNI, which the more extreme among then wanted to ban. Moreover, officers in the group had begun to express concern for the army's reputation because more and more senior officers were being appointed to positions in government and economic enterprises that presented them with many illegal opportunities to add to their incomes. As the wealth of the generals closest to Suharto grew visibly, officers in the militant group associated themselves with the growing protest against corruption made by the Action Fronts and a section of the press. Members of such Action Front circles as the students' front, KAMI, and the graduates' front, KASI, regarded these generals as dynamic and vigorous leaders who aimed to use the army's power to "modernize" Indonesian society. The completion of the purge of the Sukarnoists left the relatively dashing leaders of the "New Order militants" as the only visible source of dissidence in the army.

An open rift arose between the militants and the government over the question of what role the political parties would be permitted under the New Order. The strongly anti-Sukarnoist outlook of the militant officers had led several among them to take extremely harsh measures against the PNI, especially in Sumatra, where the party was banned in Aceh, North Sumatra, and South Sumatra during 1967. Although Suharto had approved the purge of the PNI conducted by Jasin in East Java and had not complained about the effective control exercised over the party by Dharsono in West Java and by Solihin in South Sulawesi, he clearly disapproved of action taken by the three commanders in Sumatra that seemed aimed at the dissolution of the PNI. After the government had made its position clear, the commanders of Aceh and South Sumatra refrained from imposing formal bans on the PNI, although they continued to put pressure on its leaders to keep their party in "voluntary" liquidation. The volatile Sarwo Edhie, on the other hand, openly questioned the government's approach,[18] and in December 1967, the chief of staff of

18. In a disgruntled mood after an interview with the acting commander of the army, General Panggabean, on 9 October 1967, Sarwo Edhie asked a journalist, "What will happen to the instructions we have been given, as well as our own convictions, that we must bring about a victory of the New Order if I am now instructed to embrace the PNI which follows Sukarno's teachings? Isn't this a contradiction?" (*Harian Kami*, 13 October 1967).

the interregional command in Sumatra, Brigadier General J. Muskita, felt it necessary to take personal command of Sarwo Edhie's troops to ensure acceptance of government policy. The commanders in Aceh and South Sumatra retained their posts and were permitted to continue their policy of unofficial persecution of the PNI. Sarwo Edhie, however, was transferred to West Irian during 1968 and at the beginning of 1970 to the Armed Forces Academy, where he had no troops under his command.

While Sarwo Edhie had been repressing the PNI in North Sumatra, his colleagues, Dharsono and Kemal Idris, had been agitating in favor of an election law designed to reduce drastically the role of the political parties. In 1968 they advocated a major overhaul of the political system, including the dissolution of the existing parties and the creation of two new parties based on the Action Fronts and the younger generation. But they were not able to win widespread support for their outspoken views from their military colleagues, and when Dharsono, without Suharto's approval, began to enforce the implementation of a modified version of his two-party scheme in local assemblies in West Java at the beginning of 1969, Suharto moved against them. In February, Kemal Idris was "promoted" to the interregional command in East Indonesia with headquarters in Makassar; shortly afterward Dharsono was appointed as ambassador to Thailand. Although Dharsono was succeeded as commander of the Siliwangi division by Witono, who had earlier shared some of his attitudes, the back of the "radical" opposition had been broken and Suharto's supremacy further secured.

By 1969 all important command positions in the army were filled by men who fully accepted Suharto's authority. Officers who had risen to high positions under Yani had been transferred to nonmilitary roles and the potentially dangerous group of militants dispersed. Suharto relied on officers who, like himself, had little vision of a really "new order" for Indonesia and were primarily concerned with stabilizing the existing system. Although Sukarnoist feeling had been strong in the Brawijaya division and various "militant New Order" sentiments were common in the Siliwangi division, the dissent that had been apparent in these quarters had arisen as much from a sense of being left out in the division of power, prestige, and spoils in Jakarta as it had from ideology. In full control of the government machinery, Suharto dispensed patronage widely, with the result that his leadership gained a broad base of support. While his closest confidants continued to be his old colleagues from the Diponegoro division and the West Irian campaign, the other divisions were well represented in the military elite.[19] By assuring officers from these divisions that their interests were not being neglected, Suharto was able to undermine the bases of support of his potential rivals.

Having gained unchallenged supremacy within the army, Suharto moved to complete the consolidation of his authority in the other branches of the armed forces during the last three months of 1969. Under Sukarno the four services had operated more or less independently of each other because the president expected the air force, navy, and police to balance the power of the army. The air force, like the Diponegoro division in the army, had been thoroughly purged because of the involvement of prominent officers in the coup attempt and therefore had limited political significance after 1966. But the navy and police, like the Brawijaya, had no major involvement in the Thirtieth of September Movement and were largely unaffected by the ensuing purges; thus their political vitality was little diminished by them. Concerned that the army leadership would seek to dominate the armed forces as a whole, the navy and police leadership threw in their lot with the president during 1966 and were consequently in a very vulnerable position when he fell in March 1967. Nevertheless, Suharto refrained from precipitating a crisis by moving against them until he had secured firm control over the army.

During 1966 the police commander, Sutjipto Judodihardjo, conducted a mild purge within the police force. By the middle of the year, 713 of the force's 125,000 members had been dismissed or suspended, including 2 senior officers and 35 middle-ranking

19. Among the "moderate" Siliwangi officers to gain important positions were Umar Wirahadikusumah (commander of Kostrad, 1965; deputy commander of the army, 1967; chief of staff of the army, 1969); Amir Machmud (regional commander in Jakarta, 1965; minister for internal affairs, 1969); and Sugih Arto (assistant for intelligence, 1965; attorney general, 1966). The Brawijaya was represented by Basuki Rachmat (minister for internal affairs, 1966–1969); Sarbini (minister for veterans' affairs, 1966); Sumitro (deputy for operations, 1967; chief of staff of Department of Defense and Security, 1969; deputy commander of Kopkamtib, 1969; commander of Kopkamtib, 1973); and Jasin (deputy chief of staff of army, 1969).

officers.[20] The majority of those purged were low-ranking members of the force, mainly in East and Central Java, where policemen had sometimes sided with the PKI in small-town politics. The police force did not finally succumb to army pressure to purge its more outspoken Sukarnoist officers until the latter part of 1967. In August, the former police commander in Jakarta, Brigadier general Sawarno Tjokrodiningrat, was arrested, the current commander in Central Java was replaced, and, under the New Orderization process in East Java, the regional commander, Sumarsono, and several of his colleagues were arrested. Finally, in 1968, Sutjipto was relieved of his command and replaced by Commissioner General Hugeng Imam Santoso, his first deputy, who was usually regarded as a "PSI type."

As the police force wilted under army pressure, the navy stood firm, backed by its marine corps, the Kko. With the unyielding support of the Kko commander, Lieutenant General Hartono, the navy commander, Admiral Muljadi, refused to carry out a purge of the extent needed to satisfy the army's demands. The Kko, with its main base in East Java, had resisted the New Orderization process conducted by Jasin. Referring to the conduct of the purge, Rear Admiral Sujatno, the commander of the 5th Naval Region based in Surabaya, had paid lip service to the principle of New Orderization, but added, "I am not fully convinced that the attempt will be successful if we continue to use PKI and Old Order tactics, in which violence, intimidation, prejudice, and beating up are carried to extremes."[21] Shots had been exchanged between "individuals" in the Kko and army troops at Probolinggo in June 1967,[22] and during the RPKAD's operations some of its members were injured in a grenade explosion at Wonokromo[23] and shots reportedly were fired at Jombang.[24] The RPKAD commander, Brigadier General Willy Sujono, admitted that his troops had exchanged fire with "uniformed individuals," implying that

20. *Angkatan Bersenjata,* 26 July 1966.
21. *Kompas,* 7 September 1967.
22. A spokesman for the Brawijaya division said that there had been no conflict between the army and the Kko, but "what recently happened was the result of a conflict between individuals." He added that no one had been killed in the incident (*Surabaya Post* 16 June 1967).
23. Ibid., 19 August 1967.
24. *Harian Kami,* 12 September 1967.

they were members of the armed forces, presumably from the Kko.[25] But, although the navy and Kko leaders were able to defend themselves during the New Orderization campaign, they were unable to prevent the purge of their allies.

The navy continued to maintain its independence until the end of 1969, as was very apparent in the steady stream of outspoken left-nationalist criticism of the new government printed in the bi-weekly newspaper, *El Bahar,* published from an office in a building owned by the Kko. *El Bahar* was edited by Commodore R. S. Puguh, the secretary to the navy and a nephew of Sukarno's. Suharto, however, had been only biding his time. After Hartono was replaced as Kko commander in September 1968 and appointed as ambassador to North Korea in 1969 and Muljadi was replaced as navy commander at the end of 1969 in preparation for posting as ambassador to the Soviet Union, the long-delayed purge took place. Muljadi was succeeded by Rear Admiral Sudomo, an old colleague of Suharto's, who had commanded the naval force during the West Irian campaign, and several officers, including Puguh, the former minister for maritime affairs, Rear Admiral Jatidjan, and the head of the Naval Information Center, Commodore Sjamsu Sutjipto, were placed under house arrest. At the same time, the Kko's relative autonomy was eliminated by its closer integration into the naval command structure.

The army's ascendancy over the other three services had been facilitated by the increasingly run-down condition of their supplies and equipment. During the Guided Democracy period, the navy and air force had been heavily dependent on aid from the USSR and other Communist countries for their armaments, but after 1965 new aid was not available from these sources. When the navy commander, Muljadi, visited the Soviet Union in the latter part of 1967 to discuss the possibility of obtaining naval spare parts, he was told that supplies would be made available only on a cash basis. The new government's foreign-financed program of economic stabilization and rehabilitation meant that funds were not available for armaments purchases and certainly not from the Soviet Union. As a result, the navy and air force, which depended on a more advanced technology than did the

25. *Surabaya Post,* 21 September 1967.

army, were unable to keep their equipment in working order. Early in 1970, the new chief of staff of the air force, Air Vice Marshal Suwoto Sukandar, said that only 15 to 20 percent of the air force's airplanes could fly because of the unavailability of spare parts from the Soviet Union.[26] Later in 1970 the navy's inspector general said that only 40 percent of the navy's vessels could be used,[27] and in 1971 a parliamentary commission reported on the "extremely sad" state of the navy's fleet.[28]

With the final breaking of the navy's remaining political power, no barrier remained to Suharto's complete domination over the armed forces. In October 1969, plans were announced which deprived the four services of all operational independence. To emphasize their reduced status, the army, navy, and air force commanders were henceforth known as "chiefs of staff" with the function of implementing the policies and orders of Suharto as commander of the armed forces and his deputy, General Panggabean, while the police force was given separate status within the Department of Defense and Security as a demilitarized law enforcement agency. To implement the reorganization in the regions, six integrated Regional Defense Commands (Kowilhan) were established, with army officers in charge in Java, Sumatra, and East Indonesia, while the remaining three areas were placed under the command of two naval officers and an air force officer.[29] With the successful implementation of the integration policy in 1970, interservice competition was no longer a matter of major concern for Suharto.

Suharto had shown great patience in his gradual extension of control over the army and the armed forces, following the pattern set on 1 October 1965, when he had negotiated with the troops stationed in front of the president's palace instead of fighting them. Conscious that the balance of forces was in his favor, he had persuaded the battalion commanders on that day that resistance would be futile. When the anti-Communist massacres had turned the national balance irrevocably in the army's favor, he had convinced the air force that it must sacrifice its leadership.

26. *Kompas,* 10 March 1970.
27. Ibid., 9 October 1970.
28. *Harian Kami,* 12 February 1971.
29. In 1973 the number of Kowilhan was reduced to four.

During 1966 and early 1967, he moved against key army commanders, first the leftist Rukman, then the Sukarnoist commanders in Java, and finally Mokoginta in Sumatra, while outmaneuvering Nasution in Jakarta. Having dealt with his most senior rivals, he turned to the Sukarnoist opposition, especially in East Java and in the police, then against the "ultras" among his allies in the army, especially from the Siliwangi division, and, only after fully consolidating his authority over his own force, completed the process with the subjugation of the navy and the formal organizational integration of the armed forces. Over four years, Suharto had isolated and then eliminated one source of potential opposition after another, until at the end of 1969 no effective opposition in the armed forces remained.

The Army's Grip on the Government

Although the army in fact dominated the government after 1966, it sought to associate civilians of various types with it, partly to draw on their skills and experience, partly to create an atmosphere of domestic legitimacy, and partly to create a favorable image among Western aid donors.

The appearance of a civilian-military partnership was most pronounced in the composition of the cabinet, where the military members were always in a minority, their numbers declining in successive cabinet reshuffles. In the twenty-seven-member cabinet appointed by Suharto in July 1966, six ministers were drawn from the army and another six, including the service commanders, from the other branches of the armed forces. The army representatives held the key Departments of Defense and Security and Internal Affairs, as well as important economic departments. As the army's grip on the government tightened during the next few years, however, its representation in the cabinet declined to four out of twenty-three in 1968 and three after the 1971 elections, although one more was added in 1973. The other services were represented by only one minister each from the navy and air force from 1968 and a solitary air force officer after 1971, who was replaced by a civilian in 1973.

Although civilians were in a majority in the cabinet, they lacked the political backing to exercise real power. The representation of the parties that had potential for mobilizing popular support, particularly the PNI and the NU, was increasingly overshadowed by the appointment of ministers whose qualifications were essentially technocratic. In the cabinet appointed in July 1966, the PNI and the NU were allocated two positions each, while the remaining ten civilians either lacked party affiliation or belonged to small parties with no mass base. The technocratic character of the cabinet became more evident in 1968, when the important Departments of Trade and Finance were allocated to Professors Sumitro Djojohadikusumo and Ali Wardhana, respectively, and in 1971 another four prominent economists, including Professor Widjojo Nitisastro, joined the cabinet, which by then included ten professors and several others with high academic qualifications. Although the political parties retained nominal representation, the cabinet had become essentially technocratic in nature, with its civilian members performing the functions of civil servants more than those of political leaders. Like the cabinets led by Sukarno, the cabinet under Suharto was not a decision-making body, but met mainly to hear guidelines from the president and to report to him. As members of the economic stabilization committee, the economists in the cabinet played an important role in economic policy making but, lacking political strength of their own, they had to adapt themselves to formulating and administering policies within a framework set by the generals.

The scope of the civilian ministers was further limited by the appointment of army officers to high positions in the civil service. Of the twenty departments concerned with civilian affairs in 1966, army officers held the position of secretary general in ten and a naval officer was appointed in another. Of the sixty-four directors-general appointed at the same time, fifteen were army officers and eight were from the other three services. Only two departments whose minister was not an army general had no army officers at the level of secretary general or director general, and one of these was the navy-dominated Department of Maritime Affairs.[30] The role of military men in the bureaucracy remained important in succeeding years.

30. The list of secretaries general and directors general is in *Angkatan Bersenjata*, 8 August 1966. Each department had a secretary general concerned with administration and personnel and two or three directors general concerned with the operations of the department.

While the cabinet's role in the early years of the New Order was essentially one of administrative coordination, many policy decisions were made by a select group of army officers who enjoyed Suharto's confidence. The deputy commander of the army, Lieutenant General Panggabean, and the minister for internal affairs, Major General Basuki Rachmat—until his death in 1969— exercised great influence. Complete control over Indonesia's main export commodity, oil, was left in the hands of Major General Ibnu Sutowo. A new agency, the National Logistics Board (Bulog), headed by Brigadier General Achmad Tirtosudiro, was established with full control over the food grain trade, and Brigadier General Suhardiman took control of the giant trading corporation, PT Berdikari. Most important, Suharto set up his personal staff (Spri), which at the time of its formation in August 1966 consisted of six army officers and two teams of civilian specialists concerned with providing advice in the fields of economic policy and politics. By 1968 the Spri had grown to twelve and was widely regarded as the "invisible cabinet" wielding real power. Headed by Major General Alamsjah,[31] its key members included Major General Surjo, who had headed the financial section of the Koti, and three relatively junior officers who had served under Suharto during his term as commander of Central Java's Diponegoro division in the late 1950s and later in the Kostrad in the 1960s. They were Colonels Ali Murtopo and Sudjono Humardhani and Brigadier General Yoga Sugama. Sudjono Humardhani had a background in military financing, and Ali Murtopo and Yoga Sugama were intelligence officers. Ali Murtopo also headed an all-purpose outfit known as Opsus (Special Operations), which had been set up originally in the Kostrad where it was involved in secret contacts with Malaysia during the confrontation campaign. In response to growing public criticism of the "invisible cabinet," Suharto formally dissolved the Spri in 1968, but its main members continued to wield as much influence as before.

31. Very wealthy himself, Alamsjah was the epitome of the military entrepreneur with numerous interests in the commercial world. Originally from South Sumatra, where he had served as an intelligence officer under Colonel Ibnu Sutowo, among others, he had crossed to Jakarta when South Sumatra seemed on the point of joining the PRRI rebellion. He joined Suharto's staff in 1960 and in 1965 was appointed as seventh assistant to the army commander, with responsibility for the army's finances.

The dominant position of army officers in the central government was accompanied by a similar growth in army representation in regional administration. At the beginning of 1966, twelve out of twenty-four provincial governors were army officers, including those in such important provinces as Jakarta, West Java, and East Java. By 1968 the number of army officer had risen to sixteen, and a naval officer, Lieutenant General Ali Sadikin of the Kko, was governor of Jakarta. After the 1971 elections, the number of civilian governors fell to four out of twenty-six.

The number of army officers appointed to positions in the regional administration increased also at the level of *bupatis* and mayors. In East and Central Java, military officers quickly replaced PKI and PKI-linked mayors and *bupatis* in 1965, and during the next few years many more civilians were replaced not only in these regions but throughout Indonesia. Between 1965 and 1968 the number of civilian *bupatis* and mayors fell from 15 to 3 in West Java, 38 to 19 in Central Java and Yogyakarta, and 33 to 20 in East Java, out of 23, 40, and 37 respectively. By 1969 the number of military *bupatis* and mayors had risen to 147 out of 271 throughout Indonesia.[32] After the 1971 elections the proportion reached about two-thirds.[33]

The army's domination of the government machinery at all levels enabled it to set the tone of the entire administration. Even though positions of authority were shared with civilians, the civilians had to fit into a system in which power lay with the military. Control of the administration meant not only that the army had strong influence over government policies at all levels, but also that officers could distribute benefits and dispense patronage to their military colleagues and civilian friends. Appointments throughout the administration became dependent on the approval of army officers, and power over the issuing of licenses, granting of contracts, and determination of projects enabled the army to reward those who accepted military domination and to penalize those who did not. Further, the army's power to make appointments in the bureaucracy enabled it to find lucrative and prestigious positions and favored business opportunities to compensate recalcitrant officers removed from military commands.

32. Information from the Department of Internal Affairs.
33. See Tinker and Walker 1973:1104.

10 | The Emasculation of the Political Parties

The emergence of the army to a position of unchallenged domination of the government had been welcomed enthusiastically by a small section of civilian political opinion and accepted as an unavoidable reality by most of the rest. In the wake of the turbulence of the preceding period, army rule seemed at least to guarantee a more stable political climate. Further, many civilians hoped that in the new atmosphere the army would feel the need to seek popular acceptance and support by associating civilians with the regime. Political stabilization in the long run, it seemed, would require the setting up of a new political framework within which civilian groups could be accommodated. However, in the accommodation that eventually emerged, popular participation through the political parties had no important place.

The role the existing political parties would be permitted under the New Order, however, was initially uncertain. Army officers in general had little respect for most of the party politicians who had been prominent during the Guided Democracy period, and they regarded the political parties as patronage machines serving limited sectional interests. Having gained control of the government for themselves, the army leaders had no intention of handing power over to the political parties in the name of "democracy." A small but articulate group of senior officers, who were influenced by members of the banned PSI and who cooperated closely with students and intellectuals in Action Fronts such as the KAMI and KASI, believed that firm action should be taken to prevent the reemergence of the parties as significant forces in national and local politics and that the army should rely on the Action Fronts for civilian support. On the other hand, it was widely appreciated, especially by regional and local commanders in Java, that the established parties had real roots in society which gave them a potential for rallying popular opposition to the government and made it difficult for the army simply to push them aside. Most of the army leaders were therefore reluctant to provoke a head-on collision with the parties, which might lead to further political upheaval and would certainly increase the difficulties of regional and local military commanders responsible for the maintenance of law and order. Officers in the latter group were usually not especially sympathetic to the aspirations of the political parties, but they were in no hurry to move against them.

The argument put by the antiparty "militants" was based on the belief that the army leadership was committed to "modernization" and "development," while the parties stood for "sectional interests" inimical to national goals. In this view, the repression of the parties would allow the government to carry out its program unencumbered by the need to give concessions to the "vested interests" represented by the party politicians. In place of the existing political parties, they envisaged the formation of new civilian organizations recruited from members of the younger generation, who had participated enthusiastically in the movement against Sukarno and the Old Order. Unlike the old parties, which were rooted in the habits and communal loyalties of the past, the new civilian forces were expected to give full support to the government's program of modernization. Further, it was clear, although not stated explicitly, that the new organizations would lack the popular support of the old parties, especially outside the main cities, and would therefore be in no position to obstruct policies that failed to meet with their approval.

Although the drastic attack on the parties advocated by the militants was rejected by the "moderates" around Suharto in 1967 and 1968, some of the ideas of the militant approach to military-civilian relations continued to be influential. After the upheaval and tension of the eighteen months preceding Sukarno's dismissal, the army leadership did not want to create another period of strain and uncertainty by unnecessarily provoking the political parties. It is clear in retrospect that many of the army moderates shared the militants' contempt for the party leaders and did not abandon the long-run goal of destroying the old parties, but they regarded the problem as less urgent and chose gradual means. Instead of direct repression, they eventually engineered the defeat of the parties at their own game in the 1971 general elections. Establishing its own civilian organization to contest the elections, the army ensured that its civilian arm scored an overwhelming victory, which reduced independently organized civilian influence to insignificant proportions. At the beginning of 1973, the old parties "voluntarily" dissolved themselves and formed two new "parties" under government-endorsed leadership.

Election Plans and the Move to Reform the Party System

Even though the army tightened its grip on the government in 1966 and 1967, the political parties continued to represent real forces in society. Despite the attenuated role played by the non-Communist parties in Jakarta politics during the Guided Democracy period, the masses in the rural areas continued to identify themselves with one or other of the political parties. In Java the NU drew support from *santri* peasants through the influence of rural *kiyais* (religious teachers), and the PNI held the loyalty of a large part of the *abangan* community, who continued to regard PNI-sympathizing officials in the regional administration as their patrons. Although the Masyumi had been banned in 1960, its former leaders were still respected and continued to wield influence, especially in the Outer Islands. Similarly, the Protestant and Catholic parties retained their bases of support among the Christian community, and the small Muslim parties and the secular Murba and IPKI could rely on pockets of support in particular regions. The terrorized and intimidated remnants of the PKI's mass base continued to retain a sense of separate identity, although they had no organizational vehicle for their aspirations.[1]

The general recognition of the parties' hold on the loyalties of a wide section of the people was reflected in the parliament (DPR-GR) and the MPRS. Of the DPR-GR's 242 members after the expulsion of PKI representatives in 1966, 178 had party affiliations, 102 being direct party representatives and 76 representing party-affiliated "functional groups," such as trade unions, peas-

1. The link between identification with sociocultural *aliran* (stream) and support for political parties has been discussed most fully by Geertz. See especially Geertz 1959.

ants' organizations, and other bodies. Even after new members were appointed by the government at the beginning of 1967 in preparation for the final drive against Sukarno, the ratio between party and party-affiliated members and unaffiliated functional group members was still 5:2 in favor of the parties. Similarly, in the MPRS the political parties were well represented.

The army-dominated government wanted to act in a "constitutional manner" by gaining for its program the endorsement of the institutions provided by the 1945 Constitution which it professed to uphold. Anxious to avoid giving the impression that they had usurped President Sukarno's powers illegally and wanting to win party support against the president, the army leaders were not in a strong position to withstand pressure from the parties to hold general elections. The established parties, with their well-entrenched rural organizations, could be expected to do well in elections, while the army's civilian allies in the urban-based Action Fronts were unlikely to grow into major electoral forces. Further, it was not improbable that supporters of Sukarno would be well represented in an elected parliament. Thus the army was reluctant to give in to the demands for early elections put forward at the MPRS session in June and July 1966, but agreed to a compromise which delayed elections until July 1968.[2] As part of the compromise, the army leaders secured the agreement of the parties to a further MPRS decision calling for a law to "simplify" parties, mass organizations, and functional groups.

The army leadership's lack of enthusiasm for elections was very apparent in August 1966, when a seminar was held at Bandung, attended by senior army officers and civilian advisers, to formulate a political program for the army. Accepting the fact that elections would have to be held in accordance with the MPRS decision passed the previous month, the army seminar gave its assent, but with the proviso that "it is very clear that the Panca Sila forces must be victorious in the General Elections."[3] In order to ensure the success of "Panca Sila forces," the seminar adopted a

2. At the MPRS session in 1966, such army spokesmen as Major General Basuki Rachmat favored a three-year delay before holding elections, while the Muslim parties—supported by General Nasution—favored elections in 1967. See unpublished records of fourth General Session of the MPRS. For Nasution's view, see his interview with a Japanese journalist in June 1966 in Achmad, ed. 1966:41.

3. Angkatan Darat 1966a:49.

proposal for an electoral system calculated to be unfavorable for the political parties.

The seminar's policy in regard to the electoral system was derived largely from the proposals put by the economist, Sarbini Sumawinata, a former leading member of the PSI and old associate of the influential Major General Suwarto, the PSI-leaning commandant of the Army Staff and Command College where the seminar was held. Recognizing that "despite the faults and weaknesses of the political parties, it cannot be denied that they are a reality among the political and social forces in society," Sarbini warned the radical opponents of the parties that "the reality of these political forces will not just disappear as a result of an official ban." Instead Sarbini proposed an electoral system designed to enable new political forces to challenge the predominance of the old parties and their leaders. Sarbini's main proposal was that the elections should be based on the "district system" of single-member constituencies rather than proportional representation.[4] Under the old proportional representation system based on provincewide constituencies, the well-organized existing parties would be certain to win an overwhelming majority of seats. Candidates placed high on party lists would be guaranteed election because of their party identification rather than their personal qualities. Under the "district system," locally accessible and popular nonparty candidates would have a chance of winning. Moreover, the parties would be under pressure to select candidates who had local support rather than the Jakarta-based leaders who normally headed party lists under proportional representation. In a further move against Jakarta-based party leaders, the seminar accepted the proposal of a residency provision requiring candidates to live in their constituency for at least one year before the elections.[5]

Following the army seminar, two electoral bills and a third bill dealing with political parties, mass organizations, and functional groups were drawn up and presented to the parliament early in 1967. The general elections bill provided for single-member con-

4. Sarbini's speech in Angkatan Darat 1966b. Sarbini prepared his speech in consultation with another PSI figure, Sudjatmoko (interview with Sarbini Sumawinata, 18 January 1971).
5. Angkatan Darat 1966a:53–54.

stituencies with each constituency based on a *kabupaten* or town. The second bill, dealing with the structure of the MPR, DPR, and regional assemblies, provided that only half the members of each body would represent political parties, with the other half representing functional groups—of which half would be appointed to represent the armed forces, giving the armed forces a quarter of the seats in each body. The third bill set conditions for the recognition of parties, functional groups, and mass organizations and was aimed at reducing the number of parties.[6]

The three bills were strongly criticized in the DPR-GR, where the parties were well represented. The parties demanded an electoral system based on proportional representation, opposed the allocation of a quarter of the seats to the armed forces, and criticized the proposed conditions for recognition of political parties. It soon became clear that there was little prospect that the bills would be passed unamended by the parliament. Although some of the government's advisers urged that party opposition be overcome by adopting the bills by presidential decree, Acting President Suharto preferred to make concessions to the parties rather than antagonize them. A series of meetings between the government and the party leaders was held, which on 27 July 1967 produced what was termed a "packet" or package deal in which both sides gave concessions. The parties conceded the government the right to appoint one-third of the members of the MPR and 100 of the 460 members of the DPR, including civilian as well as armed forces representatives. The government agreed to adopt proportional representation with party lists in provincewide constituencies, and the residency requirement was abolished.[7] The "packet" established the broad principles for redrafted legislation, although the details remained to be settled.

The government's concessions to the parties were substantial. The proposals of the army seminar, which had been supported by the militantly anti-Sukarnoist officers as a move to reduce the role of the parties, were largely abandoned. The reversal of the army leadership's policy toward the electoral laws signified an important change of emphasis in its approach to the political parties. The army leaders now calculated that if the parties were given a

6. The three bills are in Sekretariat DPR-GR 1970:175–245.
7. *Nusantara*, 31 July 1967.

prominent position in the legislatures as well as representation in the cabinet and other organs of government, they would quickly adjust themselves to army dominance and gain an interest in supporting the regime against challenges to it, just as they had supported Sukarno in the past. At the regional level, life would be made much easier for the local military authorities, who were more interested in maintaining a calm and orderly atmosphere than in launching a radical attack on the parties in the interests of the abstract concepts of "renewal" and "modernization." Moreover, the July 1967 package deal necessitated a further rewriting of the bills, a time-consuming process, as Suharto was well aware. The new delay in the passage of the legislation completely ruled out the possibility that elections could be held by the following July as required by the MPRS. Thus Suharto had effectively secured a release from the schedule set by the MPRS in 1966, while at the same time winning the gratitude of the parties because of his willingness to grant concessions.

The government's concessions to the parties caused much disappointment for the antiparty militants, not only among civilians in the Action Fronts, but also in the army. Before the compromise was announced, a number of important generals, including Nasution and the Siliwangi commander, Dharsono, had strongly supported the retention of the "district system" of single-member constituencies.[8] Opposition to the government's compromise with the parties was particularly strong in the Siliwangi division of West Java. In West Java, unlike Central and East Java where the PNI and NU had strong bases of support, the currently legal parties were weak. The Masyumi had been the province's largest party until it was banned in 1960. Further, sympathy for the PSI, which had been banned together with the Masyumi in 1960, was relatively widespread among Siliwangi officers, who were generally better educated and more cosmopolitan in outlook than officers of other divisions.[9] Many Siliwangi officers shared the PSI's dislike of the parties, which had been prominent during the Guided Democracy period, and the relative weakness of these parties in rural West Java made it easier to contemplate severe measures against them.

8. Ibid., 6, 8 May 1967.
9. See Gregory 1970.

In response to the government's compromise with the parties, a plan for a "Dwipartai" (two-party) system was propagated in West Java during 1967, with the full support of the Siliwangi commander, Dharsono, and his colleague, the Kostrad commander, Kemal Idris. The plan envisaged the dissolution of the existing parties and their replacement by two new parties, both committed to modernization and development, but differing over the programs they offered to achieve their goals. Although the central government followed Dharsono's efforts with not unsympathetic interest, it was not prepared to permit him to take action against the parties in West Java that would undoubtedly provoke an extremely adverse reaction from the parties everywhere else. In the face of the constraints imposed in Jakarta, Dharsono modified his plan by proposing a "Dwigrup" system, in which the existing parties would not be dissolved but would form themselves into two groups. At the beginning of 1969, two-group systems suddenly began to appear in the local legislatures of several West Java *kabupaten* as a result of heavy military pressure on the unwilling parties. Dharsono's strong-arm methods had finally run counter to the government's strategy of seeking the parties' cooperation, and, when protests were made by party leaders in Jakarta, Dharsono was ordered to stop the implementation of the Dwigrup system.[10] The episode provided the central army leadership with the opportunity it had been awaiting to disperse the potentially dangerous group of New Order militants. After his colleague, Kemal Idris, was sent as interregional commander for East Indonesia with headquarters in far-off Makassar, Dharsono was posted as ambassador in Bangkok, and the movement to restructure the political system without the old parties disintegrated.

Meanwhile, the continuing debate in the DPR-GR on the details of the electoral legislation had not been unwelcome to Suharto. The MPRS decision of 1966 had obliged the DPR-GR to pass legislation by 5 January 1967 so as to allow one and a half years for technical preparations for the elections by 5 July 1968, but the proposed laws were not debated in parliament until February 1967,

10. The armed forces newspaper, *Angkatan Bersenjata,* commented that Dharsono's "concrete efforts ... have not succeeded in showing the results we expected" (28 February 1969, translated in *Indonesian Current Affairs Translation Service,* hereafter cited as *ICATS*).

and the July 1967 "packet" had necessitated a further redrafting of the bills. During 1967 it had become clear that it would be technically impossible to hold the elections on time, and when the MPRS met again in March 1968 and appointed Suharto as full president, the opportunity was taken to set a new target date. The government proposed a postponement of five years, but the parties again succeeded in forcing a compromise obliging the government to hold elections by 5 July 1971, while agreeing to the election of Suharto for a full five-year term.

Although agreement had been reached in July 1967 on the basic principles of the electoral laws, the government and parties continued to disagree on several relatively minor issues. Discussion of the bills continued during 1968 and through most of 1969 as the settlement of old "crucial points" was followed by the emergence of new "crucial points." At the end of 1969 the deadlock was suddenly broken. As rumors spread that the government was deliberately bringing up new "crucial points" as a pretext for a further postponement of the elections, Suharto suddenly called meetings with party leaders in October 1969. Reportedly against the advice of his main political advisers, including Major General Ali Murtopo, Suharto told the party leaders that the government was determined to hold elections by the mid-1971 deadline laid down by the MPRS, and during the next month the parties gave way on the remaining issues. On 22 November 1969, the General Elections Law and the Structure and Position of the MPR, DPR, and DPRD Law were passed unanimously by the DPR-GR.[11] Suharto's concern for the legitimacy of the regime apparently outweighed the advantages seen by several senior advisers in further procrastination.

The Parties before the Elections

The government's revised thinking in regard to the electoral laws was reflected in its approach to the individual parties. Having concluded in mid-1967 that the danger of early elections had been avoided, the government no longer gave priority to the reform of the electoral system and the reduction of the party leaders' influence. The new strategy accepted the important role the parties could play in integrating the masses into the political

11. The laws are in Sekretariat DPR-GR 1970:249–318.

system. It recognized that the government could operate more smoothly with the support of the party leaders, whose participation in Jakarta politics, it was hoped, would persuade their supporters in the regions that their interests were not being neglected. By ensuring that the main political groups felt represented within the system, the government hoped to avoid the possible consequences of the alienation of important sections of the national community. While the mass base of the PKI remained unrepresented, the government sought to provide the PNI and NU leaders with places within the system, and a new party was established to represent former supporters of the banned Masyumi. But the army leaders wished to ensure that the parties did not develop to the point where they could threaten the army's control of the government. While offering the parties a role in the system, steps were taken to ensure that they were headed by amenable leaders prepared to cooperate closely with the government.

Of the major parties, the PNI had been most identified with President Sukarno in the past, with the result that it was deeply distrusted by the anti-Sukarnoists in the army and their civilian allies in the Action Fronts. The PNI, however, had a large mass base, especially in Central and East Java, where adherents of the party were well represented in the regional bureaucracy and much of the *abangan* community continued to support the party. Moreover, as a non-Muslim party identified with President Sukarno, the PNI could be expected to draw support from part of the banned PKI's clientele in the rural areas. Despite pressure from the Action Fronts, the Muslim parties, and sections of the army to ban the PNI, Suharto preferred to maintain the party for the time being, partly as a link between the government and a large section of the people and also as a means of balancing the Muslim parties. Suharto's policy toward the PNI was aimed at reforming its leadership while preserving its mass base.

Shortly before the 1965 coup attempt, the PNI leadership had split into two factions. The main body of the party remained loyal to the general chairman, Ali Sastroamidjojo, who was prepared to go along with Sukarno's Nasakom policies. The anti-Communist dissidents aligned themselves with the party's first chairman, Hardi, and the Central Java provincial leader, Hadisubeno. After the coup, with encouragement from the military authorities, in April 1966 the Hardi-Hadisubeno faction took control of the party at a "Unity Congress" held in Bandung at the behest of Suharto. Although Ali and his supporters knew that Suharto's purpose in urging the holding of the congress was to arrange their replacement by their rivals, they felt the circumstances gave them little choice but to attend. With the presence of Ali and his colleagues legitimating the proceedings, army officers ensured that the rival group won all major positions in the party leadership. Pressure was applied in the selection of delegates, whose credentials were checked by soldiers at the doors of the conference hall. Delegates were under no illusion about what to expect if they made the wrong choice. Addressing the opening of the congress, Suharto said that the party's outlook "must always be in accord with the wishes of the people." If not, he said, "It will be corrected by the people; it will even be put to death by the people themselves."[12] On the final day, the congress approved the appointment of Osa Maliki Wangsadinata as general chairman and Usep Ranuwidjaja as general secretary. Both were prominent members of the Hardi-Hadisubeno faction.[13]

Despite the purge of Ali and his colleagues, the party soon came under pressure again as it continued to oppose moves against President Sukarno during 1966 and early 1967. While such party leaders in Jakarta as Osa and Usep were convinced of the need to work in harmony with the new government and were ready to distance themselves from the fallen president, other leaders in the regions were in continual touch with the party's grass-roots support and continued to feel that the party's identification with Sukarno was an asset, especially in view of the promise of early elections. The army leadership was willing to take a tolerant view of the party's attachment to Sukarno, provided it purged itself of leaders who were unwilling to accept the army's dominance in the new political order. Some regional commanders, however, particularly in Sumatra, attempted to mobilize Muslim support for a policy aiming to eliminate the PNI. Although not identical with the Siliwangi group headed by Dhar-

12. Radio Republik Indonesia broadcast, 25 April 1966.
13. For detailed discussion of internal conflict in the PNI see Nazaruddin Sjamsuddin 1970 and McIntyre 1972.

sono and Kemal Idris, those regional commanders shared some of their attitudes.

An area of major concern for the army leadership was East Java, Sukarno's home province, where sympathy for him was strong, both in the political parties and in the armed forces. Unlike the PNI in Central Java, where the party was headed by the anti-Communist dissident Hadisubeno, the most prominent party leaders in East Java had continued to side with Ali Sastroamidjojo and were regarded with disfavor by the army. In 1967, as part of his New Orderization campaign, the East Java regional commander, Jasin, took stern measures against the PNI. Under pressure from Jasin, the provincial party leader, Sundoro Hardjoamidjojo, quickly replaced Sukarnoists among local party and mass organization leaders and suspended Pemuda Marhaen leaders from party membership, while Jasin banned all public activities of the party and its mass organizations, "froze" several local branches and student organizations, and arrested those who obstructed what was called "crystallization." Despite these measures, Sundoro explained that "the PNI is not angry but extremely grateful for the commander's initiative in sincerely assisting the PNI in carrying out its internal purge."[14] Early in 1968, Jasin permitted the reconstructed party to resume its activities except in four areas, but the party did not begin to function normally again until later in the year.

The strong measures taken by Jasin in East Java remained within the guidelines set by Suharto, who wanted to preserve the PNI under amenable leadership. But the measures taken by Brigadier General Ishak Djuarsa and Brigadier General Sarwo Edhie in Sumatra went much further. In the strongly Islamic province of Aceh the regional commander, Ishak Djuarsa, encouraged Muslim organizations to apply so much pressure on the small branch of the PNI that the party felt compelled to disband itself "voluntarily" in April 1967. When Ishak Djuarsa was transferred to the South Sumatra command shortly afterward, similar pressures were applied by Muslim organizations to the PNI there, with the result that the party disbanded itself in that region in September 1967. In North Sumatra, where the PNI was relatively

14. *Nusantara*, 4 October 1967.

strong, the newly appointed commander, Sarwo Edhie, "froze" the party in September as part of his campaign to eliminate Sukarnoist elements in the province.

The measures taken against the PNI in Aceh, North Sumatra, and South Sumatra resulted in effective bans on the party in these areas. They therefore contradicted the government's policy of reforming rather than eliminating the PNI and constituted a direct challenge to the authority of the army leadership. Suharto was then forced to take action to preserve the PNI in Sumatra. On 30 September, the interregional commander for Sumatra, Major General Kusno Utomo Widjojokerto, ordered that all the activities of the PNI and its mass organizations be "frozen" throughout Sumatra. Kusno Utomo appeared to be endorsing Sarwo Edhie's policy, but in fact his order was directed from Jakarta and aimed at preventing Sarwo Edhie from taking even more drastic measures. The acting commander of the army, General Panggabean, declared that "up till now the government continues to recognize the PNI/Front Marhaen as one of the components of the New Order,"[15] and in December, Suharto again emphasized that "measures against the PNI in Sumatra . . . have no other purpose than to assist the PNI/Front Marhaen to accelerate its crystallization in adjusting itself to the New Order."[16] In April 1968, Kusno Utomo revoked his order "freezing" the party in Sumatra, and shortly afterward Sarwo Edhie was relieved of his command. Nevertheless, in the two regions where the PNI had "dissolved" itself, the party was not reactivated until 1969 in South Sumatra and 1970 in Aceh.

Suharto aimed to preserve the party under amenable leadership, but this goal was suddenly threatened when the general chairman, Osa Maliki, died of a heart attack in September 1969. Widely respected in all sections of the party, but lacking a strong personal base of support, the mild and flexible Osa had been something of a figurehead leader because real control remained in the hands of Hardi and Hadisubeno, who became the main rivals for the succession. Hardi, a Jakarta lawyer who had been deputy prime minister from 1957 to 1959, took over the functions of the general chairman until a party congress could be held, but

15. Ibid.
16. Ibid., 4 December 1967.

he was unable to establish a warm relationship with Suharto's political advisers, who suspected him of aspiring to cooperate with the other parties against the military. Suharto had known Hadisubeno personally for many years. In the late 1950s, Hadisubeno had been mayor of Semarang, where Suharto, as the Diponegoro division commander, had his headquarters.

By the time the party congress was held in Semarang in April 1970, it was clear that the government wanted Hadisubeno to be elected. The president's personal assistant, Ali Murtopo, was assigned the task of ensuring his victory. Hadisubeno had strong support in Central Java, but the East Java leaders and many of the Outer Island branches preferred Hardi. As delegates passed through Jakarta on their way to Semarang the pro-Hardi party newspaper, *Suluh Marhaen,* complained of "briefings" by members of Ali Murtopo's Opsus organization, who told delegates that "the boss wants so-and-so to be general chairman" and "if so-and-so is not elected general chairman, the PNI will have difficulties in surviving."[17] Similarly, in East Java, Hardi's ally, Sundoro, claimed that delegates from his province had been called by local army commanders, who told them that the president wanted Hadisubeno to be elected.[18] In his address at the opening of the congress, President Suharto declared that the government would not interfere in the PNI's internal affairs,[19] but many delegates whose sympathies had originally been with Hardi decided to vote for Hadisubeno, who was elected as general chairman.

Hadisubeno's qualities were well suited to the government's strategy. On the one hand, he was an established party leader with a strong personal base of support and a colorful personality capable of appealing to the party's supporters. On the other, he was not the type of leader who could be expected to lead the party into confrontation with the authorities. Suharto's advisers calculated that he could draw back into the political system those of the party's supporters who had been alienated during the years since 1966. After his election as party leader, Hadisubeno turned to traditional PNI themes designed to attract the Sukarnoist wing of

17. *Suluh Marhaen,* 10 April 1970 (translated in *United States Embassy Translation Unit Press Review;* hereafter cited as *USE*).
18. *Harian Kami,* 14 April 1970 (*USE*).
19. *Suluh Marhaen,* 16 April 1970 (*USE*).

the party. In his first postelection speech he appealed to the anti-*santri* sentiments of many of the party's supporters in warning against the activities of "sarong-wearers" who wanted to undermine the Panca Sila, and, in a reference to the former president, he called on party members "not to forget who 'dug up' Panca Sila."[20] In later speeches Hadisubeno continued to stress the party's links with "Indonesia's best son,"[21] and called for the release of PNI supporters still in prison.[22]

Hadisubeno was careful to avoid a confrontation with the government. Accepting his critics' accusations that earlier he had supported Sukarno, he told a rally in Solo that "it is true I was Sukarno's lackey in the past and now I am Suharto's lackey."[23] By rallying the PNI's traditional supporters while avoiding criticism of the government, Hadisubeno aimed to demonstrate the PNI's mass support in the hope that after the elections Suharto would ask a PNI leader to accept the position of vice-president. With the prospect of the vice-presidency dangling before him, the army leaders expected that Hadisubeno would do nothing to oppose the government, while, behind the scenes, the party was becoming dependent on financial support channeled through the Opsus and the Bank Umum Nasional, the PNI-owned bank that had been saved from collapse by the Opsus in 1967.

Government intervention to secure preferred leadership in the PNI was accompanied by moves to control the leadership of the new Muslim party established in 1968. Since the dissolution of the Masyumi in 1960, a major section of the Islamic community, especially in West Java and the Outer Islands, had been unrepresented by a political party. Although some supporters of the Masyumi transferred their allegiance to the NU or the small Muslim parties, the majority continued to regard themselves as part of the Masyumi "stream," even though there was no political party to coordinate their activities. Excluded from political participation during the Guided Democracy period, Masyumi sympathizers

20. *Kompas,* 25 April 1970 (*USE*).
21. Ibid., 13 July 1970 (*USE*).
22. *Pedoman,* 23 April 1970 (*USE*); *Kompas,* 23 June 1970. The PNI leader and minister of state, Sunawar Sukowati, estimated that four to five hundred PNI members had been arrested during the "crystallization" process (*Kompas,* 28 May 1970 [*USE*]).
23. *Indonesia Raya,* 23 December 1970 (*USE*).

welcomed the overthrow of Sukarno's government and expected, as uncompromising opponents of the Old Order, to regain their earlier prominence. Their high hopes during 1966, however, turned to frustration in later years as they realized that the predominantly Javanese *priyayi* army leadership regarded them as potential troublemakers, bent on turning Indonesia into an Islamic state.

The often dogmatic and firebrand Masyumi leaders, with their base of support in the Outer Islands, had considerable potential for rallying opposition to the secular government in the name of Islam. As Muslim alienation from the government grew, the pro-Masyumi elements often took the lead in violent demonstrations against the Chinese minority, gambling casinos, and Christian schools and churches. Regarding themselves as thrust into a corner by a government that had betrayed Islamic principles in a land where the overwhelming majority called themselves Muslim, leaders of organizations in the Masyumi stream represented a threat to the government's goal of political stability. Thus it was in the government's interest to seek to integrate former supporters of the Masyumi into the new political order. The army leaders decided to permit the formation of a new Muslim party, but at the same time took measures to prevent its falling under the control of former Masyumi leaders.

The atmosphere after 1965 had encouraged Masyumi leaders to approach the government several times seeking recognition. These efforts were not viewed with sympathy by most army officers, who continued to blame the Masyumi for the support some of its leaders gave to the PRRI revolt in 1958 which cost the lives of several thousand soldiers. In reply to a letter from the former Masyumi general chairman, Prawoto Mangkusasmito, in January 1967, Suharto bluntly justified Sukarno's order dissolving the party, "which did not officially condemn the deeds of its members" who supported the PRRI revolt. Suharto concluded, "Legal, political, and psychological factors have led the armed forces to the opinion that the armed forces cannot accept the rehabilitation of the former political party, Masyumi."[24]

By the first part of 1967, the efforts to revive the Masyumi had

24. Prawoto's and Suharto's letters are in Solichin Salam 1970:66, 69–70.

come to a standstill, but in May Suharto let it be known that the government would not object to the formation of a new party based on mass organizations in the Masyumi stream, of which the largest was the social welfare and educational organization, Mohammadiyah. Efforts to form such a party were delayed, largely because of difficulties encountered in winning government approval for its leadership. The committee formed to establish the new party was aware that the government would not accept former Masyumi leaders of the stature of Mohammad Natsir, Sjafruddin Prawiranegara, and Prawoto, but was unclear on the government's attitude to less senior Masyumi figures who had not been closely identified with the PRRI revolt. Several proposals were rejected by Suharto's military advisers during the latter part of 1967. A further proposal was rejected in February 1968, but immediately afterward negotiations took place that resulted in government recognition for the party, known as Partai Muslimin Indonesia or Parmusi, under the general chairmanship of Djanarwi Hadikusumo, with Lukman Harun as general secretary. Both were Mohammadiyah leaders with none of the charismatic qualities of the former Masyumi leaders. All former Masyumi leaders were excluded from the party's leadership, among whom some, including one of the chairmen, Djaelani (Djoni) Naro, appeared to be government nominees. The party was recognized on 20 February 1968.[25]

The party's supporters were very disappointed at the government's attitude, but were won over by what they understood to be Suharto's willingness to permit the party to elect its own leadership later. When the party's first congress was held in November 1968, however, the government informed the delegates that it would not approve a change in leadership. Nevertheless, the delegates elected Mohammed Roem, who had been a very senior but relatively moderate leader of the Masyumi, as general chairman, while several of the leaders appointed in February, including Naro, failed to hold their positions. Despite overwhelming support from the party, Roem decided not to take office without government approval. Thus, while the party's supporters seethed

25. The problems encountered in the formation of the Parmusi are discussed in detail in Samson 1968, Ward 1970:chap. 3, Solichin Salam 1970, and Sapartini Singgih 1972:chap. 2.

with anger, its leadership continued to avoid direct confrontation with the government.

Although Djanarwi and his colleagues remained in office, they continued to regard the old Masyumi leaders with much respect. Especially after the passage of the electoral laws at the end of 1969, they turned increasingly to former Masyumi figures, both in Jakarta and in the regions, to mobilize support for the Parmusi. A General Elections Committee was established, headed by Roem, former Masyumi figures were appointed to leadership positions in the regions, and preparations were made to include senior Masyumi leaders in the party's list of candidates for the elections. At the same time, Parmusi spokesmen in the regions adopted an increasingly critical line toward the government.

Suddenly, on 17 October 1970, Naro announced that he had taken over the general chairmanship of the Parmusi and appointed one of the party secretaries, Imran Kadir, as general secretary. During the previous months, Naro and Kadir, whose relations with the president's assistant, Ali Murtopo, were warm, had strongly criticized the reemergence of Masyumi figures in the party and the party leadership's readiness to adopt a "confrontative" attitude to the government. During the next weeks, the minister for interal affairs, Amir Machmud, and the head of the Bakin, Lieutenant General Sutopo Juwono, were entrusted by Suharto with settling the Parmusi's "internal" dispute. On 14 November a minister of state, M. S. Mintaredja, was appointed as general chairman, and shortly afterward a presidential decision was issued establishing a new Parmusi board. It appeared that the conflict within the Parmusi had been provoked by Naro, with the encouragement of members of Ali Murtopo's Opsus. They had not envisaged that Naro would retain the general chairmanship of the party, but had hoped to create circumstances enabling the government to step in with its "compromise" candidate.

Like the intervention in the internal affairs of the PNI that led to Hadisubeno's election, the government's aim regarding the Parmusi was to place the party under a leader unlikely to challenge the government. Mintaredja, however, was no Hadisubeno who could bow to the government on one side while rallying party supporters on the other. Moreover, the transparency of the government's tactics alienated many Parmusi supporters from the party.

The third major party was the Nahdatul Ulama (NU). Formed in 1926 as a religious and social organization, the NU acquired political functions only during the Japanese occupation, when the original Masyumi was established with a membership covering a wide range of Muslim bodies including the NU. After 1945, the NU remained part of the Masyumi, which became a political party, but in 1952 the NU decided to break away and form its own party. Relying on conservative religious leaders in the villages of Java to mobilize its supporters, the NU quickly established itself as a major force. The leaders of the NU believed their task was to further the cause of Islam by ensuring that the party was well represented in the government, the legislatures, and the adminis-tration of religious affairs. Largely unconcerned with conven-tional political issues, the NU leaders gained a reputation for op-portunism because they adjusted themselves to whatever political changes took place. The party general chairman, Idham Chalid, had served as a deputy prime minister during the parliamentary period, deputy chairman of the MPRS during Guided Democracy, and a cabinet minister under Suharto. The NU leaders consis-tently pursued their goal of ensuring that the Muslim community was well represented.

The NU had been as much a part of Sukarno's Nasakom system as had the PNI and PKI, and the party's top leadership had hesi-tated to side openly with Suharto against Sukarno in 1966. Thus, when the NU held its first post-1965 congress in 1967, some se-nior army officers gave encouragement to Idham Chalid's main rival. However, the rural *kiyais* from East and Central Java, who made up most of the delegates to the congress, gave overwhelm-ing support to Idham. Although such strongly anti-Sukarnoist and reform-oriented leaders as Subchan and Imron Rosjadi were elected to the party leadership, they were still no match for the old guard, with its seemingly immutable base among the rural *kiyais.*

As the army leaders revised their strategy toward the political parties in the middle of 1967, they became less concerned with purging the parties of Old Order supporters than with working out a basis for cooperation in which the parties would not chal-lenge the army's dominant role. If, in the spirit of the army semi-nar of August 1966, army officers had been alienated by the NU's opportunism, by mid-1967 this quality began to appear in another light. After assessing the character of the NU's "old-guard" leaders, Suharto's advisers concluded that if they were given status and funds for their religious and other activities, Idham and his colleagues would support Suharto just as they had supported Sukarno earlier. In contrast with the PNI and Parmusi, the NU did not suffer the indignity of Opsus intervention in its internal affairs in order to produce amenable leadership.

Golkar and the Elections

President Suharto's advisers had been hesitant and uncertain about the desirability of holding elections in 1971 as scheduled by the MPRS, and the president did not make it clear to the party leaders that the elections would in fact be held until October 1969. The government's apparent aim in holding elections was to give the parties a sense of participation in the political system without threatening the army's grip on the government. The government expected to gain legitimacy, while the parties remained divided and manageable in parliament. Meanwhile, the parties were expected to be so preoccupied with confronting each other in the election campaign that they would be unwilling to challenge the government on other issues.

In deciding to go ahead with the elections, the government seemed to accept the commonly held view that the results would simply confirm the parliamentary status quo, in which some 60 percent of the seats were held by party representatives.[26] Although the government planned to develop the Joint Secretariat of Functional Groups (Sekber-Golkar or Golkar) as its own party, it apparently had little expectation of creating an electoral machine capable of seriously undermining the established parties. In August 1970 the Golkar general chairman, Major General Suprapto Sokowati, admitted that he did not expect Golkar to "win" but said he would be satisfied with third place,[27] and as late as April 1971 another Golkar leader, Sumiskum, cited a Bakin re-

26. This was the assumption of many speakers at a seminar held at the University of Indonesia in January 1970. See, for example, the speeches of Mochtar Lubis and Alfian in Dewan Mahasiswa Universitas Indonesia 1970. See also Polomka 1971:207.

27. *Abadi*, 29 August 1970 (*USE*).

port predicting that the Golkar would be one of the "Big Three" when the election results were announced.[28] Although 100 of the DPR's 460 seats were to be filled by appointment, the government still seemed pessimistic about the Golkar's prospects of winning the 131 elected seats (36 percent of the elected seats) in order to reach a majority. It was rumored that *bupatis* and mayors had been assigned "quotas" of 30 percent to be mobilized for the Golkar, which, even if fulfilled, would still leave the government with less than a majority.

The interventions carried out by Ali Murtopo's Opsus in the internal affairs of the PNI and the Parmusi were therefore necessary from the government's point of view in order to guarantee that potentially hostile groups did not gain control of organizations still capable of rallying substantial mass support. Further, the cultivation of the PNI leader, Hadisubeno, gave rise to speculation that the army leaders had decided to adopt the PNI as the "junior partner." Drawn from much the same Javanese *abangan* background, the army and PNI leaders "understood" each other in a way that excluded the Muslim leaders and the "modernists" of the Action Fronts. Obliged to hold elections but fearing that they lacked an effective vote-getting organization of their own, the army leaders seemed to be relying on the PNI to block whatever challenge might be offered from the Muslim quarter, while suppressing signs of independence in the Parmusi and buying off the NU leadership.

During the first half of 1967, a group of secular, anti-Sukarnoist intellectuals, most of whom had been prominent supporters of the Action Fronts, had set up an "independent group" which they hoped would eventually develop into a political party allied to the army.[29] Initially encouraged by the generals close to Suharto, the "independent group" lost this backing after the compromise on the nature of the electoral legislation in mid-1967 that made it inevitable that the elections due in 1968 would be postponed. In place of the "independent group," the government appointed its nonparty civilian supporters as functional-group (*golongan karya*

28. *Harian Kami*, 19 April 1971 (*USE*).
29. Among them were Mashuri (director general of higher education), Omar Khayam (director general of radio, TV, and films), Sudjatmoko, Bujung Nasution (a leader of the Graduates' Action Front, KASI), Fuad Hasan, and Sulaiman Sumardi (both of the University of Indonesia).

or Golkar) representatives in the parliament. The concept of functional-group representation had developed under Guided Democracy, but in practice most of the functional group members of the DPR-GR represented "functional" organizations such as labor, peasant, business, and religious bodies which were in fact affiliated to political parties. New appointments and replacements in 1967 and 1968 led to a sharp increase in "pure" functional group representatives without party affiliation, who then numbered 92 together with 75 armed forces representatives, although they were still outnumbered by the 247 party representatives. By "purifying" the functional group fraction of party ties in the DPR-GR, the government had taken the first step toward establishing a "government party" in parliament.

Outside parliament the government looked to the Joint Secretariat of Functional Groups which had been established by army officers in October 1964, to coordinate anti-PKI organizations within the National Front. By 1968 some 249 bodies had joined, including organizations for labor, peasants, civil servants, women, youth, intellectuals, artists, and religion. Although nearly all the affiliated bodies were civilian, the most influential were led by army officers including Brigadier General Suhardiman's SOKSI, Major General Sugandhi's MKGR, and Major General Isman's Kosgoro,[30] and the central leadership of the Sekber-Golkar was dominated by army officers, led by the general chairman, Sokowati, a senior officer of the Department of Defense and Security. With its very heterogeneous membership, the Sekber-Golkar was a coordinating "joint secretariat" rather than a federation capable of imposing policies on its affiliates, who had been drawn together originally by their opposition to the PKI. As already noted, Suharto's political advisers, headed by Ali Murtopo, were not optimistic about the prospects of turning the Sekber-Golkar into an effective electoral machine and for this reason were inclined to seek a further postponement of the elections. With the passage of the electoral laws, however, Ali Murtopo was given the task of ensuring that the Sekber-Golkar performed effectively in the elections.

30. The SOKSI was an army-sponsored "trade union." The Musjawarah Kekeluargaan Gotong Rojong (MKGR) and Koperasi Serba Usaha Gotong Royong (Kosgoro) were military-sponsored commercial and welfare organizations based in East Java.

Bypassing the old Sekber-Golkar organizations, the Golkar electoral strategy was devised by a committee recruited by Ali Murtopo and consisting largely of former activists in the Action Fronts. Convinced of the need to "modernize" Indonesian politics by reducing the role of the "traditional" parties, the members of the committee, known as the Body to Manage the General Elections (Bapilu), were secular in outlook and included a disproportionate number of Catholics.[31] Realizing that the Golkar could not develop the popular roots of the parties in the year and a half available before the elections, the Bapilu strategists made no attempt to build it into a political party with a coherent ideology of its own, but instead set out to create a patronage machine that would win over supporters from other parties. The Golkar did not seek to present a program that could unite former supporters of the PNI, the Muslim parties, and even the PKI, but aimed to create conditions in which political party adherents of all sorts felt it to be in their interests to switch their vote to the Golkar.[32]

The Golkar adopted different means to deal with each of its rivals. In facing the PNI, the Golkar used the Kokarmendagri, an association of employees of the Department of Internal Affairs from which the PNI had previously drawn much of its support. During 1970 it became apparent that the minister for internal affairs, Amir Machmud, was determined that his department would become the backbone of the Golkar. Although the minister continued to claim that officials were still permitted to belong to parties,[33] he stated that those who favored parties would be dismissed and made clear that party membership would be, at the very least, an obstacle to promotion.[34] As the election drew closer, civil servants were pressed to sign statements of "monoloyalty" to the government, implying support for the Golkar, and local government officials were assigned "quotas" of votes to be mobilized

31. See Ward 1974:chap. 2.
32. The report of the MPRS leadership refers to "the fact of the involvement of the government apparatus from the top to the bottom to achieve success for Golkar" (MPRS 1972:57). This official report, prepared under the guidance of the MPRS chairman, General Nasution, was banned by the Kopkamtib in October 1972.
33. *Kompas*, 29 September 1970 (*USE*).
34. *Kompas*, 8 April 1970 (*USE*). See report from East Java in *Duta Masyarakat*, 9 July 1970 (*USE*), and Ward 1974:33–34.

for the Golkar in their district, so that even when a local official's heart remained with the PNI or another party, his interest clearly dictated that he work for a Golkar victory. By pulling to its own side those who had once formed the backbone of the PNI, the Golkar was able to destroy much of the PNI's electoral influence.

The Muslim parties posed a different problem for the Golkar strategists who, like the majority of army officers, were secular in outlook and distrusted by Muslim leaders. During 1970, attempts were made to woo influential *kiyais* by financing overseas tours and providing funds for their *pesantrens,* and in January 1971 the more-or-less moribund Association to Improve Islamic Education (GUPPI), was revived when over eight hundred *kiyais* were invited to attend a conference which appointed the distinctly *abangan* Major General Sudjono Humardhani as its "patron" and heard an address by the president. In a disparaging attack, the pro-Parmusi newspaper, *Abadi,* claimed that some *kiyais* had been attracted by the promise of an audience with the president, others had been offered pilgrimages to Mecca at the GUPPI's expense, and a group of *kiyais* from West Java, who had been involved in a forgery scandal, had been assured that prosecutions against them would be dropped.[35]

While the Golkar strategists sought to attract support from influential local leaders through the Kokarmendagri and GUPPI, the military applied direct pressure on voters, especially in the villages. Those most susceptible to "intimidation" were former supporters of the PKI who realized that they were still vulnerable to arrest and worse. Although the electoral legislation specifically deprived former members of the PKI and its mass organizations of the right to vote, only 2,123,747 citizens were excluded from the electoral rolls,[36] whereas the PKI had claimed some 20 million supporters in 1965. Reporting on the election in rural Central Java, R. W. Liddle wrote, "Former PKI members were called into subdistrict military headquarters and instructed to vote for Golkar."[37] K. E. Ward noted that in East Java "known ex-PKI folk were readily available as the first persons to be drafted into Golkar," while in the former Communist stronghold area south of

35. *Abadi,* 27 January 1971 (*USE*).
36. Nishihara 1972:12.
37. Liddle 1973:299.

Blitar it was reported that "Golkar got every vote."[38] The other parties were not exempt, and their spokesmen complained of "intimidation" in the form of the arrest of local leaders alleged to have infringed electoral regulations, visits by local officials and military men, and raids on houses of party activists in Central Java in unsuccessful attempts to find arms.[39] Among those arrested during the election campaign on the fantastic accusation of "involvement in the Communist coup attempt" were the Parmusi chairman in Central Java and the private secretary of the chairman of the DPR-GR and NU leader, A. Sjaichu.

The measures taken by the government and the army to bolster up the Golkar proved more effective than had initially been expected. As the campaign expanded early in 1971, the parties began to react against the Golkar's "bulldozer" tactics. The party leaders, who in 1969 had pushed the government into agreeing to hold elections, suddenly found themselves on the brink of disaster. The previously amenable Hadisubeno threw caution to the winds as he launched a vigorous anti-Golkar campaign exploiting to the full the PNI's link with the late President Sukarno. Responding to a Kopkamtib ban on the dissemination of Sukarno's teachings, Hadisubeno challenged the government to dissolve the PNI if it wanted to implement the prohibition,[40] and, in growing desperation, his speeches became increasingly defiant, culminating in his celebrated claim that "Ten Suhartos, ten Nasutions and a cartload of generals don't add up to one Sukarno."[41] Hadisubeno's attempt to regain ground for his party was tragically cut short when he collapsed and died at the end of April. Meanwhile, the NU had also taken up the challenge, and although Idham Chalid remained in the background, the hitherto pliable Sjaichu joined younger leaders, especially Subchan and Jusuf Hasjim, in attacking the government. A meeting of seven hundred religious leaders at Jombang in East Java issued a *fatwa* (religious decision) declaring it obligatory for Muslims to vote for Muslim parties.[42] Of the three main parties, only the Parmusi under Mintaredja

38. Ward 1974:166.
39. For detailed allegations, see Samsuddin et al. 1972:chap. 9.
40. *Harian Kami,* 16 January 1971 (*ICATS*).
41. Ward 1974:134, 152.
42. *Kompas,* 21 April 1971.

held back in attacking the authorities. When the party's regional chairman in Central Java was arrested, Mintaredja even expressed approval of the government's action.[43]

On 5 July 1971, the Golkar scored an overwhelming victory, winning 62.8 percent of the votes and 236 of the elected seats, giving the government a huge majority in the DPR. The leading party in all twenty-six provinces, the Golkar won less than 50 percent of the votes in only three provinces and less than 60 percent in only three more. Apart from West Java, where it won 76 percent of the votes, the Golkar met relatively stiff opposition in Java. In Central Java, where the NU polled 23 percent and the PNI 19 percent, the Golkar won only 50.3 percent, while in East Java, where the PNI was reduced to 5 percent, the NU won 35 percent and the Golkar 54.9 percent. In cosmopolitan Jakarta, the Golkar won only 46.7 percent. There were also pockets of resistance in the Outer Islands. In Aceh, where the Muslim parties polled well, and Maluku, where the Parkindo and Parmusi provided the main opposition, the Golkar also failed to win 50 percent of the votes. Everywhere else the Golkar victory was overwhelming; in Jambi, Bengkulu, Central Kalimantan, and Bali, it won more than 80 percent of the votes, while in Southeast Sulawesi it scored 92.35 percent.[44]

The only party to withstand the Golkar onslaught was the NU, which, with 18.7 percent, bettered its 1955 performance when it won 18.4 percent of the votes. Relying on the *kiyais* in the rural areas, the NU persuaded Muslim villagers, especially in East Java, that the elections were a test of faith. In contrast, the PNI, which had been the leading party in 1955 with 22.3 percent, was reduced to 6.9 percent in 1971 because its traditional following in the regional bureaucracy felt forced to show its "monoloyalty" to the government and Golkar.[45] The Parmusi, the heir to the Masyumi that won 20.9 percent in 1955, suffered along with the PNI, winning only 5.4 percent. Unlike the NU, the PNI and Parmusi had both been demoralized by government interference in the

43. Nishihara 1972:36.

44. The full results are in Samsuddin et. al 1972 and Van Marle 1974.

45. In explaining the PNI's loss, Hindley suggests that the party "appears to have lost much of its raison d'etre. It had been the party of government, of patronage, of non-revolutionary, non-santri people, but by 1971 these characteristics had been assumed by Golkar" (1972:65).

selection of their leaders, so that many party supporters had been
unwilling to campaign.

Despite its electoral success, the Golkar was essentially a creation of the military authorities and had little sense of separate
identity. Lacking both a party organization of its own and roots in
society, the Golkar was a temporary federation of heterogeneous
organizations mobilized by the army with the intention of weakening the parties. Conceived as an electoral machine designed to
undermine the strength of opponents rather than create a new
focus of loyalty and identification, the Golkar showed no signs of
developing into a means of channeling civilian aspirations upward. The Golkar "bulldozer" had done its job of leveling the
ground previously occupied by the parties, but it was an unsuit-
able tool for construction.

The Golkar's overwhelming victory drastically reduced organized civilian opposition to the regime. The PNI and the Parmusi
lay in ruins, while the NU, despite its vigorous campaign, remained under the amenable leadership of Idham Chalid and his
colleagues. At the NU's congress at the end of 1971, Idham called
for a return to the "spirit of '26," the year of the NU's foundation
as a social and religious body—implying that the NU might soon
shed its political functions. In the face of considerable opposition
within each party, the government began to press the parties to
dissolve themselves voluntarily or revert to earlier nonpolitical
roles, and finally, in January 1973, two new parties were formed
in place of the old parties. The Development Unity party (Partai
Persatuan Pembangunan), under the leadership of Idham Chalid
and Mintaredja, replaced the old Muslim parties, and the Indonesian Democratic party (Partai Demokrasi Indonesia) was formed
as a result of the fusion of the former nationalist and Christian
parties. Both parties were under leadership largely amenable to
the government's wishes and received subsidies from the government to finance their operations.[46]

The collapse of the political parties was accompanied by the
mooting of a new concept, the "floating mass." In September 1971
the Central Java commander, Major General Widodo, apparently
prompted by Ali Murtopo, suggested that the political parties be

46. *Berita Buana,* 13 March 1974 (*ICATS*).

banned from carrying out activities in the villages, and soon the concept of the floating mass was widely disseminated by Ali Murtopo's colleagues from the Golkar.[47] According to the floating mass concept, the mass of the people would be "floating" voters permitted to express their political preferences in general elections once every five years. Between elections they would have no political role and therefore, in theory, would be able to devote all their efforts to economic development. Unable to organize their supporters in the rural areas, the parties would eventually wither away. Although the Golkar, too, would not be permitted to organize in the villages, it in fact had relied on the local administration and the military to mobilize its votes and could expect to do so again in future elections.

The floating mass concept was never officially endorsed by the government and, in deference to civilian feeling, was excluded from the "general outline of state policy" adopted by the MPR in 1973. Further, in 1975 legislation banning the parties and the Golkar from establishing branches in the rural areas was amended to permit all three organizations to place representatives in each village. Although the floating mass concept was no longer emphasized, the roles of the army and the parties remained much the same. The army leaders introduced a new formulation—*tut wuri handayani*—to describe their relationship with nonmilitary organizations and the people in general.[48] The Javanese phrase refers to the guidance given by a parent to a child learning to walk, where the parent does not actually support the child but is always ready to save him from falling.

47. See Ali Moertopo 1973:85–86 for an authoritative explanation. For further discussion, see Ward 1974:188–191.
48. See Suharto's speech on Armed Forces Day, 5 October 1974, in *Berita Buana*, 7 October 1974 (*ICATS*).

11 | The Army's Economic Interests

The army's domination of political life was justified ultimately by the government's promise of economic development. In contrast with Sukarno, who had sought legitimacy by promising to continue the "1945 Revolution" and the "struggle" against "imperialism," Suharto offered "stabilization" and "development." Reflecting the New Order's ideological stress, Suharto's cabinet was entitled the "Development" cabinet, in contrast with Sukarno's "Dwikora" cabinet connoting struggle against Malaysia. The army claimed not only the role of "stabilizer" but also that of "dynamizer," and perceived that its own mission required it to play an important role in the economy. Taking the view that economic development had been obstructed in the past because civilian-dominated governments had been unable to transcend the sectional interests on which the political parties were based, the army presented itself as a truly national force identified with the interests of the community as a whole and therefore most fitted to rule.

The army leaders believed that military rule would ensure the maintenance of political stability needed for economic development. They hoped that stability would encourage investment—both foreign and domestic—in an expanding modern sector of the economy, such as in extractive industries, large-scale manufacturing, and commerce. The government's role was seen largely in terms of creating conditions favorable for the exploitation of new commercial opportunities by foreign investors and Indonesian business interests. In the long run, economic development was expected to bring about a general uplift in the living standards of the mass of the people. The army's conception of economic development was thus primarily oriented toward the interests of the elite and the white-collar middle class. In the new circumstances

military officers, already experienced in commercial and bureaucratic activities during the Guided Democracy period, would be
well placed to benefit from the new policies introduced after
1966, and, in association with Chinese businessmen and foreign
investors, they did increasingly dominate commercial life.

The expansion of commercial opportunities was of vital importance for the army's role as a stabilizer. Inheriting a chaotic
administration and a declining economy, the new government
felt that it had little prospect of raising adequate funds for the
armed forces by conventional means, but it was very aware that
the failure of earlier governments to provide for the economic
well-being of military personnel had led to discontent and contributed to open rebellion. In these circumstances, the army
leaders decided to permit the continuation of practices that had
become well established during the early 1960s, whereby the
army resorted to raising its own funds to supplement what was
available from the state budget, while many individual officers
and men were permitted to engage in their own economic pur-
suits to supplement their salaries. By retaining the system of
"unconventional" financing of the armed forces, the military-
dominated government was able to create the impression that
defense and security expenditure was being held back in the
interests of the economic development program, when in fact
the government's budget allocation for defense and security in
the late 1960s covered only about a third to a half of actual
expenditure—a fact that was never stated officially.[1] The army
leaders knew it was vital that the opportunities for fund raising
by military entrepreneurs should expand, so that the members
of the armed forces, especially in the regions, would remain
satisfied. At the same time, the practice of unconventional financing created vested interests in the continuation of a system
which placed individual officers in positions where they could
amass much personal wealth.

1. In an editorial on 4 March 1970, the armed forces' newspaper, *Angkatan
Bersenjata,* said that the armed forces' budget covered only slightly more than half
of its operating requirements (translated in *United States Embassy Translation Unit
Press Review,* hereafter cited as *USE*). Earlier, the deputy to the commander of the
army in charge of administration, Major General Hartono, said that only 40 percent of the army's needs were covered by the official budget (*Pedoman,* 30 September 1969), and in 1970 the naval chief of staff said that only 30–40 percent of the
navy's requirements were met by the government (*Indonesia Raya,* 28 March 1970).

The Army's Fund Raising

Under the system of unconventional financing, selected officers at all levels were placed in positions where they could raise funds on behalf of the army. At the highest level, such huge enterprises as the state oil corporation, the national food-trading agency, and a giant general trading corporation were placed under the control of senior army officers. In addition, many enterprises were formed to supplement the funds of particular military units and sections, and similar arrangements were made in the regions, where military officers became involved in a wide range of business activities. The chief responsibility of these military entrepreneurs was to ensure a steady flow of funds into the army's coffers without causing disruption in the economy. The methods they used were left largely to their own discretion, although they were expected to avoid "excesses" which brought the military into public disrepute. They were permitted to reap off part of the proceeds as a reward for their efforts, provided they did not take "too much." In conducting their operations, military-sponsored enterprises were frequently given favored treatment by army officers occupying key positions in the bureaucracy.

By far the most important source of funds for the army during the early phase of the New Order was the state oil corporation, Pertamina. During the 1960s, oil provided about a third of Indonesia's export earnings and about two-thirds after the price rises of 1973 and 1974. Formed as Permina in 1957 when the army chief of staff, Major General Nasution, ordered his second deputy, Colonel Ibnu Sutowo, to take over a disused field in the north of Sumatra, the company's activities expanded with capital provided by a Japanese business group. During the Guided Democracy period, the three foreign oil corporations—Caltex, Stanvac, and Shell—together with foreign enterprises in other fields were put under considerable pressure by the government. After protracted negotiations leading to the 1963 oil agreements, the foreign companies gave up the concessions they had held since colonial times and accepted what were, in effect, profit-sharing arrangements with three state-owned Indonesian companies, one of which was Permina. After 1966 the army-dominated Permina absorbed the other two Indonesian companies and was renamed Pertamina in 1968. Having bought out Shell at the end of 1965, Pertamina continued the profit-sharing contracts with Caltex and

Stanvac, but introduced a new system of production-sharing contracts for new companies engaged in offshore exploration. In contrast with the liberalization of investment conditions in other fields after 1967, the production-sharing contracts were less attractive to the major international oil corporations than the earlier profit-sharing arrangements, with the result that the big corporations held back while contracts were taken up in 1966 and 1967 by small and relatively unknown companies, which in some cases seemed more interested in speculation than exploration. By 1968, however, the major international corporations had revised their attitudes, and after Mobil signed a production-sharing contract in October 1968, the others quickly followed. By 1975 more than fifty production-sharing contracts had been signed with thirty-five companies. Oil production—still mainly from onshore fields operated by Caltex and Pertamina—had risen from 174 million barrels in 1966 to 476 million barrels per year in 1975.[2]

Pertamina's activities soon expanded into fields outside oil production. It participated in the Far East Oil Trading Company established in Japan in 1965 and the Tugu Insurance Company in Hong Kong. It made huge investments in several petrochemical projects, including fertilizer plants. In 1970 it formed PT Krakatau Steel in association with the Department of Industry to complete construction of the Cilegon steel plant abandoned by the USSR in 1966. In the 1970s it invested in a project to establish an industrial estate and tourist facilities on Batam Island near Singapore and participated in a large rice estate in South Sumatra. Apart from these and many other projects, Pertamina's funds were used for a wide range of noneconomic purposes, such as to build a first-class hospital in Jakarta, a television studio in Medan, a sports stadium in Palembang, a mosque at the University of Indonesia, and the Bina Graha building for the president's office. The most important use to which Pertamina's funds were put during the early period of the New Order was to supplement the funds available to the armed forces and the military leadership.

Although Pertamina was a state-owned corporation, in practice it operated more like a private corporation run by Ibnu Sutowo, who was responsible only to the military leadership. Though formally responsible to the minister for mining, Ibnu Sutowo insisted on complete autonomy. When Slamat Bratanata, the minister appointed in July 1966, sought to exercise control over the oil industry by, among other things, insisting on the allocation of contracts through a system of open tenders and objecting to Pertamina's refusal to transfer taxes collected from Caltex on the government's behalf to the government, Suharto transferred the directorate for oil and natural gas away from the Department of Mining and placed it directly under his own authority until Bratanata was dismissed in 1967. Bratanata's successor apparently accepted Pertamina's right to conduct its operations in its own way, and even when a Board of Commissioners, consisting of senior ministers, was established in 1972, Ibnu Sutowo's autonomy remained virtually unrestricted. Only in 1975, when Pertamina was unable to meet short-term foreign debt commitments of around $1.5 billion, was Ibnu Sutowo's autonomy in running Pertamina seriously challenged, and in 1976, after an enquiry revealed debts of over $10 billion, he was replaced by another army officer.

Pertamina's financial affairs have been clouded in secrecy. Balance sheets were never published and profits were unannounced. Although its taxation payments to the government rose from 15 percent of the government's domestic revenues in 1967 to more than 50 percent after the 1973 price rise, it was clear that a large part of Pertamina's profits, especially in the early phase, was not transferred to the government. The secrecy surrounding the financial affairs of Pertamina was intended to disguise its role as a major source of funds at the disposal of the military leadership. In the competitive atmosphere of Guided Democracy, the army had developed its financial independence, and this pattern continued under the New Order. Obtaining a substantial part of its funds and foreign exchange requirements directly from Pertamina, the army sought to free itself from domestic criticism and foreign pressure by creating the impression that military expenditure was less than it really was. The funds made available by Pertamina enhanced the power of the army leaders, who were able to distribute rewards according to political requirements without being subject to bureaucratic controls and international pressure. As long as Ibnu Sutowo continued to supply the funds required by the military leaders, they had no interest in restricting his autonomy in running Pertamina. In the 1970s, however, their dependence on him decreased as the government's sources of "orthodox" funds expanded. As a result, Ibnu Sutowo's position became vulnerable when Pertamina fell into financial difficulties in 1975.

Another important fund-raising agency was the National Logistics Board (Bulog), concerned with trading in essential commodities, of which the most important was rice. Founded in 1966 as the National Logistics Command, Bulog was dominated by army officers. Headed originally by Brigadier General (later Lieutenant General) Achmad Tirtosudiro, a senior officer whose career was spent largely in military financing and logistics, Bulog was controlled by army officers in its central administration and regional branches. Until 1970, Bulog's main responsibility was the purchase of rice for civil servants and members of the armed forces, whose salaries were paid partly in kind. In 1970, following severe price fluctuations, it was given the additional task of creating a buffer stock in order to stabilize prices both for the producer and the consumer. Bulog's operations were financed by credit from the Bank of Indonesia. According to the official Commission of Four's inquiry into corruption in 1970, Bulog had never made a satisfactory report on its utilization of credit and other financial transactions.[3] Bulog's domestic purchases were not made directly at the village level, but through middlemen—mostly Chinese— and its sales on the open market were also made through private traders. Bulog quickly acquired considerable notoriety as a center of corruption.

Much of Bulog's funds were used for speculation in addition to rice purchasing. For example, when Bulog's credit from the Bank of Indonesia was obtained in 1968 at a rate of 3 percent per month, private banks were offering depositors around 10 to 15 percent. As a result, it became the practice for Bulog officials, like officials in many other government agencies, to place government funds under their control in private banks illegally or to invest in other short-term speculative projects. Among the private banks in Jakarta where Bulog funds were deposited was the Bank Dharma Ekonomi, a subsidiary of the army-controlled trading corporation, PT Berdikari. Similar practices were almost universal in the regions, as in North Sumatra, where the lieutenant colonel in charge of Bulog placed funds in the Bank of Sumatra, which had another lieutenant colonel among its directors.[4]

3. *Sinar Harapan*, 22 July 1970.
4. *Harian Kami*, 4, 7 October 1967.

One of the consequences of using Bulog's funds for speculation was a reluctance on the part of Bulog officials to make purchases in the early part of the harvesting season because they preferred to leave funds for as long as possible in more profitable fields. In 1967, Bulog delayed making purchases during the main harvesting season in the first part of the year with the intention of buying heavily during the dry-season harvest in the middle of the year, but a poor midyear harvest meant that by October only 280,000 tons had been bought, compared with a target of 597,000 tons, and Bulog had no stocks as prices rose rapidly at the end of 1967 and in early 1968.[5] One of Bulog's difficulties had been a series of private bank crashes after August 1967, including the crash of the Bank of Sumatra and others in which Bulog funds had been deposited. According to the Bulog head, Achmad Tirtosudiro, Bulog's operations had been hampered by "administrative irregularities" involving Rp 1.3 billion ($800,000).[6] A more serious disaster hit Bulog in December 1968 when the Bank Dharma Ekonomi "unexpectedly crashed," as Achmad Tirtosudiro put it.[7] During the first nine months of 1969, Bulog's domestic procurements amounted to only 156,000 tons, compared with a target of 420,000 tons, so that prices fell in the early part of the year to the detriment of peasants and rose to very high levels in the latter part of the year to the advantage of rice traders, as Bulog waited for imports to supplement its inadequate stocks.[8]

As the sole importer of rice, Bulog relied heavily on imports, which usually greatly exceeded domestic purchases. Indeed, it

5. Arndt wrote, "With quite inadequate stocks built up in the first half of the year, and with domestic supplies unexpectedly reduced by drought and import supplies almost unprocurable in the second half, the government . . . lost control of the situation after September. But for substantial PL 480 shipments which arrived in the nick of time in December and January, the situation would have been even more serious" (1968:9).

6. *Kompas*, 29 September 1967.

7. Ibid., 20 March 1970.

8. According to Arndt, "Actually Bulog bought very little rice in April and in the first half of May, reportedly owing to administrative difficulties" (1969a:6). Later Arndt reported, "Bulog, handicapped by administrative difficulties and by what proved to be excessively high quality standards, made virtually no domestic purchases between January and May" (1969b:11). An anonymous contributor to the *Bulletin of Indonesian Economic Studies* (*BIES*) wrote, "The intended price support policies failed to materialise principally owing to a lack of understanding of the policy by those charged with implementing it" (6 [March 1970], 2). It would appear that in fact more than "administrative difficulties," "excessively high quality standards," and "lack of understanding" was impeding Bulog's performance.

sometimes appeared that Bulog had a vested interest in maintaining the high level of rice imports as, for example, in 1968, when some 838,000 tons were imported, while about 60,000 tons went unpurchased in South Sulawesi, and again in 1970, when imports reached 1,051,000 tons, while the unpurchased South Sulawesi surplus rose to more than 72,000 tons.[9] In 1970, Bulog's policy of high imports combined with its tardiness in commencing domestic purchases led to a fall in rice prices below the stipulated "floor" price in many areas, including East Java, Yogyakarta, Aceh, North Sumatra, and West Sumatra. Again in 1972 prices fell below the floor price in several important rice-producing areas.[10] The high level of food imports, on the other hand, meant that there were plenty of opportunities for Bulog agents to obtain "commissions" from prospective foreign suppliers,[11] while domestic purchases below the "floor" price opened up opportunities for local Bulog officers to make personal profits.

Although Bulog's performance in procuring and distributing rice left much to be desired, it was very successful in providing opportunities to raise funds for the army as well as individual officers. Bulog's inability to repay credit resulted in losses for the government, but at the same time its fund-raising capacity enabled the government to make smaller budget allocations to the armed forces than would otherwise have been necessary. Nevertheless, Bulog's performance came under increasing criticism within government circles because of its failure to maintain adequate prices for farmers and its periodic inability to prevent steep rises in prices for urban consumers.[12] In the late 1960s Bulog's

9. See *Berita Yudha*, 14 October 1968 (*ICATS*), and *Nusantara*, 28 November 1970 (*ICATS*), for references to the surpluses in South Sulawesi, and table in *BIES* 7 (March 1971), 18–19, for import figures for rice and the rice substitute, bulgur.

10. Grenville 1973:5.

11. Sullivan wrote, "A common gambit was to approach an American rice shipper or dealer in Texas cotton as a representative of General Suharto empowered to make rice purchases—providing appropriate credits could be obtained from the American government. Implicit in these approaches was a tacit (or direct) agreement for a percentage of the sale as a bonus for the Indonesian military man. . . . Many times they carried vaguely worded letters signed by Suharto, which American diplomats came to refer to as 'hunting licences' " (1969:317–318).

12. One indication of growing concern was the tone of the weekly newspaper *Chas*, which was known to be close to army intelligence and Bakin elements. See, for example, the comments on Bulog in the issues for the third week of October (*USE*) and the first week of November 1969 (*ICATS*).

failure in the rice-trading field was apparently more than compensated for by its success as a fund raiser, but by the 1970s, as alternative sources of funds for the armed forces were developed, the government showed increased concern with Bulog's poor performance in the politically sensitive area of price stabilization. When Bulog was again caught with inadequate stocks at the end of 1972, prices rose sharply, leading to a new round of inflation which caused considerable discontent in the cities and threatened to undermine the government's economic achievements generally. In the wake of the 1972–1973 crisis, Achmad Tirtosudiro lost his position, but was rewarded for past services with an appointment as ambassador to West Germany. After 1973, Indonesia's very favorable foreign exchange position enabled Bulog to build up a large buffer stock which was used to prevent excessive price fluctuations.

A less successful army-sponsored business venture was PT Berdikari, a limited liability company owned by the government. PT Berdikari was set up in 1966 to take over two of the "old order" trading corporations, PT Karkam and PT Aslam, which had owed their spectacular business success largely to the patronage of President Sukarno, Jusuf Muda Dalam, and others. The turnover of the two companies was estimated to equal three times that of all six state trading corporations put together. The new corporation was headed by Brigadier General Suhardiman, a protégé of the former army commander, Yani. Suhardiman had led the army-sponsored "trade union," SOKSI, in its fight against the Communist party's SOBSI during the Guided Democracy period, and he also headed one of the state trading corporations, P. N. Djaja Bhakti. As head of Berdikari, Suhardiman was responsible directly to Suharto, who instructed him to "endeavor to bring about the expansion of the two enterprises so that they grow larger than when they were taken over, in order to benefit the nation, the revolution, and society."[13] In fact, Berdikari's main purpose was to raise funds for the army leadership.

Suhardiman set out on an ambitious program of expansion. Offices were established at overseas trading centers, and several subsidiary companies were set up, including the Bank Dharma Ekonomi. With military backing, Suhardiman was able to sidestep bureaucratic obstacles, such as the ban imposed by the trade min-

13. *Angkatan Bersenjata,* 24 May 1966.

ister, Sumitro, in 1968 on the import of cars valued at more than $2,000. Berdikari, which had acquired rights as the sole importer of Mercedes Benz cars to Indonesia, continued to import the cars through Jakarta's port, and eventually the trade minister withdrew the regulation.[14]

Suhardiman worked closely with the Taiwan-oriented section of the Chinese business community. In 1967 a mission of Taiwanese businessmen visited Jakarta and an Indonesian group visited Taiwan. The Taiwan government had offered credit of $20 million, apparently conditional on Indonesia's changing its vote in favor of China's admission to the United Nations. When Indonesia continued to support China's admission, the offer of long-term credit was withdrawn, but short-term credit of $10 million was offered to Suhardiman's group, presumably in the hope that they would work to secure a change in Indonesia's vote in 1968. In the latter part of 1968, however, Suhardiman suddenly fell from favor. Rumors spread that he had been arrested, and early in 1969 it was announced that he was attending an "upgrading" course at the Seskoad. It seems that Berdikari had expanded its operations too rapidly and toward the end of 1968 its bank, Bank Dharma Ekonomi, had collapsed, causing losses not only to Berdikari, but also to other government agencies, such as Bulog, which had deposited funds in the bank. During 1969, PT Berdikari's activities were cut drastically and its staff reduced by half.

The big sources of military funds in the late 1960s were Pertamina, Bulog, and—for a short time—Berdikari. Meanwhile, a wide range of smaller scale fund-raising activities were conducted by military personnel. In the absence of adequate funds from the government budget, individual sections and units of the army, as well as other branches of the armed forces, had set up "welfare foundations" and other enterprises to finance their own operations and supplement the incomes of their members. As a result, some sections, such as logistics, prospered, while other less wellplaced units were barely able to maintain themselves. In 1969 the army leadership decided to take steps toward the further centralization of fund-raising activities in order to be in a better position to allocate resources rationally within the army. The foundations

14. See Rice 1969:202, *Kompas*, 27 August 1968 (*USE*), and *Api Pantjasila*, 4 September 1968 (*USE*).

and other bodies run by the eight major directorates attached to the army headquarters were replaced with registered private companies owned by the army and coordinated by another army enterprise, PT Tri Usaha Bhakti.[15] Among the companies affiliated to Tri Usaha Bhakti were an automobile assembling plant, a battery factory, clothing and shoe factories, several rice mills, the Bank Gemari, Zamrud Airlines, and several forestry projects in Kalimantan and Ambon conducted as joint ventures with foreign enterprises.

Although the foundations run by sections of the army attached to the headquarters were rationalized and coordinated after 1969, many other foundations continued to operate. The largest was the Yayasan Dharma Putra Kostrad set up by Kostrad. This foundation had been established in 1964 by Suharto, the Kostrad commander at the time. Its daily operations were managed by Brigadier General Sofjar, who was the driving force behind its rapid expansion after 1966.[16] The foundation cooperated closely with an influential Chinese businessman, Liem Siu Liong, who had a close business relationship with General Suharto dating back to Suharto's period as commander in Central Java. Together with Liem, Sofjar established the Bank Windhu Kencana and, with credit obtained from its own bank, the foundation established the Seulawah and Mandala airlines. The foundation also operated subsidiaries engaged in film distribution, building construction, and other fields including several crumb rubber plants.[17] The foundation was able to finance its expanding operations largely through its bank, which easily attracted deposits from businessmen aware of the influence of its patrons. The "Kencana" complex of companies, which was connected with the business interests of the Suharto family through Liem Siu Liong, became one of the largest business groups in Indonesia.

Another important army-sponsored body was the Army Central Cooperative Board (Inkopad), with its affiliates in the regions. Inkopad's income came from a wide range of sources. In 1967 it took over the construction of Jakarta's second "international-class"

15. *Kompas*, 28 August 1969.
16. Shortly before he died in 1973, Sofjar was chief of staff of Kostrad and general chairman of the Indonesian Chamber of Commerce and Industry.
17. See *Ekspres*, 3 October 1970, pp. 7–8.

hotel, which had been commenced under the sponsorship of Jusuf Muda Dalam. As a joint venture with a Hong Kong company,
the hotel, Kartika Plaza, was opened in 1970. In another joint
venture, Inkopad cooperated with a Japanese company engaged
in fishing in the Arafura Sea, while in North Sumatra the interregional military command appointed Inkopad as the sole exporter
of vegetables and fruit. Although Inkopad did not appear to have
played an active role in managing the projects with which it was
associated, it was able to acquire the permits, licenses, and other
facilities required by the active partners, who were usually Chinese or foreign.

In the regions, local commanders were left to their own devices
in raising funds for local needs. In Sumatra and other export-
producing areas, army-protected smuggling was important, especially in the first few years after 1966. According to one study of
military enterprises, "The range of activities undertaken is limited
only by the imagination of the military commanders."[18] A major
field of activity was the use of military vehicles and ships for the
transport of passengers and freight; in Java the RPKAD was involved in the Pemuda Ekspres bus line, which competed with the
Kko's Bhumyanca line. A foundation sponsored by the Siliwangi
division set up PT Propelat in 1970, which became a major contractor for Pertamina's construction projects in West Java. Rice
milling and building construction were common army enterprises,
and many cinemas were owned by army units or other branches
of the armed forces. It was also common for military units and
foundations associated with them to establish their own banks,
such as the Bank Bukit Barisan in Medan and the Bank Brawijaya
in Surabaya. One of the most imaginative fund-raising initiatives
was taken by a police foundation, which presented bullfighting in
Jakarta in 1969. Most of these military-sponsored enterprises
were in fact operated by Chinese businessmen, with the military
partners ensuring that the necessary licenses and "facilities" were
available and providing "protection" when illegal activities were
involved. If in the 1950s Chinese businessmen used Indonesian

18. Rieffel and Wirjasaputra 1972:106–107. For descriptions of military fund
raising in North Sumatra, see the articles by Robert Keatley in the *Wall Street
Journal*, 2 May 1967 (translated in *Nusantara*, 17 May 1967), and by Jack Foisie in
the *Los Angeles Times*, 3 July 1969 (translated in *Pedoman*, 18 August 1969).

partners as "frontmen" in the so-called "Ali-Baba" concerns, by the late 1960s it had become common to refer to "Baba-Ali" enterprises in which army officers stood behind the Chinese managers.

Private Interests of Army Officers

One consequence of the involvement of army officers in fund raising was the spread of a "commercial" orientation within the officer corps. The officers assigned to fund raising acquired money-making skills, which they used on behalf of the army and increasingly on their own personal behalf. If originally army officers had been forced into commercial activity by necessity, they soon adjusted themselves to their new responsibilities. Many officers felt much more at home dealing with Chinese and foreign businessmen than commanding troops in the field. The commercial ethos spread rapidly outside the circle of the officers concerned directly with managing armed forces enterprises. Officers appointed to positions in the bureaucracy became equally involved with Chinese partners in private business concerns, and regional military commanders often had their own private sources of funds.

The army leadership showed no sign of disapproving of the trend. Instead it adopted the view that it was perfectly natural for officers to exploit their official positions for personal gain. As in the patrimonial states of traditional Java, where officials obtained their incomes from benefices rather than salaries, army officers were expected to make the most of their appointments in the bureaucracy and other government agencies, which were often seen as rewards for earlier loyalty. Provided they performed their functions effectively, objections were not raised if they enriched themselves on the side. The officers involved in bodies that made substantial purchases commonly demanded "commissions" from suppliers. Similarly, it was normal to obtain "commissions" from applicants for contracts, especially in the construction industry, and not unusual for construction companies to be owned by relatives of government officials. The wives of army officers became increasingly active in the commercial world.

An example was set by the large trading company, CV Waringin, whose directors included General Suharto's business associate, Liem Siu Liong, and Suharto's foster brother, Sudwikatmono.[19] Reportedly Waringin had obtained a vast quantity of credit from the government, enabling its activities to grow rapidly, and it had been favored by officials who, in one instance, permitted it to export more than five times its coffee export quota in 1967.[20] Apparently, CV Waringin had obtained some of its privileges by underhanded means—in 1970 the Commission of Four's inquiry into corruption named it as one of five cases that should be given priority.[21] However, at a meeting with students in July 1970, President Suharto said that CV Waringin had already repaid credit of Rp 60 million that had apparently been outstanding for some time, and proceedings were never initiated against the company.[22] Mrs. Tien Suharto, the president's wife, was also active in the business world as head of the "charitable" Our Hope Foundation (Yayasan Harapan Kita). The foundation owned several companies and was associated with Liem Siu Liong in PT Bogasari, which set up several flour mills in 1970 and 1971 with credit from the Bank of Indonesia which it reportedly received five days after submitting its application.[23] The president's young brother, Probosutedjo, was another member of his family to achieve outstanding business success during the New Order period. His business interests included construction, glass manufacturing, a compost plant, cooking oil, a chicken farm, and the clove importing company, PT Mercu Buana. In 1970, PT Mercu Buana and a firm controlled by Liem Siu Liong, PT Mega, were given monopoly rights by the government to import cloves. Explaining the success of the president's family in business, Probosutedjo admitted at a press conference that it had been "good fortune" to be related to

19. On Waringin, see *Nusantara,* 12 February 1971. Later in 1971 the editor of *Nusantara,* T. D. Hafas, was charged under the colonial "hate-sowing delicts" with having insulted the government and the president in articles published between 25 June 1970 and 12 February 1971. Significantly, he was not charged with libel. Eventually he was convicted and sentenced to one year of imprisonment. The Dutch laws provided for sanctions against persons who expressed "feelings of enmity, hate or disdain toward the Government of the Netherlands or that of the Netherlands Indies."

20. *Mahasiswa Indonesia,* 101, (May 1968). The report mentioned rumors that credit of Rp 500 million had been provided by the government for CV Waringin.

21. *Sinar Harapan,* 18 July 1970.

22. *Indonesia Raya,* 15 July 1970.

23. See the conflicting reports in *Nusantara,* 11 February 1971, and *Merdeka,* 16 February 1971. *Merdeka*'s report was intended to refute that of *Nusantara,* but it in fact confirms the essence of *Nusantara*'s allegations.

the president. Although he denied that the president had given his family special favors, he agreed that government officials dealing with them would have known their family connections.[24]

The head of Pertamina, Ibnu Sutowo, was another general with extensive private business interests. In 1970 he told a *Time* magazine correspondent, "I'm big in tobacco exports, drugstores, a textile factory, rubber estates and have interests in six or seven companies." Emphasizing how easy it was for a man in his position to add to his income, he said, "I personally stay out of anything connected with oil. But people are happy to deal with me because they know who I am." As an example, he related how a Singapore contractor had obtained rocks from an Indonesian quarry after Ibnu Sutowo had obtained the necessary permission from the Indonesian authorities. "I just arranged it," he told the correspondents, and without investing a cent, he obtained 50 percent of the profits on the deal.[25] Ibnu Sutowo's son, Ponco, followed his father's example. As head of the PT Adhiguna Shipyard, he arranged for it to obtain the contract to service Pertamina's shipping fleet.[26]

Other senior officers performed similar roles for foreign investors. The new foreign investment law of 1967 opened the way for a rapid inflow of foreign capital in the late 1960s which turned into a flood in the 1970s. By 1971 only $222 million had been invested (apart from investment in oil), but by 1973 this figure had jumped to almost $1 billion, and Japanese investment had overtaken American. The typical arrangement was for the investment to take the form of a joint venture in which the Indonesian side consisted of a partnership between senior military officers and Chinese businessmen.

The commercial activities of army officers and their Chinese business associates often led to what were referred to as "excesses" by those in authority. One of the most spectacular was the so-called "BE Scandal" of 1968. The opportunity for the fraud was provided by the large gap in the price paid by importers for foreign exchange originating as aid from foreign governments and the price of foreign exchange available from other sources,

24. *Kompas*, 29 September 1976.
25. *Time*, 31 August 1970, p. 42. See also Louis Kraar 1973.
26. *Tempo*, 6 March 1976.

such as exports. The foreign exchange arising from aid (known as BE) was sold to importers at a low rate, but its use was limited to the import of priority goods, whereas foreign exchange from other sources could be used for any purpose, but was sold at a higher rate. During 1968 a number of importers with good connections in the government bought BE foreign exchange for the import of goods on the priority list, but, after forging the necessary shipping documents, did not import the goods. The dollars obtained at the low BE price were used either to import more profitable consumer goods not on the priority list or resold in Jakarta at the much higher open market rate. After the practice had been uncovered by the newly appointed minister for trade, Sumitro, in August, the attorney general, Sugih Arto, estimated that the amount of credit misused during June, July, and August amounted to $35 million, or about one-third of the foreign exchange allocated for imports during that period. He admitted that the practice may have commenced much earlier, and others estimated that the total amount misused during 1968 may have been around $100 million.[27] This figure compared with $350 million made available by foreign governments in 1968, of which about $275 million took the form of balance of payments support through the BE scheme.

The BE Scandal was not only of enormous dimensions, but involved aid supplied by foreign governments. Thus action had to be taken to reassure foreign creditors that aid would not be misused again. Thirty-five importers, apparently all of them Chinese, were deregistered, and Sugih Arto imposed a temporary ban on all Chinese leaving the country. Despite these measures, he announced in the middle of September that only one of the importers had been caught, while the rest had fled, presumably abroad.[28] Although reports stated that several government officials were detained at the time, none was ever charged and tried, nor were any of the importers. In 1970, however, Sugih Arto announced that a "peaceful settlement" had been reached and that seven of the unnamed "manipulators" who had been responsible for the misuse of $22.1 of the $35 million had agreed to import priority goods of that value and would also pay a fine of

27. *Berita Yudha*, 1 October 1968.
28. *Nusantara*, 16 September 1968 (*USE*).

Rp 25 or about six cents per dollar misused.[29] It was widely believed that the main reason for not bringing the "manipulators" to court was that many had business connections with prominent military leaders.

Another major "excess" settled "peacefully" involved a firm known as PT Mantrust that had a subsidiary in Japan known as the Mexim Company. Mantrust had been an important supplier for the armed forces during the early 1960s and had strong ties with officers in the army's logistics section, some of whom later occupied important positions in Bulog. When students asked the Bulog head, Achmad Tirtosudiro, why Bulog had awarded a contract to Mantrust in 1967, he replied that he had known Mantrust's directors for many years and trusted them.[30] Under the contract, Mantrust received credit from both Bulog and the Bank of Indonesia to establish factories to produce artificial rice. The credit included $2.5 million in foreign exchange to import equipment from Japan. But no preliminary survey was made to assess whether the artificial rice would be acceptable to public taste, and it was more expensive to produce than had been anticipated. In 1969, Mantrust obtained the $2.5 million in foreign exchange at the low BE rate, but purchased equipment worth only $1.8 million, the remaining $700,000 reportedly being sent back to Jakarta for sale at the high open market rate. The scandal broke in August 1969, when two directors of Mantrust's affiliate in Japan were arrested for violating Japan's foreign currency regulations.[31] Immediately, President Suharto's personal assistant, Sudjono Humardhani, was sent to Japan, where he met the Japanese finance minister, Takeo Fukuda, and shortly afterward the two businessmen were released. Although the 1970 Commission of Four's inquiry into corruption called on the Indonesian government to prosecute the company, the government took the view that only Japanese law had been broken and that Indonesia had suffered no loss.[32] Under the patronage of Achmad Tirtosudiro, Sudjono Humardhani, and another of the president's personal assistants, Surjo, Mantrust continued to prosper.

29. *Kompas*, 11 February 1970, 25 July 1970. The exchange rate was $1 equals Rp 376.
30. *Mahasiswa Indonesia*, 77 (December 1967).
31. *Kompas*, 13 August 1969, *Mahasiswa Indonesia*, 7 September 1969.
32. *Kompas*, 13 September 1969.

The biggest "excess" of 1970 involved a company with which
Surjo was associated. In 1968 the Indonesian government established a scheme known as "Bimas Gotong Royong," under which
foreign companies were made responsible for introducing the
"Green Revolution" on a wide scale. The foreign companies undertook to provide seeds, fertilizers, and other inputs, including
the aerial spraying of pesticides, while the government undertook,
through Bulog, to collect credit repayments from the peasants on
behalf of the foreign companies.[33] Among the companies involved were such well-known corporations as Ciba, Hoechst, and
Mitsubishi, as well as the internationally unknown Coopa Trading
Establishment registered in Liechtenstein. Coopa's Jakarta "representative" was an Indonesian Chinese, Arief Husni (Ong Seng
Kheng), the manager of the Bank Ramayana, with which Surjo
and Suharto's brother Probosetedjo, were closely associated.

In the first three months of 1970, newspaper allegations were
made that although Coopa had failed to supply fertilizers for its
projects, the government had paid it on the basis of forged documents. Coopa allegedly had received payment of $711,000 for
200 tons of diazinon which had not arrived at the beginning of
1969, and again at the end of 1969 it had been paid for urea
which had not been distributed.[34] The government took the view
that Coopa had been guilty only of "technical" violations of the
law and decided that as Coopa had contracted to supply credit of
$13 million, the matter was better settled out of court.[35] Later in
the year the Commission of Four placed the Coopa case among
the urgent cases that should be taken to court, but its recommen-
dation was not heeded by the government.

The Bimas Gotong Royong program led to a substantial increase in rice production through the introduction of new seed
varieties, but it was also very profitable for the companies involved
which were guaranteed payment by the government. The rush to

33. See Rieffel 1969, Hansen 1972, Meares 1970.
34. *Indonesia Raya,* 5 January, 6, 7, 31 March 1970, *Nusantara,* 2 March 1970
(*USE*).
35. *Pedoman,* 4 March 1970, *Kompas,* 4 March 1970. The minister for information, Air Vice Marshal Budiardjo, even described the case as a "blessing in disguise" and hinted that the critics of Coopa were speaking for foreign companies
that had been unable to participate in the Bimas Gotong Royong program. The
editor of *Indonesia Raya,* Mochtar Lubis, was also head of a consulting agency
(Indoconsult) for prospective foreign investors.

increase the area covered by the Bimas Gotong Royong program after the first Ciba project in 1968–1969 suggested that the program was also profitable for some Indonesian officials, who seemed more concerned to expand the scope of the program than to ensure its effective implementation.[36] Bulog proved unable to enforce repayments by the peasants, leaving the government with the debt, rumored to be about Rp 25 billion ($60 million),[37] and in May 1970 it was announced that the scheme would be abandoned. The "excess" of the Coopa case had highlighted the failure of the program, which was causing the government large losses and giving rise to considerable resistance among the peasantry.

One type of activity carried out by military officers which the army leaders sought to suppress was unauthorized smuggling. Although in the early years of the New Order some regional commanders in export-producing areas continued to condone smuggling conducted to raise funds for the army, steps were taken to repress smuggling by individuals for their own profit. Unlike some other forms of "unorthodox" fund raising, smuggling had directly disruptive consequences on the economy and deprived the central government of revenue. During 1967, smuggling had become an area of major concern for the government, and in August Acting President Suharto ordered that "all foundations, cooperatives, and enterprises associated with any of the armed forces" must "observe all valid requirements and regulations"; he also ordered that "all ships and airplanes owned or operated by armed forces units must load and unload nonmilitary cargoes at ports staffed by customs officials."[38] During the following years, the form of smuggling changed from the "physical" to

36. In 1968 the program covered 300,000 hectares. This rose to 1,650,000 for the first 1969 crop and 3,475,000 for the second crop. According to Selo Soemardjan, the private secretary to the sultan of Yogyakarta (minister for the economy, finance, and development), "As a result of incomplete organizational planning, even after due corrections and improvements after every season, the implementation of the program did not meet the expectations of both the government and the people. Ineffective communication with the farmers at the grass roots made many of them reluctant to work actively in the program, difficulties in transportation resulted in dissatisfactory and untimely distribution of fertilizers down to the villages, rehabilitation of neglected irrigation networks could not keep pace with the increasing areas of rice fields in need of water, and finally the marketing of the increased rice production, not well prepared in advance, confused the price and turned only an insignificant net profit into the hands of the farmers" (1971:7–8).

37. *Kompas*, 26 October 1971.

38. Ibid., 26 April 1967.

the "administrative." As the army disciplined its members, the smuggling of export products declined, and it became less common for army-owned ships to unload commercial cargoes on lonely beaches in the middle of the night. Nevertheless, smuggled goods continued to enter the country through the main ports, where customs officials were in league with high-level army officers. In place of "physical" smuggling the goods went through the proper procedures, but it was arranged "administratively" that import duties and other charges be overlooked.[39] In 1971 a large-scale "administrative" smuggling racket was discovered by the reform-minded chief of police, General Hugeng Imam Santoso. Hundreds of expensive cars were being imported duty-free through Jakarta's port, Tanjung Priok. The smuggling ring was said to be headed by a young Chinese working in league with customs officials, but they clearly had backers in the military elite. Far from being congratulated for his exposure of the case, Hugeng was dismissed from his post a few days later.[40] Hugeng rejected an offer of appointment as ambassador to Brazil.

During the 1970s the dependence of the armed forces on "unconventional" sources of funds declined as the government's capacity to raise "conventional" revenue through taxation improved. The army's "official" budget trebled between 1969 and 1973[41] and rose sharply during the following years, when oil price rises led to an enormous increase in government revenues generally. In the late 1960s a major general's official salary was no more than Rp 15,000 (about US $40) per month, but by 1975 it had risen to more than Rp 100,000, and similar increases were made for all ranks.[42] Although the need for military units and individual officers to depend on "unconventional" sources had greatly declined, old habits die hard. Unchallenged by political groups outside the army, military men continued to use their positions in the government to further their personal business interests.

39. In 1972 the Department of Finance estimated that Indonesia lost $1 million per day through smuggling, of which 80 percent was "administrative" and 20 percent "physical" (*Kompas*, 1 November 1972).

40. Hugeng announced the discovery of the racket on 9 September 1971 (*Kompas*, 10 September 1971) and was dismissed four days later (ibid., 15 September 1971).

41. *Nusantara*, 18 January 1973 (translated in *Indonesian Current Affairs Translation Service*).

42. Booth and Glassburner 1975:19.

Corruption

What was considered as an "excess" by those within the system was often regarded as yet another manifestation of "corruption" by those on the outside. The Dutch sociologist, W. F. Wertheim, has suggested that it was only after the creation of the Napoleonic state in Europe that officials were expected to keep their private business separate from their public activities and even later that the distinction between public and private accounts was transferred to the colonies. During the early period of Dutch rule in Indonesia, the salaries paid by the Dutch East Indies Company were very nominal because officials were expected to seize the opportunities open to them to carry out private business, and eventually "these perquisites of office were considered so normal that instead of receiving a nominal salary, an annual 'office charge' had to be paid to the Company."[43] In traditional Java, officials were similarly rewarded by being placed in positions which they were expected to exploit for their own benefit. All the land was "owned" by the sultan, who apportioned it as benefices for loyal officials. Like the contemporary village head, who is allocated the use of land rather than a salary, "payment of officials [was] essentially in the form of specified benefices allotted by the ruler for the period of tenure of each particular office." As B. R. O'G. Anderson has pointed out, residual influences of the old appanage system are still present. He writes, "Corruption on a large scale typically takes the form of the allotting of the 'surplus' of certain key sectors of the economy to favored officials or cliques of officials." In addition, "The corruption is typically used to finance a whole subsection of the administrative apparatus," and "Cuts and commissions are often standardised enough to be called benefices in the traditional sense."[44]

Like the ancient sultans and their officials, who did not regard themselves as "corrupt" but were careful to avoid excessive exactions from the peasantry over whom they ruled for fear of creating political difficulties for themselves, the rulers of the New Order sought to avoid "excesses" but did not accept the charge

43. Wertheim 1964:124–131.
44. Anderson 1972b:33, 49.

of "corruption."[45] When Ibnu Sutowo told the *Time* correspondent that he had made money in his "spare time" by using his influence in the government to secure deals for foreign companies, he expected to be admired for his skill rather than accused of corruption.[46] For the army leaders, the provision of contracts, credit, and licenses for colleagues, friends, and relations or in exchange for "commissions" was normal business practice. To them the term "corruption" covered activities of a quite different sort carried on typically by low-level officials behind the backs of their colleagues, such as embezzling funds or misusing government property.

Beginning in 1967, students and a section of the press increasingly took up the issue of "corruption," which they thought threatened the achievement of the New Order's stated goals. In particular, they singled out generals close to the president including Ibnu Sutowo, Alamsjah, Surjo, Suhardiman, Sudjono Humardhani, and Achmad Tirtosudiro.[47] While Suharto continued to remain above criticism, they noted that "there are signs which suggest that Pak Harto is surrounded by a cordon consisting of elements whose integrity cannot be relied upon."[48] Student alienation continued to grow after 1967, aggravated by courageous revelations and allegations in several newspapers. The most outspoken were Mochtar Lubis' *Indonesia Raya* and T. D. Hafas' *Nusantara* together with the student newspapers, *Harian Kami,* edited by Nono Anwar Makarim, and *Mahasiswa Indonesia,* edited

45. After meeting the president in August 1970, the youth leader, Arief Budiman, wrote, "Corruption has its limits if they want it to survive. The limit is that corruption should not be so great as to obstruct economic development. If it obstructs development to the point, for example, where peasants can no longer grow rice because fertilizer is unavailable so that the price is extremely high, then it will no longer be only the youths in the cities who go into action but also the youths in the villages. This means a people's revolt or social revolution. Thus, if the corruptors are clever (and in Indonesia they are indeed clever enough), I think they will not violate this 'code of ethics.' Clever corruptors will not destroy the nation, they will keep the nation alive although very thin" (*Kompas,* 8 August 1970).

46. *Time,* 31 August 1970, p. 42. For a stinging attack on Ibnu Sutowo in response to the interview, see the editorial in *Indonesia Raya,* 9 September 1970, entitled "Not Corruption?"

47. See, for example, the "Hati Nurani Rakjat" column in *Mahasiswa Indonesia,* 59 (July 1967), 67 (September 1967), 77 (December 1967).

48. According to Ismid Hadad of *Harian Kami* in *Nusantara,* 18 May 1967. See also the article by Arief Budiman in *Kompas,* 11 March 1968 (*USE*).

from Bandung by Rahman Tolleng. Early in 1970, large demonstrations occurred in Jakarta in protest against a sudden increase in the prices of oil products—almost exactly four years after the demonstrations that culminated in the fall of Sukarno. Again in July and August 1970, student demonstrations occurred in the capital, while *Indonesia Raya* and *Nusantara* attacked the corruption of senior army officers in a way that was unprecedented since the army had come to power.[49]

Despite the much-publicized "excesses," the government continued to react to public criticism as if the key problem was the petty corruption of underpaid low-level officials. Receiving a delegation, Suharto said, "I feel that the presence of corruption is not due to a corrupt mentality, but is a result of economic pressures. Thus, we must eliminate the basic cause first."[50] As public dissatisfaction mounted, the government felt compelled to establish several agencies to investigate accusations of corruption, although in practice usually only the small cases ended in court proceedings. During the entire period of the New Order until 1976, only two generals were put on trial for corruption. The first, Brigadier General Sudarman, had been head of the BPU Timah managing nationalized tin mines since the Guided Democracy period and had apparently failed to cement his ties with the dominant military group around Suharto. He was convicted in 1969 and sentenced to two and a half years of imprisonment. The other officer, Major General Hartono Wirjodiprodjo, had been an important supporter of Suharto and had risen to the position of deputy to the commander of the army with responsibility for administration and finance. He was accused of using his position in a way that brought the Indonesian government into international disrepute by facilitating the smuggling of arms to Biafra during the Nigerian civil war and also, reportedly, to Israel. He was tried in camera by a military court and sentenced to two years of imprisonment, which he served at his home.

Although the 1945 Constitution provided for a Financial Inspection Board (BPK), the body established during the Guided Democracy period had been ineffective because of its subservi-

49. It was widely believed that the confidence with which *Indonesia Raya* and *Nusantara* attacked the generals close to Suharto was derived from their belief that they had the support of reform-minded elements within the army.

50. *Kompas*, 13 August 1970.

ence to the president, who appointed its chairman to the cabinet in 1964 and insisted on its reorganization in conformity with the Nasakom principle in 1965. In 1966, Lieutenant General Suprajogi was appointed as chairman of the BPK, but the board did not actively investigate minor cases of corruption until 1967. In the meantime, Suharto had set up a body known as the Team to Regularize State Finances (Pekuneg) in April 1966, headed by Surjo. The Pekuneg's primary function was to collect incriminating material about members of the old government, such as Jusuf Muda Dalam and Chaerul Saleh, and it succeeded in recovering irregular funds held by them in Indonesia and abroad. After a period of inactivity following the trial of Jusuf Muda Dalam in 1966, the Pekuneg was reactivated in April 1967, when the public became more disturbed about corruption among high officials. Although Surjo's ability to recover the irregular funds of Sukarno's ministers was recognized, he was not the most appropriate choice to head a body intended to reassure the public that the government was serious in its intention to suppress high-level corruption under the New Order.

In order to further assuage public doubts and growing cynicism about the government's anticorruption drive, a Team to Eliminate Corruption (TPK) was appointed in December 1967, under the leadership of the attorney general, Sugih Arto, and including several journalists, such as T. D. Hafas of *Nusantara,* and representatives of the Action Fronts. Following the establishment of this team, several relatively minor officials were tried during 1968. Explaining why all those brought to court were "small fish," Sugih Arto said, "For the time being the cases of the 'big fish' cannot be finalized because of technical difficulties."[51] During 1968, 172 cases were investigated, but none involved members of the armed forces.[52] At the beginning of 1970, one of Sugih Arto's deputies, Brigadier General Ali Said, said that the TPK had completed the investigation of 144 cases during 1969, but he admitted that among the uncompleted cases were those involving CV Waringin, the "BE manipulators," Bank Dharma Ekonomi, Pertamina, Bulog, and several dozen more.[53]

In response to the student demonstrations of January 1970, the

51. *Nusantara,* 25 January 1968.
52. *Pedoman,* 30 January 1969 *(USE).*
53. *Kompas,* 3 February 1970.

government appointed a Commission of Four on 31 January to inquire into corruption and ways of overcoming it. Headed by the former prime minister and respected PNI figure, Wilopo, its members were the veteran Catholic party leader, I. J. Kasimo, a former rector of the Gajah Madah University, Johannes, and the PSII politician, Anwar Tjokroaminoto. The former vice-president, Mohammed Hatta, who had refused the chairmanship of the commission, was appointed as its adviser, while the head of Bakin, Major General Sutopo Juwono, acted as its secretary. Although the government's purpose in appointing the commission was primarily to take the heat out of the situation in January 1970, its members were by no means nonentities who would not dare to raise embarrassing questions. Moreover, the secretary, Sutopo Juwono, was one of the few leading generals whom the student leaders respected.

During the next five months, the commission presented a series of recommendations to the government, dealing with Pertamina, Bulog, foreign investment in forestry, and the administration in general. After submitting its final recommendations at the end of June, the commission was dissolved, and the government announced that its proposals would be summarized by the president in his annual report to the DPR-GR on 16 August. The failure of the government to publish the full report of the commission caused widespread disappointment among students and in other disaffected circles. Suddenly, the newspaper, *Sinar Harapan,* published the commission's proposals in full over a number of days beginning on 18 July.[54] *Sinar Harapan*'s editor, Aristides Katoppo, had obtained a copy of the commission's report from a source close to the commission, and the government felt that it could not take action against either the source of the leak or the newspaper concerned without giving the impression that it wanted the report suppressed. Moreover, reformist and other dissident elements in the army itself had probably indicated their wish to see the report published so as to embarrass Suharto's colleagues.[55] In response to the commission's recommendations, the president issued a decision requiring officials to submit lists of their private property to him, and he publicly defined the role of his personal assistants as

54. See *Sinar Harapan,* 18 July 1970 to 24 July 1970.
55. The governor of the Military Academy at Magelang, Sarwo Edhie, was reported to have called for the publication of the report (*Pedoman,* 13 July 1970).

entailing no executive powers. In addition, an anticorruption law
and a law regulating the activities of Pertamina were soon passed.

The most crucial of the commission's recommendations was its
request to the government to give priority to five cases of corruption involving Coopa, CV Waringin, PT Mantrust, the Department of Religion, and the PN Telekom. The civilians involved in
the PN Telekom case were put on trial in July, and a high official
of the directorate for haj affairs in the Department of Religion
soon followed, but the Coopa, Waringin, and Mantrust cases were
ignored. Referring to the commission's request in his speech on
16 August, President Suharto said, "Cases where there is enough
evidence of violation of the law have already been placed before
courts. Certainly in cases where there is not enough evidence and
there are not enough grounds for prosecution it is difficult to
force them before the courts."[56]

In the wake of the publication of the Commission of Four's
report in *Sinar Harapan,* small-scale student demonstrations took
place, and on several occasions student delegations were received
by the president and other high officials. However, when students
planned to hold a "night of meditation" in one of Jakarta's main
streets on 15 August, shortly before the Independence Day celebrations, the army through the Kopkamtib banned all demonstrations and made it clear that the limits of its tolerance had been
reached. Although the demonstrations stopped and newspapers
like *Indonesia Raya* and *Nusantara* suddenly eased the tone of their
criticism, the government felt the need to defuse the corruption
issue further by bringing cases to court immediately. It was perhaps a measure of the gap between the government's conception
of corruption and that of the students that the cases brought
forward by the attorney general several days after the president's
speech involved nine minor officials in the State Electricity Corporation. Four of them were charged with embezzling funds ranging
between Rp 20,000 and Rp 34,000 (about $90), while the remain-
ing five were accused of taking sums of less than Rp 2,000 (about
$5), the lowest being Rp 150 (about 40 cents).[57]

56. Suharto's speech, 16 August 1970, in *Indonesia Magazine,* no. 5 (1970), 30.
57. *Harian Kami,* 26 August 1970 *(USE).* A few days later, a delegation of youths
insulted the attorney general by presenting him with a paper medal for his efforts
to fight corruption *(Nusantara,* 29 August 1970 [*USE*]), and *Indonesia Raya* bitterly
proposed that he and his officials be buried in the Heroes' Cemetery at Kalibata
when they died *(Indonesia Raya,* 26 August 1970 [*USE*]).

In their approaches to the "corruption" issue, the government and its critics were talking about different matters. While the students and the critical press were concerned with the misuse of power by the president's closest colleagues in the government, the government persisted in viewing corruption as dishonesty on the part of minor officials. In the long run, the government argued, when economic development leads to higher living standards, civil servants will receive adequate incomes and no longer need to be corrupt. On the other hand, the government's critics argued that it was not poverty that led Ibnu Sutowo, Surjo, and the president's wife to add to their incomes by irregular means, but the absence of institutional checks on their power. According to the critics, if high-level corruption were permitted to continue unhindered, the nation would never reach the level of economic development that would permit low-level officials to live on their salaries.

A Comprador Class?

The economic policies introduced by the government in 1966 and afterward brought great benefits to the commercial enterprises with which army officers were associated. The government's policies created conditions favorable for foreign investment, which was attracted by price stability, the liberalization of foreign trade, the incentives and guarantees of the 1967 investment law, and, most important, the evidence that the generals were firmly in control. The sharp rise in foreign investment was channeled mainly through joint ventures, in which the Indonesian partner had military connections and often contributed little more than arranging the necessary approval from the government. Basing their economic strength on political influence rather than entrepreneurial skill, members of the Indonesian military elite acquired the characteristics of a "comprador" class whose interests ran parallel with those of the foreign corporations with which they were associated. Rewarded with a share in the profits that enabled them to live in a style similar to that of their foreign partners, the private interests of the comprador elements in the elite were well served by the new strategy of economic development.[58]

58. See the argument of Mortimer 1973.

The domination of the expanding modern sector of the economy by foreign investors and their comprador partners was not challenged by established domestic business interests. The Chinese trading community, which had been permitted by the Dutch to dominate "middle-level" trade during the colonial period, continued to enjoy a subordinate but symbiotic relationship with the ruling elite after independence. Lacking a mass political base of their own, Chinese businessmen had furthered their interests by attaching themselves to influential politicians, bureaucrats, and, especially under the New Order, army officers. Rather than being threatened by the influx of foreign capital after 1967, many Chinese, through their association with military-backed enterprises, became partners in tripartite arrangements with foreign enterprises and Indonesian military officers, and thus part of the comprador class. On the other hand, the small groups of indigenous businessmen, who had looked especially to the Muslim parties, and to a lesser extent, the PNI, to further their interests, found themselves without political influence as a result of the decline of the parties during the 1960s. Lacking political weight, indigenous entrepreneurs were unable to prevent the introduction of policies that led to the increased availability of imported consumer goods competing with local manufactures and the entry of foreign corporations competing with indigenous enterprises. The circumstances were certainly not propitious for the emergence of a "national bourgeoisie."

Nevertheless, army interests were not wholly identified with the emerging comprador class. The comprador element, which set the tone of much commercial activity, was not completely predominant. In particular, the nature of cooperation with foreign companies in the oil industry was ambiguous in contrast with many joint ventures in forestry and manufacturing, where the Indonesian partner was hardly more than a well-rewarded agent for foreign interests. Dealing in a commodity in great and rising international demand, the Indonesian state oil corporation, Pertamina, gradually came to behave as a giant oil corporation in its own right. From 1968 or 1969 onward, after the major international companies had accepted production-sharing contracts of a sort they had initially rejected, Pertamina was able to bargain from a position of growing strength. The resulting contracts were certainly generous and were quickly looked on with favor by the international companies, but their introduction showed that Pertamina could not be dismissed as a mere agent of foreign interests. That Pertamina could act in its own interests and those of the Indonesian state against those of foreigners was shown more clearly when Indonesia joined the other oil-producing countries in sharply raising oil prices in 1973 and 1974. Further, at the beginning of 1974, Pertamina unilaterally increased the share of oil produced by foreign companies that had to be surrendered to the Indonesian corporation. The capacity of Pertamina to further its own interests at the expense of the foreign companies was even more apparent following the dismissal of Ibnu Sutowo early in 1976. Negotiations conducted by his successor, Major General Piet Harjono, led the major producer, Caltex, and then the other companies, to agree to a sharp increase in Indonesia's share in oil profits.[59]

The role of the comprador element within the military was to some extent balanced by a feeling within the officer corps that some of its members were making too much of a good thing. Army officers in general certainly accepted and welcomed the wide commercial opportunities open to them, but some, especially those of a more "professional" orientation, were disturbed by the damage done to the army's reputation as a result of unrestrained profiteering in association with Chinese businessmen and foreign investors. Priding themselves as the bearers of the spirit of the revolution, many officers were worried by the willingness of their colleagues to enter business arrangements highly favorable to foreign interests. These officers were inclined to support government moves to strengthen Pertamina's independence and curb "excesses" in the field of foreign investment generally.

The presence of strong nationalist feeling combined with a growing sense of professionalism within the army served to limit the freedom of the comprador element, but by no means gave the economic nationalists full control. Although Pertamina maintained a substantial degree of independence from the international companies with which it worked and curbs of one sort or another were gradually applied to foreign investment in other fields, the eco-

59. See *Far Eastern Economic Review*, 27 February 1976.

nomic system continued to be one in which foreign capital was invited to invest on easy terms. Through Pertamina the government sought to keep a key sector of the economy under its control, placing substantial funds at its and the military leadership's disposal, while nationalist sentiment was to some extent assuaged. However, the dominant element in the government was not interested in extending the area under direct supervision through state enterprises at the expense of the private interests of members of the military and business elite who were associated in joint ventures with foreign investors. Despite Pertamina's example, the government did not show much interest in establishing similar corporations to bargain from a position of relative strength with foreign investors in such fields as forestry and fishing, which were left open to joint ventures in which the Indonesian partner usually played no significant managerial role. In a sense, Pertamina's autonomy in its relations with foreign interests made it easier for the government to leave other fields open to arrangements in which the Indonesian partners played unqualified comprador roles. A balance was struck in which the oil industry and some other fields were reserved to the public sector, while other profitable areas were left open to private interests. Pertamina maintained its own independence (despite the private profiteering of some of its officials), but it supported a system in which comprador relationships were predominant.

The army's claim to rule was based on the promise of economic development. It presented itself as the guardian of the national interest in contrast with the narrow sectional interests it claimed were represented by the civilians who previously held power. The generals promised a level of integrity in government that they claimed had been absent during the Guided Democracy and Parliamentary Democracy periods. However, the involvement of many army officers both in fund raising on behalf of the armed forces and in all kinds of private business concerns, including those controlled by foreign interests, raised doubts about their own degree of commitment to the national goals they espoused. As "excess" followed "excess," it became increasingly clear that more than just a few individuals among the top army generals were giving priority to private interests, but rather that the entire system was designed primarily to serve the interests of the military elite and the civilian bureaucrats and business groups—both domestic and foreign—closely linked with it. If in 1967 critics could distinguish between Suharto and the powerful "corruptors" on whom he was forced, in their view temporarily, to rely, his failure to take action against high-level corruption in later years suggested that he was as much involved in the abuses as were his colleagues. Moreover, the involvement of army officers in the huge expansion of foreign investment was undermining the nationalist credentials of the regime. During the first half of the 1970s, cynicism about the government and its goals became very widespread in many civilian circles.

12 | Policies and the Struggle for Power

The New Order government had come to power in the chaos surrounding the disintegration of the Guided Democracy system. Under Guided Democracy, bureaucratic norms had atrophied as inflation raged out of control and political competition reached a point where the polarization of rival forces made administrative reform impossible. Military men had become deeply involved in business activities, and, after taking power in 1966, the chief concern of many senior officers was to create conditions conducive to expanding commercial opportunity which they hoped to exploit in association with their business partners. The military elite, however, was aware of a need to exercise restraint in order to keep the system functioning smoothly, and many officers of a relatively "professional" orientation were concerned to develop a more orderly system in which bureaucratic and professional standards were respected. In the early years of the New Order, the "political" and "financial" generals in the president's immediate circle were given a very free hand, but by the first half of the 1970s there were signs that their predominance was being challenged by reform-minded officers interested in establishing a more orderly system. At the same time, the civilian "technocrats" attempted to extend their authority over economic policy, and the foreign minister, Adam Malik, sought to resist encroachments made by several military groups into the field of foreign affairs.

The military reformers did not form a distinct group, but consisted of officers who held many common attitudes. They were not advocates of radical change, but sought to preserve the system by its regularization. Like their military rivals, they wanted the army to remain in control. But they feared that the long-term viability of the system might be threatened if the "financial" and "political" officers continued to ride roughshod over whatever obstacles stood in the path of their immediate goals and interests. The reformers were usually not puritanically opposed to the involvement of military men in private business activities, but were concerned that a continuous stream of "excesses" would eventually undermine the legitimacy of military domination of the government and obstruct the economic development that the regime was committed to achieve. Some were concerned, too, that the image won by the army during the revolution as the custodian of the spirit of nationalism might be besmirched by the too open association of military-backed enterprises with foreign capital. Not only was this more "professional" group worried about civilian alienation from the regime as a result of the unbridled activities of many members of the military elite, but they were even more concerned about the prospect that resentment would spread within the military itself as younger officers contrasted the exhortations of the army leaders with their practice.

A major factor strengthening the hand of the reform-minded officers arose from the passage of time. Since independence the army had been dominated by its "1945 Generation," the officers—often with a background in the Japanese-sponsored Peta—who led the guerrilla struggle against the Dutch. Aged in their late twenties and early thirties at the time of the transfer of sovereignty at the end of 1949, they continued to occupy command positions through to the 1970s, when more and more of them began to face retirement. Meanwhile, a new generation was rising through the ranks. During the revolution, a small group of young officers had received formal military training at the military academy established in Yogyakarta. During the early 1950s, recruitment was discontinued, but in 1957 the National Military Academy (renamed the Indonesian Armed Forces Academy, or Akabri, in 1966) was opened at Magelang in Central Java to provide officer recruits with a professional military education. In contrast with the 1945 Generation of officers, who had won their spurs on the battlefield, the members of the "Magelang Generation" were selected partly on the basis of examination results and other formal tests of attainment and potential. They were therefore drawn almost entirely from families that could afford to provide their sons with a full high school education. Further, in contrast with the members of the 1945 Generation, who were mainly Javanese, the "Magelang" recruits were drawn from all parts of Indonesia. By the mid-1970s several officers trained at the Yogyakarta academy—of whom the most prominent was Major General Sajidiman Surjohadiprodjo, the deputy chief of staff of the army in 1973—had obtained senior appointments, while officers of the Magelang Generation were moving up to the ranks of major and lieutenant colonel.

The gradual transformation of the army from a force of former guerrilla fighters to one of academy-trained professionals gave the reform-minded group of officers among the 1945 Generation a growing base of support. Not all the members of the Magelang Generation, of course, were dedicated to regularization and reform. Many, no doubt, accepted the values of the business-oriented officers of the older generation and were only waiting for the day when they, too, would get their share of the booty. But their middle-class origins and the professional military training they had undergone oriented many of them toward order, discipline, and regularity. Moreover, they were conscious that they eventually would inherit the mantle passed on from the older generation, and many were concerned that it should be in good condition. A belief was growing that if curbs were not soon applied to the freewheeling activities of the "financial" and "political" generals close to the president, the problems of maintaining control would be multiplied in the future. While it is not possible to assess with certainty the extent of dissatisfaction in the middle and lower ranks of the army, it was clear that a mood in favor of reform was developing.

Rivalry in the Army

During the four years after 1965, one of Suharto's central concerns was to consolidate his control over the armed forces. Moving against rivals and potential rivals one at a time, he purged the army of both Sukarnoists and extreme anti-Sukarnoists, while undermining the autonomy of the other three services. This process was completed with the final integration of the armed forces under a single command at the end of 1969. By then all command positions in the army as well as the other services were filled by officers appointed since 1966. Many potential dissidents had been appointed to prestigious and often lucrative posts in the bureaucracy or army headquarters, some had been forced reluctantly to accept diplomatic postings abroad, and a few had been arrested. In consolidating his hold over the armed forces, Suharto had relied more on his powers of patronage than on the capacity to coerce.

In leading the government, Suharto relied heavily on a small group of advisers drawn from the army. In 1966, Suharto had established a personal staff (Spri), consisting of army officers, which grew from six to twelve members by 1968. Headed by Major General Alamsjah, the members of the Spri were allocated fields of responsibility such as finance, politics, foreign intelligence, domestic intelligence, social welfare, and general elections affairs, as well as "general affairs" and "special affairs."[1] During 1967 it had become apparent that the members of the Spri together with several other generals close to Suharto—the acting commander of the army, Lieutenant General Panggabean, the minister for internal affairs, Major General Basuki Rachmat, and the head of Pertamina, Major General Ibnu Sutowo—were exercising a determining influence on government policy. After the expression by students, sections of the press, and other civilian groups of strong resentment against the existence of an "invisible government," Suharto dissolved the Spri at the time of the appointment of a new cabinet in June 1968.

The dissolution of the Spri, however, did not lead to a diminution in the influence of its most powerful members. Alamsjah had been appointed in February 1968 as state secretary with control over the president's staff, and Yoga Sugama, who had been the Spri officer responsible for domestic intelligence, was soon appointed as head of the state intelligence body, Bakin. Further,

1. The members of the Spri at the time of its dissolution in 1968 were: Major General Alamsjah (coordinator); Brigadier General Sudjono Humardhani (economy); Colonel Ali Murtopo (foreign intelligence); Brigadier General Yoga Sugama (domestic intelligence); Major General Surjo (finance); Brigadier General Abdul Kadir Prawiraatmadja (social welfare); Brigadier General Slamet Danudirdjo (economic development); Brigadier General Nawawi Alif (mass media); Brigadier General Sudharmono (general); Brigadier General Sunarso (politics); Brigadier General Isman (mass movements); and Brigadier General Jusuf Singadikane (national projects) (*Kompas*, 13 June 1968).

Generals Surjo, Sudjono Humardhani, and Ali Murtopo were appointed as personal assistants (Aspri) to the president, and Ali Murtopo's Opsus organization continued to carry out "special operations" for the president, such as watching over developments in the political parties and ensuring favorable outcomes in the 1969 Act of Free Choice in West Irian and the 1971 general elections. Moreover, the status of other senior generals close to Suharto remained unchanged.

These "political" and "financial" generals exercised great influence over the patronage system. They played a major role in determining appointments in both the military hierarchy and the government administration. Furthermore, they concerned themselves with the implementation of policy, particularly in such fields as foreign investment, the allocation of construction contracts, and the opening of other business opportunities that had implications for the smooth functioning of the patronage machine. Thus many officers were beholden to them for important appointments or profitable business opportunities, while officers still active in the military field looked to the president's advisers to ensure for them a bright future. Although the dominant group of presidential advisers did not—apart from General Panggabean, as deputy commander and later commander of the armed forces—exercise direct control over troops, their closeness to the president gave them influence over the troop commanders.

The dominant "Aspri group"—headed by Ali Murtopo and Sudjono Humardhani after Alamsjah had been gradually eased out of his earlier preeminent position[2]—did not command universal loyalty among the troop commanders. Although many regional commanders owed their appointments to the endorsement of the Aspri group, they often resented the activities of the political and financial generals which caused difficulties for troop commanders responsible for security and the maintenance of law and order. Political moves leading to popular dissatisfaction, such as

2. Alamsjah's decline commenced in 1968, when he assured Suharto that Japan was ready to provide Indonesia with increased economic aid. Assuming that the aid would be forthcoming, Suharto visited Japan immediately after his appointment as full president by the MPRS in March 1968. Suharto was extremely embarrassed when he discovered during the visit that Alamsjah had been misinformed about the readiness of the Japanese to provide the aid (see Weinstein 1972:632–637). Alamsjah was sent as ambassador to the Netherlands in 1971.

heavy-handed interventions in the affairs of the political parties or policies upsetting to the Muslim community, were viewed with concern by many field officers, not because they had special sympathy for the political parties or the Muslim community, but because they would be responsible for repressing any outbreaks of discontent provoked by such measures. Similarly, army officers in general did not disapprove of their colleagues engaging in business activities with Chinese or foreign partners, but they were worried when blatant profiteering led to student demonstrations or when mismanagement in rice procurement resulted in peasant unrest and shortages in urban areas. By the early 1970s, many field officers were looking to the deputy commander of the armed forces and head of Kopkamtib, Lieutenant General Sumitro, the new head of Bakin, Lieutenant General Sutopo Juwono, and the deputy chief of staff of the army, Major General Sajidiman, to express their point of view. While the commander of the armed forces, General Panggabean, was closely associated with the Aspri group, Sumitro became increasingly recognized as the leader of the "Hankam group" of military "professionals" in the Department of Defense and Security. Further, Sumitro, as a former Brawijaya officer, and Sajidiman, formerly in the Siliwangi division, attracted the support of officers who resented the prominence of so many officers, like Ali Murtopo and Sudjono Humardhani, from Suharto's own Diponegoro division.

The rivalry between the president's political and financial advisers on one side and General Sumitro's supporters on the other largely took the form of intraelite jostling for position. After Ali Murtopo's great success in molding the Golkar into an effective electoral force in 1971, the Hankam generals moved quickly to prevent the Golkar from developing into an extramilitary base of power for Ali Murtopo, and when the Golkar's first congress was held in September 1973, Major General Amir Murtono, the nominee of the Hankam group, was elected as general chairman. On the other hand, when General Sumitro proposed the appointment of his protégé, Major General Charis Suhud, as deputy commander of the Kopkamtib in mid-1973, Suharto decided instead to appoint the former chief of staff of the navy, Admiral Sudomo, who had close ties with Ali Murtopo. Although the members of the Aspri group enjoyed a warmer relationship with the president than did their rivals, he was careful not to favor them to the point where the military professionals felt alienated. A careful balance was maintained, in which both groups were rewarded in the present and had grounds for optimism about the future.

Presiding over a system of balancing vested interests, Suharto seemed in the early 1970s to be in a position to maintain his regime indefinitely. As long as foreign aid, foreign investment, and oil income continued to provide increasing resources available for distribution, it seemed that the rival groups in the army could be held together through the judicious allocation of material satisfactions. Sharp rivalries continued within the military elite, but those who lost out in the struggle for power were expected to abide by the "rules of the game," which required that they accept defeat rather than attempt to mobilize open opposition to the regime. Moreover, defeat was usually made palatable by a prestigious and lucrative civilian appointment, whereas those who refused to cooperate faced the prospect of arrest.

The patronage system worked well in holding rival groups together within the armed forces, but it tended to aggravate civilian discontent. The huge influx of foreign capital provided vast new business opportunities for military men and their civilian partners, but it also threatened the position of indigenous Indonesian entrepreneurs, who lacked both capital and military connections. When the initial period of mainly American investment in mining projects was followed in the early 1970s by mainly Japanese investment in manufacturing, opportunities narrowed for Indonesian enterprises. Many, most prominently in textiles, were forced by foreign competition to close down, while the workers who lost their jobs in the old labor-intensive factories were not absorbed in the new capital-intensive plants.[3] A sense of resentment was spreading, particularly against Japanese capital and such Indonesian officials as Sudjono Humardhani and Ibnu Sutowo, who were most closely associated with it.

Growing discontent over "foreign domination" of the economy

3. By 1973 the government had approved foreign investment projects amounting to about $3 billion. Japan's share of approvals had risen to 20 percent, overtaking the American share of 19 percent. Foreign investment actually implemented had risen from $222 million between 1967 and 1971 to almost $1 billion in 1973 (Grenville 1974:12).

was expressed most openly by students. Student restiveness, particularly over the issue of corruption, had first appeared in 1967 and had led to demonstrations in 1970. New manifestations of student and youth discontent broke out toward the end of 1971, when the president's wife sponsored the "Beautiful Indonesia" project—a pleasure park depicting life in all of Indonesia's provinces. Such youth leaders as Arief Budiman saw the expensive project as a symbol of official wastefulness and a return to the "prestige projects" of the Sukarno era. In the latter part of 1973, immediately after the fall of the military-led government in Thailand in October, student opposition to the government broke out again. The Thai military had appeared well entrenched, but a few days of student rioting had been enough to bring about its "miraculous" overthrow. If the analogy with the Indonesian situation was not perfect, there were enough similarities for the developments in Bangkok to have a dramatic impact on the atmosphere in Jakarta.

Toward the end of October, a meeting of students at the University of Indonesia issued the "Petition of 24 October," which protested against "the violation of law, raging corruption, the abuse of authority, rising prices, and unemployment" and called for a review of the existing strategy of development which benefited only the rich.[4] A fortnight later when the youthful and sympathetic Dutch minister for development cooperation, Drs Pronk, arrived on an official visit, he was greeted by student demonstrators, who handed him a statement which declared "that we do not take pride in the results of foreign aid and foreign capital in the form of tall buildings and hotels, Coca Cola, nightclubs, etc. In the meantime more people are without jobs, homes, and land, our small textile industry has died, our forests have become barren, and our oil fields depleted."[5] During the next few weeks, numerous small-scale delegations visited government offices to protest against overreliance on foreign capital and conspicuous high living. The unusually liberal atmosphere encouraged strong press criticism of foreign investment and government economic policy in general.

4. *Pedoman,* 3 November 1973 (translated in *United States Embassy Translation Unit Press Review,* hereafter cited as *USE*).
5. *Indonesia Raya,* 12 November 1973 (*USE*).

The sudden outburst of student protest had taken place against a background of growing uncertainty caused by two other developments. On 5 August the most serious anti-Chinese riot of the New Order period had broken out in Bandung, when, following a minor traffic accident, mobs rampaged through the city from about 4 P.M. until 1 A.M., damaging about fifteen hundred shops and houses, including almost all the shops in the central part of the city. The most striking aspect of the riot, however, was the failure of the army to move into action against the rioters. Troops had not appeared until fairly late in the evening and even then had not taken firm measures. The conclusion seemed inescapable that many members of the armed forces in West Java had at least sympathized with the rioters, and it was rumored that soldiers had participated in the destruction and looting. Although the government blamed the "underground Communist party,"[6] nineteen members of the Siliwangi division were arrested, including two lieutenant colonels and several other officers, as well as several civilian leaders of the Siliwangi Youth Wing (Angkatan Muda Siliwangi), an organization sponsored by some Sundanese officers in the Siliwangi division.[7] Ethnic Sundanese officers had apparently encouraged the rioting as a means of protesting against the government's practice of favoring Chinese and foreign corporations at the expense of indigenous enterprises. Aware of the sympathy felt by ordinary soldiers and junior officers for the feelings of the anti-Chinese rioters, the Siliwangi leadership had hesitated to order troops into action. The army leadership's grip was far less secure than it had appeared to be before the riot, and there was speculation about the extent to which the apparent lack of discipline in West Java could be found in other areas.

As the apparent lack of unity and discipline within sections of the army raised questions about its capacity to deal with mass discontent, a new issue was gathering momentum. On 31 July the government had introduced a draft bill providing for uniform

6. Lacking convincing evidence to demonstrate Communist involvement, the chief of staff of Kopkamtib, Admiral Sudomo, claimed that the PKI was now using "OTB tactics"—*organisasi tanpa bentuk* (organization without form).

7. A Siliwangi spokesman announced that these officers and soldiers were suspected of involvement in the 1965 coup attempt (*Kompas*, 26 October 1973) but the general understanding was that the real reason was their involvement in the riot (*Tempo*, 27 October 1973).

marriage and divorce regulations for members of all religions. The bill was the culmination of years of pressure from women's organizations that were concerned to gain legal protection not provided by Islamic law and was supported by Christian and secular organizations. The decision to introduce the legislation appears to have originated with Ali Murtopo's staff, who regarded it as an issue to be exploited in furthering the process of "secularizing" political Islam. Although some Muslim politicians, such as Mintaredja and Naro, supported the legislation, it was vehemently opposed by most of the Muslim community, whose religious leaders vied with each other in identifying more than a dozen points where the proposed law conflicted with Islamic law.[8] In Jakarta, hundreds of demonstrating Muslim students stormed the floor of the parliament during the minister of religion's address on the bill on 27 September, while in the provinces some Muslim leaders began to talk of a "holy war."

The new atmosphere toward the end of 1973 was very unfavorable for the government, as challenges increased from both secular and Muslim quarters. General Sumitro, commander of the Kopkamtib, seemed unconcerned. As students attacked dealings with Chinese and Japanese businessmen, Sumitro not only refrained from taking repressive measures, but in November he visited university campuses in West, Central, and East Java, where, echoing a phrase from the president's National Day speech on 16 August, he promised "a new pattern of leadership," including "two-way communication." At the same time, together with the head of the Bakin, Sutopo Juwono, he approached Muslim leaders and offered to work out a new draft marriage law to replace the bill introduced earlier with Ali Murtopo's endorsement. Supported by field officers, who wished to avoid undue provocation of the Muslim community, the new draft became the basis of the law which was eventually passed with Muslim support

---

8. Among other points, the proposed law provided for civil marriages and marriage between Muslims and non-Muslims, restricted grounds for divorce, and prevented a man taking a second wife without the permission of the first. The former Masyumi leader, Sjafruddin Prawiranegara, complained that the law did not recognize the husband as the "head of the family." He declared, "The freeing of women from their obligation to obey their husbands is what is leading to free sex, hippy culture, marijuana, and narcotics" (*Harian Kami*, 26 September 1973). For a thorough analysis of the proposed law, see Mohammed Kamal Hassan 1975:chap. 5.

at the end of December. With the Thai precedent very much in mind, Sumitro was consciously distancing himself from the regime by cultivating Muslim opinion and implicitly encouraging students and the press to attack policies associated with Ali Murtopo and his supporters.

The Japanese prime minister, Tanaka, was due to arrive on a state visit on 14 January 1974. That an intense struggle for power was taking place within the military elite became apparent during the first two weeks of 1974. Although the maneuvers and counter-maneuvers were carried out in private, there were enough public indications of friction to create the expectation that "something might happen" during Tanaka's visit. After two long meetings with the president on 1 and 2 January, a worried Sumitro, accompanied by a smiling Ali Murtopo, denied rumors that he was planning to change the national leadership and claimed that there was no rivalry between himself and Ali Murtopo.[9] It appeared that the president, with Ali Murtopo's strong support, had insisted that Sumitro make the statement to the press, and the rumor spread that Suharto had already decided to dismiss Sumitro once the current tension had subsided. During the next fortnight, Sumitro sought to bolster his position among his own supporters and win the support of such dissidents as Nasution and the disgruntled governor of the Military Academy, Sarwo Edhie, who was about to be sent as ambassador to South Korea. On 11 January Sumitro and Nasution separately visited the small Central Javanese town of Magelang, where the Military Academy is located, apparently to hold discussions with the Military Academy's governor.[10] Although it was not clear what Sumitro was planning, he was not passively accepting the reprimand given to him by the president on 2 January.

It can be surmised that Sumitro hoped that the student protest against Tanaka's visit could be used to weaken the position of Ali Murtopo and Sudjono Humardhani, both of whom were identified in the public mind with a pro-Japan outlook.[11] In the days before Tanaka's arrival on the fourteenth, the restraints usually imposed by the Kopkamtib were further loosened when students

9. See report and photograph in *Kompas*, 3 January 1974.
10. Ibid., 14 January 1974.
11. Sudjono was generally regarded as the overseer of Japanese investment in Indonesia, while Ali Murtopo had put forward the idea of a "Tokyo-Jakarta-Canberra axis" in the context of declining American power in Southeast Asia.

demonstrated at Ali Murtopo's office and burned effigies of Tanaka and Sudjono Humardhani in Jakarta and Bandung. On the
morning after Tanaka's arrival, thousands of students marched
through the city and leaflets were distributed calling for the dissolution of the Aspri, the reduction of prices, and the suppression of corruption.[12] In the afternoon, however, the student
demonstration turned into an uncontrolled riot in which the
main participants were youths and children from Jakarta's slum
areas, who burned Japanese and other cars, wrecked the show-
rooms of the Toyota-importing Astra Motor Company (with
which the president's wife was said to be associated), attacked a
Coca Cola plant, and the following day burned and looted the
huge Senen shopping complex. On the first day of the riot,
troops took no firm action, and foreign correspondents were
amazed to see General Sumitro addressing demonstrators in a
friendly tone from a jeep in front of the Japanese embassy.[13]
Not until the second day did troops fire on looters, killing about
a dozen, at the Senen complex.

It seems clear that General Sumitro had let it be known that
repressive action would not be taken if students organized a large
demonstration during Tanaka's visit. Possibly Sumitro hoped that
a massive demonstration of anti-Japanese feeling would enable
him to demand that the president curb the powers of the archi-
tects of Indonesia's Japan policy, and rumors circulated that he
was planning to present Suharto with a fait accompli by arresting
Ali Murtopo and Sudjono Humardhani. Perhaps his strategy was
modeled on Suharto's own use of demonstrating students in
March 1966 to force President Sukarno to accept the dismissal of
Subandrio and other ministers. Whatever Sumitro's plan was, it
backfired when the student demonstration in the morning turned
into a two-day riot.[14] Not only did it cease to be feasible to envis-

12. The three demands were entitled the "Tritura '74," echoing the slogan of
the demonstrations against President Sukarno almost exactly eight years earlier.
See Chapter 6 above.
13. Sumitro reportedly told the demonstrators that the government was good,
but "certainly there are some people among us who are not good" (*Kompas*, 16
January 1974).
14. It was later rumored that the rioting had been instigated by Ali Murtopo's
agents as a means of discrediting Sumitro. These allegations were made by a
Yogyakarta student, Aini Chalid, at his trial (ibid., 29 July 1975 [*ICATS*]). See also
Far Eastern Economic Review, 11 October 1974.

age further student demonstrations against Ali and Sudjono, but Sumitro himself was put on the defensive as accusations were made that he had irresponsibly created a situation that threatened the interests of the army as a whole. While Sumitro had much support in military circles for his endeavor to curb the role of the Aspri group, army officers quickly closed ranks in the face of a general breakdown of law and order.[15]

The so-called Malari incident (Malapetaka Januari or January Disaster) demonstrated that the apparent unity of the army rested on fragile foundations and that sharp rivalries could easily rise to the surface in a crisis. Although the government sought to blame the affair on disgruntled remnants of the Socialist and Masyumi parties that had been banned by Sukarno in 1960,[16] it was clear that the main challenge came from within the army itself. In the aftermath, Sumitro was dismissed immediately as commander of the Kopkamtib and shortly afterward "resigned" as deputy commander of the armed forces after reportedly rejecting appointment as ambassador to Washington. His ally, Sutopo Juwono, was appointed as ambassador to the Netherlands, Sarwo Edhie took up his appointment as ambassador to South Korea, Charis Suhud was made head of the Indonesian contingent in Vietnam, and Sajidiman was transferred to the National Defense Institute.[17] As the new deputy commander of the armed forces, Suharto selected the army chief of staff and former Diponegoro commander, Su-

15. For a more complete discussion of the background to the affair, see Crouch 1974. For a different interpretation, which denies that the army was seriously split, see Sundhaussen 1977.

16. See Ali Murtopo's press statement, *Angkatan Bersenjata*, 22 January 1974 (translated in *Indonesian Current Affairs Translation Service*, hereafter cited as *ICATS*), and Marzuki Arifin 1974. Among those arrested were former PSI leaders, Subadio Sastrosatomo and Sarbini Sumawinata. Other detainees regarded as "PSI-oriented" were the lawyer Adnan Bujung Nasution, the university lecturer Drs Dorodjatun Kuntjorojakti, the Golkar official Rahman Tolleng, the chairman of the League of Human Rights, H. Princen, and student leaders, Sjahrir and Hariman Siregar. Several young Muslim activists were also arrested together with many student leaders. In addition, several Sukarnoists were detained, including Sukarno's nephew, Rear Admiral (retired) Puguh, a former minister, Mardanus, and Major General Suadi. All except Sjahrir had been released by late 1976.

17. In February the government denied rumors that Sumitro and two senior retired officers, General Nasution and Lieutenant General Djatikusumo, had been arrested (*ICATS*, 14 February 1974).

rono, while control of the Kopkamtib was placed in the hands of the trusted Admiral Sudomo. Another old associate of Suharto's from the Diponegoro division, Lieutenant General Yoga Sugama, was reappointed as head of the Bakin, a post he had vacated in favor of Sutopo Juwono in 1969. Although Suharto sought to create a public impression of standing above the factional struggle by formally dissolving the positions of Aspri, it was apparent that Ali Murtopo, Sudjono Humardhani, and Surjo remained as close advisers to the president.

The challenge launched by Sumitro and the military professionals against the dominance of the "political" and "financial" generals around Suharto had failed. However, the relatively mild action taken against Sumitro and his most prominent supporters suggested that a significant section of the officer corps continued to sympathize with their views and that Suharto was not prepared to antagonize these officers further by taking more drastic action against their leaders. The appointment of General Surono as deputy commander of the armed forces was an attempt to reassure these officers because Surono, although a Diponegoro officer loyal to Suharto, was also in some ways a military technocrat.[18] In response to the riot, the government took limited steps to meet the demands of its critics. It immediately introduced a set of regulations designed to curb "high living" on the part of officials, and in the months that followed, stricter controls were imposed on foreign investment, policies were introduced to provide greater opportunities for indigenous businessmen, and a few measures were taken to ameliorate the conditions of the poor. Although the military reformers had suffered a setback, many remained in important positions from which they and their supporters continued to challenge the groups closest to the president. In seeking to curb the "excesses" of the business-oriented generals, the reform-minded officers were attacking groups in the army which had also been in conflict with the civilian technocrats responsible for economic policy formulation.

18. Surono had been governor of the military academy in Magelang for several years until 1966, when he was appointed as commander of the Diponegoro division. As governor of the academy, he had personal contact with many of the new generation of "professional" officers now rising through the military hierarchy and was apparently respected by them.

The Technocrats and Military Entrepreneurs

Inheriting an economy in which the modern sector had been thrown into disarray by the previous government's economic policies and the political upheaval of 1965–1966, the new government needed to restore order and stability in the economic as well as the political sphere. Conscious of their own lack of expertise in the field of economic policy making despite their well-developed money-making skills, the generals recruited civilian experts to administer the economy for them, within limits which they themselves set. The most prominent of the technocrats originally belonged to a special team attached to General Suharto's Spri, but in 1967 and 1968 most of them were appointed to senior positions in the government, and by 1971 all the top technocrats were ministers in the cabinet.[19]

The military leaders hoped that the technocrats would formulate stabilization policies, creating a favorable climate for business and the restoration of confidence on the part of the Western states and Japan, which were expected to become major sources of capital—both public and private—for the government's program of economic development. The government envisaged the rapid expansion of modern commerce and industry together with the growth of the export sector based on raw material exploitation, especially in the Outer Islands. It also intended that its economic policies should strengthen political stability by meeting the consumption needs of the urban "middle class" and avoiding mass discontent due to food shortages. In this system, political stability was to be maintained, while lucrative economic opportunities for the military-dominated elite and the middle classes in general were to be created.

The New Order government inherited an economy over which the old government had lost almost all control. In early 1966, prices were rising at a rate of about 50 percent per month, foreign exchange reserves were exhausted, and debt repayments due in 1966 amounted to a sum almost equal to expected export earnings. Industrial production was falling because the inability to

19. The Spri economists were Widjojo Nitisastro, Ali Wardhana, Emil Salim, Mohammed Sadli, and Subroto. Ali Wardhana was appointed to the cabinet in 1968 and the others in 1971. In addition, their old mentor from the University of Indonesia, Sumitro, was appointed to the cabinet in 1968.

finance essential imports forced factories to operate well below capacity. Exports had been declining for years as the infrastructure of roads, harbors, and marketing facilities deteriorated. As the purchasing power of civil service salaries fell to an absurd level, the administration became riddled with corruption and extraordinary inefficiency.[20] The fierce struggle between the component elements of the old government had prevented it from pursuing self-consistent economic policies. Each group concentrated on maneuvering to enhance its political position, and none could afford to risk losing ground by identifying itself with unpopular economic policies that imposed sacrifices on important sections of the community. The government found itself able neither to cut expenditure nor raise revenue. As a result, not only did expenditure always exceed revenue, but the deficit alone exceeded total revenue in both 1964 and 1965.

Although the new government's capacity to impose unpopular measures was much greater than that of the previous government, its powers in 1966 were limited. The army was not fully united, the other services enjoyed a measure of autonomy which, although decreasing, remained significant, and the political parties retained considerable mass support. While there was a general consensus that severe measures were required to restore the economy, the government was anxious to avoid the imposition of excessive hardships on politically important groups. Suharto and his colleagues were aware of the danger of mass disaffection, which might be exploited by their rivals not only among civilians and the other services but in the army itself. Thus there was no question of a drastic program to mobilize domestic resources. Instead the government turned abroad for assistance and thus opted for measures to restore the economy that were within its political and administrative capacity.

The government's initial goals were "stabilization" and "rehabilitation," which involved stopping the runaway inflation, restoring international solvency, and rehabilitating the infrastructure.

20. See the frank statements of the sultan of Yogyakarta on 4 and 12 April 1966, in *Statement-Statement Politik Waperdam Bidang Sospol/Menteri Luar Negeri dan Waperdam Bidang Ekubang*. Commenting on the statements, Arndt and Panglaykim wrote that "a picture of economic breakdown has been revealed to the Indonesian people and to the world which can have few parallels in a great nation in modern times except in the immediate aftermath of war or revolution" (1966:1).

The new program was heavily dependent on the inflow of capital and consumer goods from abroad, which could be obtained only by meeting the conditions set by the international financial institutions and foreign creditors. The new economic policy was introduced in a series of measures commencing in October 1966. Formulated by the economists from the University of Indonesia who had been recruited to Suharto's personal staff, the measures were introduced with an eye to the reaction of the International Monetary Fund (IMF) and the governments of the Western states and Japan. The initial October 1966 measures were prepared in consultation with an IMF mission in Jakarta. The new policy reflected the outlook of the IMF, emphasizing stabilization and liberalization as essential prerequisites for development. It involved balancing the budget, a tight credit policy, reliance on market forces, the setting of a "realistic" exchange rate through de facto devaluation, and finally, encouragement to the private sector and especially private foreign investment.[21] The Indonesian government's willingness to adopt these policies was a major factor influencing the IMF mission in Jakarta to recommend substantial aid to Indonesia and the readiness of the Western governments and Japan to supply the aid. In 1967, the United States, Japan, and other Western states formed the Inter-Governmental Group on Indonesia (IGGI) to coordinate their aid policies, and in the following years aid inflows increased vastly, overtaking in the early 1970s the $2.4 billion debt inherited from the Sukarno years. About two-thirds of the aid came from the United States and Japan. This large increase in resources soon made the government's new economic approach effective in controlling inflation, correcting the balance of payments deficit, and promoting the rapid development of the modern sector of the economy.

The dependence of Indonesia's development program on outside support meant that the foreign creditors in the IGGI and IMF were in a position to put heavy pressure on the Indonesian government's technocrats to accept policies they recommended. One American radical has argued that the technocrats had been more or less "brainwashed" by the North American education they all had experienced and that this had blinded them to the

21. For a sharp critique of the IMF approach, see Payer 1974. For a laudatory account by a former IMF official in Jakarta, see Tomasson 1970.

alternative paths of development open to Indonesia.[22] The Suharto government, however, was in no position to carry out the
mobilization of domestic resources that would free it of dependence on foreign aid, and the economists would not have been
free to experiment with such an approach. The government had
neither the administrative machinery nor the means of coercion
necessary for such a program, which would have required an
ideologically committed army quite different from Indonesia's.
The government much preferred to rely on foreign aid rather
than attempt a draconian overhaul for which it was in no way
fitted.[23] The alternatives open to the government's economic advisers were severely limited by the nature of the power holders in
the government. Far from feeling coerced by the IMF, the government's economic advisers were glad to have its backing in their
efforts to persuade the government to accept policies which were
expected to be unpopular politically. As one of them said, "We
think the same way IMF people think."[24]

Despite the government's official adoption of the program
urged on it by its economic advisers and the IMF, not all of these
policies were fully implemented in practice. The widespread involvement of army officers and army units in commercial activities
had created powerful interests that would have been impeded by
a strict implementation of the new economic program. Although
the impression was created that "General Suharto, conscious that
the military was ill-equipped for the job, insisted on leaving economic policy making to civilians,"[25] in fact the policies actually
implemented often deviated considerably from those recommended by the technocrats. H. W. Arndt's observation that "the
itch to interfere on the part of civil and military officials, high and
low, has tended to make a mockery of the proclaimed policy of
greater reliance on market forces"[26] applied equally well to all

22. Ransom 1970.
23. Contrasting the conditions of Indonesia with those of China, where "the
Chinese Communist Party is fully dominant," Sadli pointed out in May 1966 that
"governments in Indonesia are always coalitions" which "are unable to squeeze out
great amounts of national savings with the result that development requirements
will always need much foreign assistance." See Sadli's speech at a seminar at the
University of Indonesia in Universitas Indonesia 1966.
24. Weinstein 1972:624.
25. Arndt 1972:19.
26. Ibid., p. 26.

fields of economic policy. The "itch to interfere," however, was not just a cultural predisposition of Indonesian officialdom, but an essential feature of a system in which military and civilian officials raised the supplementary funds needed for their own remuneration and the operations of their unit or department. In particular, the participation of the military in commercial activity led to distortions that could not be dismissed as unfortunate "excesses," but were at the heart of the New Order. The policies that the economists persuaded the government to enunciate in Jakarta were often more effective in influencing the attitudes of foreign creditors than in regulating Indonesian economic life.

A major limitation on the capacity of the government's economic advisers to allocate funds according to technocratic criteria during the early period of the New Order was their lack of control over much of the funds at the government's disposal and particularly revenue from oil. An important instrument of economic policy making in the hands of the technocrats was the government's annual budget, which was intended to control government revenues and expenditures, but in fact the early budgets bore little relationship to the actual state of government finances. Although the new government's budget was characterized "by ruthless cuts in allocations, not least to the armed forces,"[27] actual military expenditure may have increased because the army and other services continued to raise at least half of their operating funds from Pertamina and other military-controlled commercial enterprises. Similarly, most if not all government departments operated their own "welfare funds" or "foundations," which allocated supplementary salaries to civil servants from money raised through a wide range of legal, semilegal, and illegal activities. Although the "official" budgeted salary of cabinet ministers in 1970, for example, was only Rp 17,000 per month, their actual remuneration was estimated to be between Rp 80,000 and Rp 100,000, and similar "unofficial" supplements were made to the salaries of officials at all levels, as well as such perquisites as housing and automobiles.[28] In the regions semilegal taxes were im-

27. Ibid., p. 20.
28. See editorial in *Pedoman*, 13 February 1970, and the article entitled "The Gap as High as the Heavens between 'Official' and 'Unofficial' Salaries," in *Kompas*, 21 September 1970.

posed to supplement funds made available by the central budget and to pay salaries when central government funds failed to arrive on time.[29] Thus it is doubtful, at least in the early years of the New Order, whether the official budget raised more than half the revenues actually utilized by the government apparatus, with the result that the technocrats were handicapped in using the budget for the rational allocation of resources in the interests of economic development.

The capacity of the technocrats to influence the balance of payments was also limited. The important measures that they introduced to reform the multiple exchange rate in 1966[30] affected only part of total "actual" exports and imports because a significant quantity of foreign trade continued to take place outside the formal system. Export earnings from Indonesia's main export commodity, oil, were controlled by the army-dominated Pertamina, which retained an undisclosed proportion of its foreign exchange income and contributed only its "net" export income to the national reserve. Moreover, during 1967 and 1968, an estimated $200 million of goods were "exported" through smuggling backed by military officers, although the quantity declined in later years. On the import side military personnel were involved in smuggling luxury goods into the country on behalf of "foundations" operated by armed forces' units, and "manipulations" in the form of underinvoicing and other irregularities were commonly practiced with the backing of army officers—as in the cases of the scandals uncovered by the minister of trade, Sumitro, in 1968, and the police chief, General Hugeng, in 1971.[31]

The guidelines formulated by the technocrats were often ignored in the case of foreign investment, too. Although a Technical Team for Foreign Capital Investment, headed by the technocrat, Mohammed Sadli, was established in 1967 to investigate applications by investors, its powers were only advisory, and it was in a weak position to recommend restrictions on projects with which powerful army officers were associated. In the case of investment in the oil industry, the team was not even consulted. Even when restrictions were imposed, as in the case of joint ventures in for-

29. See Mitchell 1970.
30. See Glassburner 1971:434–437.
31. See Chapter 11 above.

estry, contractual obligations limiting the felling of trees, requiring replanting, and the establishing of processing facilities were rarely observed, and there was little effective supervision of the quantity of exports on which royalties to the government were calculated.[32] Although the foreign investment law adopted in 1967 referred to the desirability of foreign investment "in the fields and sectors where investment of national capital cannot or cannot yet be undertaken in the near future," many projects were approved which competed directly with established Indonesian companies, such as in shoe polish, ink, glass, soft drink, and milk production. In many cases, the foreign investments took the form of joint ventures in which a "sleeping" Indonesian partner had military connections.

The key field of rice production and marketing was another area in which the influence of the technocrats was limited. The Five Year Development Plan drawn up by the technocrats in 1969 provided for a 47 percent increase in rice production through the introduction of new high-yield seeds requiring assured supplies of water and a packet of inputs including fertilizers and pesticides. However, the reliance of the government on foreign companies in the Bimas Gotong Royong program had opened opportunities to members of the military elite, with the result that technocratic requirements in the implementation of the Green Revolution were subordinated to commercial considerations. Although the scheme resulted in a rapid increase in rice production, the hostility it engendered among the peasantry and their refusal to repay credit led to the abandonment of the scheme in 1970 and its replacement by a voluntary, domestic-financed program in which much more attention was paid to local requirements.[33]

In the case of marketing, the state rice-marketing agency, Bulog, was firmly in army hands. Bulog's rice-purchasing policies, which were often influenced by military fund-raising considerations, had failed to prevent erratic price fluctuations, to the detriment of producer and consumer alike, and prices had risen

---

32. See Manning 1971. According to Manning, "Realised royalties have been considerably less than those expected on the basis of realised exports. . . . If the struggle of one major Indonesian 'non-business' concessionaire with the East Kalimantan government over failure to pay royalties is any guide, then the capacity of the politically influential to resist payment may have been a significant factor" (p. 45).

33. See Chapter 11 above.

sharply at the end of 1967 and 1969, when Bulog found itself without adequate stocks. Only in 1970 was Bulog given the function of maintaining price stability in order to ensure adequate incentives for peasants while holding prices down for urban consumers. During 1972 a poor harvest and an unanticipated rice shortage on the international market again left Bulog without adequate stocks at the end of the year. Although some of Bulog's problems lay outside its control, one of the most serious was the tendency of many members of its army-dominated staff to utilize their positions either to raise funds for the army or for personal gain. Bulog was thus a poor instrument for technocratic policy implementation.

Following Bulog's failure in 1972, one of the technocrats, Subroto, the minister for manpower, transmigration, and cooperatives, pushed the proposal that rice purchasing at the village level should be carried out by cooperatives called Village Unit Enterprises (BUUD), which would then sell to Bulog. The plan was adopted by the government in March 1973, but at the same time governors of rice-producing provinces were set purchasing targets to be met by the BUUDs. In East Java, for example, the provincial government was obliged to supply 400,000 tons to the national stock of 900,000 tons. In order to reach the target, *bupatis* (heads of districts) were set quotas to fill, and they in turn set quotas for their *camats* (heads of subdistricts). Measures were taken to prevent the movement of rice across regional boundaries, and peasants were forced to sell to BUUDs at prices well below those obtaining in the urban markets. These restrictions provided opportunities for local authorities—often including military personnel—to siphon off part of BUUD stocks for highly profitable private sale in the towns, and in many areas military personnel traveled with rice trucks illegally carrying rice across regional boundaries.[34] As conditions not only in East Java but in all rice-producing areas grew increasingly chaotic, the government abandoned its policy at the beginning of July. Whatever merits the technocratic proposal to purchase rice through village cooperatives may have had, its combination with the setting of targets led

34. After the policy had been abandoned, General Sumitro declared that "today there are no more members of the Armed Forces acting as guards on rice trucks" (*Kompas*, 19 July 1973 [*ICATS*]).

to innumerable abuses in which local military personnel were usually prominent.[35]

The technocrats had little power during the early period of the New Order to ensure that their policies were implemented as planned when military interests were involved. Nevertheless, they played a major role in determining the broad strategy of economic policy and in formulating the details of particular policies. Initially, their influence was based largely on technical expertise, which enabled them to propose policies to overcome the complex economic crisis that the government immediately faced. They formulated policies to control inflation, maintain balance in foreign payments, and create a favorable climate for foreign investment. Further, by giving the technocrats a prominent say in policy formulation, the government was able to win and maintain the confidence of foreign governments and international financial institutions on which it relied for much-needed funds.

The position of the technocrats as the government's chief economic policy advisers, however, was not unchallenged. From time to time they came under criticism for their alleged subservience to the dictates of the IMF and the Western aid donors. The technocrats' efforts to promote greater order in state finances naturally brought them into conflict with the generals controlling bodies like Pertamina and Bulog, who sought to preserve their autonomy. The most articulate group opposing the technocrats was headed by Ali Murtopo, who set up his own "research" institute, the Center for Strategic and International Studies. Its members often criticized the technocrats' approach, particularly their alleged willingness to follow Western advice blindly. The antitechnocratic views of Ali Murtopo's colleagues were also voiced in the newspaper, *Merdeka,* and the weekly, *Ekspres,* both owned by the former minister for information, B. M. Diah. The attacks on the technocrats from this quarter reached their peak in late 1973, when General Sumitro appeared to be siding with them against Ali Murtopo.[36]

Despite the regular assaults by their rivals, there were signs that the authority of the technocrats was gradually increasing during

35. See McCawley 1973:2–6, *Tempo,* 9 June 1973, *Kompas,* 24 May 1973 (*ICATS*).
36. See *Tempo,* 1 December 1973, *Far Eastern Economic Review,* 10 December 1973, p. 19, 4 February 1974, pp. 10–12.

the 1970s, when some of their most powerful adversaries were removed from key posts. The pursuit of a rational import policy had been obstructed by the notorious corruption of customs officials working hand in hand with politically influential importers, but in 1972 the long-entrenched director general of customs, Padang Sudirgo, was replaced by Major General Slamet Danudirdjo, an army officer who had worked closely with the technocrats as one of the deputy chairmen of the National Development Planning Board (Bappenas). Although the energetic Slamet was soon replaced by another army officer, the removal of Padang Sudirgo was warmly welcomed by the technocrats.

The technocrats won an even bigger victory in 1973, when President Suharto finally replaced Achmad Tirtosudiro as head of Bulog. The apparent preoccupation of Bulog officials with private trading and speculation had made a mockery of the government's endeavors to stabilize rice prices. Despite growing dissatisfaction with Bulog's performance and its reputation as a "nest of corruption," Achmad had retained his post through several crises, but was finally dismissed following the sharp rises in rice prices at the end of 1972 which undermined the general price stability prevailing since 1968. Although Achmad was replaced by his deputy, Bulog's performance after 1973 was more satisfactory from the technocratic point of view.

Finally, in 1975 the great bastion of unorthodox fund raising, Pertamina, and its head, Ibnu Sutowo, came under attack. Encouraged by the enormous increase in oil income—especially after 1973—Ibnu Sutowo had set out on a very ambitious program of expansion. Not only did Pertamina's operations in oil production, refining, and marketing expand, but it ventured into a wide range of other activities, including petrochemicals, fertilizers, a steel plant, a rice estate, an industrial estate, transport, real estate, and tourism. Since at least 1971, Pertamina had been borrowing substantial sums commercially on the international money market without express approval from the ministers responsible for economic affairs. At the insistence of the aid-providing countries in the IGGI, the president issued a regulation in 1972 requiring that further medium-term borrowing by Pertamina should have the approval of the minister of finance. Thus effectively cut off from medium-term funds, Ibnu Sutowo turned to the short-term money market, presumably in the expectation that increasing oil revenues would enable Pertamina to make payments on schedule and obtain further short-term financing. In addition, it seems that a large long-term loan was expected from the Middle East. In early 1975, however, Pertamina was caught in a liquidity crisis which prevented it from repaying a short-term loan of $40 million. In the inquiry that followed, it was revealed that Pertamina's short-term debts amounted to $1.5 billion and estimated that it had been unable to pay about $800 million (Rp 330 billion) as taxes to the government. Ibnu Sutowo's massive miscalculation provided his military rivals and the civilian technocrats with an opportunity for which they had long been waiting. After Pertamina's initial default in February 1975, the Bank of Indonesia made the payment and raised international loans to cover further repayments. At the same time, Pertamina's right to borrow abroad was withdrawn and several committees were formed to examine the corporation's operations, including one headed by the reform-inclined chief of staff for administration of the Department of Defense and Security, Lieutenant General Hasnan Habib. Nevertheless, Ibnu Sutowo retained his position, with the public support of Ali Murtopo, until early in 1976 when further investigations revealed huge commitments for oil tankers that brought the total debt to more than $10 billion—a sum considerably more than the total government debt contracted during both the Sukarno and Suharto periods. The Pertamina debt imposed an enormous unanticipated burden on the economy and forced the government to move funds away from other important areas. At the same time, Pertamina's inability to pay numerous domestic creditors led to a series of local business failures. In the wake of the new revelations and accusations of personal profiteering, Ibnu Sutowo was finally relieved of his position and replaced by Piet Harjono, an army officer with long experience as a senior official in the Department of Finance, who was willing to work closely with Sadli, the minister for mining.[37]

The growing importance of the technocrats had resulted in part from economic growth. Despite distortions caused by pressure from military interests, the government's economic achievements

37. See Arndt 1975a:3–8, *Far Eastern Economic Review*, 30 May 1975, pp. 51–58; Glassburner 1976.

had been substantial. Aided by huge credits from the Western countries and Japan and growing private investment, the government achieved an average annual rate of growth of about 7 percent between 1967 and 1976, while industrial production rose rapidly. Exports rose from $595 million in 1967 to $4,671 million in 1974–1975. Rapid economic growth led to a sharp increase in government revenues from Rp 142 billion in the 1969–1970 budget to Rp 671 billion in 1973–1974 and, after the huge rise in oil revenues due to the price increases after 1973, to Rp 2496 billion in the 1975–1976 budget estimates. Even when inflation is taken into account, the funds available to the government had expanded vastly. This enormous increase in available resources greatly strengthened the position of the civilian technocrats. The vastly increased funds at their disposal widened the scope for allocating funds according to technocratic criteria in a way that had seemed inconceivable a few years earlier.

The technocrats had also been supported by many foreign governments, particularly the United States, and international institutions like the World Bank and the IMF, which preferred the technocrats' liberal orthodoxy to the unpredictability of the military entrepreneurs. The American government also seemed inclined to side with the technocrats and their military supporters because of the tendency of some of the military entrepreneurs to draw closer to Japan. Initially, the expansion of the Indonesian economy, and especially the oil boom, had provided Indonesia with the possibility of reducing its dependence on its creditors, but the revelation of Pertamina's enormous debts again underlined the government's need for foreign support. The government's resulting susceptibility to foreign pressure thus worked to the technocrats' advantage.

The removal of several of the technocrats' main military rivals, however, in fact reflected the growing influence of the more technocratically inclined professional officers in the armed forces rather than the technocrats' own political power. The rapid expansion in resources available to the government, which had increased the scope of the technocrats' authority, had also strengthened the regularization-oriented groups in the army at the expense of the generals who were primarily concerned with business activities. The rise in orthodox revenues enabled the government to increase defense allocations and official military salaries sharply, with the result that it was able to reduce its own and the army's dependence on the military-run enterprises raising unorthodox revenues, so that their managers no longer seemed indispensable. The growth in the influence of the professional officers was, of course, greatly facilitated by the manifest blunders committed by such key military entrepreneurs as Achmad Tirtosudiro and Ibnu Sutowo. Further, growing public dissatisfaction with corruption, foreign domination of the economy, and the failure of economic development to improve the lot of the mass of the people—as expressed in rioting in Bandung in 1973 and Jakarta in 1974—tended to persuade some military officers of the need to give the technocrats more scope and authority to pursue policies designed to alleviate mass resentment.

By the middle of the 1970s, the cabinet ministers formally responsible for government policy exercised more control over the administrative machinery than they had in the early years of the New Order. Steps had been taken to exercise stricter supervision over foreign investment, and the resources available to the government for allocation through the budget had vastly increased. The technocrats in the cabinet and other high government positions, however, still had not gained full control over the economy. Enterprises backed by military officers continued to dominate the private sector and still obtained favors from military men in the government.

Conflicting Foreign Policy Orientations

The struggle between the civilian technocrats and the business-oriented generals was accompanied by a parallel conflict between the foreign minister, Adam Malik, and various military groups. Unlike the fairly consistent alignments that characterized the struggle over economic policy, however, Adam Malik's position was attacked from several different directions. Adam Malik, a former ambassador to the Soviet Union, had been a leader of the so-called "national-Communist" Murba party, which had spearheaded attacks on the PKI in the name of Sukarnoism in 1964. Losing favor with Sukarno, he had been demoted in a cabinet reshuffle early in 1965, but was appointed as a deputy prime minister and foreign minister in March 1966, when Suharto was anxious to maintain the appearance of continuity with the past. As foreign minister, Malik supported the government's policy of approaching the West for funds but wanted to avoid excessive dependence on the aid-providing states. He sought to broaden the range of Indonesia's long-run options by fostering regional solidarity within Southeast Asia and resisting moves to make a complete break with the Communist countries. His efforts to steer an "independent and active" course of nonalignment, however, were regularly challenged by army officers, who often placed security considerations above all else and in many cases expected to obtain immediate economic benefits from a policy of closer cooperation with the United States.

The New Order government sharply reversed the previous regime's foreign policy. Sukarno's conception of a world in which the Nefos and Oldefos were locked in conflict was abandoned together with the policies associated with it. Instead of holding the projected Conference of New Emerging Forces, Indonesia rejoined the United Nations. The mooted "axis" with China, North Vietnam, North Korea, and Cambodia was forgotten as anti-Chinese demonstrations led to the suspension of diplomatic relations with China, while the confrontation of the Nekolim standing behind Malaysia was ended when the new government sought economic assistance from the West. Although the new policies were presented as a "return" to Indonesia's "independent and active policy" of nonalignment, in fact the government leaned heavily toward the West. The turn to the West and Japan was due primarily to economic exigencies. Although more than half of Indonesia's foreign debt was owed to Communist countries, it seemed clear after 1965 that they would not be the major source of new economic aid, while the Western nations, especially the United States, regarded the change of government in Jakarta as an opportunity to expand Western political and economic influence and Japan was anxious to secure raw materials for its own use.

Indonesia's top foreign policy objective after Suharto had taken power in March 1966 was to end the confrontation campaign against Malaysia. In this there was no difference of opinion between the new foreign minister and the army officers advising Suharto, although some conflict arose when the terms of the settlement were negotiated. Both sides realized that Indonesia would have little chance of obtaining much-needed funds from the Western countries and Japan if the confrontation campaign were allowed to continue. At the end of May 1966, Adam Malik held formal talks at Bangkok with Tun Razak of Malaysia, which resulted in an agreement to normalize relations "immediately" on the understanding that Kuala Lumpur would permit the people of Sabah and Sarawak to "reaffirm" their status in Malaysia by holding general elections. The military members of the Indonesian delegation were very dissatisfied with what they felt were humiliating concessions given by the foreign minister, particularly his willingness to recognize Malaysia before rather than after elections were held in Sabah and Sarawak.[38] During the next two months, responsibility for policy toward Malaysia was taken out of Adam Malik's hands, when Ali Murtopo and his colleagues secured Malaysia's approval of a secret annex to the public agreement which contradicted its text by postponing the establishment of diplomatic relations until after the holding of elections in Sabah and Sarawak. The annex was apparently needed not only to win President Sukarno's acquiescence but to assuage a sense of wounded national pride felt as much in the armed forces as in the community at large. Although diplomatic relations were not formally restored immediately after the agreement was signed on 11 August 1966, Adam Malik's concessions were implemented in effect when "unofficial" diplomatic offices were established by each country in the other's capital. Eventually full diplomatic relations were restored in August 1967, after elections had been held in Sabah but not in Sarawak.

Despite the new warmth between Indonesia and the Western countries, the government sought to avoid giving the impression of moving into the Western camp. Concerned to maintain a nonaligned image and keep long-term options open, Adam Malik resisted pressure in 1966 and 1967 to break diplomatic relations with China, but his policy was challenged from several quarters, including sections of the military. Anti-Chinese demonstrations and rioting had become common following the 1965 coup attempt when Muslim and other groups took the opportunity provided by upset conditions to express their resentment at the alleged complicity of China in the Gestapu affair and the relative wealth of the three-million-strong Chinese minority.[39] The demand to break diplomatic relations was supported publicly by several regional military commanders, including Brigadier General Ishak Djuarsa in Aceh (and later South Sumatra) and Major General Jasin in East Java.[40] Moreover, the group around Brigadier General Suhardiman of PT Berdikari was actively canvassing support for recognition of the government in Taipeh in the expectation of obtaining substantial business advantages.[41] In 1966 and the first part of 1967, Adam Malik was able to convince Suharto and the other top generals that relations should be maintained with China. Only when a renewed outbreak of anti-Chinese rioting in Jakarta coincided with the takeover of the Chinese Ministry of Foreign Affairs in Peking by an "ultraleft" group in the middle of 1967 during the Cultural Revolution, did the Indonesian government come to the conclusion that the expected long-term benefit of maintaining diplomatic relations was outweighed by their politically destabilizing consequences in the short run. When the decision to withdraw Indonesia's embassy staff from Peking was taken in October 1967, however, Adam Malik quickly coined the term "frozen" to describe the state of diplomatic relations between the two countries, thereby blocking moves to recognize Taiwan and facilitating the possible "normalization" of relations in the future.

Although diplomatic relations were not officially "broken," the two governments continued to regard each other with hostility. As international attitudes to China began to change in the early 1970s, especially after President Nixon announced in 1971 his

39. See Coppel 1975:chaps. 3, 4. Van der Kroef has argued that China played an important role in the "coup attempt." As evidence he cites newspaper reports that appeared several weeks before 1 October about Chinese arms being smuggled into Indonesia "via small East and West Java ports and fishing villages as well as in crates ostensibly containing building materials for Sukarno's Conefo project" (1971:6). The report, in the *Sabah Times* (Jesselton) of 14 September 1965, was based on "Bangkok and Hong Kong sources." It is not clear why the military participants in the Thirtieth of September Movement needed outside arms assistance. Nevertheless, given the PKI's close relationship with China, it is not improbable that the Chinese embassy was forewarned of the party's plans.

40. *Nusantara,* 1 December, 5 September 1967.

41. Suhardiman made an unpublicized visit to Taiwan in December 1966 (interview with Suhardiman, 23 August 1973).

intention of visiting Peking, Adam Malik began to hint publicly at the possibility of improving relations with China. In February 1973, he held discussions in Paris with the Chinese foreign minister, and in October he expressed the hope that relations would be normalized within the next twelve to twenty-four months.[42] According to Adam Malik, Indonesia did not object in principle to normalization but had to take into account domestic conditions, particularly the need to "educate" the local Chinese community.[43] The military leaders continued to fear that Chinese "subversion" might lead to renewed Communist activity in Indonesia,[44] and Suharto declared that normalization would require a guarantee from China that there would be no repetition of the 1965 coup, which was allegedly aided by China.[45] Even after Malaysia's recognition of China in 1974 had been followed by the Philippines and Thailand in 1975, the military leaders continued to take the view that the reopening of the Chinese embassy would lead to divided loyalties on the part of the Chinese residing in Indonesia and a resurgence of underground PKI activity. More basically, but unstated, the regime felt that its legitimacy might be put at stake if it restored friendly relations with the power it had portrayed as the embodiment of evil throughout the previous decade.

Unable to reestablish "normal" relations with China, Adam Malik succeeded in maintaining "correct" relations with the Soviet Union as part of the preservation of Indonesia's "independent and active" policy. In the early period after the coup attempt, a few generals were attracted to the idea of simply repudiating the huge debts to the Soviet Union contracted by the previous government, but Adam Malik stressed the need to keep options open in regard to the USSR.[46] In the wake of the anti-Communist purge, the Soviet Union suspended work on aid projects, but in the latter part of 1966 an Indonesian delegation headed by Adam Malik was received in Moscow, after which a short-term agreement on the rescheduling of debt repayments was signed. The Soviet Union ap-

42. *Berita Buana*, 24 October 1973 (*ICATS*).
43. *Sinar Harapan*, 30 October 1974 (*ICATS*).
44. See General Panggabean's statement in *Kompas*, 4 March 1972.
45. *Angkatan Bersenjata*, 7 November 1974 (*ICATS*).
46. Interview with Adam Malik, 22 October 1973. Of the debt of $2,358 million at the end of 1965, $1,404 million was owing to Communist countries, including $990 million to the Soviet Union. See table in *Bulletin of Indonesian Economic Studies*, no. 4 (June 1966), 5.

parently regarded developments in Indonesia since 1965 as more a disaster for China than for itself and, after Brezhnev's mooting in 1969 of the concept of "an Asian system of security," apparently aimed at "containing" China, a Soviet economic delegation arrived in Jakarta to discuss a further rescheduling of the outstanding debt and the possible resumption of work on abandoned aid projects. The 1969 talks, however, did not produce immediate results, and it was not until August 1970 that Adam Malik signed a long-term agreement on debt rescheduling along lines similar to agreements already reached with the Western creditors and Japan. Resumption of work on the abandoned projects did not commence, and it was not until 1975 that Indonesia announced that it was willing to accept the new aid the Russians were offering.[47]

The Soviet Union seemed keen to reestablish its influence in Indonesia, but many generals, particularly in the intelligence field, continued to be suspicious of all Communist powers— whether Chinese or anti-Chinese. When the Russian delegation visited Indonesia in late 1969, an extraordinary attempt to upset the talks was made by a weekly newspaper, *Chas,* which had close ties with military intelligence officers.[48] Army intelligence officers feared that the resumption of Russian aid projects would provide opportunities for Soviet agents to assist the remnants of the PKI. The strength of this fear was illustrated again in 1971, when *Chas* warned about the dangers of permitting Soviet diplomats to visit Central Java during the election period.[49] When the Central Java military commander seemed about to ban diplomats from Communist countries from visiting his territory, the Foreign Ministry responded by restricting the rights of *all* diplomats to travel in the regions during the election campaign, evidently to avoid a military ban discriminating against Communist embassies.

Although Adam Malik did not succeed in strengthening Indo-

---

47. *Far Eastern Economic Review,* 12 December 1975, p. 48.

48. *Chas* pointed to Arab countries which, it claimed, had become dependent on the Soviet Union. It alleged that several Arab embassies in Jakarta were supporting the underground PKI and claimed that staff members of the Iraqui embassy had been arrested. Adam Malik denied the report, and *Harian Kami,* which had repeated the *Chas* story, later claimed that it "has been exploited and turned into a political instrument" by elements that wanted to undermine Adam Malik and Indonesia's "independent and active" policy. See *Chas* fourth week of September 1969 (*USE*), *Harian Kami,* 8, 12, 15 September 1969 (*USE*).

49. *Nusantara,* 22 March 1971 (*USE*).

nesia's relationship with the USSR as a counter to overreliance on the West, he was able to dampen some of the pressures from military groups, including Ali Murtopo's Opsus group, toward closer alignment with American policies. During the late 1960s many military officers were sympathetic toward the American attempt to repress Communism in Indochina. While Adam Malik continued to call for a cessation of American bombing and a settlement based on the 1954 Geneva agreement, rumors circulated in Jakarta that some generals wanted to provide Indonesian troops for service in Vietnam.[50] In response, Adam Malik declared that Indonesia had never considered the dispatch of troops except as part of a UN force after a settlement had been reached,[51] and only after the 1973 peace settlement did Indonesia agree to send troops to Vietnam as part of a four-nation supervisory contingent. Shortly after the coup against Sihanouk in Cambodia, in April 1970, rumors spread that some Indonesian generals, including Ali Murtopo, wanted to provide arms for the new Lon Nol government, and *Time* magazine referred to reports that "the Djakarta government might agree to serve as a conduit for US supplies" to Cambodia.[52] These generals had envisaged disposing of old Indonesian armaments in Cambodia in exchange for new equipment from the United States, but the plan was frustrated by Adam Malik's countermove to hold an Asian Conference in Jakarta in May 1970 to discuss the Cambodian crisis.[53] By casting Indonesia in the role of the chief mediator, Adam Malik made it inappropriate for Indonesia to become involved in supplying arms on the United States behalf to Lon Nol. Nevertheless, the army later agreed to train Cambodian military personnel.[54]

50. See *Harian Kami,* 7 August 1968 (*USE*). Polomka, who was in Jakarta at the time, wrote, "Differences over Vietnam policy were evident among Indonesian leaders during the latter part of 1967, with some influential military interests arguing that Indonesian interests would be best served by closer alignment with the United States of America, even to the extent of a possible military commitment" (1974:13).

51. *Berita Yudha,* 3 February 1969 (*USE*).

52. *Time,* 20 April 1970:23; see also *Kommunikasi,* 10 April 1970 (*USE*). Cambodian officers had been in contact with Indonesia for some time, and reportedly a secret Cambodian military mission visited Indonesia in November 1969 and January 1970. See Hindley 1971:113.

53. Apart from Indonesia, the conference was attended by Japan, South Korea, South Vietnam, Laos, Philippines, Thailand, Malaysia, Singapore, Australia, and New Zealand. See Lau Teik Soon 1972.

54. *Kompas,* 25 November 1971.

Adam Malik's concern to maintain Indonesia's "nonaligned" image was further illustrated by the policy of continuing to recognize the Hanoi government and permitting the South Vietnamese National Liberation Front to maintain an office in Jakarta. In December 1969, when Malaysia proposed that South Vietnam be invited to attend an Association of Southeast Asian Nations (ASEAN) meeting as an observer, Adam Malik unsuccessfully proposed that North Vietnam and the National Liberation Front be invited as well.[55] The foreign minister's attitude, however, was regularly challenged by military groups, especially Ali Murtopo and his colleagues. The Opsus group had attempted to revise Indonesia's policy toward South Vietnam when one of its parliamentary friends, the Parmusi leader, Djaelani Naro, introduced a resolution in the DPR-GR in October 1969 calling for the recognition of the Saigon government. In March 1970, more than trade issues were discussed when Ali Murtopo's assistant, Liem Bian Kie, led a "trade mission" to South Vietnam, but the challenge to Adam Malik's "nonaligned" stand on Vietnam did not win sufficient military support to effect a change in policy. Many officers continued to view the Communist—but nationalist—struggle against foreign forces in Vietnam with much ambivalence.[56]

Although Adam Malik largely succeeded in keeping a distance between the foreign policies of Indonesia and the United States, closer cooperation developed in the defense field. In the early years of the New Order, the aid-giving countries as a group had believed that Indonesia could not afford new military supplies, but the success of the economic stabilization program strengthened the hand of military men keen to acquire new armaments. American aid for the army's "civic mission" activities had been resumed in 1967 with the supply of road-building equipment, including bulldozers, but after President Nixon's visit to Indonesia in 1969, American military assistance expanded.[57] In 1971 the

55. See Weinstein 1972:226–228. The armed forces' newspaper, *Angkatan Bersenjata,* commented, "Meanwhile some people think that rather than make a move that is subject to misinterpretation, it is better to improve the relations among the member nations themselves" (9 December 1969 [*USE*]).

56. As an indication of pro-North Vietnamese sentiment see the laudatory editorials on the death of Ho Chi Minh in the press, including military newspapers, for example, *Angkatan Bersenjata,* 5 September 1969 (*USE*).

57. A few days before Nixon's visit, General Nasution pointedly reaffirmed his opposition to military pacts and foreign bases (*Pedoman,* 28 July 1969 [*USE*]).

United States supplied a "hot line" communications system to link the military headquarters with the regions and a military spokesman confirmed that some units of the army were using M16 rifles of the sort used by the United States in Vietnam.[58] After the cease-fire in Vietnam early in 1973, US aid in the form of airplanes and ships increased.[59] Very minor assistance was received from Australia, but the United States was effectively the sole supplier of military equipment, and its aid increased suddenly from $5.8 million in 1969 to $18 million in 1970.[60] By 1976 American military aid had risen to more than $40 million annually.[61]

Despite Indonesia's dependence on the United States and its allies for economic aid and the renewed supply of armaments and other military aid from the United States, Indonesia continued to keep its distance from its chief benefactor in the field of foreign policy. In part, Indonesia's potential for a flexible policy was strengthened by the presence of several major donors in the IGGI group. Although the United States provided about one-third of Indonesia's economic aid, Japan supplied about as much, with the remaining one-third coming mainly from the countries of Western Europe. After the boom in oil prices in 1973, Indonesia's reliance on foreign aid was further reduced and its capacity for taking an independent foreign policy stand correspondingly enhanced. Moreover, by maintaining "correct" ties with the Soviet Union and the countries of Eastern Europe, the option always remained open of seeking assistance from this quarter if Western terms became too onerous. Despite its formal "nonalignment," however, Indonesia was very lukewarm in its support for the Malaysian-sponsored policy of creating in Southeast Asia a "zone of peace and neutrality" adopted by the ASEAN in 1971. Although Indonesia had long-term aspirations to become the major power in Southeast Asia, it was particularly anxious in the short term for the United States to maintain its "presence" in the region.[62]

58. *Kompas*, 2, 3 June 1971.

59. *Kompas*, 13 February 1973, *Suara Karya*, 5 March 1973 (*ICATS*).

60. *The Age* (Melbourne), 14 July 1971, quoting *New York Times*, 12 July 1971, which reported that combat weapons began to be supplied in 1970.

61. *Far Eastern Economic Review*, 19 March 1976, p. 36.

62. On his departure from Jakarta after talks with the Indonesian leaders in February 1973, the American vice-president, Spiro Agnew, stated that he had given a guarantee that the American presence would continue in the region and that America's promises to Indonesia would be honored (*Sinar Harapan*, 7 February 1973 [*ICATS*]).

Another area where Adam Malik's approach differed from that of the security-minded generals was in regard to the scope of regional cooperation in the ASEAN which had been established in 1967 as a body to facilitate cooperation in economic, cultural, and social relations between the five member states— Indonesia, Malaysia, Singapore, Thailand, and the Philippines. Initially, its members emphasized that the ASEAN was not a military pact, but important sections of the Indonesian army showed signs that they looked forward to the formation of a military alliance consisting only of Southeast Asian nations. At the end of 1966, Lieutenant General Panggabean, the deputy commander of the army, declared that "it is necessary to form a joint defense organization of Southeast Asian states because of China's efforts to strengthen her influence in this part of the world" and added that Indonesian forces must "be able to operate in any neighboring country which requires defense assistance."[63] In an interview published in a Japanese newspaper in early 1968, Suharto envisaged the possibility of military cooperation within ASEAN although the government quickly denied that Indonesia wanted to turn the organization into a pact.[64] Again in 1970, when the Lon Nol government in Cambodia was being threatened by rebels supported by North Vietnam, General Panggabean spoke of the principle of "preemptive offensive" in the event that neighboring states were attacked by an outside power and said that instead of waiting to be attacked herself, Indonesia should "make common defense with ASEAN."[65] Indonesian delegations to ASEAN meetings increasingly included senior military officers. After the Communist victories in Indochina in 1975, the proposal to give defense functions to the ASEAN arose again in Indonesian military circles.

These moves by the military were countered by Adam Malik. Immediately after Panggabean's call for a "joint defense organization" at the end of 1966, Malik declared that "Indonesia will not join military pacts of any sort."[66] Again when Panggabean spoke of his "preemptive offensive" principle in 1970, Malik tried to

63. *Kompas*, 27 December 1966.
64. Ibid., 4 March 1968.
65. *Angkatan Bersenjata*, 7 December 1970 (*ICATS*), *Kompas*, 28 January 1971 (*ICATS*).
66. Radio Republik Indonesia broadcast, 7 January 1967.

explain that what Panggabean meant was help "in the form of ideas, prayers, and diplomatic steps" but not troops.[67] Although important elements within the army had repeatedly called for the ASEAN to take on military functions, Adam Malik and his supporters successfully persuaded President Suharto against proposing such a course. Malik was conscious of the susceptibilities of Indonesia's neighbors, who realized that Indonesia would become the dominant force in any military alliance, and he was aware of the likely negative reaction of some of the aid donors, especially sections of the American Congress, to signs of Indonesian "expansionism." Nevertheless, although the ASEAN itself did not acquire military functions, bilateral defense cooperation among its members increased.

Adam Malik's concern to avoid creating the impression that Indonesia had expansionist designs was evident again when Portugal began to take steps to divest itself of its colonies, including the eastern part of the island of Timor which it shared with Indonesia. Speaking for the government, Adam Malik said that the best way for Portuguese Timor to achieve independence was through merger with Indonesia, but the decision had to be made by the people concerned;[68] and in 1974 he assured the visiting Timorese nationalist leader, Ramos Horta, that Indonesia would not interfere in East Timorese affairs.[69] Meanwhile, Ali Murtopo sought to persuade leaders of the three main East Timorese nationalist groups voluntarily to join Indonesia. In August 1975, however, the right-wing Timor Democratic Union (UDT) carried out a coup, which was followed by a countercoup by the leftist Revolutionary Front for Independent Timor (Fretilin) and the outbreak of civil conflict, which led to defeated UDT forces seeking refuge on the Indonesia side of the border. While Adam Malik tried to assure the world that "Indonesia will not create 'another Goa,' " the defense minister, General Panggabean, warned that "Indonesia will take action if the situation there disturbs stability in this region."[70] During the next months, Indonesia held negotiations with Portugal on the future of East Timor, but at the

67. *Suluh Marhaen,* 8 December 1970 (*ICATS*).
68. *Berita Buana,* 27 November 1974 (*ICATS*).
69. *Sinar Harapan,* 17 June 1974 (*ICATS*).
70. *Tempo,* 23 August 1975.

same time it became evident that military assistance was being provided for the UDT and pro-Indonesian groups. In October the UDT and the pro-Indonesian Apodeti launched a counteroffensive with the disguised backing of units of the Indonesian armed forces. Finally, the day after the American president, Gerald Ford, visited Jakarta on 6 December, Adam Malik announced that Indonesian "volunteers" had entered Timor to restore order. During the next months, Indonesian troops continued operations against Fretilin forces, and despite the official incorporation of East Timor in the Republic of Indonesia in July 1976, the resistance movement remained substantial. Worried that the leftist Fretilin might be infiltrated by Communists and establish close ties with Communist countries, the army leaders had felt that Indonesia's own security required the merger of East Timor with the republic. Although Adam Malik had initially sought to avoid military intervention, policy in the end was determined by the military leaders.

Part of the military dissatisfaction with Malik's policies arose from the tendency of some officers to place "security" above all other foreign policy considerations. Many officers were sympathetic toward American efforts to bolster up anti-Communist regimes in the region and were not averse to Indonesia's cooperating with the Americans in providing assistance to governments threatened by Communist insurgencies. Concern for the security of Indonesia's neighbors lay behind General Panggabean's proposal to form a military alliance among Southeast Asian nations and his repeated calls for increased military cooperation among ASEAN members after 1967. In the domestic field also, the overriding concern of many army officers for "security" was apparent. The call to break diplomatic relations with China and the continued "freezing" of relations since 1967 were supported by military men who believed that the Chinese embassy would be a source of subversion. Similarly, many officers, especially in the intelligence field, were reluctant to accept the proposed renewal of economic aid from the Soviet Union because of their fear that Russian technical experts might engage in political activities. The 1975 military intervention in Portuguese Timor was also motivated by the fear that an independent Timor would become a source of subversion in Indonesia itself.

Malik's military opponents were not always motivated only by concern for security considerations, however. In some cases, their policy differences with the foreign minister arose as much, if not more, from anticipated side benefits of new policies rather than from the overt foreign policy issues themselves. Thus, some of the advocates of sending Indonesian troops to Vietnam foresaw that the adoption of the policy would result in a large inflow of funds and armaments from the United States. Similarly, the plan to send arms to the Lon Nol government in Cambodia was conditional on the American government's supplying new replacements, while the advocates of expanding the ASEAN's functions into the military field probably expected material support from the United States. Brigadier General Suhardiman's attempts in 1967 to have the government take a pro-Taiwan stand were clearly linked to the promise of substantial credits from the Taiwan government, which were to be channeled through the business association he had formed, and the later approaches by the Opsus group to Taiwan were also motivated by business as well as political considerations.

Adam Malik was thus regularly under attack. Although forced to give much ground to his military rivals, he succeeded in defending the general line of his policy. An important factor was his ability to win the confidence of foreign governments, especially the United States, which wanted to avoid the impression that it was supporting a military regime in Indonesia. Although Adam Malik opposed policies that drew Indonesia into open military cooperation with the United States, the dominant group of American policy makers apparently preferred him to the military men who wanted to replace him. President Suharto was aware of the need to present a favorable image abroad and appreciated Malik's value in sustaining the impression that Indonesia was ruled by a "military-civilian partnership." Perhaps the most important factor favoring Adam Malik in his efforts to resist pressures toward greater alignment with the West was the enduring sense of nationalism found not only in civilian circles but also in many sections of the armed forces. The sensitivity of much of the officer corps to the dangers of foreign dependence had its origins in the army's early experience of fighting for independence from Dutch rule and the later involvement of the CIA in the regional rebellion of 1958. Moreover, army officers have always been conscious of Indonesia's potential as a "great power" in the Southeast Asian context and have tended to regard the involvement of the big powers in the region as an obstacle to the fulfillment of their aspirations. Although Indonesia accepted, and indeed welcomed, the involvement of American military forces in Southeast Asia, their presence has been seen as a temporary necessity while Indonesia builds up her own military power.

13 | Conclusion: The Army and Politics

The Indonesian army differs from most armies that have seized political power in that it had never previously regarded itself as an apolitical organization. From the army's beginnings in 1945 as a guerrilla force to combat the return of Dutch colonial rule until the consolidation of its political power under the New Order, Indonesian army officers have always concerned themselves with political issues and for most of the period actively played important political roles. Having participated fully in the nationalist struggle against Dutch rule, most officers continued to feel that their voices should be heard in postindependence political affairs. After the imposition of martial law in 1957, their right to participate was given formal recognition through appointments to the cabinet, the parliament, and the administration. During the Guided Democracy era, the army became one of the two major organized political forces, which, with President Sukarno, dominated the politics of the period. Finally, the army's drive against the PKI in 1965 and its success in easing President Sukarno out of office left it as the dominant force in Indonesian politics.

The growth of the army's nonmilitary role was accompanied by an ideology justifying its new activities. After the introduction of martial law in 1957, General Nasution had formulated the concept of the Middle Way, according to which army officers participated actively in affairs of government but did not seek to achieve a dominant position.[1] During the Guided Democracy period, the army's perception of itself as an active participant in day-to-day politics and other nonmilitary fields became deeply engrained. At its first seminar, held in April 1965, the army produced a doctrine which declared that the armed forces in

1. See Lev 1966:191–192.

Indonesia formed both a "military force" and a "social-political force." As a "social-political force," the army's activities covered "the ideological, political, social, economic, cultural, and religious fields."[2] The lack of limitations on the army's political role, in contrast with the earlier Middle Way concept, was even more marked at the army's second seminar, in August 1966, when the army leaders were stepping up the pressure on President Sukarno to resign himself to the fact of military domination of the government. The seminar declared that: "The army, which was born in the cauldron of the Revolution, has never been a dead instrument of the government concerned exclusively with security matters. The army, as a fighter for freedom, cannot remain neutral toward the course of state policy, the quality of the government, and the safety of the state based on Panca Sila. The army does not have an exclusively military duty but is concerned with all fields of social life."[3] During the New Order period, this doctrine became known as the Dwi Fungsi (Dual Function) of the armed forces and later, in Sanskritized form, as the Dwi Dharma (Dual Duty)—referring to the military and "social-political" roles played by the armed forces. The army's continued domination of the state during the 1970s was justified on the grounds that civilians still needed the strong leadership that only the army could provide.

The army rose to power by outstaying its less institutionalized rivals. Based mainly in Java during the revolution, it extended its organization to cover all of Indonesia during the early 1950s, and in the early 1960s its power was enhanced by the sharp increase in numbers and armaments that accompanied the West Irian and Malaysia campaigns. Financed by state funds supplemented by its own commercial activities, the army developed its political organization to meet its responsibilities under martial law and established itself as a major autonomous political force. By the end of the 1950s, army officers had entered the political elite at the national, regional, and local levels, and during the early 1960s they became firmly entrenched in the government apparatus. Backed by a nationwide organization and, ultimately, the power to coerce, army officers were well placed to take advantage of the opportunities that presented themselves in 1965 and after.

2. Angkatan Darat 1965:Main book, chap. 3.
3. Angkatan Darat 1966a:19.

As the army's power grew, its rivals were neutralized one after another. The non-Communist political parties had been largely discredited together with the parliamentary system in the 1950s, leaving the PKI as the main organized civilian counterweight to the army during the first half of the 1960s. The intense competition between the army and the PKI after 1963 culminated in the coup attempt and army-instigated massacres of 1965, in which the army used its physical power to eliminate the PKI as a political force. In the aftermath, President Sukarno was left as the main obstacle to army domination. In the drawn-out maneuvering between October 1965 and March 1967, the army leaders gradually divested the president of his allies, while Sukarno held back from forcing a showdown that might have thrown the nation into civil war. After the elimination of the PKI and the dismissal of Sukarno, the army's domination of the government was unchallenged, and in the following years the remaining centers of independent power in the political parties and other civilian organizations were completely subjugated.

The elimination of autonomous centers of civilian power was accompanied by the consolidation of authority within the armed forces. The revolutionary army had consisted of heterogeneous guerrilla units with strong local roots but a weak sense of hierarchy. The army had lost many of its more extreme officers of both the left and the right after the Madiun revolt and the formation of the Darul Islam, but the postindependence military was far from a unified force, and it was not until the Outer Islands rebellion of the late 1950s resulted in a further shedding of dissident elements that the leadership was able to establish its unchallenged authority. The entry of army officers into a wide range of "civilian" activities during the Guided Democracy period, however, led to a new form of politicization. Many officers acquired extramilitary loyalties and commitments which inhibited the army leadership from exploiting its political potential to the full. In these circumstances, President Sukarno manipulated interservice rivalries and used his ability to gain the personal loyalty of important army officers to undermine the cohesion of the armed forces. But the situation changed dramatically on 1 October 1965, when the assassination of the army commander and his closest colleagues created an atmosphere which permitted the new army commander to gain almost universal support from his colleagues for his attack on the PKI despite the president's disapproval.

In asserting the army leadership's power after 1965, Suharto used a combination of coercion and political pressure. The application of physical violence against the mass base of the PKI and the arrest of hundreds of thousands of PKI sympathizers placed the army leaders in a position of dominance, which enabled them to use less drastic measures to consolidate their power against other rivals. Backed by the threat of coercion, which continued to be used against supporters of the PKI and the more militant of the president's followers, Suharto adopted the Javanese principle of *alon alon asal kelakon* (slow but sure) in applying pressure to other groups that stood in the way of the army leadership's rise to full power. By persuading key regional commanders in the army to accept transfers to prestigious but powerless positions during 1966, while encouraging the propaganda campaign against the president, Suharto prepared for the watershed of early 1967, in which Sukarno's remaining senior military allies reluctantly accepted the president's loss of power in exchange for assurances that his fall would not mark the commencement of a new purge aimed at his military supporters. In establishing his authority within the army and over the armed forces, Suharto recognized the need of his rivals to save face. Not only did he avoid punitive action against them, but he often rewarded their willingness to cooperate by giving them prominent and lucrative diplomatic or administrative appointments.

Visible political competition among the political parties, the four services, and rival groups in the army continued for several years despite the army leadership's unchallenged preeminence. By 1969, however, open factionalism within the army had ceased with the transfer of the remaining "New Order militant" commanders from key positions, and open interservice rivalry ended with the reorganization and integration of the armed forces and the replacement of the service commanders. Having thus established full control over the entire armed forces, Suharto then moved on to deal with the political parties, which, despite heavy pressure, had continued to enjoy a measure of independence and remained as potential rallying points for civilian opposition to the regime. Agreeing in 1969 to the parties' demand for general elections, the army leaders then ensured that the elections were held under conditions which guaranteed the parties' crushing defeat. The elections served to enhance the government's legitimacy while dealing a heavy blow to the last remnants of organized civilian strength. By 1971, the regime had extended its control over all potential bases of organized opposition—both military and civilian.

The subjugation of the remaining relatively autonomous centers of power was accompanied by a decline in open political competition between clearly identifiable military factions. The complete ascendancy of the army leadership meant that the most important struggles for influence took place within the military elite among generals whose power rested on their capacity to win the confidence of their fellow generals rather than on their ability to mobilize organized support from outside the elite. Contenders for influence among the senior generals did not question the army's continued domination of the government or Suharto's leadership, but concerned themselves mainly with appointments and the division of the spoils of power. The "political" and "financial" generals close to Suharto were able to exercise great influence over appointments to key positions and the allocation of rewards, which they used to ensure that troop commanders remained loyal to the regime. Nevertheless, there were sharp rivalries among the generals in the president's circle of advisers, and several fell from power after losing the confidence of their colleagues and the president. Of those who lost out in the intraelite power struggles, none was in a position to mobilize support against the regime, and the only attempt to exploit mass discontent, in January 1974, failed. Most dissidents were glad to accept the ambassadorships and similar posts offered to them.

The commercial ethos that had spread among army officers after the imposition of martial law in 1957 became dominant a decade later with the final accession of the army to full power. The troop commanders who had set the tone of the army during the revolution and the early 1950s were superseded by, or themselves became, the managers, bureaucrats, and businessmen in uniform who directed the army in the 1960s. The rapid expansion of the army's role in politics, the economy, and civilian administration had provided the setting for a transformation of the army's ethos in which the youthful freedom fighters of the revolutionary period turned their minds to the pursuit of material satisfactions as they approached middle age. While the troop commanders were occupied with the West Irian and Malaysia campaigns, many of their colleagues concerned themselves with fund raising on their own and the army's behalf in association with Chinese businessmen. Following the dramatic events of 1 October 1965, which thrust to the fore a troop commander with a strong business sense and a flair for political maneuver, the stage was set for a further increase in the commercial activities of army officers. Under the New Order, army officers occupied key economic posts in the bureaucracy and controlled the vital fields of oil production and the rice trade, while the private business activities of military men were able to expand in association with the inrush of foreign corporations.

The New Order government's proclaimed goal of "economic development" was perceived largely in terms of the growth of the modern sector of the economy. The initial "stabilization" of the economy was followed by a large influx of foreign funds, leading to a rapid expansion of business opportunities which could be exploited by those with political influence. Enterprises with which army officers were associated obtained favorable treatment when seeking licenses, credits, and contracts and were able to avoid tax obligations and other regulations, with the result that the policies formulated by the technocrats in Jakarta were often distorted at the point of implementation. The rapid expansion of commercial opportunities through the influx of foreign aid and private capital was of crucial importance to the new government in achieving political stability because it enabled the army to raise funds for its own operations and provided officers with material satisfaction derived from their private activities. The government's encouragement of private business activity created conditions in which military-backed enterprises prospered and contented military men acquired a stake in the regime.

The expansion of the modern commercial sector of the economy and the sharply increased inflow of foreign capital directly served the interests of the military elite and their civilian associates, but it also helped create a broader civilian base of support for the regime. During the Guided Democracy period, the professional and salaried members of the urban middle class had failed to prosper because civil service salaries fell to absurdly low levels and private commerce declined. The expansion of economic activity after 1966 brought increased revenues, which enabled the government to pay substantial supplements to the salaries of senior and professional civil servants and later to increase sharply "official" salaries at all levels, while the rapid growth of private business activity, especially the establishment of new foreign-financed industries, opened up numerous well-paid employment opportunities to the educated and the technically qualified. The urban middle class of Jakarta and the main regional cities was able to benefit from the increased availability of consumer goods and other modern facilities in the late 1960s, and as a result the New Order was for them an improvement on the Old Order.

While the policies of the new government favored part of the urban middle class, the free rein given to military-backed commercial activities gave rise to resentment in other civilian quarters. In the cities, students and sections of the press protested against high-level corruption and the apparent willingness of senior generals to sacrifice "national interests" to do business with foreigners, while indigenous businessmen complained about competition from military-backed firms, foreign enterprises, and increased imports of consumer goods. The irregular purchasing policies of the army-dominated rice-trading agency, Bulog, contributed to urban hardship when prices rose and rural hardship when prices fell, while the corruption-ridden endeavor to expand the Green Revolution through the Bimas Gotong Royong program provoked so much opposition among peasants that it had to be abandoned. Symbolizing the army's grip on the economy, the state oil corporation, Pertamina, became a major target of civilian resentment as it channeled much of the nation's rising oil revenues into the army's coffers and to other military-sponsored purposes. The feeling became widespread that "economic development" served primarily the interests of the military and their Chinese and foreign business partners, while the mass of the people in the urban slums and rural areas were neglected.

The decline of the political parties and the absence of other civilian organizations able to countervail the army's power meant that the system grew less capable of responding to popular discontent. When the emasculated political parties ceased to serve as channels to carry nonelite aspirations upward, popular resentments were deprived of institutional means of expression and army officers felt free to pursue their commercial interests with little concern for civilians harmed by their policies. Because they controlled the means of coercion and the distribution of patronage, the military leaders of the government were rarely under pressure to take account of civilian interests. But the failure of the government's program of economic development to bring about improvements for the mass of the people meant that popular frustration and discontent continued to spread, while the government showed no signs of being capable of tackling the basic long-term problems of growing unemployment, overpopulation, and poverty. Despite the government's achievement of political "stability," it had no program to cope with the inevitable growth of popular discontent which it faced except to rely on the instruments of repression.

Although civilian frustration was acute, there seemed to be no prospect of removing the military from control of the government. The institutionalization of military power had proceeded over more than two decades, while alternative political organizations had atrophied, grown demoralized, or been crushed. The vigilance of the army's security apparatus ensured that the PKI could not revive itself and that other organized opposition could not develop. The prospect of the emergence of revolutionary opposition to the government seemed slight, not only because of the government's capacity to nip all signs of dissent in the bud but because of the weakness of revolutionary tradition. Although isolated protest movements had been common in the rural areas during the colonial period and the village masses had been partially mobilized to fight the Dutch after 1945, the Javanese peasantry had shown few signs of rebelliousness during the 1950s and 1960s and the PKI had won widespread support not as a revolutionary party but as an organization defending the interests of the poor within the existing system. Armed resistance to the government had been confined to regional revolts in which militant Muslims played a major role. If past experience is a guide, militant Islam in the regions outside Java may represent a greater short-run threat to the government than Communist-led revolutionary movements based in Java.

Although the army's grip on the government seemed unchallenged, there were, nevertheless, signs that the position of the dominant group of "political" and "financial" generals was becoming increasingly insecure. As the 1945 Generation of generals who had fought as guerrillas against the Dutch reached retiring age, a new generation of academy-trained officers was rising to middle-level positions. These officers often had a stronger sense of commitment to "professional" military values. Although many had acquired much of the ethos of the older generation, others seemed likely to be concerned that the unrestricted pursuit of commercial interests at the expense of mass needs and nationalist sentiment would give rise to political challenges to the army in the long run. While some of these officers favored meeting the spread of mass discontent with increased repression, others were more inclined to work with the civilian technocrats in the government to promote orderly administration in the interests of economic development. Although there seemed to be little possibility that army officers would carry out a far-reaching program of social transformation in the interests of the masses, the prospects of limited reform were not negligible as troop commanders were confronted with increasing civilian frustration engendered by the policies of the "political" and "financial" generals in Jakarta and their allies in the regions.

Appendix | Institutions and Organizations

State Institutions

Under the *1945 Constitution,* reintroduced by President Sukarno in 1959, the supreme source of authority is the *People's Consultative Assembly* (Majelis Permusyawaratan Rakyat, MPR), which is obliged to convene at least once every five years to elect the president and determine the "broad outline of state policy." In 1960, the president appointed a *Provisional People's Consultative Assembly* (Majelis Permusyawaratan Rakyat Sementara, MPRS) to carry out the functions of the MPR until elections could be held. The MPRS convened six times (including one special session). After the 1971 elections, the MPR convened for the first time in 1973.

The 1945 Constitution also provides for a *People's Representative Council* (Dewan Perwakilan Rakyat, DPR) or parliament. In 1960 a provisional parliament known as the *Gotong Royong (Mutual Assistance) People's Representative Council (DPR-GR)* was appointed. It was replaced by an elected DPR after the 1971 elections. The *cabinet* is responsible to the president, not to the parliament.

At the provincial level the administration is headed by a *Governor* appointed by the president. Each province is divided into districts headed by a *mayor* in the case of *towns* and a *bupati* in the case of *kabupaten* covering rural areas. The *kabupaten* are further divided into subdistricts called *kecamatan* headed by an appointed *camat*. At the bottom of the administrative structure is the *village* with an elected head known as *lurah* in most of Java and other terms elsewhere. In 1970 there were 26 provinces and 271 towns and *kabupaten*.

The Armed Forces

The structure of the armed forces has changed from time to time. The armed forces consist of the army, navy, air force, and police, each headed by a *commander* between 1962 and 1969 and a *chief of staff* before 1962 and after 1969. Before 1967 the commanders of the four services were directly responsible to the president as *supreme commander,* while administrative coordination was the responsibility of the *chief of staff of the armed forces* until 1966, when that position was abolished. In 1969 operational authority over all four services was transferred to the *commander of the armed forces,* a position created in 1967. In practice the commander of the armed forces has also held the position of *minister of defense and security,* leaving the *deputy commander* effectively at the top of the military hierarchy.

In 1969 integrated *Regional Defense Commands* (Kowilhan) were established to place all army, navy, and air force troops under a single command in each region. Six commands were formed, but these were reduced to four in 1973.

The Army

The commander was assisted by a *general staff* consisting of a *deputy commander* (since 1966), three *deputies* (responsible for operations, administration, and extramilitary activities), and seven *assistants* (for intelligence, operations, personnel, logistics, political affairs, extramilitary activities, and finance). After 1969 the commander and deputy commander were called *chief of staff* and *deputy chief of staff* respectively and the three positions of deputy were abolished.

There are seventeen *Regional Military Commands* (Kodam), each headed by a *regional commander.* The most important were the four in Java—Jakarta, West Java (*Siliwangi*), Central Java (*Diponegoro*), and East Java (*Brawijaya*). Before the reorganization of 1969, the Kodams outside Java were coordinated by three *Interregional Commands* (Koandah) for Sumatra, Kalimantan, and East Indonesia.

Each regional commander has his own general staff headed by a deputy (*chief of staff*) with seven assistants concerned with the same fields as the assistants on the headquarters general staff. The territory of the Kodam was divided into three or four *Resort*

Military Commands (Korem). Beneath the Korem, *District Military Commands* (Kodim) were placed in towns and *kabupaten,* while at the *kecamatan* level there was a small *Rayon Military Command* (Koramil). Apart from these "territorial" troops, the Kodams on Java have *infantry brigades* trained for conventional military operations.

The *Army Strategic Reserve Command* (Kostrad) did not have troops of its own, but elite battalions in the infantry brigades of the Kodams were assigned to the Kostrad when required. In addition, the army's elite force, the *Army Paracommando Regiment* (RPKAD), was transferred to the Kostrad at the end of 1965.

The Other Forces

The other three forces are similarly organized with a general staff and regional commands, as well as special commands, such as the navy's *Armada* and the air force's *Operations Command.* Further, all three services had their own elite ground forces—the navy's *Commando Corps* (Kko), the air force's *Mobile Troops* (PGT), and the police's *Mobile Brigade* (Briged Mobil, Brimob).

Internal Security Bodies

The army regional commanders acquired wide powers after the declaration of martial law in 1957, when they were designated as *Regional War Authorities* (Peperda) responsible to the army *Central War Authority* (Peperpu) until 1959 and then to the *Supreme War Authority* (Peperti). With the lifting of martial law in 1963, the Peperti and Peperda were dissolved.

In September 1964 army regional commanders (with several unimportant exceptions) acquired new security powers as *Regional Authorities to Implement Dwikora* (Pepelrada). The Pepelrada were responsible to the *Supreme Operations Command* (Koti). The Koti and Pepelrada were abolished in July 1967.

The *Operations Command to Restore Security and Order* (Kopkamtib) was established in October 1965. With the abolition of the Pepelrada regulations, army regional commanders were appointed as *Special Executors* (Pelaksana Khusus, Laksus) of the Kopkamtib in August 1967.

During the Guided Democracy period the main civilian intelligence body was the *Central Intelligence Board* (BPI). This was dissolved in 1966 and replaced by a new body that began to function in 1967 and was later known as the *State Intelligence Coordinating Body* (Bakin).

Political Parties

Under Guided Democracy there were ten legal parties after the enforced dissolution of the Muslim *Masyumi* and the *Indonesian Socialist party* (Partai Sosialis Indonesia, PSI). The three largest parties were the nationalist *Indonesian National party* (Partai Nasional Indonesia, PNI), the Muslim *Nahdatul Ulama* (NU) and the *Indonesian Communist party* (Partai Komunis Indonesia, PKI). Of the seven minor parties, two were Muslim—the *Syarikat Islam party of Indonesia* (Partai Syarikat Islam Indonesia, PSII) and the *Islamic Education Union* (Persatuan Tarbijah Islamijah, Perti), two were Christian—the *Catholic party* (Partai Katholik) and the *Protestant party* (Partai Kristen Indonesia, Parkindo), one was nationalist—the *Indonesia party* (Partai Indonesia, Partindo), one had ties with army officers—the *League of Upholders of Indonesian Freedom* (Ikatan Pendukung Kemerdekaan Indonesia, IPKI), and one had its origins as a Marxist party—the *Murba party*. The PKI was banned in 1966 and Partindo suppressed. In 1968 a new Muslim party, the Indonesian Muslim party (Partai Muslimin Indonesia, Parmusi) was formed. Thus nine parties competed in the 1971 elections with the army-sponsored *Joint Secretariat of Functional Groups* (Sekretariat Bersama Golongan Karya, Sekber-Golkar), which was later called simply Golkar. In 1973 the nine political parties were reduced to two—the *Development Unity party* (Partai Persatuan Pembangunan, PPP) representing the former Muslim parties and the *Indonesian Democracy party* (Partai Democracy Indonesia, PDI) representing the other parties.

Bibliography

Books, Monographs, Theses, Articles

Ali Moertopo 1973. *Some Basic Thoughts on the Acceleration and Moderniza-tion of 25 Years' Development* (Centre for Strategic and International Studies, Jakarta).

Anderson, B. R. O'G. 1972a. *Java in a Time of Revolution* (Cornell University Press, Ithaca).

——. 1972b. "The Idea of Power in Javanese Culture," in C. Holt, ed., *Culture and Politics in Indonesia* (Cornell University Press, Ithaca).

Anderson, B. R. O'G., and Ruth McVey. 1971. *A Preliminary Analysis of the October 1, 1965, Coup in Indonesia* (Modern Indonesia Project, Cornell University, Ithaca).

Anonymous. 1970. "Survey of Recent Developments," *Bulletin of Indonesian Economic Studies*, 6 (March), 1–16.

Arndt, H. W. 1968. "Survey of Recent Developments," *Bulletin of Indonesian Economic Studies*, no. 10 (June), 1–28.

——. 1969a. "Survey of Recent Developments," *Bulletin of Indonesian Economic Studies*, 5 (July), 1–16.

——. 1969b. "Survey of Recent Developments," *Bulletin of Indonesian Economic Studies*, 5 (November), 1–28.

——. 1972. *Australia and Asia: Economic Essays* (Australian National University Press, Canberra).

——. 1975a. "Survey of Recent Developments," *Bulletin of Indonesian Economic Studies*, 11 (July), 1–29.

——. 1975b. "Development and Inequality: The Indonesian Case," *World Development*, 3 (February–March).

Bartlett, A. D. III, R. J. Barton, J. C. Bartlett, G. A. Fowler, Jr., and C. F. Hays. 1972. *Pertamina: Indonesian National Oil* (Amerasia, Jakarta).

Boerhan and Soebekti. 1966. *Fakta dan Latarbelakang G.30.S.* (Kosgoro, Jakarta).

Booth, Anne, and Bruce Glassburner. 1975. "Survey of Recent Developments," *Bulletin of Indonesian Economic Studies*, 11 (March), 1–40.

Brackman, Arnold. 1969. *The Communist Collapse in Indonesia* (Norton, New York).

Britton, Peter. 1973. "The Indonesian Army: 'Stabiliser' and 'Dynamiser,' " in Rex Mortimer, ed., *Showcase State: The Illusion of Indonesia's 'Accelerated Modernisation'* (Angus & Robertson, Sydney).

Budiardjo, Carmel. 1974. "Political Imprisonment in Indonesia," in J. Taylor et. al., *Repression and Exploitation in Indonesia* (Spokesman Books, London).

Bunnell, F. P. 1966. "Guided Democracy Foreign Policy: 1960–1965: President Sukarno Moves from Non-alignment to Confrontation," *Indonesia*, no. 2 (October), 37–76.

Castles, Lance. 1974. "Economic Recovery under the New Order: Miracle or Illusion?" in Oey Hong Lee, ed., *Indonesia after the 1971 Elections* (Oxford, London).

Coppel, Charles. 1975. "The Indonesian Chinese in the Sixties: A Study of an Ethnic Minority in a Period of Turbulent Political Change" (Ph.D. thesis, Monash University).

Crouch, H. A. 1971. "The Army, the Parties and Elections," *Indonesia*, no. 11 (April), 177–192.

———. 1972. "Military Politics under Indonesia's New Order," *Pacific Affairs*, 45 (Summer), 206–219.

———. 1974. "The '15th January Affair' in Indonesia," *Dyason House Papers*, 1 (August), 1–5.

Dake, A. C. A. 1973. *In the Spirit of the Red Banteng: Indonesian Communists between Moscow and Peking* (Mouton, The Hague).

Dharmawan Tjondronegoro. 1966. *Ledakan Fitnah Subversi G-30-S* (Matoa, Jakarta).

Feith, Herbert. 1962. *The Decline of Constitutional Democracy in Indonesia* (Cornell University Press, Ithaca).

———. 1963a. "Dynamics of Guided Democracy," in Ruth McVey, ed., *Indonesia* (Human Relations Area Files Press, New Haven).

———. 1963b. "Indonesia's Political Symbols and Their Wielders," *World Politics*, 16 (October), 79–97.

———. 1964. "President Sukarno, the Army and the Communists: The Triangle Changes Shape," *Asian Survey*, 4 (August), 969–980.

———. 1968a. "Suharto's Search for a Political Format," *Indonesia*, no. 6 (October), 88–105.

———. 1968b. "A Blot on the 'New Order's Record: The Fate of 80,000 Political Prisoners in Indonesia," *New Republic*, 13 April.

Feith, Herbert, and Lance Castles, eds. 1970. *Indonesian Political Thinking: 1945–1965* (Cornell University Press, Ithaca).

Geertz, Clifford. 1959. "The Javanese Village," in G. W. Skinner, ed., *Local, Ethnic and National Loyalties: A Symposium* (Southeast Asian Studies, Yale University, New Haven).

———. 1960. *The Religion of Java* (Free Press of Glencoe, New York).

———. 1968. *Islam Observed: Religious Development in Morocco and Indonesia* (Yale University Press, New Haven).

Gibson, Joyce. 1965. "Survey of Recent Developments," *Bulletin of Indonesian Economic Studies*, no. 1 (June), 1–12.

Glassburner, Bruce. 1971. "Indonesian Economic Policy Since Sukarno," in Bruce Glassburner, ed., *The Economy of Indonesia: Selected Readings* (Cornell University Press, Ithaca).

——. 1976. "In the Wake of General Ibnu: Crisis in the Indonesian Oil Industry," *Asian Survey,* 16 (December), 1099–1112.

Gordon, Bernard. 1966. *The Dimensions of Conflict in Southeast Asia* (Prentice-Hall, Englewood Cliffs).

Gregory, Ann. 1970. "Factionalism in the Indonesian Army," *Journal of Comparative Administration,* 2 (November).

Grenville, Stephen. 1973. "Survey of Recent Developments," *Bulletin of Indonesian Economic Studies,* 9 (March), 1–29.

——. 1974. "Survey of Recent Developments," *Bulletin of Indonesian Economic Studies,* 10 (March), 1–32.

Hansen, G. 1972. "Indonesia's Green Revolution: The Abandonment of a Non-Market Strategy Toward Change," *Asian Survey,* 12 (November), 932–946.

Hatta, Mohammed. 1965. "One Indonesian View of the Malaysia Issue," *Asian Survey,* 5 *(March), 139–144.*

Hauswedell, P. C. 1973. "Sukarno: Radical or Conservative? Indonesian Politics, 1964–1965," *Indonesia,* no. 15 (April), 109–144.

Hindley, Donald. 1962. "President Sukarno and the Communists: The Politics of Domestication," *American Political Science Review,* 61 (December), 915–926.

——. 1964. "Indonesia's Confrontation of Malaysia: A Search for Motives," *Asian Survey,* 4 (June), 904–913.

——. 1966. *The Communist Party of Indonesia, 1951–1963* (University of California Press, Berkeley).

——. 1967. "Political Power and the October 1965 Coup in Indonesia," *Journal of Asian Studies,* 26 (February), 237–249.

——. 1970. "Alirans and the Fall of the Old Order," *Indonesia,* no. 9 (April), 23–66.

——. 1971. "Indonesia 1970: The Workings of Pantjasila Democracy," *Asian Survey,* 11 (February), 111–120.

——. 1972. "Indonesia 1971: Pantjasila Democracy and the Second Parliamentary Elections," *Asian Survey,* 12 (January), 56–68.

Hong Lan Oei. 1968. "Indonesia's Economic Stabilisation and Rehabilitation Programme: An Evaluation," *Indonesia,* no. 5 (April), 135–174.

Horn, R. C. 1971. "Soviet-Indonesian Relations Since 1965," *Survey,* 17 (Winter), 216–232.

——. 1973. "Indonesia's Response to Changing Big Power Alignments," *Pacific Affairs,* 46 (Winter), 515–533.

Hughes, John. 1968. *The End of Sukarno* (Angus & Robertson, London).

Janowitz, Morris. 1964. *The Military in the Political Development of the New Nations* (University of Chicago Press, Chicago).

Jones, Howard. 1971. *Indonesia: The Possible Dream* (Harcourt, Brace, Jovanovich, New York).

Kahin, George McT. 1952. *Nationalism and Revolution in Indonesia* (Cornell University Press, Ithaca).

——. 1964. "Malaysia and Indonesia," *Pacific Affairs*, 37 (Fall), 253–270.

Karni, Rahadi S. 1974. *The Devious Dalang: Sukarno and the So-called Untung Coup: Eyewitness Account by Bambang S. Widjanarko* (Interdoc, The Hague).

Kraar, Louis. 1973. "Oil and Nationalism Mix Beautifully in Indonesia," *Fortune*, 89 (July).

Lau Teik Soon. 1972. *Indonesia and Regional Security: The Djakarta Conference on Cambodia* (Institute of Southeast Asian Studies, Singapore).

Legge, J. D. 1972. *Sukarno* (Allen Lane, Penguin Press, London).

Lev, D. S. 1966. *The Transition to Guided Democracy: Indonesian Politics, 1957–1959* (Modern Indonesia Project, Cornell University, Ithaca).

Liddle, R. W. 1973. "Evolution from Above: National Development and Local Leadership in Indonesia," *Journal of Asian Studies*, 32 (February), 287–309.

Mackie, J. A. C. 1967. *Problems of the Indonesian Inflation* (Modern Indonesia Project, Cornell University, Ithaca).

——. 1970. "The Report of the Commission of Four on Corruption," *Bulletin of Indonesian Economic Studies*, 6 (November), 87–101.

——. 1974. *Konfrontasi: The Indonesia-Malaysia Dispute, 1963–1966* (Oxford University Press, London).

Manning, C. 1971. "The Timber Boom with Special Reference to East Kalimantan," *Bulletin of Indonesian Economic Studies*, 7 (November), 30–60.

Marzuki Arifin. 1974. *Peristiwa 15 Januari 1974* (Publishing House Indonesia, Jakarta).

McCawley, Peter. 1973. "Survey of Recent Developments," *Bulletin of Indonesian Economic Studies*, 9 (November), 1–27.

McIntyre, Angus. 1972. "Divisions and Power in the Indonesian National Party, 1965–1966," *Indonesia*, no. 13 (April), 183–210.

McVey, Ruth. 1963. "Indonesian Communism under Guided Democracy," in A. D. Barnett, ed., *Communist Strategies in Asia: A Comparative Analysis of Governments and Parties* (Praeger, New York).

——. 1965. "The Strategic Triangle: Indonesia," *Survey*, no. 54 (January), 113–122.

——. 1968. "Indonesian Communism and China," in Tang Tsou, ed., *China in Crisis*, Vol. 2 (University of Chicago Press, Chicago).

——. 1970. "Nationalism, Islam and Marxism: The Management of Ideological Conflict in Indonesia." Introduction to Sukarno, *Nationalism, Islam and Marxism* (Modern Indonesia Project, Cornell University, Ithaca).

——. 1971a. "PKI Fortunes at Low Tide," *Problems of Communism*, 20 (January).

——. 1971b. "The Post-Revolutionary Transformation of the Indonesian Army" (Part I), *Indonesia*, no. 11 (April), 131–176.

——. 1972. "The Post-Revolutionary Transformation of the Indonesian Army" (Part II), *Indonesia,* no. 13 (April), 147–181.

Meares, L. A. 1970. "A New Approach to Rice Intensification," *Bulletin of Indonesian Economic Studies,* 6 (July), 106–111.

Mitchell, David. 1970. "Wanokalada: A Case Study in Local Administration," *Bulletin of Indonesian Economic Studies,* 6 (July), 76–93.

Mohammed Kamal Hassan. 1975. "Contemporary Muslim Religio-Political Thought in Indonesia: The Response to New Order Modernisation" (Ph.D. dissertation, Columbia University).

Mortimer, Rex. 1968. "Indonesia: Emigre Post-Mortems on the PKI," *Australian Outlook,* 22 (December), 347–359.

——. 1969. "Class, Social Cleavage and Indonesian Communism," *Indonesia,* no. 8 (October), 1–20.

——. 1971. "Unresolved Problems of the Indonesian Coup," *Australian Outlook,* 25 (April), 94–101.

——. 1972. *The Indonesian Communist Party and Land Reform, 1959–1965* (Monash Papers on Southeast Asia, Monash University, Melbourne).

——. 1973. "Indonesia: Growth or Development?" in Rex Mortimer, ed., *Showcase State: The Illusion of Indonesia's 'Accelerated Modernisation'* (Angus & Robertson, Sydney).

——. 1974. *Indonesia Communism under Sukarno: Ideology and Politics, 1959–1965* (Cornell University Press, Ithaca).

Mozingo, David. 1965. *Sino-Indonesian Relations: An Overview, 1955–1965* (Rand Corporation, Santa Monica).

Nasution, A. H. 1967. *Menegakkan Keadilan dan Kebenaran,* Vols. I and II (Seruling Masa, Jakarta).

——. 1971. *Kekaryaan ABRI* (Seruling Masa, Jakarta).

Nazaruddin Sjamsuddin. 1970. "Partai Nasional Indonesia dan Kepolitikannja pada Masa Terachir ini" (Drs. thesis, Universitas Indonesia).

Nishihara, Masashi. 1972. *Golkar and the Indonesian Elections of 1971* (Modern Indonesia Project, Cornell University, Ithaca).

Nugroho Notosusanto. 1966. *40 Hari Kegagalan G-30-S* (Staf Pertahanankeamanan, Jakarta).

Nugroho Notosusanto and Ismael Saleh. 1968. *The Coup Attempt of the "September 30th Movement" in Indonesia* (Pembimbing Masa, Jakarta).

Oey Hong Lee, ed. 1974. *Indonesia after the 1971 Elections* (Oxford University Press, London).

Paget, Roger. 1967. "The Military in Indonesian Politics: The Burden of Power," *Pacific Affairs,* 40 (Fall-Winter), 294–314.

Panglaykim and Arndt, H. W. 1966. "Survey of Recent Developments," *Bulletin of Indonesian Economic Studies,* no. 4 (June), 1–35.

—— and K. D. Thomas. 1967. "The New Order and the Economy," *Indonesia,* no. 3 (April), 73–120.

Pauker, Ewa. 1964. "Has the Sukarno Regime Weakened the PKI?" *Asian Survey,* 4 (September), 1058–1070.

Pauker, G. J. 1959. "Southeast Asia as a Problem Area in the Next Decade," *World Politics,* (April), 325–345.

——. 1962. "The Role of the Military in Indonesia," in J. J. Johnson, ed., *The Role of the Military in Underdeveloped Countries* (Princeton University Press, Princeton).

——. 1965. "Indonesia in 1964: Towards a 'People's Democracy'?" *Asian Survey,* 6 (February), 88–97.

——. 1967. "Towards a New Order in Indonesia," *Foreign Affairs,* 45 (April), 503–519.

——. 1969. "The Rise and Fall of the Communist Party of Indonesia," in Robert Scalapino, ed., *The Communist Revolution in Asia: Tactics, Goals and Achievements* (2d ed., Prentice-Hall, Englewood Cliffs).

——. 1971. "The Gestapu Affair of 1965," *Southeast Asia,* 1 (Winter-Spring), 43–58.

Payer, Cheryl. 1974. "The International Monetary Fund and Indonesian Debt Slavery," in Mark Selden, ed., *Remaking Asia* (Pantheon, New York).

Penny, D. H. 1965. "Survey of Recent Developments," *Bulletin of Indonesian Economic Studies,* no. 2 (September), 1–15.

Polomka, Peter. 1969. "The Indonesian Army and Confrontation: An Inquiry into the Functions of Foreign Policy under Guided Democracy" (M.A. thesis, University of Melbourne).

——. 1971. *Indonesia since Sukarno* (Penguin, Harmondsworth).

——. 1972. "The Indonesian Army and Foreign Policy: A Reappraisal," *Asia Quarterly,* no. 4, pp. 363–382.

——. 1974. "Indonesia's Future and Southeast Asia," *Adelphi Papers,* 104 (International Institute of Strategic Studies, London).

Posthumus, G. A. 1972. "The Inter-Governmental Group on Indonesia," *Bulletin of Indonesian Economic Studies,* 8 (July), 55–66.

Pye, L. W. 1962. "Armies in the Process of Political Modernisation," in J. J. Johnson, ed., *The Role of the Military in Underdeveloped Countries* (Princeton University Press, Princeton).

Ransom, David. 1970. "The Berkeley Mafia and the Indonesian Massacres," *Ramparts,* 9 (October), 28–29, 40–49.

Rice, Robert. 1969. "Sumitro's Role in Foreign Trade Policy in Indonesia," *Indonesia,* no. 8 (October), 183–212.

Rieffel, Alex. 1969. "The Bimas Programme of Self-Sufficiency in Rice," *Indonesia,* no. 8 (October), 103–134.

—— and A. S. Wirjasaputra. 1972. "Military Enterprises," *Bulletin of Indonesian Economic Studies,* 8 (July), 104–108.

Roeder, O. G. 1969. *The Smiling General* (Gunung Agung, Jakarta).

Samson, A. A. 1968. "Islam in Indonesian Politics," *Asian Survey,* 8 (December), 1001–1017.

——. 1975. "Indonesia," in R. N. Kearney, ed., *Politics and Modernization in South and Southeast Asia* (John Wiley, New York).

Samsuddin, A., Tarman Assam, Masmimar, Ignatius Sukardjasman, and

R. Hidajat. 1972. *Pemilihan Umum 1971* (Ikatan Pers Mahasiswa Indonesia, Jakarta).

Sapartini Singgih. 1972. "Partai Muslimin Indonesia: Berdiri dan Perkembangannja hingga 1970" (Dra. thesis, Universitas Indonesia).

Selo Soemardjan. 1971. "Imbalances in Economic Development—The Indonesian Experience," in S. S. Hsueh, ed., *Development in Southeast Asia: Issues and Dilemmas* (Southeast Asia Social Sciences Association, Hong Kong).

Sloan, Stephen. 1971. *A Study in Political Violence: The Indonesian Experience* (Rand McNally, Chicago).

Soedjatmoko. 1967. "Indonesia: Problems and Opportunities" and "Indonesia and the World," *Australian Outlook*, 21 (December), 263–306.

Solichin Salam. 1970. *Sedjarah Partai Muslimin Indonesia* (Lembaga Penjelidikan Islam, Jakarta).

Sullivan, J. H. 1969. "The United States and the 'New Order' in Indonesia" (Ph.D. dissertation, American University).

Sundhaussen, Ulf. 1971. "The Political Orientation and Political Involvement of the Indonesian Officer Corps, 1945–1966: The Siliwangi Division and the Army Headquarters" (Ph.D. thesis, Monash University).

——. 1972. "The Military in Research on Indonesian Politics," *Journal of Asian Studies*, 31 (February), 355–365.

——. 1977. "The Military in Indonesia," in L. W. Pye and K. D. Jackson, eds. *Political Power and Communications in Indonesia* (University of California Press, Berkeley and Los Angeles).

Suripto. 1969. *Surat Perintah 11 Maret* (Grip, Surabaya).

Tinker, Irene, and Millidge Walker. 1973. "Planning for Regional Development in Indonesia," *Asian Survey*, 13 (December), 1102–1120.

Tomasson, G. 1970. "Indonesia: Economic Stabilisation, 1966–1969," *Finance and Development*, December.

Usamah. 1970. "War and Humanity: Notes on Personal Experience" (translated by Helen Jarvis), *Indonesia*, no. 9 (April), 89–100.

Utrecht, Ernst. 1969. "Land Reform in Indonesia," *Bulletin of Indonesian Economic Studies*, 5 (November), 71–88.

——. 1975. "An Attempt to Corrupt Indonesian History," *Journal of Contemporary Asia*, 5, no. 1.

Van der Kroef, J. M. 1965a. "Indonesian Communism's 'Revolutionary' Gymnastics," *Asian Survey*, 5 (May), 217–232.

——. 1965b. *The Communist Party of Indonesia* (University of British Columbia Press, Vancouver).

——. 1966. "Gestapu in Indonesia," *Orbis*, 9 (Summer), 458–487.

——. 1971. *Indonesia since Sukarno* (Donald Moore for Asia Pacific Press, Singapore).

Van Marle, A. 1974. "Indonesian Electoral Geography under Orla and Orba," in Oey Hong Lee, ed., *Indonesia after the 1971 Elections* (Oxford, London).

Vatikiotis, P. J. 1961. *The Egyptian Army in Politics: Pattern for New Nations?* (Indiana University Press, Bloomington).

Walkin, Jacob. 1969. "The Muslim-Communist Confrontation in East Java, 1963–1965," *Orbis*, 12 (Fall).

Ward, K. E. 1970. *The Foundation of the Partai Muslimin Indonesia* (Modern Indonesia Project, Cornell University, Ithaca).

———. 1974. *The 1971 Election in Indonesia: An East Java Case Study* (Monash Papers on Southeast Asia, Monash University, Melbourne).

Weatherbee, D. E. 1966. *Ideology in Indonesia: Sukarno's Indonesian Revolution* (Southeast Asian Studies, Yale University, New Haven).

Weinstein, F. B. 1969. *Indonesia Abandons Confrontation* (Modern Indonesia Project, Cornell University, Ithaca).

———. 1972. "The Uses of Foreign Policy in Indonesia" (Ph.D. dissertation, Cornell University).

Wertheim, W. F. 1964. *East-West Parallels: Sociological Approaches to Modern Asia* (van Hoeve, The Hague).

———. 1966. "Indonesia before and after the Untung Coup," *Pacific Affairs*, 39 (Spring-Summer), 115–127.

———. 1969. "From Aliran to Class Struggle in the Countryside of Java," *Pacific Viewpoint*, 10, 1–17.

———. 1970. "Suharto and the Untung Coup—The Missing Link," *Journal of Contemporary Asia*, 1 (Winter).

Wibisono, Christianto. 1970. *Aksi2 Tritura: Kisah Sebuah Partnership* (Departemen Pertahanan-Keamanan, Jakarta).

Wijarso. 1970. "Oil in Indonesia: In Review and Prospect," *Pacific Community*, 1 (July).

Willner, A. R. 1970. "The Neo-Traditional Accommodation to Political Independence," in L. W. Pye, ed., *Cases of Comparative Politics: Asia* (Little, Brown, Boston).

Documents, Official Publications, Unofficial Publications
Documents

Boyce, P., ed. 1968. *Malaysia and Singapore in International Diplomacy: Documents and Commentaries* (Sydney University Press, Sydney).

MPRS. 1972. *Laporan Pimpinan MPRS Tahun 1966–1972* (MPRS, Jakarta).

Muhono, ed. 1966. *Himpunan Ketetapan MPRS dan Peraturan Negara jang Penting Bagi Anggauta Angkatan Bersenjata* (Jakarta).

Sekretariat DPR-GR. 1970. *Undang-Undang Pemilihan Umum.*

"Selected Documents Relating to the 'September 30 Movement' and Its Epilogue," *Indonesia*, no. 1 (October 1966).

Supolo Prawotohadikusumo, ed. 1967. *Dari Orde Lama Menudju Orde Baru* (Pantjuran Tudjuh, Jakarta).

Sutjipto, ed. 1966. *ABRI Pengemban Suara Hati Nurani Rakjat*, Vols. I and II (Matoa, Jakarta).

Military Publications

Angkatan Darat. 1965. *Doktrin Perdjuangan TNI 'Tri Ubaya Çakti.'*

———. 1966a. *Sumbangan Fikiran TNI-AD Kepada Kabinet Ampera.*

——. 1966b. *Amanat/Pidato Pra-saran Dalam Seminar AD Ke-11/1966.*

Koti (Komando Operasi Tertinggi). 1965. *Rangkaian Pidato dan Pernjataan2 Resmi Disekitar Peristiwa 'Gerakan 30 September'* (Jakarta).

Panitia Penyusun Sejarah Kostrad. 1972. *Kostrad Dharma Putra* (Jakarta).

Puspenad (Pusat Penerangan Angkatan Darat). 1965. *Fakta2 Persoalan Sekitar 'Gerakan 30 September'* (Jakarta).

Publications of the Departemen Penerangan (Department of Information)

Kabinet Ampera (List of members of Ampera Cabinet, Speeches by Sukarno on 25 July 1966 and 28 July 1966).

Keterangan Pemerintah Pada Sidang Pleno DPR-GR Tanggal 4 Maret 1967 Mengenai Penjerahan Kekuasaan Pemerintahan (Speech by Suharto on 4 March 1967).

Pengumuman Presiden Republik Indonesia/Mandataris MPRS/Panglima Tertinggi ABRI, Tanggal 20 Februari 1967.

Statement-Statement Politik Waperdam Bidang Sospol/Menteri Luar Negeri dan Waperdam Bidang Ekubang (Statements by Adam Malik and the sultan of Yogyakarta, on 4 and 12 April 1966).

Susunan Kabinet Republic Indonesia 1945–1970 (Pradjna Paramita, Jakarta 1970).

President Sukarno's Speeches
Published by Departemen Penerangan:

"Tjapailah Bintang-Bintang Dilangit," 17 August 1965.

"Nekolim Musuh kita jang terbesar," 16 October 1965.

"Binalah Kesatuan dan Persatuan Nasional Progresif Revolusioner atas Dasar Pantja Azimat Revolusi," 23 October 1965.

"Nawaksara," 22 June 1966.

Speeches on 25 July 1966 and 28 July 1966 in *Kabinet Ampera.*

"Djanganlah Sekali-kali Meninggalkan Sedjarah," 17 August 1966.

Mimeographed speeches, Sekretariat Negara (State Secretariat)

Pidato pada Sidang Paripurna Kabinet di Bogor, 6 November 1965.

Amanat Peringatan Isr'a dan Mi'radj di Istana Negara, Jakarta, 20 November 1965.

Amanat pada Pembukaan Sidang Pimpinan MPRS ke-X, 6 December 1965.

Amanat pada Pembukaan Konperensi para Gubernur Seluruh Indonesia, 13 December 1965.

Amanat pada Hari Ulang Tahun Perwari, 17 December 1965.

Amanat dihadapan para Mahasiswa HMI di Bogor, 18 December 1965.

Amanat dihadapan KAMI, Jakarta, 21 December 1965.

Amanat di Sidang Paripurna Kabinet Dwikora dengan dihadiri djuga oleh Wakil2 dari Mahasiswa2 dan Wartawan, 15 January 1966.

Amanat pada Rapat Kerdja Komando Utama ALRI, 1 February 1966.

Amanat pada Rapat Umum Front Nasional, 13 February 1966.

Amanat pada Peringatan Sapta Warsa GSNI, 28 February 1966.

Amanat pada Rapat Umum Wanita Internasional, 8 March 1966.

Amanat pada Sidang Kabinet Paripurna, 11 March 1966.
Amanat pada Penutupan Musjawarah Kesenian Nasional, 30 June 1966.
Sambutan Presiden Sukarno Pada Penutupan Sidang Umum ke-IV MPRS 1966, 6 July 1966.
Amanat dihadapan Delegasi Angkatan '45, 6 September 1966.

Trials
Published
Jusuf Muda Dalam trial: *Proses Jusuf Muda Dalam* (Kedjaksaan Agung Bidang Chusus, Jakarta, 1967).
Njono trial: *G-30-S Dihadapan Mahmillub 1 (Perkara Njono)* (Pusat Pendidikan/Kehakiman AD, Jakarta).
Subandrio trial: *G-30-S Dihadapan Mahmillub 3 (Perkara Dr. Subandrio)*, Vols. I and II (Pusat Pendidikan Kehakiman AD); Lieutenant Colonel Ali Said and Lieutenant Colonel Durmawel Ahmad, *Sangkur Adil, Pengupas Fitnah Chianat* (Ethika, Jakarta) (prosecution and defense speeches, judgment).
Untung trial: *G-30-S Dihadapan Mahmillub 2 (Perkara Untung)* (Pusat Pendidikan Kehakiman AD, Jakarta).
Unpublished
Muljono trial: "Hasil Sidang Mahmillub ke-II dalam Pemeriksaan Terdakwa/Tertuduh Ex Major Moeljono Soerjowardojo di Djogjakarta," 1 vol., typescript.
Omar Dhani trial: "Mahkamah Militer Luar Biasa: Perkara Omar Dhani, Ex Laksamana Madya Udara," 3 vols., typescript.
Sjam trial: "Mahkamah Militer Luar Biasa: Putusan, Perkara Sjam," mimeographed judgment.
Sudisman trial: "Mahkamah Militer Luar Biasa: Perkara Sudisman," 2 vols., typescript.
Supardjo trial: "Mahkamah Militer Luar Biasa: Perkara M.S. Supardjo, Bridgjen TNI," typescript of closing speeches, judgment, and other documents.
Utomo Ramelan trial: "Mahkamah Militer Luar Biasa di Surakarta, Perkara Utomo Ramelan," 2 vols., typescript.
Wirjomartono trial: "Mahkamah Militer Luar Biasa: Requisitor dan Vonnis, Perkara Wirjomartono," typescript of judgment, etc.

Miscellaneous
Achmad, D. S., ed. 1966. *Wawantjara Djenderal dengan Wartawan* (Rilan, Solo, 1966).
Dewan Mahasiswa Universitas Indonesia. 1970. *Seminar Pemilihan Umum dan Masalah2 jang Ditimbulkan* (Jakarta).
Djawaban Tertulis Djenderal A.H. Nasution untuk (Penulisan Buku) H.P. Jones (made available by General Nasution).
KAMI. 1966. *The Leader, the Man and the Gun* (Jakarta).

People of Indonesia, Unite and Fight to Overthrow the Fascist Regime (Foreign Languages Press, Peking, 1968).

Report of Fact-Finding Commission appointed by President Sukarno on 24 December 1965 to inquire into postcoup massacres (unpublished). Universitas Indonesia. 1966. *Kebangkitan Semangat '66: Mendjeladjah Tracee Baru* (Jakarta).

Newspapers, Periodicals (with political affiliations)

Jakarta

Abadi: Muslim, Masyumi orientation
Api Pantjasila: IPKI.
Angkatan Bersenjata: Armed Forces
Berita Buana: Army
Berita Yudha: Army
Duta Masyarakat: NU
Ekspres: Independent
El Bahar: Navy
Harian Kami: "1966 Generation"
Harian Rakjat: PKI
Indonesia Magazine: Sponsored by Mrs. Suharto
Indonesia Raya: Independent
Komunikasi: Protestant
Kompas: Catholic
Merdeka: Independent-nationalist
Nusantara: Independent
Pedoman: PSI orientation
Pelopor: Sekber-Golkar, pro-Sukarno
Sinar Harapan: Protestant
Suara Karya: Golkar
Suluh Marhaen: PNI
Tempo: Independent

Yogyakarta
Suluh Indonesia: PNI

Surabaya
Manifesto: Army
Obor Revolusi: NU
Pewarta Surabaya/Nusa Putera: PSII
Surabaya Post: Independent

Bandung
Mahasiswa Indonesia: PSI-oriented students
Mimbar Demokrasi: Muslim-oriented students

Others

Antara Ichtisar Tahunan, 1964, 1965–1966.
Bulletin of Indonesian Economic Studies (BIES).
Far Eastern Economic Review.
Radio Republik Indonesia: news broadcast monitored by the Indonesian Embassy, Canberra. Mimeographed.

Translations

(The letters *USE* or *ICATS* after newspaper references indicate that the source is a translation.)
Indonesian Current Affairs Translation Service (ICATS).
United States Embassy Translation Unit Press Review (USE).

Index

Abangan, 36, 155, 201, 227, 247, 254, 265, 268
Abdul Kadir Prawiraatmadja, 307
Achadi, A. M., 195
Achmad Tirtosudiro, 243, 278–279, 281, 289, 294, 327, 330
Achmad Wiranatakusumah, 70
Achmadi, 55, 161, 168, 195
Action Fronts, 141, 160, 197, 217, 235–236, 248, 251, 254, 265, 267, 296. *See also* KAMI; KAPPI; KASI
Adjie, Ibrahim, 163, 168–171, 173, 177–178, 181, 183–184, 208, 230
Agnew, Spiro, 338
Aidit, D. N., 49–50, 67, 77, 87, 89–90; and coup attempt, 83, 100, 102–105, 109–111, 116–117, 121, 129, 133; after coup attempt, 140, 145, 161
Aini Chalid, 315
Air force, 58, 73–74, 84, 86, 91, 200, 202; and coup attempt, 83, 92, 98, 100, 103, 107, 117–118, 122, 130–133, 140. *See also* Armed forces, conflict within; Omar Dhani; Rusmin Nurjadin; Sri Muljono Herlambang
Alamsjah Ratu Perwiranegara, 229, 243, 294, 307–308
Ali Murtopo, 131, 243, 307–309, 326, 328, 336–337, 340; and confrontation, 74, 204, 206, 332; and coup of 11 March, 181, 183–184, 190; and elections, 253, 258, 262, 265–267, 271–272; and 15 January Affair, 313–317
Ali Sadikin, 85, 244
Ali Said, 296
Ali Sastroamidjojo, 31–32, 171, 184, 201, 254–256
Ali Wardhana, 242, 318

Amir Machmud, 167, 170, 181, 188, 190–191, 195, 237, 262, 267
Amir Murtono, 309
Anderson, Benedict, 101, 126, 293
Andoko, 92
Ansor, 92, 146–147, 152, 172, 225. *See also* Youth organizations
Anwar Tjokroaminoto, 297
Anwas Tanuamidjaja, 98
Arief Budiman, 294, 311
Arief Husni (Ong Seng Kheng), 290
Arief Rahman Hakim, 182–184
Aristides Katoppo, 297
Armed forces, conflict within, 34, 52, 84, 137–138, 159, 192–193, 198–199, 213–214, 219, 228, 237–241, 306, 319, 346–347. *See also* Air force; Navy; Police
Armunanto, 195
Army: in administration, 22, 24, 33–35, 39–41, 48, 76–77, 199, 242, 244, 275, 306, 344, 348–349; as agent of modernization, 22, 199, 235, 246, 251, 267, 273; in business, 22–23, 34–35, 38–41, 274–305, 308–310, 321–330, 345, 348–350; in cabinet, 34, 47, 76–77, 241; and confrontation, 59–62, 69–75; as conservative elite, 22–23, 35–36, 41, 199, 299–303; internal rivalries, 22, 27–33, 35, 52–54, 60, 79–82, 171, 177–178, 184, 228–237, 241, 346, 348; and Islam, 37, 146, 153, 260–264, 268, 309, 313; and party politicians, 26–27, 35, 140–141, 235–236, 241–242, 245–272; size, 51, 98; territorial organization, 222, 345. *See also* Army officers; Nasution, Abdul Haris; PKI, and army; Suharto; Sukarno, and army

Army (cont.)
   leaders (Guided Democracy period);
   Sukarno, after coup attempt; Yani,
   Achmad
Army officers, professional and technocratic, 25, 28–30, 209, 304–306,
   309–310, 317, 329–330, 352; New
   Order militants, 180–181, 184–186,
   190–191, 198–199, 212–214, 217,
   228, 234–236, 241, 245–247, 250–
   252, 254–257, 347; pro-Sukarno, 30,
   34, 83–84, 158–159, 163–164, 178–
   180, 192, 197–198, 203, 208–210,
   212–215, 217, 229–233, 236; social
   background, 36–37
Arndt, H. W., 279, 319, 321
Artati Marzuki Sudirgo, 174
Arudji Kartawinata, 174
ASEAN, 337–340, 342
Astrawinata, Achmad, 77–78, 194–195
Azahari, A. M., 60

Bakin, 223, 262, 264, 280, 297, 307,
   309, 313, 317, 356
Banks, military-sponsored, 259, 278–
   279, 281–284, 290, 296
Basuki Rachmat, 80–81, 128, 131, 151,
   188–189, 210, 237, 243, 248, 307
Berdikari, PT, 243, 278, 281–282, 333
Bimas Gotong Royong, 290–291, 324,
   350
BPI, 60–61, 86, 162, 223, 355
BPS, 65–66, 76, 78, 82, 330
Brackman, Arnold, 105, 123, 150
Bratanata, Slamat, 277
Brawijaya, 309, 354; and coup attempt,
   100–101, 113, 131, 143, 146–147,
   154; "New Orderization," 232–233,
   236, 238; and Sukarno, 209–210,
   214–216. See also Army, internal ri-
   valries
Britain, 44, 56–57, 59, 61, 67. See also
   Foreign investment, British
BTI, 87, 224–225
Budiardjo, 290
Bujung Nasution, 265, 316
Bulog, 243, 278–282, 289–291, 296–
   297, 324–327, 350

Cakrabirawa, 97, 110, 120, 167, 182,
   186, 189–190, 200

Cambodia, 331, 336, 339, 342
Catholic party, 141, 247, 356
Chaerul Saleh, 48, 64–66, 77, 98, 117,
   120, 165–166, 199, 296; and Barisan
   Sukarno, 168, 171, 173, 180; and
   coup of 11 March, 184, 186, 188–
   189, 191, 193–195, 197, 200
Chalid Mawardi, 172
Charis Suhud, 309, 316
China, 67–68, 78, 81, 89, 92–93, 95,
   161, 187, 282, 331–334, 339–340
Chinese: anti-Chinese outbursts, 146,
   149, 260, 312, 331–333; business-
   men, 38, 41, 274, 278, 282, 284–290,
   300–301, 309, 312–313, 349–350; in
   Kalimantan, 224, 227; physicians,
   109; volunteers, 60–61, 72
Chou En-lai, 89–90
Civil war, threat of, 32, 132, 145, 198–
   199, 211, 219, 221, 346. See also
   Armed forces, conflict within
Confrontation, 44–45, 51, 55–63, 67–
   76, 78–81, 95, 102, 204–206, 331–
   332, 345. See also Koga; Kogam; Kolaga
Cornell Paper, 101–103, 107, 112–113, 115
Corruption, 21, 31, 40, 52, 66, 232,
   235, 293–299, 311, 319, 326, 330,
   350; measures against, 40, 80, 286,
   289–290, 295–298
Council of Generals, 97, 104, 106–108,
   110–111, 115–116, 118, 120, 125,
   127, 133
Coup attempt, 92, 96, 97–135, 137,
   143–144, 237, 333–334, 346

Dachjar Sudiawidjaja, 78
Dake, A. C. A., 105, 119–122
Darul Islam, 28, 54, 346
Defense budget, 31, 38, 59, 274, 277,
   292, 322, 330
Des Alwi, 74
Dewanto, Ignatius, 92, 133
Dharsono, Hartono Rekso, 181, 208,
   210, 212–214, 234–236, 251–252,
   255–256
Diah, B. M., 65, 326
Diponegoro, 227, 237, 243, 309, 316–
   317, 354; and coup attempt, 100–
   101, 112–117, 123, 129, 131, 143–
   145, 147–150, 230, 232

Djarnawi Hadikusumo, 261–262
Djatikusumo, 316
Djuanda Kartawidjaja, 47–48, 51, 56, 59, 77
Djuhartono, 96, 167–168
Dorodjatun Kuntjorojakti, 316
Dual Function, 24, 345
Dul Arief, 126

Economic conditions, 21, 55, 95–96, 164–165, 204, 274, 318–319
Economic development, 51, 55, 59, 273, 299, 302, 305, 318, 349–352
Elections, 223, 248–253, 264–272, 308, 335, 347–348
Emil Salim, 318

Fahmi Idris, 185
Feith, Herbert, 45
Fifteenth of January Affair, 223, 313–317, 330, 348
Fifth force, 87–94, 96, 103
Ford, Gerald, 341
Foreign aid, 56–58, 96, 204, 288, 319–321, 329, 331–332, 334–335, 338
Foreign investment, 273–276, 287, 290, 299–303, 311–312, 317, 320, 323–324, 329–330, 349–350; American, 39, 63, 68, 287, 310; British, 39, 60, 63, 68; Dutch, 34, 38–39; Hong Kong, 284; Japanese, 275, 284, 287, 310, 313
Foreign relations, 44, 67–68, 330–343. See also Confrontation
Fuad Hasan, 265
Fukuda, Takeo, 289

Gatot Subroto, 53
Gatot Sukrisno, 126
Gerwani, 102–103, 138, 140
Golkar, 96, 167, 264–272, 309, 356

Hadisubeno Sosrowerdojo, 201, 254–259, 265, 269
Hafas, T. D., 286, 294, 296
Hardi, 201, 254–255, 257–258
Hariman Siregar, 316
Harjono, M. T., 81, 99, 107
Hartawan Wirjodiprodjo, 195
Hartono, 175, 188, 193, 238–239
Hartono Rekso Dharsono. See Dharsono, Hartono Rekso

Hartono Wirjodiprodjo, 274, 295
Hasnan Habib, 328
Hassan Basri, 60
Hatta, Mohammed, 59, 117, 210, 297
Henk Ngantung, 78
Heru Atmodjo, 98, 118, 128
Hindley, Donald, 50, 270
HMI, 67, 157, 165, 185
Horta, Ramos, 340
Hugeng Imam Santoso, 238, 292, 323
Hughes, John, 122
Husni Thamrin, 185

Ibnu Subroto, 89
Ibnu Sutowo, 40, 78, 80, 165, 199, 243, 275–278, 287, 294, 299, 307, 310, 327–328, 330
Ibrahim Adjie. See Adjie, Ibrahim
Idham Chalid, 171–172, 193, 200, 263–264, 269, 271
IGGI, 320, 327, 338
IMF, 56–58, 320–321, 326, 329
Imran Kadir, 262
Imron Rosjadi, 263
Indigenous businessmen, 300, 310, 312, 317, 350
Ipik Gandamana, 174
Ishak Djuarsa, 143, 234–236, 256, 333
Ismael Saleh, 112
Isman, 266, 307
Ismid Hadad, 294 /

Japan, 276, 289, 308, 314–315, 329, 331, 338. See also Foreign aid; Foreign investment, Japanese
Jasin, 233–235, 237–238, 256, 333
Jatidjan, 239
Javanese values, 199–200, 215–216, 222, 228, 347. See also Traditional politics
Johannes, 297
Jones, Howard, 62, 150
Jusuf, Mohamad, 188–189
Jusuf Hasjim, 269
Jusuf Muda Dalam, 194–195, 197, 199, 211, 281, 284, 296
Jusuf Singadikane, 307 /

KAMI, 165–166, 169, 174, 181–186, 194, 197, 210, 212–213, 235, 245

KAPPI, 184–185, 187, 194–195, 197, 210, 212–213
KASI, 197, 235, 245, 265
Kasimo, I. J., 297
Katamso, 100, 144–145, 148
Kemal Idris, 72–73, 166, 180–181, 183–186, 189–190, 193–194, 208, 212–213, 234–236, 252, 256
Kennedy, Robert, 57
Kko, 85, 193, 198, 210, 214–215, 238–239, 244, 284, 355. See also Hartono
Koga, 61, 70–71
Kogam, 175, 183
Kolaga, 71–73, 84, 123, 181
Kopkamtib, 160, 174, 222–223, 267, 269, 298, 309, 312–314, 316–317, 355
Kostrad, 47, 71, 81, 100, 125, 130–132, 141, 148, 229, 243, 283, 355. See also Kemal Idris
Koti, 47–48, 54–55, 61–62, 76–77, 80, 95, 141, 161, 170, 172–173, 175, 355
Kusno Utomo Widjojojkerto, 257

Latief, A., 104, 110, 115–116, 123–125, 128
Le Duc Tho, 67
Legge, J. D., 82, 89, 93
Leimena, Johannes, 48, 77, 85, 88–89, 120, 127–128, 132, 185, 188–189, 191, 193, 200
Leo Wattimena, 118, 132–133
Letter of 11 March, 189, 191–192, 201–202, 214
Liddle, R. W., 268
Liem Bian Kie (Jusuf Wanandi), 337
Liem Siu Liong (Sudono Salim), 283, 285–286
Lubis Affair, 33, 72, 180
Lukman, M. H., 50, 77, 111, 140, 145, 161
Lukman Harun, 261

Macapagal, Diosdado, 56
Madiun Affair, 28, 84, 346
Magelang generation, 305–306, 352
Magenda, A. E. J., 60–61
Mahmillub, 101, 103, 106, 108–109, 112, 125, 161, 173, 211
Makmun Murod, 173
Malaysia, 334, 337–339. See also Confrontation

Malik, Adam, 64–66, 200, 204–206, 304, 330–342
Manning, C., 324
Mardanus, 316
Marjono, 114
Martadinata, Eddy, 84–85, 91, 98, 128, 130, 132, 137, 168, 174–175
Martial law, 22, 24, 32–34, 38–40, 46–50, 54, 59, 76, 139, 222, 344–345, 355
Mashuri, 212, 265
Massacres, 135–136, 141–143, 147, 151–158, 227, 346
Masyumi, 33, 48, 165, 169, 179, 185, 197, 247, 251, 254, 259–263, 270, 300, 313, 316, 356
McVey, Ruth, 101, 124, 190, 211
Middle class, 23, 273, 318, 349–350
Middle Way, 24, 39, 344–345
Mintaredja, M. S., 262, 269–270, 313
Mochtar Lubis, 264, 290, 294
Mokoginta, Achmad Junus, 88, 90, 173, 209, 230–231, 241
MPR, 250, 272, 353
MPRS, 47–48, 91, 194, 231, 247–248, 353; 1966 session, 201–203, 207, 212–213, 248, 251–252; 1967 session, 105, 216–219, 234; 1968 session, 220, 253
Muljadi, 175, 193–194, 212–213, 216–217, 238–239
Muljono Surjowardojo, 114–115, 144, 149
Murba party, 64–66, 78, 82, 185, 247, 330, 356
Murnadi, Benny, 74
Mursjid, 119–120, 122, 125, 128–129, 137, 175–176, 193, 229, 231
Muskita, J., 81, 236

Naro Djaelani, 261–262, 313, 337
Nasakom, 43–44, 48, 66, 92–93, 129, 157, 162–164, 173, 192, 207, 254, 263; Nasakom cabinet, 77, 82; Nasakomization, 67, 78, 95, 146, 296; Nasakomization of the armed forces, 87–91, 94
Nasution, Abdul Haris, 24, 28, 32–33, 37, 46–47, 84, 140, 183, 193, 229, 275, 344; and confrontation, 60–62, 72, 80, 205; and corruption, 40, 80,

Nasution (*cont.*)
   232; and coup attempt, 99, 107, 125,
   128, 131; dismissal as minister, 174–
   177, 179; and New Order, 248, 251,
   267, 314, 316, 337; and PKI, 49, 79–
   80, 91; and Seventeenth of October
   Affair, 30, 177, 209; and Suharto,
   40, 124–125, 136–137, 141, 166,
   168, 177, 201, 208, 217, 228, 231–
   232, 241; and Sukarno, 49, 52–55,
   79–80, 201, 208, 217; and Yani, 52–
   55, 60, 79–81, 93–94
National Front, 34, 141, 167–168, 170–
   171, 173, 186, 195, 266
Natsir, Mohammad, 261
Navy, 73–74, 84–86, 98–99, 130, 136,
   200, 202, 217, 239. *See also* Armed
   forces, conflict within; Kko; Martadinata, Eddy; Muljadi
Nawawi Alif, 307
Netherlands, 46–47, 293, 300, 311. *See
   also* Foreign investment, Dutch;
   Revolution
Newspapers: Abadi, 268; Angkatan
   Bersenjata, 139–140, 150, 170; Berita Indonesia, 65–66; Berita Yudha,
   139–140; Chas, 280, 335; El Bahar,
   215, 239; Harian Kami, 294, 335;
   Harian Rakjat, 65, 102–103; Indonesia Raya, 290, 294–295, 298; Mahasiswa Indonesia, 294; Merdeka, 65–
   66, 286, 326; Nusantara, 286, 294–
   296, 298; Sinar Harapan, 297–298;
   Suluh Marhaen, 258
Ngadimo, 113
Nixon, Richard, 333, 337
Njono, 102–104, 106, 108–109, 111,
   139, 161, 173
Njoto, 49, 77, 103, 109–111, 121, 140,
   161–162
Nono Anwar Makarim, 294
NU, 48, 65, 141, 162, 205, 300, 356; in
   cabinet, 200, 242; and PKI, 64, 95,
   143, 145–146, 152, 154, 227; and Su-
   karno, 159, 171–172, 202, 210, 217.
   See also Ansor
Nugroho Notosusanto, 112

Oei Tjoe Tat, 174, 194–195
Oloan Hutapea, 227
Omar Dhani, 25, 61, 70–73, 84, 91–93,
   161, 174, 200, 212; and coup at-
   tempt, 98, 100, 115, 117–119, 122,
   128, 132–133, 137–138, 140
Omar Khayam, 265
Opsus, 259, 342. *See also* Ali Murtopo
Osa Maliki Wangsadinata, 201, 255,
   257

Padang Sudirgo, 327
Palmos, Frank, 142
Pandjaitan, D. I., 99, 107, 127
Panggabean, Maraden, 73, 223, 235,
   240, 243, 257, 307–309, 339–341
Panglaykim, 319
Pardede, Peris, 103, 108–109, 111,
   161
Parkindo, 48, 247, 270, 356
Parman, S., 81, 99, 106–107, 110
Parmusi, 259–262, 265, 268–271, 337,
   356
Partindo, 78, 162, 187, 195, 356
Patronage, 30, 237, 243, 245, 267, 270,
   307–308, 310, 348, 351
Pauker, Ewa, 68
Pauker, Guy, 68, 108
Pemuda, Marhaen, 92, 147, 256. *See
   also* Youth organizations
Pemuda Rakyat, 77, 102, 138–139, 157
Pepelrada, 76, 146, 151, 169, 172, 186,
   222, 355
Pertamina, 39, 78, 80, 243, 275–278,
   282, 284, 296–298, 300–302, 322–
   323, 326–329, 350
Peta, 25, 29–30, 37, 305
Philippines, 56–57, 334, 339
Piet Harjono, 301, 328
PKI: and army, 21, 34, 44–45, 48–52,
   55, 69, 76–80, 82, 86–96, 138–142,
   161; and China, 64, 333; and coup
   attempt, 98, 100–112, 114–117, 121,
   123, 138–140, 145, 333; dissolution
   of, 163, 192; influence in armed
   forces, 82–86; militant policy, 62–68;
   representation in government, 49–
   50, 77–78, 95; revival efforts, 221,
   224–228, 334–335, 351; and Sukarno, 34, 42–45, 48–50, 58, 66–69,
   77, 82, 93–95, 133, 135–136, 157,
   161–164, 173, 184; supporters, 247,
   254, 268. *See also* Madiun Affair;
   Massacres

PNI, 31, 65, 88, 162, 173, 184, 186–
187, 195, 205, 233, 300, 356; in cabi-
net, 242; and PKI, 64, 95, 143, 150,
152, 156; purge of, 200–201, 234–
236; and Sukarno, 48, 136, 159,
171–172, 180, 202, 210, 217, 232.
See also Pemuda Marhaen
Police, 73–74, 85–86, 130, 284; purge
of, 200, 233–234, 237–238; and Su-
karno, 136, 202, 210, 214. See also
Armed forces, conflict within; Sut-
jipto Judodihardjo
Polomka, Peter, 61, 336
Ponco Sutowo, 287
Pono, 83, 110, 116–117
Pranoto Reksosamudro, 128–132, 136–
137, 161, 229
Pratomo, 227
Prawoto Mangkusasmito, 260–261
Prijono, 185, 194
Princen, H. J. C., 225, 316
Prisoners, political, 155, 173–174, 224–
225, 259, 316
Priyayi, 36–37, 153, 260
Probosutedjo, 286–287, 290
Progressive Revolutionary Officers'
Movement, 85, 113
Pronk, J., 311
PRRI, 33, 37, 48, 53, 59, 74, 179, 243,
260, 342–343, 346
PSI, 33, 74, 166, 169, 179, 197, 249,
316, 356; influence in armed forces,
72, 180, 209, 234, 238, 245, 251
Puguh, R. S., 215, 239, 316

Rahman Tolleng, 295, 316
Ransom, D., 320–321
Razak, Tun Abdul, 205–206, 332
Revolution, 22, 24–28, 36–38, 222,
273, 305, 346, 351
Rewang, 89, 227
Roem, Mohammed, 261–262
RPKAD, 133, 148–151, 154, 188–190,
195, 233, 238, 284, 355. See also
Sarwo Edhie
Rudhito Kusnadi Herukusumo, 106
Rukman, U., 86, 128, 230, 241
Rural conflict, 21, 63–64, 68. See also
Massacres
Ruslan Abdulgani, 48, 194, 200
Ruslan Widjasastra, 227

Rusmin Nurjadin, 193, 200, 212–213,
216–217
Ryacudu, 73

Sabur, Muhamad, 120–122, 127, 171,
191
Sadli, Mohammed, 318, 321, 323,
328
Saifuddin Zuhri, 211
Sajidiman Surjohadiprodjo, 306,
309, 316
Sakirman, 49, 110, 161
Santri, 36, 64, 247, 259
Sarbini Martodihardjo, 81, 131, 175–
176, 193–194, 210, 215, 237
Sarbini Sumawinata, 249, 316
Sartono, 171
Sarwo Edhie, 75; and coup attempt,
133, 150, 154, 156; and coup of 11
March, 181, 184–186, 189–190, 194–
195; and New Order, 234–236, 256–
257, 297, 314, 316; and Sukarno,
208, 212–213
Satrio Sastrodiredjo, 78, 143
Sawarno Tjokrodiningrat, 86, 238
Sekber-Golkar. See Golkar
Selo Soemardjan, 291
Semaun, 163
Setiadi Reksoprodjo, 77, 174, 195
Seventeenth of October Affair, 29–31,
72, 177, 180, 190, 209
Sigit, 110
Siliwangi, 101, 142, 148, 209, 237, 241,
251, 255, 284, 309, 312, 354. See also
Adjie, Ibrahim; Dharsono, Hartono
Rekso
Simatupang, T. B., 28
Singapore, 58–59, 62, 72, 74, 339
Sjafe'i, Imam, 174, 195–196
Sjafiuddin, 120, 208
Sjafruddin Prawiranegara, 261, 313
Sjahrir, 316
Sjahrir, Sutan, 74
Sjaichu, A., 269
Sjam, 83, 104–105, 108–112, 115–117,
123, 126, 128
Sjamsu Sutjipto, 239
Sjarif Thajeb, 165, 174
Slamet Danudirdjo, 307, 327
Smuggling, 38, 40, 74–75, 129, 284,
291–292, 295, 323

Sobiran Mochtar, 131, 173
SOBSI, 65, 76, 90, 146
Sofjar, 283
Sokowati, Suprapto, 264, 266
SOKSI, 65, 153, 266, 281
Solihin Gautama Purwanegara, 234–235
Soviet Union, 51, 59, 62, 64, 68, 204, 239, 276, 331, 334–335, 338, 340
Special Bureau, 83, 104, 109–112, 114–117
Spri, 243, 307, 318, 320
Sri Muljono Herlambang, 55, 92, 161, 168, 175, 193–195, 197, 200
Student demonstrations: anti-corruption, 294–298, 309, 311, 313, 350; anti-Sukarno, 164, 167–168, 171–172, 179–183, 187, 189
Suadi, 188, 316
Subadio Sastrosatomo, 316
Subamia, I Gusti Gede, 194
Subandrio: after coup attempt, 98, 161–162, 167–171, 173–174, 177, 179–180; and coup of 11 March, 184–186, 188–191, 193–195, 197, 200; Guided Democracy period, 48, 55, 60–61, 77, 80, 86, 89, 109, 120; trial, 211–212
Subandrio, Mrs., 186
Subchan, Z. E., 141, 187, 263, 269
Subroto, 318, 325
Sudarman, 295
Sudharmono, 307
Sudibjo, 167–168, 194–195
Sudijono, 114
Sudirgo, 120, 223
Sudirman, General, 28, 31
Sudirman (commander of Seskoad), 81, 210
Sudisman, 103, 108–109, 111–112, 161, 226–227
Sudjadi, 214
Sudjatmoko, 249, 265
Sudjono, 87–88
Sudjono Humardhani, 243, 268, 289, 294, 307–310, 314–317
Sudomo, 155, 223, 239, 309, 312, 316–317
Sudono, 113
Sudwikatmono, 285–286
Sugandhi, 140, 266

Sugeng, Bambang, 210, 215
Sugih Arto, 224, 237, 288, 296
Sugijono, 100, 145, 148
Suhardiman, 65, 80, 199, 243, 266, 281–282, 294, 333, 342
Suharjo, 73
Suharto, 47, 125, 161–162, 166, 183, 218, 220, 242–243, 347–349; business interests, 40, 129, 283, 285–287; and confrontation, 71–72, 74, 204–206; and coup attempt, 99–100, 105–106, 119, 123–125, 128–134, 144, 148; and coup of 11 March, 181, 185, 187–191; and parties, 246, 250–265, 268; as president, 273, 277, 281, 291, 294–298, 303, 306–310, 314–319, 333, 339–340. See also Army, internal rivalries; Armed forces, conflict within; Nasution, and Suharto
Suharto, Mrs. Tien, 124, 286, 299, 311, 315
Suherman, 100, 104, 114–116, 144
Sujatno, 238
Sujono, 92, 110, 115–118, 138
Sujono Atmo, 78, 143
Sukarni, 64
Sukarno, 21–22, 43–45, 135, 229, 273, 281, 330–332, 344–347; and army leaders (Guided Democracy period), 33–34, 41–43, 45–55, 70–71, 77–82, 89–95, 237; and confrontation, 56–59, 61, 70–71, 204–206; and coup attempt, 97–101, 105, 118–122, 125–134, 137, 139–140, 144, 207, 212–213; after coup attempt, 136–141, 157–165, 167–194, 196–221, 231–232; dismissal of, 216–218; illness of, 96, 104, 109–111, 117, 133; and massacres, 216–218. See also Army officers, pro-Sukarno; Nasution, and Sukarno; PKI, and Sukarno; Yani, and Sukarno
Sukarno, Mrs. Dewi, 126
Sukarno, Mrs. Hartini, 189
Sukarno, Mrs. Haryati, 127
Sukendro, Achmad, 49, 75, 81, 107, 182
Sukirno, 131
Sulaiman Sumardi, 265
Sullivan, J. H., 280

Sultan of Yogyakarta, 176, 200
Sumantoro, 65
Sumantri, 81
Sumardi, Brigadier General, 214
Sumardi, Colonel, 152, 154
Sumardjo, 174, 184–185, 195
Sumarno Sosroatmodjo, 195–196
Sumarsono, 210, 214, 233, 238
Sumbodo, 113
Sumiskum, 264
Sumitro, 73, 208, 210, 215, 223, 233,
    237, 309, 313–317, 325–326
Sumitro Djojohadikusumo, 242, 282,
    288, 318, 323
Sunardi, Ranu, 98
Sunarijadi, 154, 208
Sunarjo, 121, 127
Sunarso, 170, 307
Sunawar Sukowati, 259
Sundhaussen, Ulf, 35
Sundoro Hardjoamidjojo, 256, 258
Sungkono, 210, 215
Supardjo, 72–73, 86, 98, 104, 110, 115,
    118–119, 123, 126–129, 132, 137,
    140
Supeno, Bambang, 209–210, 215
Suprajogi, 296
Suprapto, 81, 88, 99, 107
Surachman, 195
Surjadarma, Surjadi, 84
Surjo, 80, 243, 289–290, 294, 296, 299,
    307–308, 317
Surjosumpeno, 100, 144–145, 147–
    150, 154, 178, 208
Surono Reksodimedjo, 208, 232, 316–
    317
Sutardhio, Augustinius, 174
Sutarto, 86
Sutedja, Anak Agung Bagus, 78
Sutjipto, 141
Sutjipto Danukusumo, 85
Sutjipto Judodihardjo, 85–86, 98, 128,
    137, 168, 175, 193–194, 212–213,
    216–217, 237–238
Sutojo Siswomihardjo, 81, 99, 107
Sutomo Martoprodoto, 195
Sutopo Juwono, 223, 262, 297, 309,
    313, 316–317
Suwadji, 214–215
Suwarto, 249
Suwoto Sukandar, 240

Taiwan, 282, 333, 342
Tanaka, Kakuei, 314–315
Technocrats, 51, 57, 242, 304, 317–
    330, 349, 352
Tendean, P., 99
Thailand, 311, 334, 339
Thirtieth of September Movement. See
    Coup attempt
Timor, 340–341
Tjan, Harry, 141
Traditional politics, 44–45, 65, 79, 176,
    285, 293
Tumakaka, J. K., 186, 195
Tunku Abdul Rahman, 56–57

Ujeng Suwargana, 80–81
Ulung Sitepu, 77
Umar Wirahadikusumah, 123, 125,
    181, 237
United Nations, 38, 47, 54, 57, 72, 78,
    329, 331, 336
United States of America, 47, 55–57,
    67–68, 113–114, 204, 231, 331,
    336–338, 340–343. See also Foreign
    investment, American
Untung, 97–98, 101–102, 104–105,
    107, 110, 115–116, 120–124, 126,
    128, 131, 140
Urip Widodo, 166
Usep Ranuwidjaja, 255
Usman Sastrodibroto, 100, 114
Utojo, Bambang, 31, 215
Utomo Ramelan, 84, 102, 150

Van der Kroef, J. M., 50, 68, 88, 108,
    333
Vietnam, 63, 67, 316, 331, 336–339,
    342

Wahjudi, 110
Wahono, 186, 214
Walujo, 83, 110
Ward, K. E., 268
Waringin, CV, 285–286, 296, 298
Wertheim, W. F., 105–106, 123–125, 293
West Irian campaign, 38, 44–51,
    54–56, 58–60, 81, 84, 123, 229, 237,
    345
Widjaja Sukardanu, 151
Widjanarko, Bambang, 105, 119–122,
    131–132

Widjojo Nitisastro, 242, 318
Widodo, 145, 271
Wijono, 146, 233
Willy Sudjono, 151–152, 154, 233
Willy Sujono, 238
Wilopo, 297
Wirjomartono, 114–115
Wirjono Prodjodikoro, 88
Witono, 166, 234–236

Yamin, Mohammed, 48
Yani, Achmad, 33, 47, 52, 76, 113,
  158–159, 229–232; assassination of,
  99, 126–128, 162; and confrontation,
  59–62, 70, 72–75, 80; and PKI, 78–
  80, 88–91, 93–94; and Sukarno, 53–
  55, 65, 82, 89, 93–94, 105–107, 119–
  122, 129, 134, 136. See also Nasution,
  and Yani
Yani, Mrs., 183, 185
Yoga Sugama, 181, 190, 223, 243, 307,
  317
Youth organizations, 141, 145, 148–
  149, 151, 153, 156, 165–166, 180–
  181, 184–185, 198, 214. See also Ansor; Pemuda Marhaen

Zulkifli Lubis, 33. See also Lubis Affair

Library of Congress Cataloging in Publication Data
(For library cataloging purposes only)

Crouch, Harold A   1940–
    The army and politics in Indonesia.

    (Politics and international relations of Southeast Asia)
    A revision of the author's thesis, Monash University, Melbourne, 1975, entitled:
The Indonesia Army in politics, 1960–1971.
    Bibliography: p.
    Includes index.
    1. Indonesia—Politics and government—1950–1966.   2. Indonesia—Politics
and government—1966–   3. Indonesia—Armed Forces—Political
activity.   I. Title.   II. Series.
DS644.C76   1978   322.4'4   77-90901
ISBN 0-8014-1155-6